NA680 .F83 2007

Fuchigami, Masayuki.

World architects 51 :
 concepts & works
    2007.

250101

$97.50

WORLD ARCHITECTS 51
CONCEPTS & WORKS

AUTHOR & EDITOR: MASAYUKI FUCHIGAMI

ADP | Art Design Publishing

Contents

5	EXPLORING THE PLURALISTIC NATURE OF THE 21ST CENTURY MASAYUKI FUCHIGAMI	82	HERZOG & DE MEURON
10	WILLIAM ALSOP	88	HOK/HERMUTH OBATA KASSABAUM
16	ARO/ARCHITECTURE RESEARCH OFFICE	94	HANS HOLLEIN
22	WIEL ARETS	100	HELMUT JAHN
28	GUNTHER BEHNISCH	106	DANI KARAVAN
34	FREDERIC BOREL	112	KIM YOUNG-SUB
40	DOUGLAS CARDINAL	118	JOSEF PAUL KLEIHUES
46	RICHARD ENGLAND	124	KPF/KOHN PEDERSEN FOX
52	MASSIMILIANO FUKSAS	130	C.Y. LEE
58	FUTURE SYSTEMS	136	IMRE MAKOVECZ
64	GIGON/GUYER	142	MECANOO
70	HEIKKINEN-KOMONEN	148	RICHARD MEIER
76	HERMAN HERTZBERGER	154	ENRIC MIRALLES BENEDETTA TAGLIABUE
		160	MVRDV

166	Neutelings Riedijk	250	SOM/Skidmore, Owings & Merrill
172	NOX	256	Studio Granda
178	O'Donnell+Tuomey	262	Szyszkowitz-Kowalski
184	Gustav Peichl	268	TEN Arquitectos
190	Cesar Pelli	274	UN Studio
196	Dominique Perrault	280	Erick van Egeraat
202	Ricardo Porro	286	VSBA/Robert Venturi and Denise Scott Brown
208	Miguel Angel Roca	292	Rafael Vinoly
214	Aldo Rossi	298	West 8
220	Roto Architects	304	Tod Williams Billie Tsien
226	Sauerbruch Hutton	310	Peter Zumthor
232	Schmidt Hammer Lassen		
238	Snohetta		
244	Paolo Soleri	316	Works Index (in alphabetical order of countries / cities)

Exploring the Pluralistic Nature of the 21st Century
Masayuki Fuchigami

More than ten years have already passed since the publication of my book _Contemporary Architects: Ideas and Works_ (Shokokusha, 1995). Not only has the 20th century given way to the 21st, but world architecture has also undergone many changes. In the 1980s and 90s, there was an explosion of urban developments throughout the world. Among the first were the Paris Grand Projet, the International Building Exhibition Berlin (IBA), the London Docklands, and the Millennium Project (also in the U.K.). In addition, there were projects like the Eastern Docklands in Amsterdam and the EU-related developments in Belgium. Also, in Spain, there were projects connected to events like the Barcelona Olympics and the Seville Expo '92, and in Portugal, the Lisbon Expo '98. And finally, to cap off the 20th century, there was the Hannover Expo 2000. In terms of history, these final 20 years of the 20th century will be remembered as a period of extensive activity which provided architects from around the world with an increased number of opportunities to work irrespective of national borders.

At present, China is the most competitive market for architecture. By the end of the 20th century, there had already been a marked rise in the strength of the country's economy, leading international architects to set their sights on the Asian superpower. In fact, since Beijing was chosen as the site of the 2008 Olympics, a succession of national projects and international architectural competitions have been announced. The superstar architects who are sometimes referred to as "contemporary globalists" are an especially strong presence in Beijing. Projects like Rem Koolhaas' CCTV, Herzog and de Meuron's National Olympic Stadium (p. 82), PTW Architects' National Swimming Center, and Paul Andreu's National Theater have all captured headlines around the world. In the mercantile city of Shanghai, however, architectural development has been going on for some time in the private

1 La Grande Arche, part of the Grand Projet in Paris
2 The Potsdamer Platz development, part of the International Building Exhibition Berlin (IBA)
3 Heron Quays, part of the London Docklands project

sector, as evidenced by a multitude of projects, including Skidmore, Owings, and Merrill's Jin Mao Tower (p. 250), Kohn, Pedersen, and Fox's Shanghai World Financial Center (p.124), Norman Foster"s Juishi Corporation Headquarters, and Von Gerkan, Marg and Partner's Chinese National Museum. In other regions too, architects such as Steven Holl and MVRDV(p. 166) are involved in large-scale housing complexes, and countless Japanese architects are also rushing over to the continent.

The Era of the Contemporary Globalist

In the 20-year period that preceded the current situation, architects generally functioned at a comparable level in their respective countries. But this state of equilibrium gradually began to collapse, and around the turn of the new century in particular, change became increasingly rapid. From the perspective of an island nation like Japan, the U.S. stands out, as the number of architects who attract widespread attention in most other countries rarely exceeds one or two.

For example, Italy is known for Renzo Piano and the late Aldo Rossi (p. 214), and France for Jean Nouvel and Dominique Perrault (p.196). This is not an indictment of a certain country's architecture, but rather an indication that designers no longer function in the way they once did.

There's a reason for this. With a contemporary globalist like Piano, information can be found in every type of magazine and media, while the work of many other architects is blotted out. This trend has become even more pronounced in recent years. In British architecture, for example, you often hear about contemporary globalists like Norman Foster, Richard Rogers, and Zaha Hadid, but rarely about anyone else.

Japan is no different. From the outside, Tadao Ando and Toyo Ito might look highly visible, and SANAA and Shigeru Ban might be a little more difficult to spot in the background. But those of us who live here realize that there is much more to Japanese architecture than a few famous names. This phenomenon is similar to what happens when a Japanese baseball player joins the American major leagues. Both the local and foreign media are flooded with references to Ichiro and Matsui, but the players who stay behind are often overlooked. In other words, news about people who are leading a glamorous life in another country tends to obscure the bigger picture.

This book, _World Architects 51:Concepts & Works_, focuses not only on contemporary globalists who are active on an international scale, but attempts to provide insight into the work of architects who work within their own country. Almost all of the 51 architects featured in the previous edition of this book were involved in projects in Japan during the era of the "bubble" economy, or visited Japan for a speech, an exhibition or some other event, giving me an opportunity to meet and interview them. But in writing this book, I was only able to meet or visit about half of the architects or firms. To make up for this, I tried to choose the most unique and individualistic architects of the era.

Forging Ahead with New Architects

In this book, I have consciously avoided the architects I featured in the previous edition and focused on a wide range of designers working in a multitude of countries. In doing this, however, I realized that many of them had already become true globalists.

4   The Eastern Docklands in Amsterdam
5   Palace Sant Jordi, built for the Barcelona Olympics
6   The Portuguese Pavilion at Lisbon Expo '98

Take, for example, Herzog and de Meuron. When I was gathering material for the first book between 1990 and 1995, the firm had done little more than complete the Ricola-Europe SA Production and Storage Building, the Schutzenmatt Housing Complex, Signal Box, and the Auf dem Wolf Signal Box in the Basel area. But in the intervening ten years or so, the firm has made an amazing leap forward, and the Herzog and de Meuron that I present in this book are globalists of the highest order.

Similarly, over the last decade, the Swiss architects Gigon / Guyer (p. 64), and Peter Zumthor (p. 310) have ratcheted up their respective skills with works like Kalkriese Archaeological Museum Park and Thermal Vals – masterpieces that are sure to become part of contemporary architectural history. Along with Herzog and de Meuron, Gigon / Guyer, and Zumthor, Mario Botta and Santiago Calatrava (both included in the first book) have made a tremendous contribution to post-Le Corbusier Swiss architecture.

In addition to Switzerland and the three major architectural nations of Europe (France, Germany, England), the Netherlands has produced a host of new architects in the last ten years. Many Dutch architects have been involved in urban development, but in recent years a younger generation of designers have matured and begun to exhibit a variety of developments. Among these are also globalist-type teams that are active internationally.

In the first book, I wrote about young Dutch architects and urban planners like Jo Coenen, known for his Netherlands Architecture Institute (NAI) and KNSM Island Masterplan, and Rem Koolhaas, designer of Kunsthal and the Netherlands Dance Theater, but in this book, I concentrate on the many Dutch architects who have emerged in the interim such as MVRDV, Wiel Arets (p. 22), Neutelings Riedijk (p. 166), UN Studio (p. 274), NOX (p. 172), Mecanoo (p. 142), Erick van Egeraat (p. 280), and the colossal Herman Hertzberger (p. 76).

The Emergence of a Wide Diversity of Architects

My intention in publishing this book was not to focus solely on young architects, but to introduce both young and old architects of various types from around the world. Thus, there are renowned masters like Hertzberger, who has strived to go beyond Dutch structuralism, and Paolo Soleri (p. 244), who spent his life trying to complete his work Arcosanti in the middle of the American desert.

Some of the architects have already left us, including Enric Miralles (p. 154), the Catalan architect respected for his avant-garde work who died much too young. His later works, such as Santa Caterina Market and the New Scottish Parliament, are unforgettable for their powerful deconstructed style. The late Josef Paul Kleihues (p. 118), who was instrumental in overseeing the International Building Exhibition (IBA), was also a dedicated architect who left us with outstanding works such as the Hamburger Bahnhof Museum of Contemporary Art and the Kant Dreieck. Another late master of contemporary Italian architecture is Aldo Rossi, whose work Hotel Il Palazzo is located in Japan. His deep understanding and insight into urban architecture has exerted a notable influence on many architects, including Herzog and de Meuron.

Other designers in the book include Imre Makovecz (p. 136), famous as an advocate of Eastern European Magyar architecture; and Sauerbruch Hutton (p. 226), who have filled Germany with a colorful and fun style. And you'll also find brilliant talents like

7 The Hannover Expo 2000 site
8 The Chinese National Swimming Center (foreground) and National Olympic Stadium under construction
9 The Netherlands Architecture Institute (NAI)

Dani Karavan (p. 106), an Israeli environmental sculptor, and Richard England (p. 46), a post-modern regionalist from Malta.

Among the other regions represented here are one of the world's remotest countries, Iceland, with its sole internationally known architectural firm, Studio Granda (p. 256). From South America, there is the Argentinean regional modernist Miguel Angel Roca (p. 208), and from Canada, Douglas Cardinal (p. 40), known for his unique organic architecture. From Scandinavia, there is Snohetta (p. 238), the Norwegian firm known for the Alexandria Library, and Heikkinen - Komonen (p. 70), the Finnish firm known for the Finnish Embassy in Washington D.C., both of which are active around the globe. The wide variety of architects in the book presents an accurate picture of contemporary world architecture as well as adding spice to the mixture.

An Era of Pluralism

For the first edition, I asked Arata Isozaki to write the introduction. This was because, as the producer and commissioner of Nexus World in Fukuoka Prefecture, Face of the Town in Toyama Prefecture, and Kumamoto Artpolis in Kumamoto Prefecture, and a designer with extensive contact with foreign architects, Isozaki had a very thorough understanding of architecture around the world.

His introduction, "Decomposition, Dispersal, and Prophetic Indication of a New Transition," examined pluralistic elements in the diverse world of contemporary architecture. As I mentioned above, however, from outside a given country, it appears as if there are only a couple of noteworthy architects. Does this imply a change, or is it merely one of the contradictions inherent in pluralism? Whichever the case, it is a clear indication of the complexity of contemporary society.

In our network society, based on computers and cell phones, everyone has access to a vast amount of information. This has given rise to any number of unique creators in every field. In other words, it is an important foundation for the growth of pluralistic tendencies. Despite this, as I have said, the number of foreign architects that stand out are very few indeed. The reason lies in the media's bias toward the latest trends. At the same time, it also reflects the audience's (the public's) tendency to favor advanced information and avant-garde work.

In contemporary society, the specific and the universal are concomitant. The specific is derived from the universal, and hovers on the edge of society. This universal, pluralism cultivates specific, cutting-edge ideas and isms. In his introduction to my book, Isozaki wrote, "Someday perhaps, the pluralistic situation suggested by its richly varied content may, as if decolorized, jell into new circumstance. For now, however, the future must be left to the mind of the reader, for nothing is yet fixed – there is no established interpretation, and what could be more interesting than a time without an established interpretation?"

In rereading Isozaki's introduction, I feel that he is in essence indicating the presence of pluralistic elements and expressing his confidence that a seed will be sown that signals a transition to a new set of circumstances. And I now feel that this bed for change is something that very much agrees with me, as my own work has come to be increasingly linked with foreign architecture and architects.

10 The Rem Koolhaas Wing of Nexus World
11 The gate to the offices of Herzog & de Meuron
12 Interior of the MVRDV office

Hope for a World Architecture

When I became an independent journalist around 1990, the country was still basking in the "bubble" economy and many architects were visiting Japan. The first edition of this book was a summary of the interviews I did with most of these people. But it wasn't long after that the bubble burst and visits by foreign architects began to wane, making it difficult to meet designers in Japan. On the other hand, I began to make more trips abroad, which expanded my perspective of architecture.

In _ World Architects 51:Concepts & Works_, I have collected a wealth of information through visits to architects in other countries. Although I did manage to meet Peter Zumthor and Herzog and de Meuron in Japan, I interviewed many others at their offices, including Dominique Perrault, Hans Hollein (p. 94), MVRDV, UN Studio, Snohetta, Studio Granda, Cesar Pelli (p. 190), Helmut Jahn (p. 100), Kim Young-Sub (p. 112), C.Y. Lee (p. 130), etc. Even though I wasn't able to visit every architect's office, I did make it to about two-thirds of the over 1,000 works that are mentioned in the book.

Having originally moved into architectural writing after a career as an editor, I have always thought that the job of a journalist called for direct reports from the source. This is why I have continued to travel all around, from Europe to Asia to North, Central, and South America. And I don't think this pattern of activity is likely to change in the future. The more new architects and architecture emerge, the more inspired I'll be to go out and find them. Obtaining all of the latest information might be difficult, but I hope to continue reporting on the pluralistic circumstances of the 21st century in a variety of ways in the future.

List of Architects Discussed in the first edition of _Contemporary Architects_

European:
Architecture Studio (France)
Gae Aulenti (Italy)
Benson and Forsyth (U.K.)
Ricardo Bofill (Spain)
Mario Botta (Switzerland)
Santiago Calatrava (Spain)
David Chipperfield (U.K.)
Jo Coenen (The Netherlands)
Coop Himmelblau (Austria)
Manuel Graça Dias (Portugal)
Gunther Domenig (Austria)
Terry Farrell (U.K.)
Norman Foster (U.K.)
Piers Gough (U.K.)
Nicholas Grimshaw (U.K.)
Zaha Hadid (U.K.)
Christian Hauvette (France)
Pekka Helin (Finland)
Rem Koolhaas (The Netherlands)
Leon Krier (U.K.)
José Rafael Moneo (Spain)
Jean Nouvel (France)
Renzo Piano (Italy)
Christian de Portzamparc (France)
Richard Rogers (U.K.)
Massimo Scolari (Italy)
Alvaro Siza (Portugal)

American:
Emilio Ambasz
Arquitectonica
Asymptote
Neil Denari
Diller and Scofidio
Peter Eisenman
Frank Gehry
Steven Holl
Daniel Libeskind
Morphosis
Eric Owen Moss
Antoine Predock
Bart Prince
Michael Sorkin
Bernard Tschumi
Lebbeus Woods

Other:
Brodsky and Utkin (Russia)
Charles Correa (India)
Zvi Hecker (Israel)
Sumet Jumsai (Thailand)
Ricardo Legorreta (Mexico)
Raj Rewal (India)
Moshe Safdie (Canada)
Ken Yeang (Malaysia)

13 UN Studio's Ben van Berkel
14 The Snohetta building
15 Interviewing C.Y.Lee

photos : ©Synectics except No.9 by ©Bryan Kuo

WILLIAM ALSOP

U.K.

Born in Northampton, U.K. in 1947. Graduated from the AA School of Architecture in 1973. From 1973 to 1977, collaborated with Cedric Price. From 1973 to 1981, taught sculpture at St. Martins College of Art and Design. In 1990, established the firm Alsop and Stormer. In 2000, the firm was dissolved Alsop began his an Served as chairman of the British Architecture Foundation until 2007.

2   section

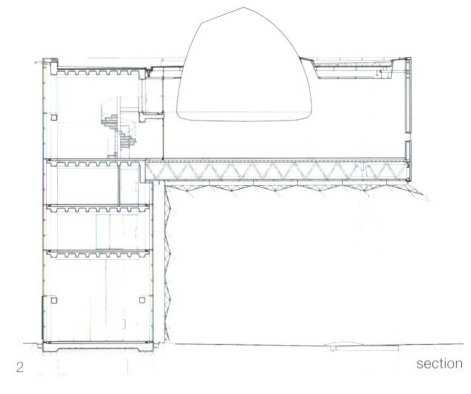

1, 2   Peckham Library   2000 / London
3, 4   Redevelopment of Potsdamer Platz / Competition
5   Cardiff Bay Visitor's Center   1990 / Cardiff, UK

4   elevation

7

8

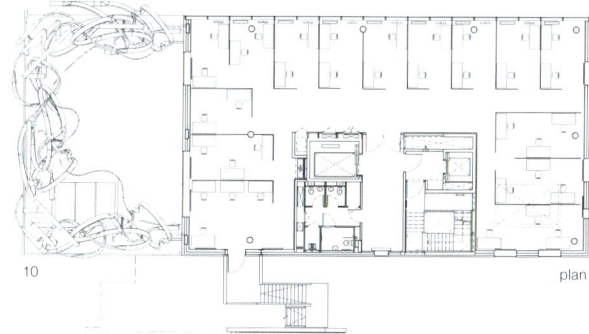

6   Ontario College of Art & Design   2004 / Toronto
    photo: ©Richard Johnson
7   Hotel du Department des Bouches du Rhone   1994 / Marseilles, France
8   Urban Entertainment Center Almere   2005 / Almere, The Netherlands
9, 10   Goldsmiths College   2005 / London
    photo: ©Roderick Coyne of Alsop & Partners
11, 12   Fawood Children's Center   2005 / North London

WILLIAM ALSOP

13

14

15

16

17

18

It was clear from the Potsdamer Platz Redevelopment competition that William Alsop was a different kind of architect. His design, based on an entomological form, resembled a grasshopper or an anthropod. The colorful and comical proposal seemed so mischievous that it was hard to take it seriously in the context of a major urban development competition. Ultimately, he lost, but after winning the Bouches-du-Rhone Prefectural Government Office Project in Marseilles in 1990, Alsop's practice not only gained a firm economic foundation, his name suddenly became familiar around the world.

Alsop's proposal, one of 156 entries, would have been completely unimaginable for a prefectural office in Japan. Le Grand Bleu (inspired by the Luc Besson film of the same name) is divided into two wings, and a small assembly hall is elevated on piloti. The larger office wing also stands on glass piloti. What's more, the entire structure is an eye-opening shade of blue. In contrast, the lobby, with a split-level, white-chalk breezeway, is a large area measuring 120 meters in length, and aided by the transparency of the glass, the interior feels expansive and comfortable. The space in Alsop's Cardiff Bay Visitor Center can also be found here as an exhibition space, and it too is elevated on piloti.

For some reason, Alsop often relies on piloti in his work. Unlike the thick, concrete Unite d'Habitation, designed by Le Corbusier and also in Marseilles, Alsop's prefectural office is a thin, steel structure. Similarly, a recent work like the Ontario College of Art and Design (OCAD) has a superstructure which is nine meters in height, 31 in width and 84 in length, and towers an astounding 26 meters above the ground. This is also supported by piloti in the form of twelve colorful, steel columns.

For the Peckham Library, Alsop also used high piloti, constructed out of long, thin steel columns leaned against the L-shaped structure. The Urban Entertainment Centre in Almere, Netherlands too features a piloti-form to elevate the hotel wing some eight meters above street level. And Heron Quays DLR Station is characterized by its tilted, piloti-like columns. In contrast, recent Alsop works such as the Colorium Office Building, Goldsmiths College, and the Fawood Children's Centre make absolutely no use of piloti. And as a gifted designer of waterfront development projects, Alsop is moving forward with the Masterplan for Rotterdam Centraal, Clarke Quay Development in Singapore, and the Fourth

13	Colorium 2002 / Dusseldorf, Germany
photo: ©Synectics	17	Clarke Quay Development / Singapore
14	Erotic Arts Museum 1997 / Hamburg, Germany	18	Heron Quays DLR Station 2003 / London
15	Victoria House Office Redevelopment 2003 / London	19, 20	The Fourth Grace / Liverpool, UK
16	Rotterdam Central Masterplan / Rotterdam	21	North Greenwich Underground Station, Jubilee Line 1999 / London

photos: Courtesy of the Architect except ©Synectics

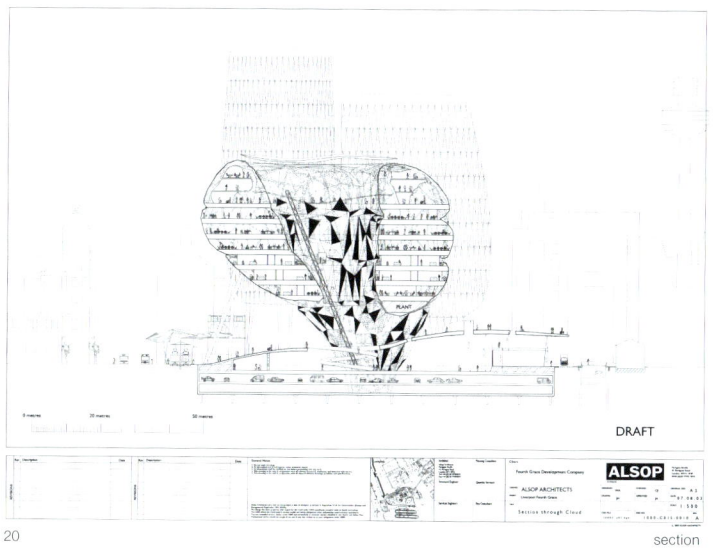

19

20 section

21

Grace project in Liverpool.
Colorful and amusing designs which invigorate a city are Alsop's forte: Along with the black-and-white pixel pattern of the OCAD, there is the brim of the red hat and the green exterior walls at Peckham Library, the deep blue of the Bouches-du-Rhone office and the North Greenwich Underground Station, and the variety of competing colors on the facades of the Colorium and Fawood buildings. Where does Alsop's playful approach come from? Alsop belongs to a generation of modern British architects who are difficult to classify according to any one school. His architectural philosophy holds that a fun design should be allowed to permeate every aspect of a building. Alsop's essential ethos is to distance himself from architecture which is based on the inflexible views that are commonly associated with trained professionals.

Alsop studied art at St. Martins College of Art and Design, and then went on to the AA School of Architecture. Because of this, he uses painting as his primary means of expression in creating a design. After graduation, he studied at Archigram and collaborated with the architect Cedric Price. Being an artistic architect, Alsop also taught sculpture at St. Martins. His senses are specially attuned to colorful and enjoyable architecture. It might also be noted that Alsop's piloti columns, like the legs of a multipede, have a definite link to the Archigram designer Ron Herron's obsession with legs in works such as "Walking City."

ARO/Architecture Research Office

USA

Firm founded by Adam Yarinsky and Stephen Cassell in 1993. Yarinsky was born in New Jersey in 1962. After graduating from the University of Virginia School of Architecture, completed a postgraduate degree at Princeton University. Cassell was born in New York in 1963. After graduating from Princeton University, completed a degree at the Harvard University Graduate School of Design. Both worked together at Stephen Holl Architects, and then left to start their own practice.

1 Colorado House   1999 / Telluride, Colorado
  photo: ©Paul Warchol
2 Martha's Vineyard House   2005 / Martha's Vineyard, Massachusetts
  photo: ©Elizabeth Felicella

ARO

plan

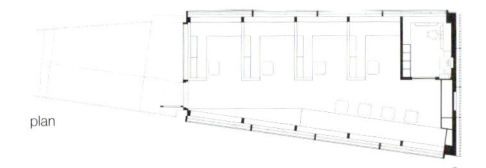

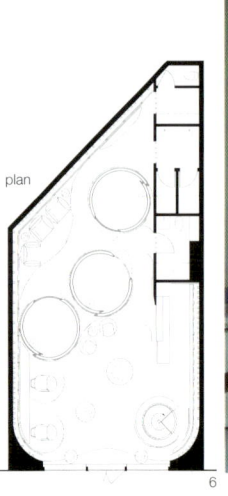

3, 4, 5 US Armed Forces Recruiting Station   1999 / New York
photo: ©Synectics

6, 7 Qiora Store and Spa   2000 / New York
photo: ©Synectics

plan

8   Capital Z Office   1999 / New York
9   PRADA NY Epicenter   2001 / New York
    photo: ©Synectics
10 SoHo Loft   1999 / New York
11 54 Thompson Street Lobby   1996 / New York

Picture Times Square at dusk. Neon signs, just beginning to come on, flash with intense colors, urging the stream of cars down Broadway. Next to the cylindrical NASDAQ sign, the most eye-catching one in the area, is a building with an exterior wall ornamented with a neon version of the American flag that towers over the meridian in the center of the expansive avenue. The ARO's (Architecture Research Office) US Armed Forces Recruiting Station, a facility which functions to induce young Americans to join the army, is a glass box located above a subway exhaust vent.

Three sides of the building are made of transparent glass, and the striped section of the flag functions as a louver or shutter, partially shutting out light in the afternoon. The idea to incorporate the Stars and Stripes in a building designed to entice new recruits into protecting the nation is magnificent, and the work is an interesting example of ARO's intuitive approach to architecture.

Based in New York, ARO is a young firm overseen by Adam Yarinsky, born in 1962, and Stephen Cassell, born in 1963. Still in their 40s, the two became friends while working together at Steven Holl Architects. Both also teach at Harvard University's Graduate School of Design. The firm employs close to 20 people, and despite its short history has a strong foundation.

Though ARO is an architecture firm, it is involved in much more than design. As the name "research office" suggests, the firm's work goes far beyond the walls of its headquarters. An important part of the operation is the collaborative relationship ARO maintains with construction firms, material and parts manufacturers, and its clients.

ARO's design process begins by clarifying a variety of information related to the physical and social context of an architecture project. Then, a given set of conditions arises out of the program, type of lot, and size of budget. After classifying and structuring this information, the firm arrives at a morphological approach. In fact, ARO's designs continue to evolve simultaneously with the actual construction of the building. Thus, the firm can verify certain architectural aspects, and using on-site alterations and minor adjustments, better resolve various design issues. To make the process work, ARO constantly receives input from the builder and gathers information from parts manufacturers.

The firm is especially skilled at studying computers models of the proposed structure and

12 Art et Industrie Gallery and Sculpture Garden   1995 / New York
13 Motown Center / Detroit, Michigan
14 Paper Wall   2000 / New York
15 Packard Hall at Colorado College   2005 / Colorado Spring, Colorado
    photo: ©Elizabeth Fellicella
16 Weston Performing Arts Center / Weston, Connecticut
17 Museum of Art and Technology / Competition
18 Flatiron Loft   1996 / New York
19 Remembrance Memorial at Columbia University
20 Modular Wall, Curved Plywood Partitions   1996
21 Corrulamp-1   2005 / New York

photos : Courtesy of the Architect except ©Synectics

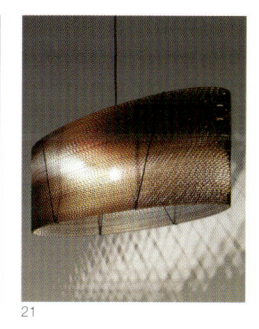

overall landscape to resolve specific design problems. With this interactive system, something intuitive is cultivated in each project. The Qiora Store and Spa, an antenna shop designed for the Shiseido Corporation, sells skin care products and cosmetics. To produce a space for customers to enjoy the spa salon, there was a special need for cleanliness. This was beautifully rendered by creating a vertical spa cabin covered with a light-blue organdy fabric against a pure white interior. It looks as if the sun is shining down into the bottom of the sea. As with the fabric in the Qiora Store, ARO makes skillful use of a variety of materials in its designs. For the Trina Showroom and Offices, the firm worked four types of fire-resistant fiber membranes into the ceiling grid using bungee cords.

In SoHo Loft, blue bahia granite was used for the interior walls, while steel shingles were applied to the exterior walls of Colorado House. In the dining hall at the Flatiron Loft, the floor was covered with an unusual material – leather. The leather tiles have a slightly deformed pentagonal shape.

The Japanese architect Shigeru Ban makes buildings out of paper tubes, but as an art space in SoHo, ARO unveiled Paper Wall. With a computer-operated laser cutter, the building's paper structure was cut and fitted together. The work symbolizes the future of ARO and the firm's principles of surveying, researching, and developing with the help of intuition.

Other ARO works in New York include the Capital Z Office, the 54 Thompson Street Lobby, the Art et Industrie Gallery and Sculpture Garden, and the PRADA New York Epicenter (a collaboration with OMA). In recent years, the firm has completed Martha's Vineyard House and Packard Hall at Colorado College. The Weston Performing Arts Center and the Motown Center are currently in progress.

WIEL ARETS

NETHERLANDS

Born in Heerlen, the Netherlands in 1955. Graduated from Technische Universiteit Eindhoven in 1983. From 1986 to 1989, taught at the Academies of Architecture in Amsterdam and Rotterdam. Served as unit master at the AA School of Architecture from 1988 to 1992. In 1994, received the Victor de Stuers Award and the Mies van der Rohe Pavilion Award for European Architecture. In 2005, awarded the Rietveldprijs.

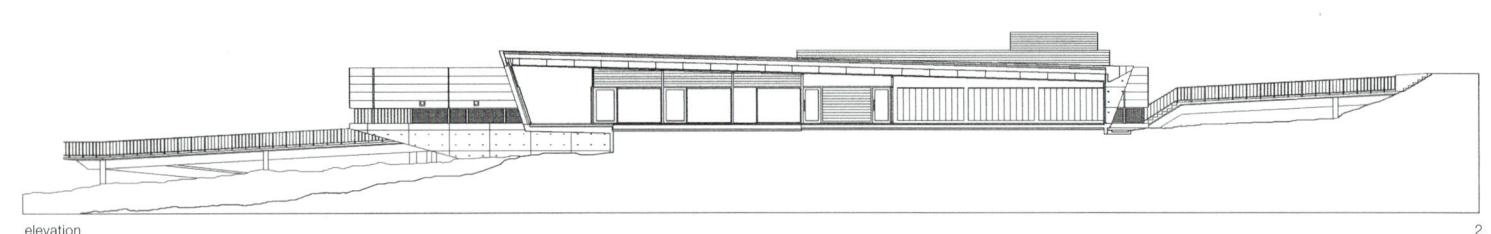

elevation

1, 2 Police Station in Vaals 1995 / Vaals, The Netherlands
 photo: ©Synectics
3 Ceramic Office Building 1995 / Maastricht, The Netherlands
 photo: ©Synectics
4 AZL Pension Fund Heduquarters 1995 / Heerlen, The Netherlands
 photo: ©Kim Zwarts
5 Maastricht Academy of Arts and Architecture
 1993 / Maastricht, The Netherlands
 photo: ©Synectics

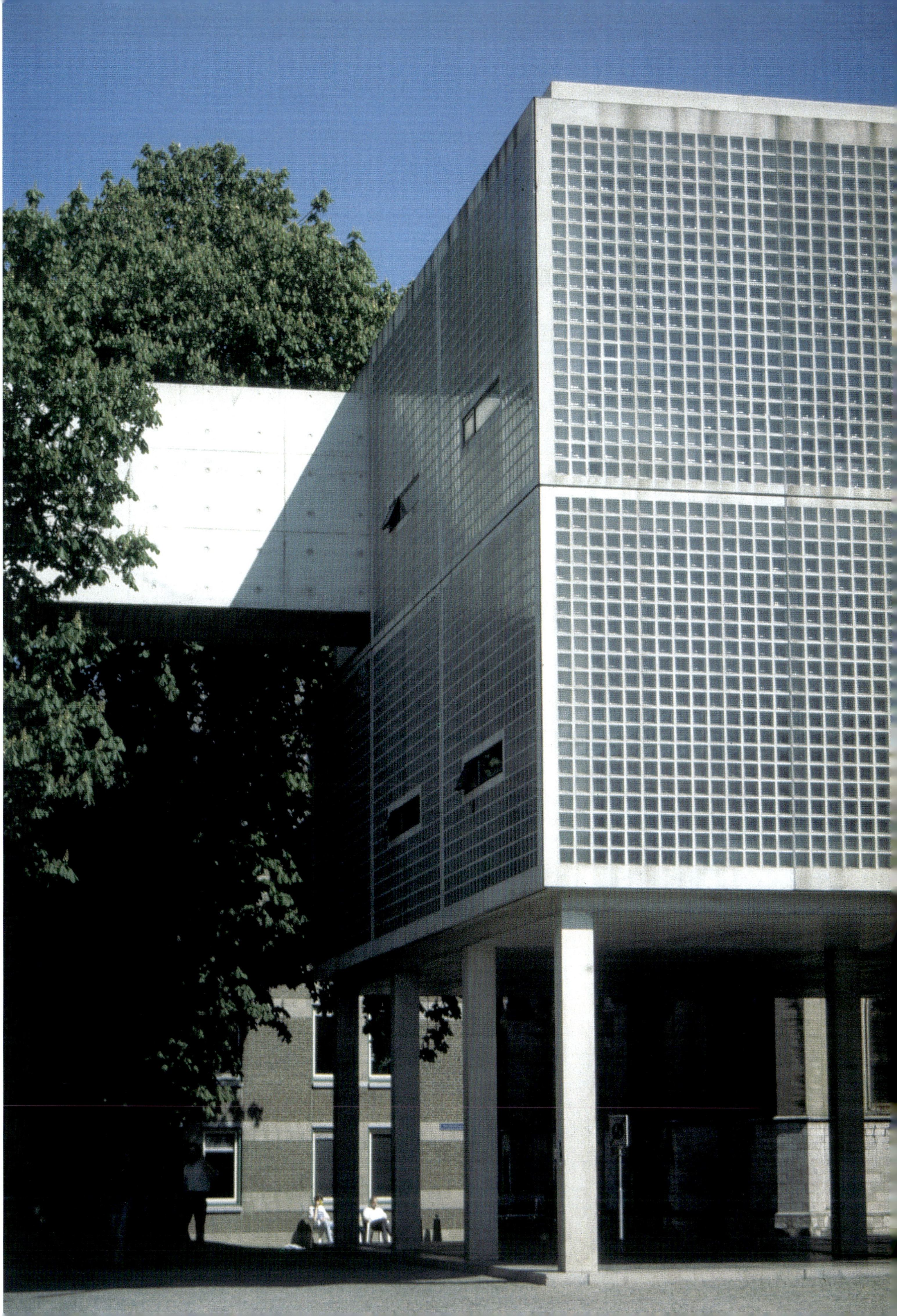

5

Wiel Arets

perspective drawing 6

perspective drawing 7

perspective drawing 8

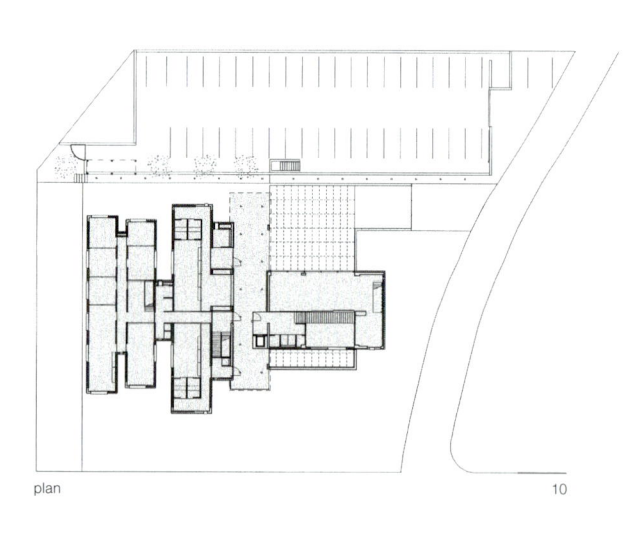

plan 10

14

6   Groningen Court Building / Groningen, The Netherlands
7   Delft Theater / Delft, The Netherlands
8   Amsterdam Academy for the Arts / Amsterdam
9, 10   Police Station in Boxtel   1997 / Boxtel, The Netherlands
   photo: ©Kim Zwarts
11   Cathedral in Ghana / Cape Coast, Ghana
12   Lensvelt Office & Factory Building
   1999 / Breda, The Netherlands
   photo: ©Kim Zwarts
13   Almere Theater / Almere, The Netherlands
14, 15   Utrecht University Library   2004 / Utrecht, The Netherlands
   photo: ©Synectics

15

Maastricht is located in the southernmost part of Holland. In a remote corner a little to the west of the city center stands one of Wiel Arets' most representative works, the Maastricht Academy of Arts and Architecture. In the middle of a grove of huge, verdant chestnut trees is an aerial bridge made of reinforced concrete. With the blue sky as a backdrop, the refreshing architectural beauty created by the combination of light, greenery, reinforced concrete, and glass blocks makes for a deeply moving scene.

After passing under the bridge, one finds a square called Herdenkingsplein. Then, looking back, a workshop with glass-block walls in a square grid is visible on the right side, and on the left is the school's old wing, or main building, and adjacent to it, a glass-block auditorium. The bridge, as one might expect, connects the auditorium and the workshop.

Arets, who pays particularly close attention to a building's skin, demonstrates an impressive prowess in his use of glass blocks in this work. The brilliant glass-block walls, which with their square pattern are enclosed in a thin concrete frame, recall the austerity of other glass houses such as Pierre Chareau's Maison de Verre and Tadao Ando's Ishihara Residence.

The use of linear space, something that Arets is deeply fond of, also creates a striking effect. With glass blocks for the floor and ceiling, and reinforced concrete for the walls, the bridge creates a strange feeling of elation rooted in one's sense that the position of the materials would normally be reversed. In the Police Station in Vaals too, two linear spaces stand parallel to each other, creating a floating sensation, with the cantilevers hanging out in space over the slanted lawn area.

Among Arets' other linear-space-based works are the Ceramic Office Building, Groningen Court Building, Delft Theater, Amsterdam Academy for the Arts, the AZL Pension Fund Headquarters, the Police Station in Boxtel, the Lensvelt Office and Factory Building, and Almere Theater. Common to all of these is a long, thin office space, slope, and a corridor – a structure with a heightened sense of perspective.

In looking at Arets' drawings, one finds similarities between his elongated, flowing form of spatial expression and the paths through hyperspace depicted by Zaha Hadid. Arets' expressions, however, are supported by a geometry of rigid right angles. The simple yet pure impression this creates is truly Andoesque, and in light of Ando's use of approach slopes, glass blocks, and reinforced concrete walls, he seems to

| 16, 17 | KNSM Tower   1996 / Amsterdam
photo: ©Synectics
| 18 | Zalmhaven Apartments Towers   2001 / Rotterdam
photo: ©Kim Zwarts
| 19 | Arena Tower / Amsterdam
| 20 | Euroborg Stadium   2006 / Groningen, The Netherlands
photo: ©Jan Bitter
| 21 | Renovation for Glass Palace 'Schunck'   2003 / Heerlen, The Netherlands
photo: ©Jan Bitter
| 22 | Hedge House Gallery   1995 / Wijlre, The Netherlands
photo: ©Jan Bitter
| 23 | Sportcampus Leidsche Rijn   2006 / Utrecht, The Netherlands
photo: ©Jan Bitter
| 24 | Stylesuite D&G fashion Store, Maastricht   2005 / Maastricht, The Netherlands
photo: ©Jan Bitter

photos : Courtesy of the Architect except ©Synectics

have exerted a strong influence on Arets. Arets later switched from these horizontally expansive linear spaces to a vertical style. Out of this emerged expressive high-rise towers such as the Zalmhaven Apartments Towers, KNSM Tower, and Arena Tower. As Arets' first high-rise building, KNSM, for example, has a unique quality created by the comprehensive use of imitation stone (made of concrete), which he conceived as a kind of black natural stone. The planar form is also complex, exuding something slightly different from the vertical mass in a run-of-the-mill high rise.

To Arets, the current age is one of increasing corporeality. This is due to the changing relationship between materials. And through advances that have been made in electronic media, human perceptions themselves have by necessity changed, making it impossible to deny that our mode of thought has also been affected. A global age in which the world can be summed up in a single image is now upon us. According to Arets, though expressions which are fundamentally clean, pure and perfect can be applied to modern architecture, people are ready to accept elements which are essentially incomplete, noisy, and disordered as part of contemporary technology. This is why, when Arets says at the beginning of his book _An Alabaster Skin_, "Architecture is the desire for purity and the effort to create perfection," he is clearly speaking of his own practice.

Wiel Arets was born in the Dutch town of Heerlen in 1955. He graduated from the Technical University in Eindhoven in 1983. In 1985, he quickly established a base of operations by opening a firm in Heerlen. Following this, he traveled to Russia, the U.S., Japan, and throughout Europe. Between 1986 and 1989, he taught at architecture schools in Amsterdam and Rotterdam. From 1988 to 1992, he served as a unit master at the AA School. After working at Columbia University in 1991 and the research institutes at Cooper Union and Berlage in 1992, Arets used his rich experience as a teacher at schools throughout the world to move into the sphere of international architecture. The scale of recent works such as Utrecht University Library, Cathedral in Ghana, Arena Tower, and Euroborg Stadium is proof that Wiel Arets has truly arrived.

GUNTHER BEHNISCH

GERMANY

Born in Dresden in 1922. Graduated from Stuttgart Technical University in 1951. Established his own firm in 1952, which in 1966 became Behnisch & Partner, and in 1989, Behnisch, Behnisch & Partner. Came to international attention in 1972 for the Olympic Park designed for the 1972 Munich Olympics. Awarded the Gold Medal from the Academy of Architecture, France in 1992. Named professor emeritus at University of Karlsruhe in 1993.

1 State Clearing Bank (B,B&P) 1997 / Stuttgart, Germany
2, 3 North German State Clearing Bank (B,B&P) 2002 / Hannover, Germany
photo: ©Roland Halbe

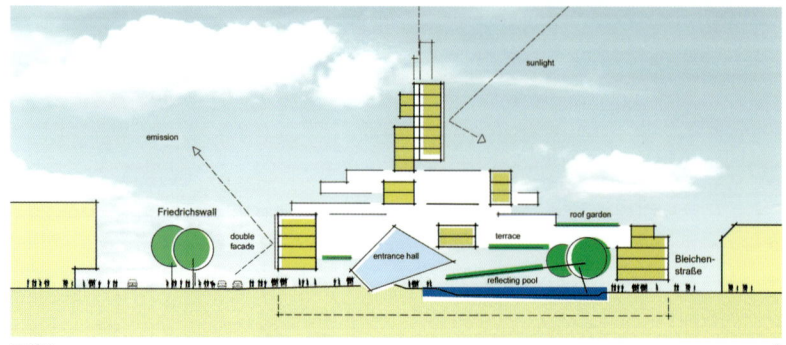

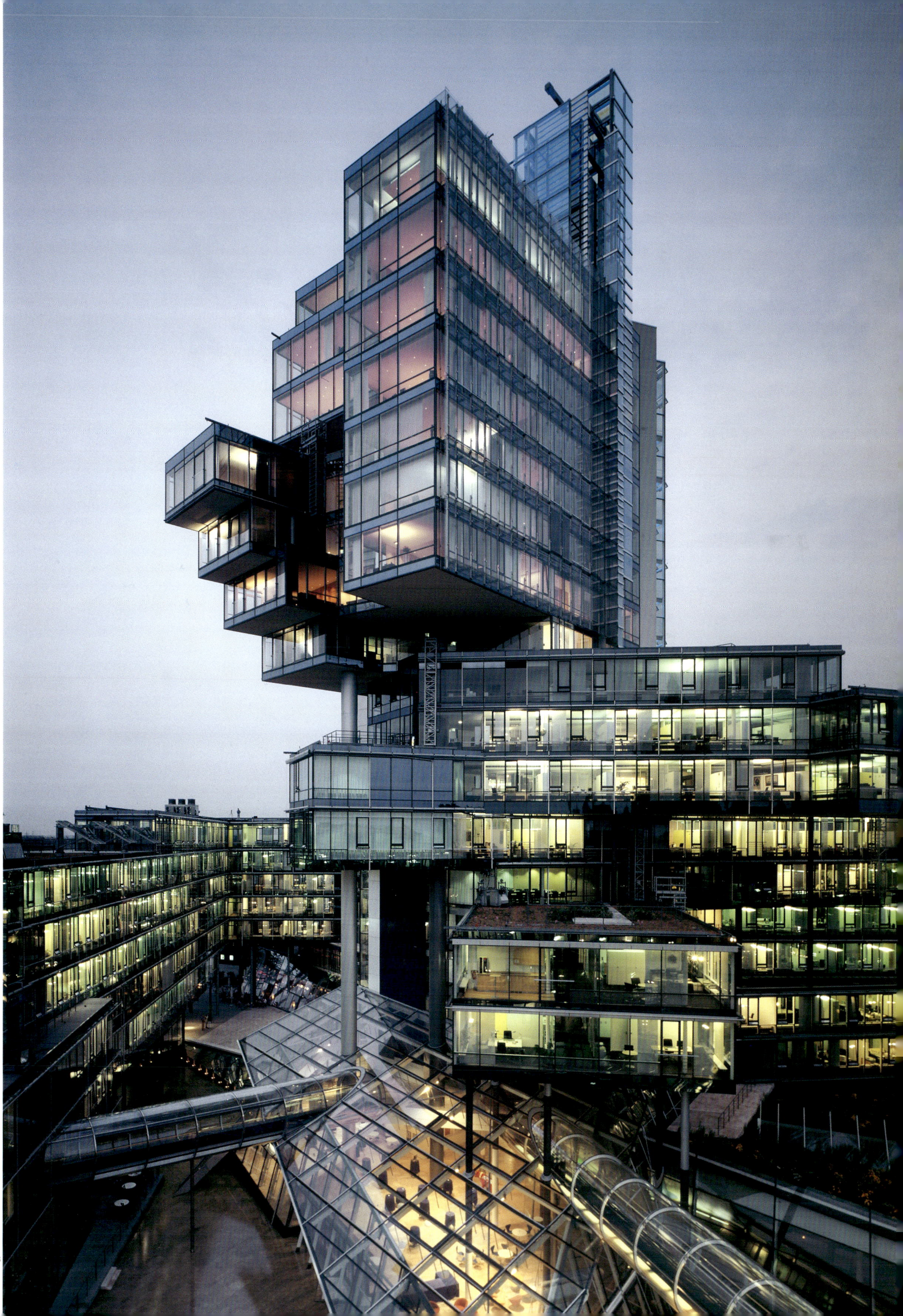

3

4 Plenary Complex of the German Bundestag (B&P)   1992 / Bonn
photo: ©Kandzia

5 Center for Cellular and Biomolecular Research University of Toronto (B,B&P)
2005 / Ontario, Canada

6 Institute for Forestry and Nature Research (B,B&P)   1998 / Wageningen, The Netherlands

7, 8 LVA State Institute Agency (B,B&P)   1997 / Lubeck, Germany

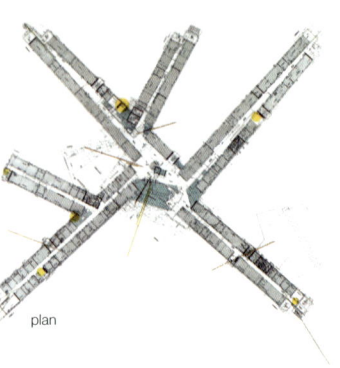

plan

9   Air Control Tower Nuremberg Airport (B&P)   1998 / Nuremberg, Germany
    photo: ©Kandzia
10 St. Benno Gymnasium (B,B&P)   1996 / Dresden, Germany
    photo: ©Kandzia
11 Geschwister Scholl Schule (B&P)   1994 / Frankfurt
    photo: ©Synectics
12 Academy of Fine Arts Berlin (B&P)   2005 / Berlin
    photo: ©Kandzia
13 Health and Spa Facilities Bad Elster (B&P)   1999 / Saxony, Germany

14 German Postal Museum (B&P)   1990 / Frankfurt
    photo: ©Synectics
15 Sky Lofts / Los Angeles
16 German Oceanographic Museum (B,B&P) / Stralsund, Germany
17 Thermal Spa Bad Aibling (B,B&P) / Bad Aibling, Germany
18 Mildred Scheel Haus (B&P)   2002 / Dresden, Germany
    photo: ©Kandzia

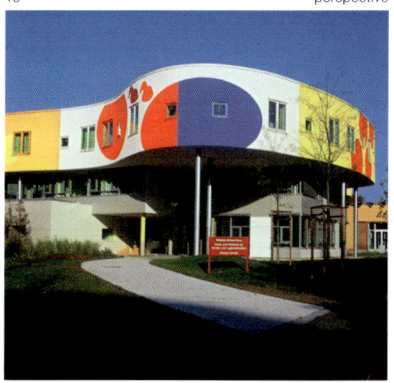

19 Museum of Fantasy (B,B&P) 2001 / Bernried, Germany
20 Olympic Park in Munich (B&P) 1972 / Munich
    photo: ©Synectics
21 Hysolar Institute Building (B&P) 1987 / Stuttgart, Germany
    photo: ©Synectics
22, 23 Genzyme Center (B,B&P) 2004 / Cambridge, Massachusetts
    photo: ©Anton Grassl
24 Reconstruction of the Bayerishe Vereinsbank (B,B&P) 1996 / Stuttgart, Germany
25 Feuerbach Station (B&P) 1991 / Stuttgart, Germany
    photo: ©Synectics

photos : Courtesy of the Architect except ©Synectics

B&P=Behnisch & Partner
B,B&P=Behnisch, Behnisch & Partner

With the design for the 1972 Olympic Park in Munich, Gunther Behnisch was catapulted to the forefront of the German architecture world. Twenty years later, in 1992, Behnisch completed the Plenary Complex of the German Bundestag just prior to the unification of Germany. Through these two national projects, Behnisch was able to established his reputation internationally.

Some of Behnisch's works, for example the Olympic Park, have been collaborations with the professional tent designer Frei Otto. With transparent tents using gigantic pieces of Plexiglas to cover the audience, or thick steel wires or groups of forested steel masts, Behnisch's early works place a strong emphasis on technique.

For the 1987 Hysolar Institute Building, on the University of Stuttgart campus, the architect used slanted windows for the stainless-steel structure to create a complex and chaotic expression, and give the work an intricate, deconstructed appearance. This was the first Behnisch building I had seen since the Olympic Park, and it was after this work that he continued to explore and refine his style. What exactly inspired this stylistic shift in Behnisch's work?

In Germany, Hugo Haering is seen as a master of organic architecture known for works such as Garkau Farm. Haering declared, "Form is not something to be imposed [on a design], but something that is waiting to be discovered."

This philosophy later came to be embodied in the postwar works of Hans Scharoun, including his Berlin Philharmonic Hall.

In Scharoun's school architecture, for example, the planes grant individual elements such as classrooms a certain degree of freedom and separation from the whole. In addition, while other architects adhered to a grid, Scharoun was a progressive designer who opted for complicated, irregular geometry. In his view, the freedom of the form was linked to the freedom of the individual in a democratic society.

This is exactly the approach that Behnisch later adopted. Carrying on Haering and Scharoun's organic orientation, Behnisch expanded his focus as an architect. And not only did he include geometric irregularity and spatial interpenetration in his work, Behnisch's philosophical stance was the same.

After seeing the Hysolar Building, I began looking for other Behnisch buildings. In Frankfurt, I visited the Geschwister Scholl Schule and the German Postal Museum; in

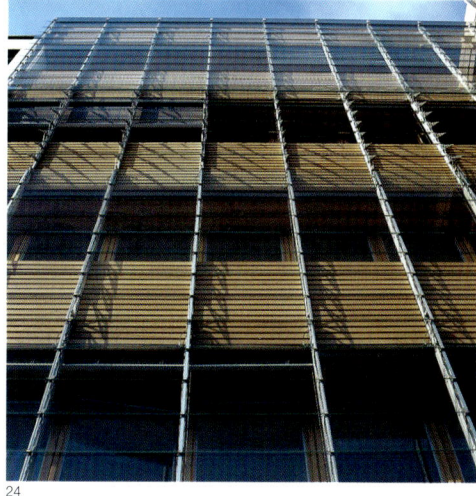

Dresden, the St. Benno Gymnasium; in Bonn, the Bundestag; in Stuttgart, Feuerbach Station and State Clearing Bank; and in Hannover, North German State Clearing Bank. There were so many works, I couldn't see all of them. After opening his own firm in Stuttgart in 1952, Behnisch designed close to 40 schools in the surrounding area alone. When one includes all of the banks and public buildings he has designed, the number of Behnisch's works is practically uncountable. Indeed, it is truly rare to find a German architect with such a large body of work.

If one looks at, for example, one of his more recent representative works, the North German State Clearing Bank, the special characteristics of Behnisch's design become apparent. The overall structure is transparent glass with an eco-design that features water and greenery, the interior of the lobby has an intricate, deconstructed style, and the offices in the building exhibit a rich range of colors. These features can also be found in other important Behnisch works such as the Academy of Fine Arts in Berlin, the Health and Spa Facilities in Bad Elster, the Museum of Fantasy, and the LVA State Institute Agency.

In 1989, Behnisch beefed up his firm by inviting his son Stefan and Gunther Schaller to join the practice, and establishing Behnisch, Behnisch and Partner. His foreign commissions also began to increase, and Behnisch opened a new branch in Los Angeles. At present, his staff exceeds 100 people, and his completed works outside of Germany include the Genzyme Center in Cambridge, Massachusetts, the Centre for Cellular and Biomolecular Research at University of Toronto, and the Institute for Forestry and Nature Research in Wageningen, The Netherlands. In addition, among his works currently in progress are Sky Lofts in Los Angeles, and the German Oceanographic Museum and the Thermal Spa Bad Aibling in Germany.

Frederic Borel

FRANCE

Born in Roanne, France in 1959. Graduated from the Ecole Spéciale d'Architecture in Paris in 1982. Worked at Christian de Portzamparc's firm from 1982 to 1985. In 1983, awarded the Lauréat PAN (Programme d'Architecture Nouvelle) and the Albums de la Jeune Architecture. In 1984, opened his own firm. Completed the Rue Ramponneau and Boulevard de Belleville housing complexes in 1989. In 1993, completed the Rue Oberkampf project and in 1999, the Rue Pelleport project. Awarded the French Arts & Culture Medal in 1999.

2   section

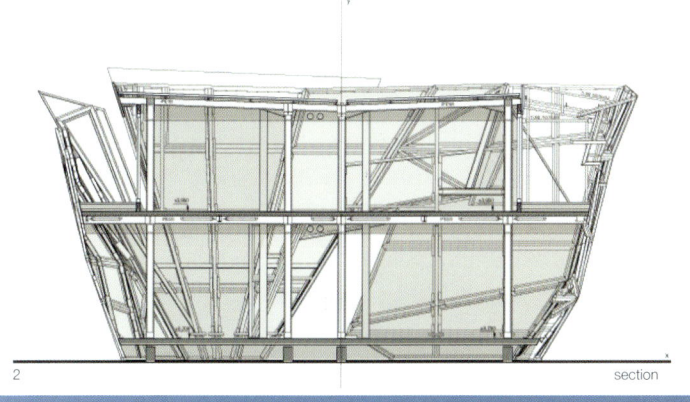

1, 2   Agen Institute for local Development   2002 / Agen, France
photo: ©Nicolas Borel
3   Dreux Theater   1994 / Dreux, France
photo: ©Nicolas Borel
4   Theater & Concert Hall in Blois   1991 / Blois, France
photo: ©Nicolas Borel
5   Nursery School on Recollects Street   2002 / Paris
photo: ©Nicolas Borel
6   Logements Paris 13 / Paris

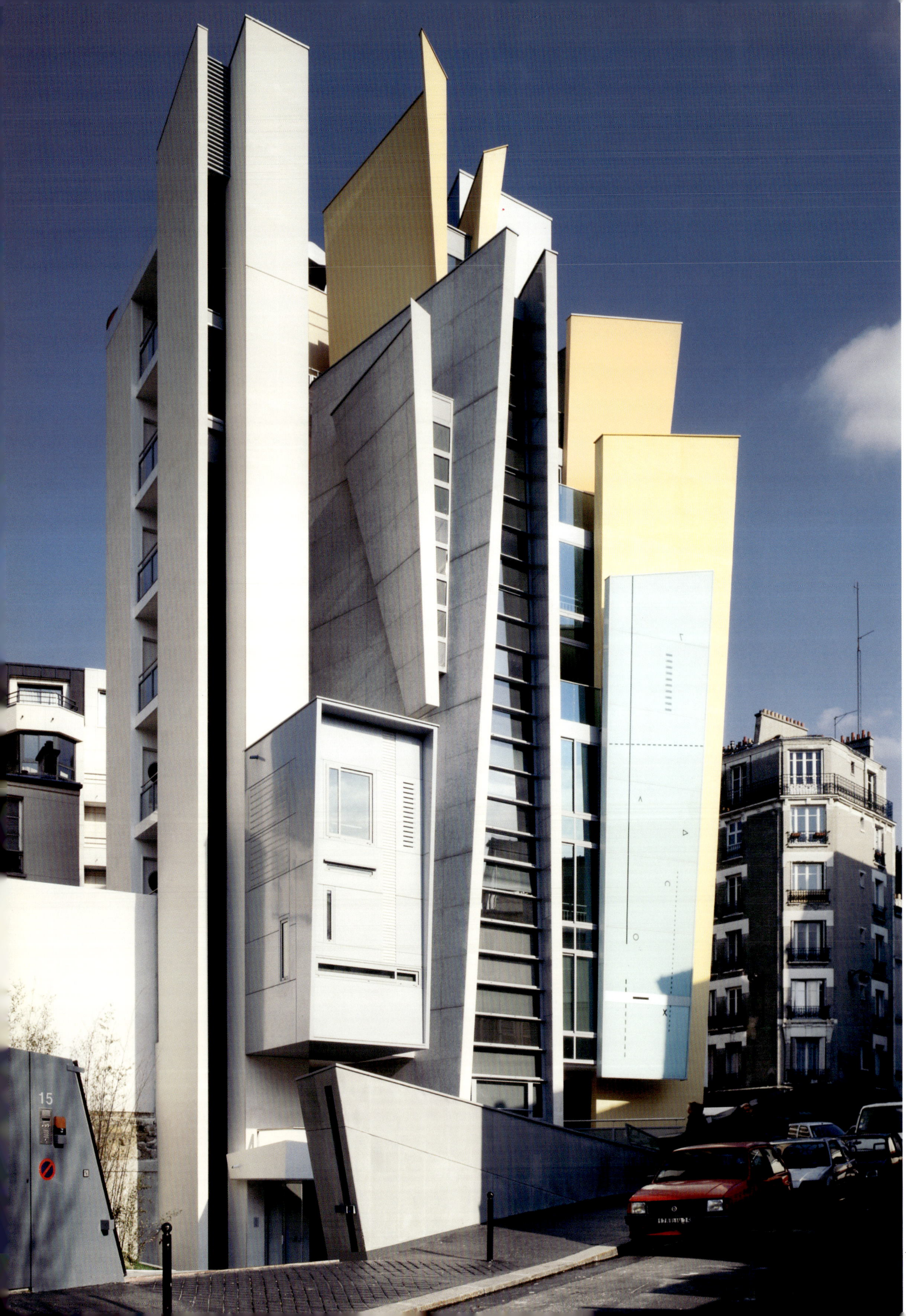
15

7, 8	Housing on Pelleport Street 1998 / Paris
	photo: ©Nicolas Borel
9, 10	Housing on Oberkampf Street 1993 / Paris
	photo: ©Nicolas Borel
11, 12	Summary Court & Regional Court in Laval
13	Tax Center at Brive 1999 / Brive, France
	photo: ©Nicolas Borel

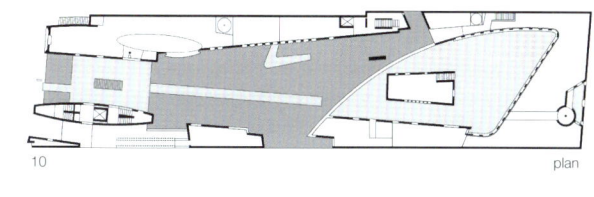

FREDERIC BOREL

As seen in important early works such as the Housing Complexes on Belleville and Ramponeau Streets, many of Frederic Borel's designs place an excessive emphasis on the vertical. This is due in part to the narrow frontage and depth of the lots in Paris. His four-year collaboration with Christian de Portzamparc has probably also had a strong influence on Borel's slender works, such as the apartment complex on Rue des Hautes-Formes. After graduating from the Ecole Spéciale d'Architecture in 1982, Borel displayed an abrupt maturity by winning the Programme Architecture Nouvelle Competition the following year. In 1984, he opened his own firm in Paris. With the Boulevard de Belleville and Rue Ramponeau Streets projects, he transformed the traditionally empty courtyards of Paris into generous spaces symbolizing a new type of architectural Epicureanism. This then led to the emergence of more radical forms in the Housing on Oberkampf and Pelleport Streets.

The Housing on Oberkampf Street is a stunning work. Comprising a post office and a residential complex for workers, the building offers a commanding view of a sunken garden from street level – another truly awesome sight. Front and center, a thin housing unit towers overhead like a black monolith; and on the left, is another thin apartment block standing atop a thin, reenforced-concrete support. These two slender buildings, which are breathtaking in their fragmentation, are connected to the main housing complex by an aerial bridge surrounded by a garden.

Another Borel work that astounded me was his Housing on Pelleport Street. Here the verticality is even more drastic. The facade, which is nearly deconstructed, is fragmented to create an irregular shape. Though the wall surfaces would ordinarily rise up in parallel with the facade, the deconstruction of the facade is notable for the sense of asymptopia and alienation it creates.

The fragmentation is not limited to Borel's verticality. It Is also seen in the four masses in the Nursery School on Recollets Street, the sinusoidal cylinders in the Summary Court and Regional Court in Laval, the white exterior walls that resemble the sails of a yacht in the Dreux Theater, and finally, a variety of forms at the Theater and Concert Hall in Blois. Because this type of fragmented volume is a response to the increasingly compact and introverted urban areas that house recent public buildings, the mass of these structures confronts

14, 15, 16 Michel Serres Science Center in Agen   1998 / Agen, France
photo: ©Nicolas Borel
17 Housing on Ramponeau Street   1989 / Paris
photo: ©Nicolas Borel
18 Architecture School Class Rooms & Streets / Paris

19 Housing on Belleville Street   1989 / Paris
photo: ©Nicolas Borel
20 School on Moskowa Street   2000 / Paris
photo: ©Nicolas Borel

photos : Courtesy of the Architect except ©Synectics

nature and the city in a calm and peaceful manner. Another excellent example is Borel's Brive Tax Center, which has the appearance of a ship floating far away from the squalid city. And while both the Agen University Office (also called the "Meteorite") and the School on Moskowa Street include touches that recall a suspended monolith, Rognes High School creates a horizontal line across the chaotic yet delicate skyline of the new town.

Borel has said he is interested in comparing cities with microcosms, and archetypal forms using a simple vocabulary with futuristic towers. In Borel's 1996 book _Densité, réseaux, évènments_ too, he writes, "Cautiously mixing color, form and material, there is a necessity to infuse some imagination into the new emotional wilderness that the contemporary city aspires to."

The frame of the Michel Serres Science Center at Agen floats above a forest with its series of V-shaped columns and is covered with colorful fragments. Here again, Borel's signature elliptical entrance is captivating. His use of sinusoidal forms hints at the influence of the great Brazilian architect Oscar Niemeyer. After his years with Portzamparc, who at the time was planning the City of Music, Borel seems to have absorbed some of the architect's references to Niemeyer's large curves with the roof and rounded walls of the hall.

Behind the elliptical entrance to the Laval courthouse, currently underway, are two towering wings with sinusoidal forms – a design that is quintessentially Borel. This futuristic form is Borel's trump card in creating architecture for the 21st century.

Douglas Cardinal

CANADA

Born in Calgary, Canada in 1934. Studied architecture at the University of British Columbia and the University of Texas, Austin, graduating from the latter in 1963. Became a member of the Royal Architect Institute of Canada in 1964. Established his own firm, Douglas J. Cardinal Architect, in Edmonton in 1964, and moved his practice to Ottawa in 1985. Received the Great Canadian Award in 1992. Joined the American Institute of Architects, Washington, D.C. Chapter in 1995. Named honorary fellow of the Royal Incorporation of Architects in Scotland.

1	St. Mary's Roman Catholic Church 1968 / Alberta, Canada
2	Nicaragua Museo de la Naturaleza / San Juan del Sur, Nicaragua
3	St. Albert Place 1976 / Alberta, Canada
4, 5	Grande Prairie Regional College 1976 / Alberta, Canada
6, 7	Edmonton Space Sciences Center 1983 / Alberta, Canada
8	Grand Traverse Band of Ottawa & Chippewa Indian Civic Center 2001 / Michigan

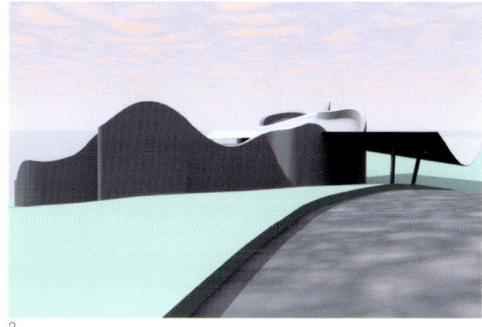

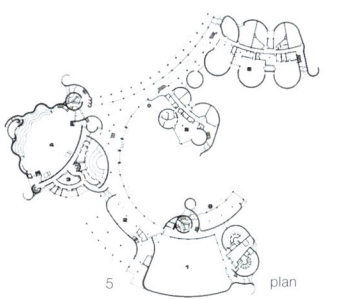

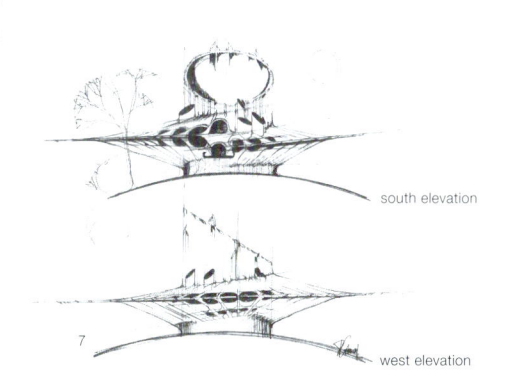

Douglas Cardinal

9 Canadian Museum of Civilization 1989 / Quebec, Canada
10, 11, 12 Cardinal Studio & Residence 1982 / Alberta, Canada

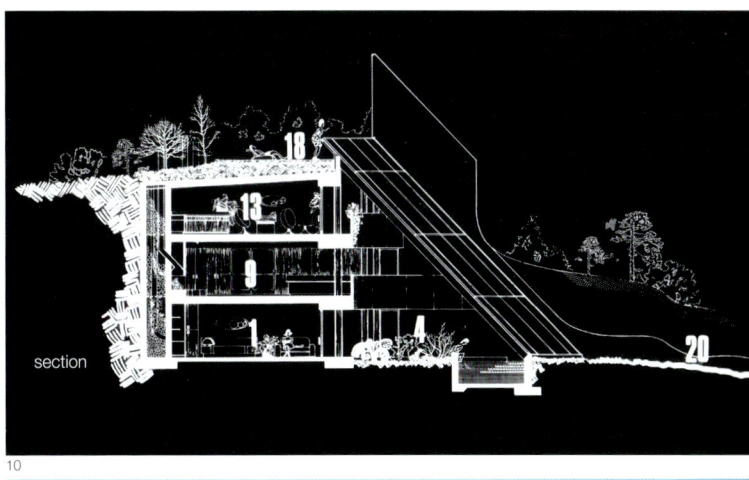

The Canadian architecture world isn't very well known in Japan. The leading light, Arthur Erickson, is remembered for serving as a judge at the Tokyo International Forum Competition, and the Isareli-born Canadian architect Moshe Safdie is fairly famous. Then there is Dan Hanganu, Richard Henriquez, Peter Rose, Patkau Architects, Bruce Kuwabara, and Forsythe and MacAllen, who until just prior to winning the Aomori Northern Style Housing Competition were virtually unknown. Architecturally, Canada is definitely far-removed, but among the most unique of the country's architects is Douglas Cardinal, who those in the know know. Cardinal, an eminent designer in Canada, is also unique for his Native American background. He has said, "I was actually raised in the construction world. I was the oldest of eight brothers and sisters, and was already helping my father make houses and furniture as a child. I think my mother just assumed that I would become an architect." The family lived in a log cabin outside of Red Deer, Alberta, and Cardinal's father worked first as a forest ranger and later as a game warden. Cardinal explains, "We lived way off the beaten track and we studied nature and our own customs."

While in his teens, Cardinal's family moved to the city, and his father began working in the hotel industry. Cardinal and two of his younger brothers devoted themselves to carpentry, helping to build hotels and bungalows, and also making furniture. This lifestyle gave Cardinal an ecological orientation and a pragmatic technique, and helped him develop into an architect. The Canadian Museum of Civilization in Ottawa is a concentration of his way of living and his experiences. Considered to be one of Cardinal's most representative works, the museum is also the best embodiment of his essence and style. The museum was actually designed as a "habitat" in accordance with the surrounding environment, and the organic design symbolizes human evolution and harmony with the earth. In terms of form, the building's organic curves reflect the rugged nature and varying elevations of the adjacent landscape.

Yet, there are also numerous architectural elements at the museum that perhaps reflect Cardinal's artistic influences. The columns and dome are reminiscent of Alberti, Michelangelo, and Palladio, while the receding steps on each successive level recall the ziggurats of Mesopotamia. And the overhangs and latticework are akin to the Prairie style of Frank

13 National Museum of American Indian
    2004 / Washington D.C.
    photo: ©Synectics
14 Ochichakkosipi Healing Lodge / Manitoba, Canada
15 Victoria Island Development / Ottawa, Canada
16 Penewobecong Heritage Center / Ontario, Canada
17 York Regional Headquarters   1992 / New Market, Canada
18 Iskotew Healing Lodge   2002 / Ottawa, Canada
19 Neeganin Round House & Park   2000 / Manitoba, Canada
20 Mono-Ya-Win Health Center / Ontario, Canada
21 Seneca Nation of Indians
    New Administration Building / Salamanca, New York
22 Fairview Elementary School   1975 / Alberta, Canada
23 First Nations University of Canada
    2003 / Saskatchewan, Canada
24 Alberta Government Services Building
    1976 / Alberta, Canada
25 Keatley Creek Interpretive Center / British Columbia, Canada

photos : Courtesy of the Architect except ©Synectics

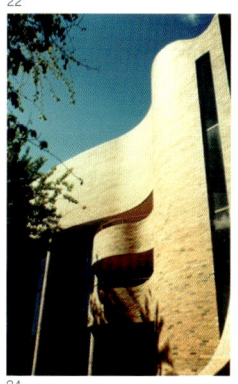

Lloyd Wright.
St. Mary's Roman Catholic Church, another curve-filled Cardinal work, was built in the architect's hometown of Red Deer in 1968. It is distinguished by a rippling, brick exterior wall and an unusual wall surface above the canopy with organically shaped holes in it. Later, around the same period in 1976, the architect completed three works, St. Albert Place, Grande Prairie Regional College, and the Alberta Government Services Building. After developing his own distinctive style and skill, Cardinal designed Cardinal Studio and Residence in 1982. Then, in 1983, he completed the Edmonton Space and Science Center, and truly coming into his own, he was selected to create the aforementioned museum. Perhaps as a graduate of the University of Texas at Austin, it was normal to embark on drives down from Alberta and over the Rocky Mountains. Always choosing a different route, Cardinal found inspiration in the landscape and natural forms he saw from the road. He says that this "on-the-road" method of education taught him that "architecture is derived from the natural environment of a place." Cardinal also says that because high-rise buildings are a male symbol, he'd like to replace them with architecture that embodies the female qualities of protection, nurturing, care, and healing.
In March 2001, he completed the Grand Traverse Band of Ottawa and Chippewa Indian Civic Center, which indeed displayed a soft, female texture, and in the fall of 2002, he also created the First Nations University of Canada. Cardinal's works are located not only in Canada, but in where he created the National Museum of the American Indian in Washington D.C. Currently, he is at work on the Keatley Creek Interpretive Center, the Museo de la Naturaleza in Nicaragua, and the New Administration Building for the Seneca Nation of Indians.

Richard England

MALTA

Born in Malta in 1937. Graduated from the University of Malta and the Polytechnic University of Milan. Teaches at the International Academy of Architecture, University of Malta, and the University of Buenos Aires. Received the Malta Architects Association Prize in 1985 and 1987, the Georgia U.S.S.R Biennale Laureate Prize in 1988, the IFRAA-AIA Award in 1991, and a few International Academy of Architecture Laureate Prizes. Awarded the Gold Medal at the Belgrade Architectural Triennale in 2000.

1 Astana Concert Hall / Astana, Kazakhstan
2 White Shadows Sculpture   2002 / Sliema, Malta
3 St. James Cavalier   2000 / Valletta, Malta
4 Central Bank of Malta   1993 / Valletta, Malta
5 LOVE Sculpture   2003 / St. Julians, Malta

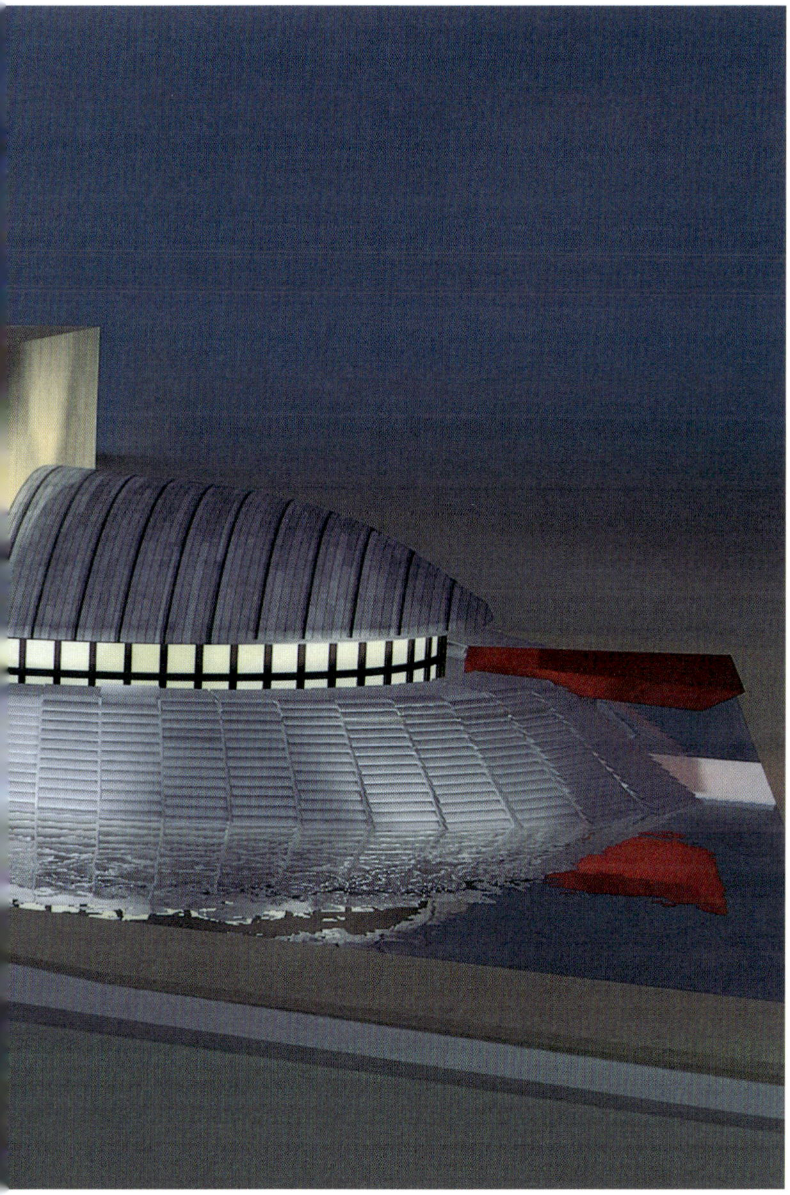

1

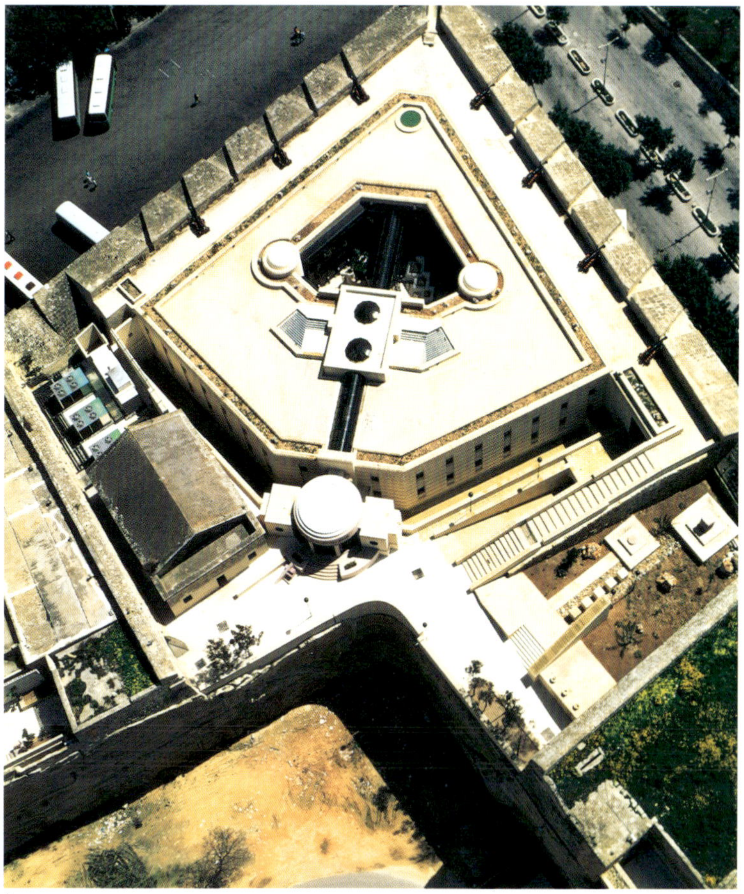

4

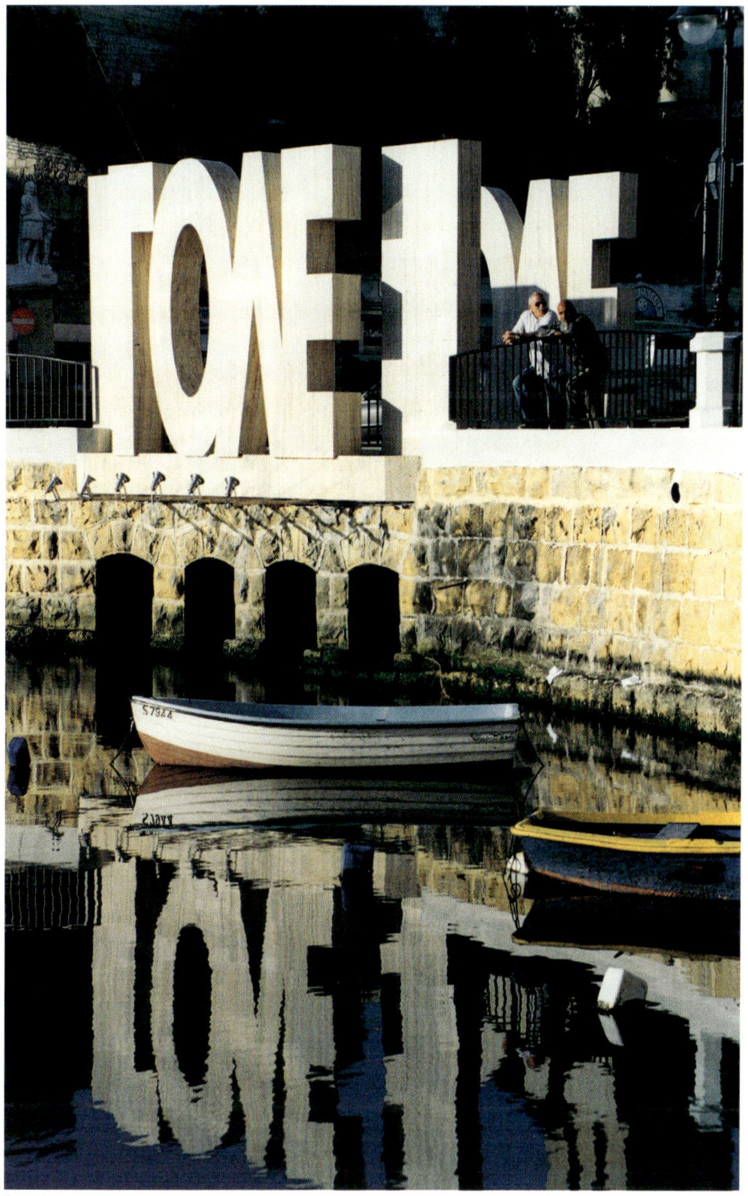

5

RICHARD ENGLAND

6   Ir-Razzett ta-Sandrina   1993 / Mgarr, Malta
7   Dar il-Hanin Samaritan   1996 / Santa Venera, Malta
    photo: ©Peter Bartola Parnis
8, 9   Hal-Farrug Church   2005 / Hal-Farrug, Malta
10, 11, 12, 13   Filfla Chapel   2006 / Wied Iz-Zurrieq Cliffs, Malta

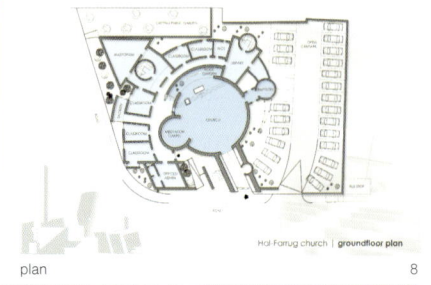

Hal-Farrug church | groundfloor plan

10

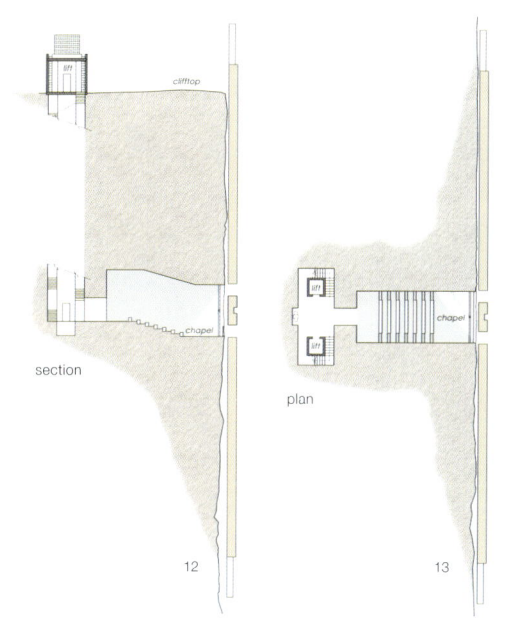

11 12 section 13 plan

49

Richard England

14 A Garden for Myriam 1982 / St. Julians, Malta
15 Church of St. Francis of Assisi 2000 / Qawra, Malta
16 Stage-set for "Le Pescatrici", Manoel Theater 2001 / Valletta, Malta
17 Millennium Chapel 2000 / Paceville, Malta

According to Richard England, "Over the last 30 years, rather than creating a revolution in architectural expression, I've worked toward evolution. I've attempted to create architecture that is founded on the philosophy of 'continuity within change,' and I've continued to work not only by observing where architecture is headed, but reflecting on where it has been."

England adds, "There is no future for architectural expression without a past." Rather than pursuing a wholly original form, England places great value on the sequence within the evolution of architecture that connects the past with the present and the future. As a metaphor, England suggests, "You don't make new trees, you make new leaves." In that sense, by returning to basics, he is calling for a complete symbiosis between architecture and environment. By skillfully adopting the "genius loci" ("spirit of place") that is peculiar to a site, the architect remains faithful to the scale of the place, and in developing a work, needs only present an expression that is requisite to the era. England was born and raised in Malta, and he graduated from the Faculty of Architecture at the University of Malta. Later, he attended the Polytechnic University of Milan, and as a student architect, went to work for Gio Ponti, one of the leading figures in modern architecture.

England is a multi-talented individual with a host of other titles besides architect, including sculptor, photographer, poet, artist, and writer. This seems to have been due in part to the influence of Ponti, who was also involved in a wide range of activities including interior, furniture, industrial and graphic design. Among England's noted sculptural works are "Love" and "White Shadows."

Currently a visiting professor at the University of Malta, in 1987 and 1988, England was commissioned to design the school's Faculty of Architecture. Though he may be from a small Mediterranean country, England's work is wide-reaching. One indication of the extent of his achievement is to note that England has served as an architectural consultant for countless national and public facilities not only in his own country, but in Yugoslavia, Saudi Arabia, Iraq, Italy, Poland, Bulgaria, a number of countries in the former Eastern Bloc including the Soviet Union, and Argentina. Recently, he has been working on the Astana Concert Hall in Kazakhstan.

As a result of his many experiences, England says something he always tries to keep in mind is that "architects cannot only serve as designers

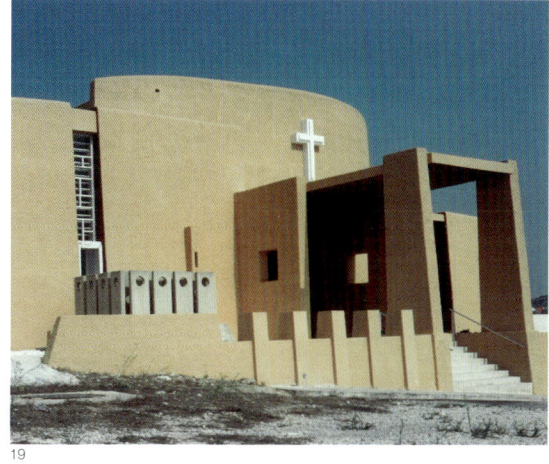

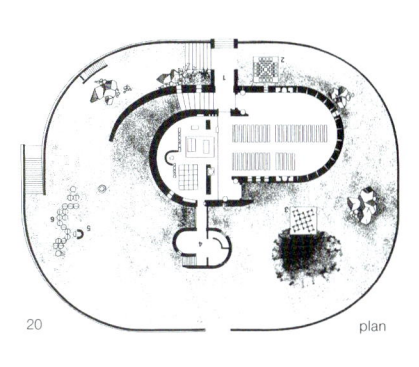

18 St. Andrew Chapel   1989 / Pembroke, Malta
19, 20 St. Joseph Church   1974 / Manikata, Malta
21 University of Malta Extension   1997 / Msida, Malta
22 Opera House / Valletta, Malta
23 Private Villa   1996 / Siggiewi, Malta
24 Tectonic Tendril / Milan

photos : Courtesy of the Architect

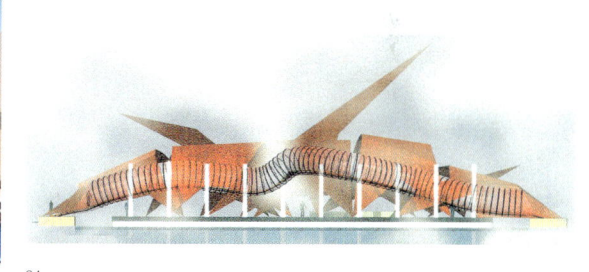

of the future, they must also be guardians of the past." His interest in the past is truly extraordinary. Because of this, England's work is imbued with a strong sense of post-modernism and in light of his origins, one can also detect a hint of something Arabic or Islamic in his architecture.

Some excellent examples include works such as St. James Cavalier, the Central Bank of Malta, Ir-Razzett ta-Sandrina, Dar il-Hanin Samaritan Chapel, and Hal-Farrug Church, with the latter three exhibiting the Arabic influence suggested by their names. In addition, there are works with mythological features such as a Garden for Myriam, the Church of St. Francis of Assisi, the Stage Set for "Le Pescatrici" at Manoel Theater, Millennium Chapel, Filfla Chapel, and St. Andrew Chapel.

Among England's other works are masterpieces of critical regionalism such as St. Joseph Church, which references "girna," the stone sheds used to store farming tools that can be found throughout the hilly landscape of Malta, and the University of Malta Extension, which, as a reflection of the pre-existing colonial-style architecture, is reminiscent of a citadel.

"I've felt this for a long time, but the weakness of the international style is that many modern architects spend too much time analyzing the link between buildings while disparaging the more important bond between building and site. For this reason, I try not only to maintain the value of the original site through my architecture, but also advocate designs which I believe will improve the site."

Architecture is always linked to a specific time and place. It must, therefore, also be suitable to the circumstances and the era. We might sum up Richard England's work with a quote from the Hungarian composer Bela Bartok: "What is new and essential must of necessity be grafted to old roots."

Massimiliano Fuksas

ITALY

Born in Rome in 1944. Opened his own firm in Rome in 1967, followed by offices in Paris in 1989, and in Vienna in 1993. Graduated from La Sapienza University in 1969. Served as a visiting professor at the University of Hannover in 1983, the State Academy of Art and Design Stuttgart in 1988, Ecole d'architecture de Paris la Villette in 1990, and Columbia University in 1990 and 1991. Awarded the Grand Prix National de l'Architecture in 1999.

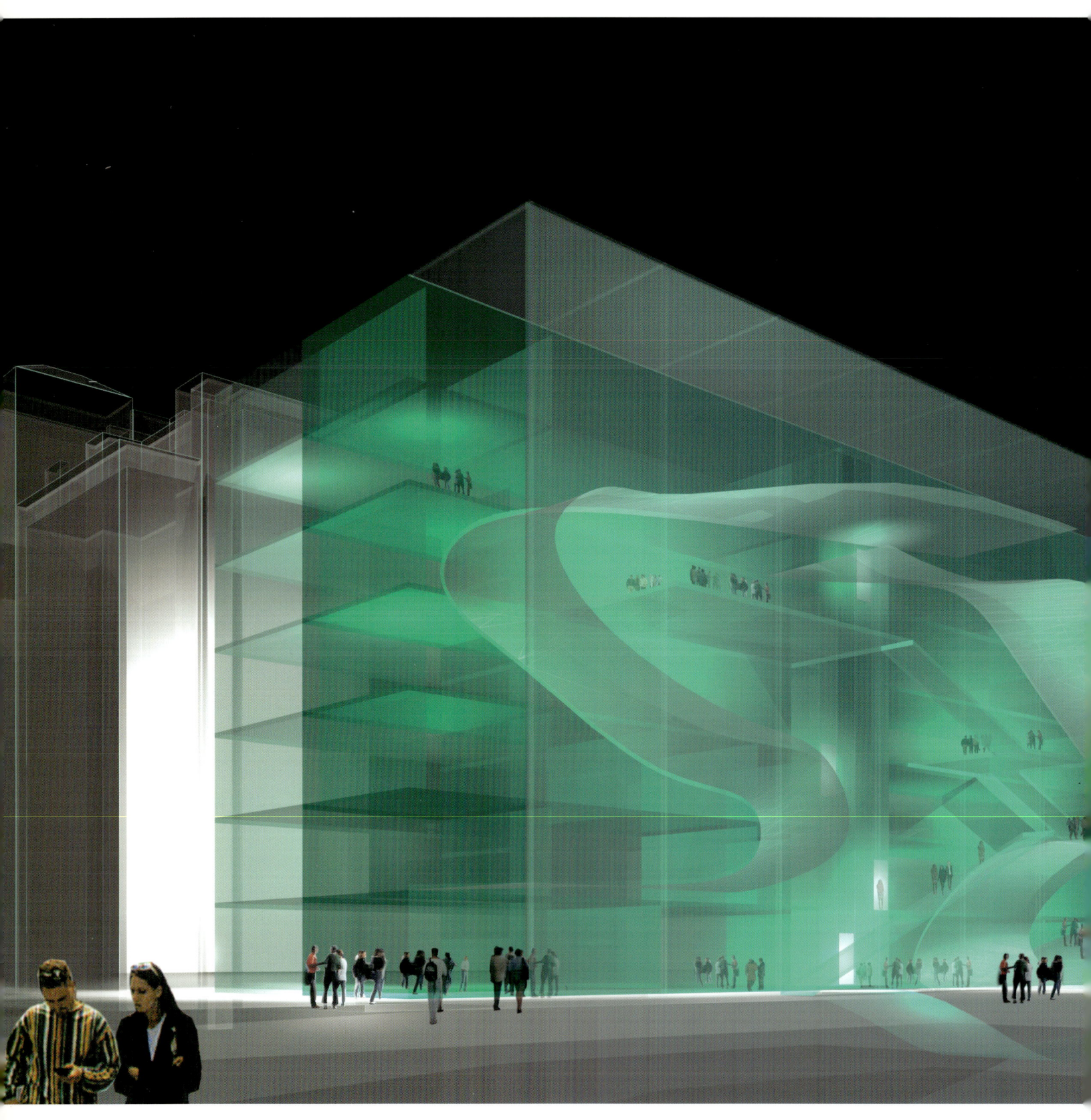

1, 2   New Italian Space Agency Headquarters / Competition
3   Sassocorvaro Sports Hall   1973 / Sassocorvaro, Italy
4   Paliano Gymnasium   1985 / Paliano, Italy
        photo: ©D.O.Mandrelli
5   Tarquinia Nursery School   1982 / Tarquinia, Italy
        photo: ©D.O.Mandrelli
6   Anagni Sports Center   1985 / Anagni, Italy

Massimiliano Fuksas

7 Cassino Town Hall   1990 / Cassino, Italy
8 Reze Cultural Center & Mediatheque   1991 / Reze, France
9 Civita Castellana Cemetery   1992 / Civita Castellana, Italy
10 Sports Complex + Parking   1993 / Paris
photo: ©Synectics
11 Entrance to the Cave Painting Museum   1993 / Niaux, France
photo: ©Jourdan
12 Saint-Exupery College   1993 / Seine-Saint-Denis, France
photo: ©Kozlowski
13 The Faculty of Law and Economics at the University of Limoges   1996 / Limoges, France
photo: ©Synectics
14 The Maison des Arts at Michel de Montaigne University   1995 / Bordeaux, France
photo: ©Synectics
15 Europark   1997 / Salzburg, Austria
photo: ©Philippe Ruault
16 Alsterfleet Office Building   2002 / Hamburg, Germany
photo: ©Philippe Ruaulta

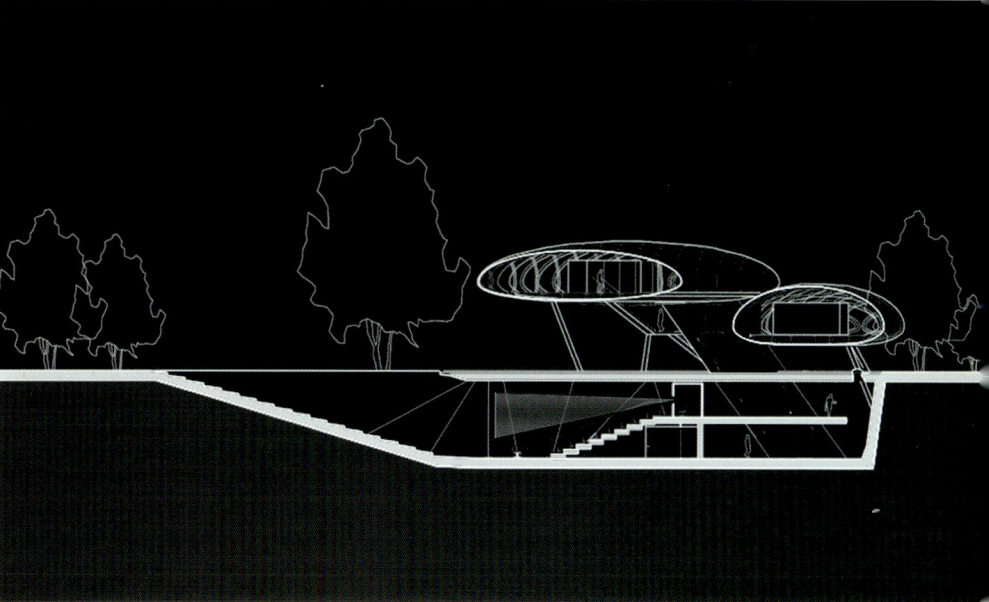

17, 18 Nardini Research & Multimedia Center 2004 / Vicenza, Italy
photo: ©Marcato Maurizio

19 Hanse-Forum Offices 2002 / Hamburg, Germany
photo: ©Philippe Ruault

20 Emporio Armani 2003 / Hong Kong
photo: ©Ramon Prat

Massimiliano Fuksas

21 Vienna Twin Towers 2001 / Vienna
photo: ©C. Drexleri

22, 23 Milan Trade Fair 2005 / Milan
photo: ©Archivio Fuksas

24, 25 New Piemonte Regional Council Headquarters / Torino, Italy

26 EUR Congress Center in Italy / Roma
CG: ©fabio_Cibinel

27 Zenith Concert Hall / Strasbourg, France
28 Queensland Gallery of Modern Art / Competition
29 Peres Peace Center 2007 / Jaffa, Israel
30 San Giacomo Parish Complex / Competition

photos : Courtesy of the Architect except ©Synectics

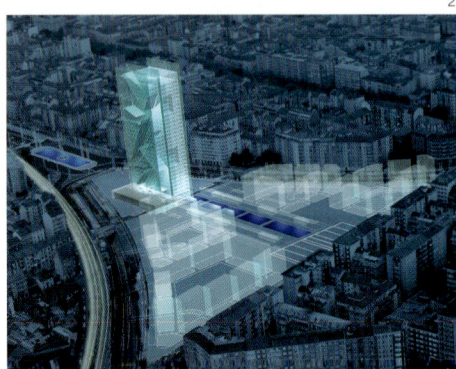

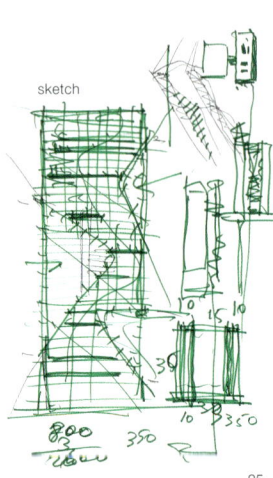

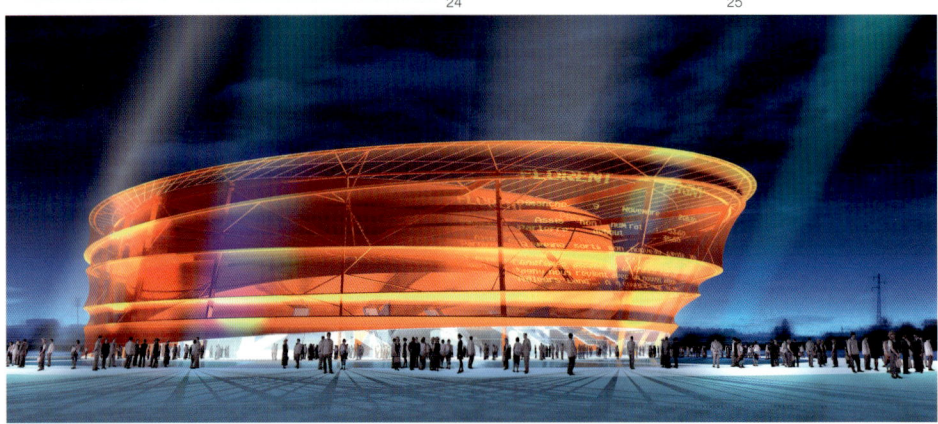

stamp 23

sketch 25

From the end of June to the beginning of July 1991, the JIA (Japan Institute of Architects) held an event called "Architect's Holiday" in Nagasaki. Workshops, led by Rem Koolhaas, Massimiliano Fuksas, Michael Rotondi, Shin Takamatsu, Atsushi Kitagawara, Nadim Karam, and others were offered at a variety of sites in the Higashi-Yamate Former Foreign Settlement.

In my role as coordinator, I was shocked at what I found when I took a peek inside Fuksas' workshop. On large sheets of paper, he had drawn a number of brilliantly colored pictures. I thought that this was perhaps his way of sketching. He struck me as an architect with a painter's heart. But I didn't find out until later that he had actually studied with that master of metaphysical painting Giorgio de Chirico and had originally intended to be a painter. Then everything made sense. The next step in Fuksas' development came in 1964, when he entered the Department of Architecture at La Sapienza University, with encouragement from his mother.

After graduation, he remained at the university to teach, and in 1973, he completed his early masterwork, Sassocorvaro Sports Hall. In the 70s, Fuksas stated, "The architect's role is to provide visions rather than details, concepts rather than drawings." He expanded on this idea by saying, "Architecture is a kind of magic. It is our duty to add 'emotional magic' of the sort you might find in a drama."

Then he made reference to his old teacher. Fuksas noted that de Chirico's abstract, metaphysical paintings are tinged with "magic proportions." His use of this architectural term helped define his own work as having "narrative" qualities. He also spoke of providing a building's residents and users with something dramatic. One finds examples of this in works such as Tarquinia Nursery School, with its three-dimensional expression and the magical aspect in its openings, and the narrative character of the facade at the Paliano Gymnasium, which was inspired by the image of a sunken ship.

While Fuksas' work of the early 1970s had an abstract quality, they were enriched by brutalism on a concrete level. At the time, Louis Kahn's Palazzo dei Congressi project, which had first been unveiled in the 60s, was enjoying great popularity, and Fuksas' Sassocorvaro Sports Hall was clearly influenced by the American architect's brutal and organic approach. Fuksas' Anagni Sports Center also exhibits similar qualities.

28

29   30

Later, Fuksas took up the concept of "fragmentation," and the brutal quality of his work was greatly weakened. His new direction can be seen in the inclined parapet in works of Cassino Town Hall, and the group of fragmented and separated wings of Civita Castellana Cemetery. Similarly, as seen in the contrast between the separated, inclined black mass and the white, reinforced concrete mass of the Reze Cultural Center and Mediatheque, Fuksas developed a variety of fragmentation methods.

In the early part of his career, while teaching at La Sapienza University, Fuksas received several commissions for projects in regional cities. These works were then completed after he left the school in 1978. Not long after, in 1982, the Paris architecture magazine _L'Architecture d'Aujour'hui_ published a feature on high-profile architects of the day, which, by placing Fuksas alongside William Alsop, Arquitectonica, Toyo Ito, Rem Koolhaas, and Jean Nouvel, helped make his name in France. In 1987, he also won a competition for the Sports Complex and Parking Lot, which became his first work in France.

Opening an office in Paris in 1989, Fuksas enjoyed great success in France in the 90s. With works such as the Entrance to the Cave Painting Museum, Saint-Exupery College, the Faculty of Law and Economics at the University of Limoges, and the Maison des Arts at Michel de Montaigne University, his practice was going very smoothly. In addition, Fuksas began to do an increasing number of foreign projects, including Europark in Salzburg, the Alsterfleet Office Building and Hanse-Forum Offices in Hamburg, the Vienna Twin Towers, Emporio Armani in Hong Kong, and the Peres Peace Center in Israel.

From recent works such as the Nardini Research and Multimedia Center, with its cutting-edge, space-capsule-like design, and Milan Trade Fair, an important work with a heavy glass roof, Fuksas has clearly moved away from the reinforced concrete of his brutalist era toward a more organic steel- and glass-based style.

Fuksas' concept of the "frame," which encloses the organic elements in his work, is a highlight of his upcoming projects. It will be interesting to watch as he completes other intriguing works such as the EUR Congress Center in Italy, the Zenith Concert Hall, the New Italian Space Agency Headquarters, and the Queensland Gallery of Modern Art.

Future Systems

UK

Future Systems principal Jan Kaplicky was born in Prague in 1937, and graduated from the University of Applied Arts in Prague in 1962. Established Future Systems after working with Dennis Lasdun, Piano and Rogers, and Norman Foster. Taught at the AA School of Architecture from 1982 to 1988. Kaplicky's partner Amanda Levete was born in Bridgend, England in 1955. Graduated from the AA School in 1982. Worked with Richard Rogers from 1984 to 1989. Joined Future Systems in 1989.

1, 2, 3   Selfridges Birmingham   2003 / Birmingham, UK
         photo: ©Richard Davis + Soren Aagaard
4   NatWest Media Center   1999 / London
5   Kafka Memorial   1966 / Praha, Czech
         photo: ©Synectics
6   French National Library / Competition

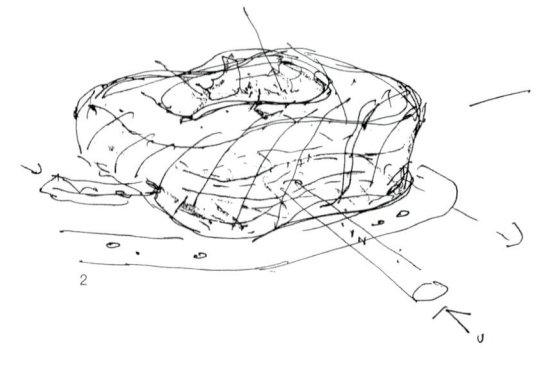

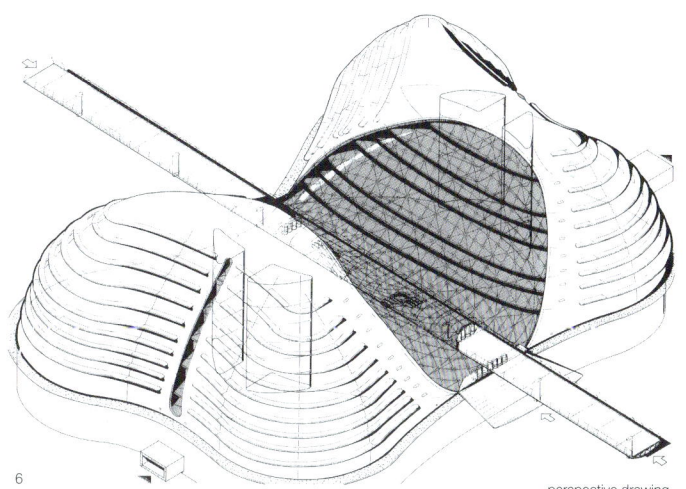

perspective drawing

FUTURE SYSTEMS

7 House in Wales   1996 / Wales, UK
8 Marni   1999 / London
9 Comme de Garcons New York   1998 / New York
  photo: ©Synectics
10 Frankfurt Mortor Show Booth Design   2003 / Frankfurt
11 Comme de Garcons Tokyo   1998 / Tokyo
   photo: ©Synectics

12 Une Petite Maison
13 Peanut
14 Blob Office Building / Competition
15 Coexistence
16 Spire
17 Doughnut House
18 Green Building

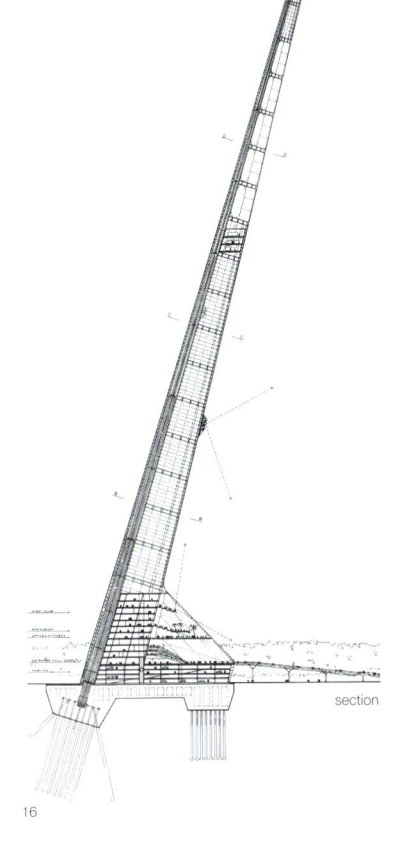

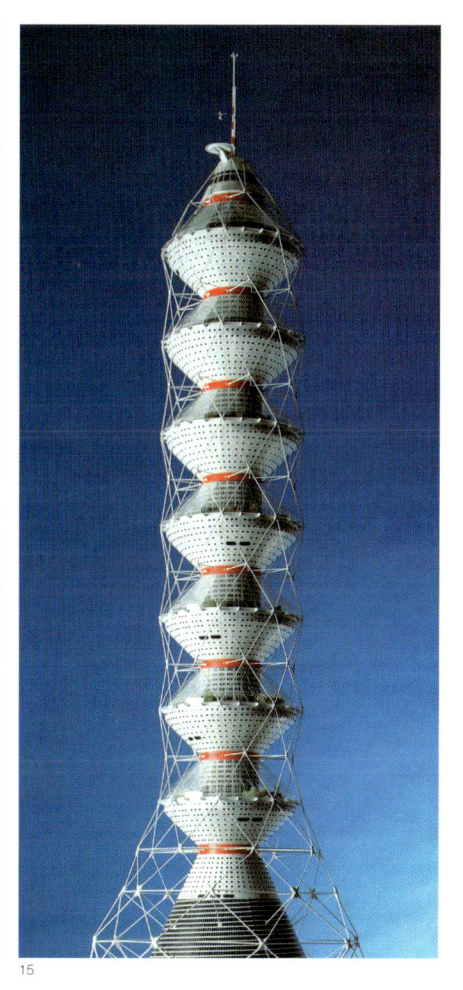

section

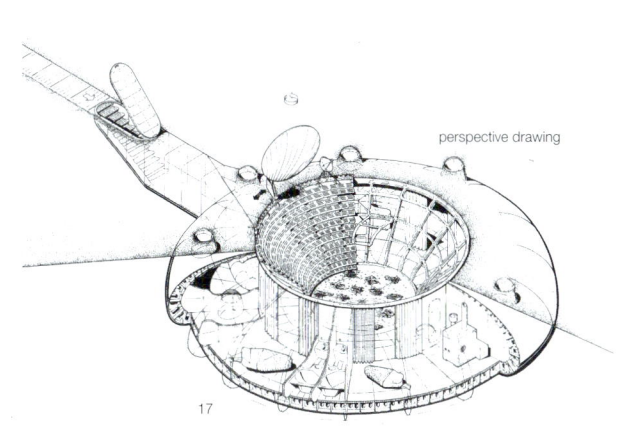

perspective drawing

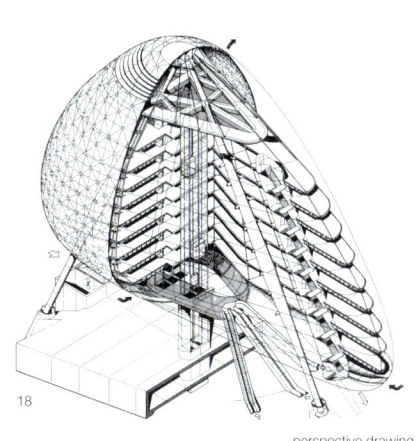

perspective drawing

61

FUTURE SYSTEMS

19	Floating Bridge 1996 / London
20	Hauer King House 1994 / London
21	JSO Project
22	River Clyde
23, 24	Green Bird

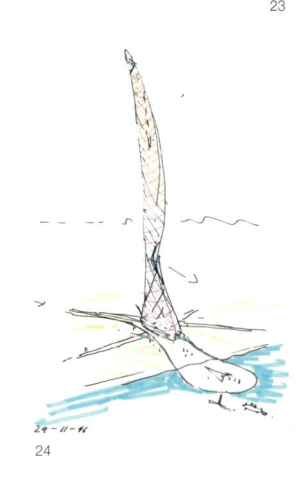

Future Systems, as might be imagined from the firm's name, is an architectural collective which designs extremely futuristic buildings and interiors. The firm's work from the early 80s is particularly attractive. Among these enormously provocative, cutting-edge buildings with hi-tech specifications are Une Petite Maison, which looks like a helicopter that swooped down onto a rock next to the sea, and Peanut, a weekend residence for two which, with its base on the shore of a lake and the end section of a crane attached to it, can be moved at will. Many of Future Systems' works offer dreams to both children and adults alike.
Later projects such as Doughnut House, an underground residence, and the Blob Office Building, are also brimming with possibilities. Other works including the super-high-rise tower Spire, a London office complex called the Green Building, and the even taller high-rise Coexistence look cool and boast fun designs. But all of these works are unfinished.
In the midst of these unbuilt projects, however, came the firm's controversial plan for the National Library of France. About 20 or 30 famous architects from around the world entered the competition. After now influential figures like Jean Nouvel and Rem Koolhaas were awarded special prizes, two finalists remained: Dominique Perrault and Future Systems. As many will remember, Perrault was ultimately declared the winner. With its organic, butterfly-like plan, Future Systems' library of the future was perhaps too revolutionary at the time. Today, in the 21st century, however, the magnificent plan could well have won.
The firm's visually impressive and highly practical designs owe much to the careful observation of nature and use of technology from other industries. At Future Systems, a balance is maintained between actual projects and research projects, which are intended to expand the scope of the firm's design work. As forerunners of Future Systems, one might cite Archigram, a similar architecture group that was also based in England. This group, which graphically expressed futuristic, cutting-edge cities and architecture, exerted a strong influence on architects around the world, though none of Archigram's works were actually built. In addition, as a constructor and architect, Buckminster Fuller had a powerful effect on Future Systems.
After graduating in 1962 from the University of Applied Arts in Prague, Jan Kaplicky, the director of Future Systems, worked

25

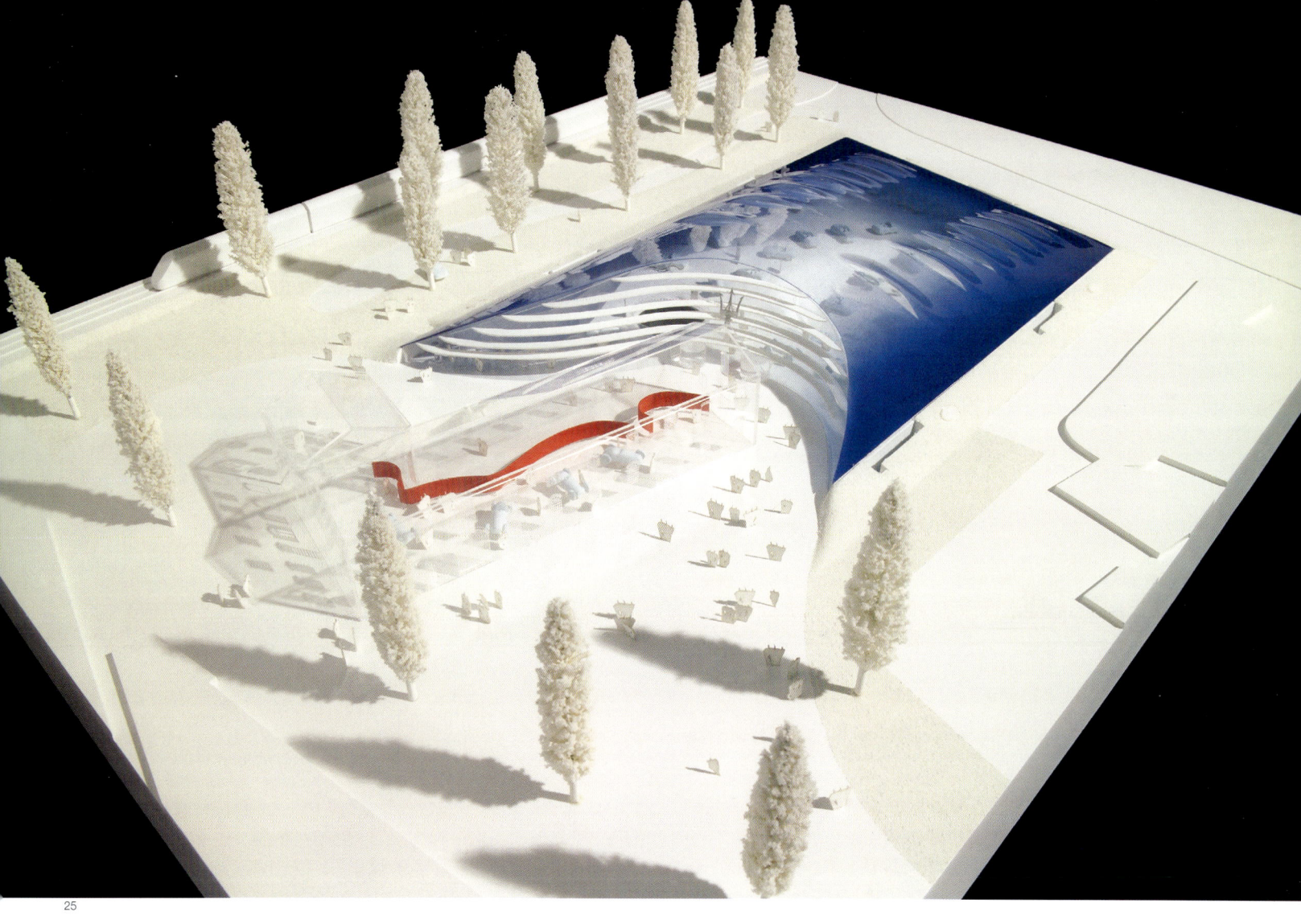

| 25 | Maserati Museum / Modena, Italy | 27 | Leamouth Bridge |
| 26 | BBC Music Center | | |

photos : Courtesy of the Architect except ©Synectics

26

27

independently for a period of two years. During this period, he designed the Kafka Memorial that serves as a marker for Franz Kafka's house. Two years after that, Kaplicky relocated to London. There, along with training he received at hi-tech architecture firms such as Piano and Rogers, and Norman Foster, Kaplicky came across the ideas of Archigram and Fuller, both of which were very much in vogue at the time. These architects' works were built on a deep knowledge of aeronautics, aerospace engineering, and ship-building technology. Their drawings also displayed a level of skill that was comparable to mechanical engineering diagrams and drafts.

Following the French Library competition, the next project that brought Future Systems international attention was the NatWest Media Center, completed in 1999. A shell construction which, with its aluminum monocoque body, resembles a UFO, the building seems to be floating in midair. The innovative design caused a stir all over the world. Made the same year, House in Wales, is an eco-residence buried in a grassy hill with a commanding view of the sea. In Japan, the work became famous when it appeared in a TV commercial featuring the actress Sayuri Yoshinaga. Other completed works soon came to include Comme de Garcons buildings in Tokyo and New York. Future Systems' largest project to date has been Selfridges Birmingham, completed in 2003. The department store, an organic form with a three-dimensional, curved exterior, has a humorous air created by an outer layer of 15,000 aluminum disks with 60-centimeter diameters. The tube-shaped escalators that intersect the building's huge atrium are also wonderfully suggestive of a futuristic space.

Other completed works include the Floating Bridge in the Docklands, and Hauer-King House and a Marni shop (all in London), and a booth design for the Frankfurt Motor Show. And with projects such as a subway station in Naples, Housing Complex in Copenhagen, and the Maserati Museum now underway, the future looks very bright for the firm.

GIGON/GUYER

SWITZERLAND

Annette Gigon was born in 1959, and graduated from the Swiss Federal Institute of Technology in 1984. From 1985 to 1988, worked with Herzog and de Meuron, and practiced independently from 1987 to 1989. Mike Guyer was born in 1958, and also graduated from the Swiss Federal Institute of Technology in 1984. From 1984 to 1987, worked at Rem Koolhaas' OMA. Established the joint practice Gigon and Guyer in 1989.

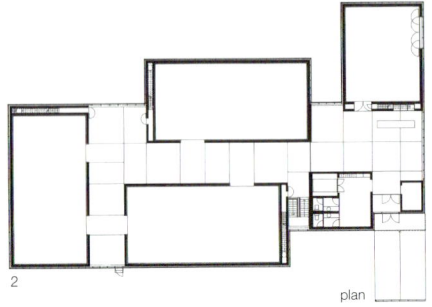

1, 2 Kirchner Museum 1992 / Davos, Switzerland
photo: ©Heinrich Helfenstein

3 Winterthur Museum 1995 / Winterthur, Switzerland
photo: ©Heinrich Helfenstein

4, 5 Liner Museum 1998 / Appenzell, Switzerland
photo: ©Heinrich Helfenstein

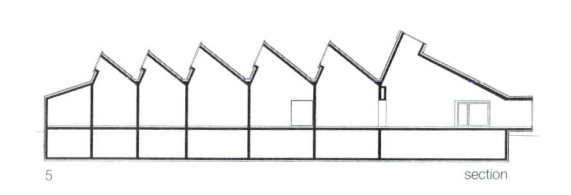

section

GIGON/GUYER

6   Oskar Reinhart Collection Museum Renovation   1998 / Winterthur, Switzerland
    photo: ©Arazebra, Helbling + Kupferschmid
7   Broelberg Residential Complex I   1996 / Kilchberg, Switzerland
    photo: ©Heinrich Helfenstein
8   Single-Family House   1994 / Zurich
    photo: ©U. Karrer
9   Switching Station   1000 / Zurich
    photo: ©Heinrich Helfenstein
10 Kalkriese Archaeological Museum and Park   2002 / Osnabruck, Germany
    photo: ©Heinrich Helfenstein

67

11 Davos Sports Center
    1996 / Davos, Switzerland
    photo: ©Heinrich Helfenstein

12, 13 Prime Tower Office Building / Zurich

14 Davos Workshop Building
    1999 / Davos, Switzerland
    photo: ©Heinrich Helfenstein

15 Restaurant Vinikus Expansion
    1992 / Davos, Switzerland
    photo: ©Heinrich Helfenstein

16 Renovation and Extension of the
    Appisberg Complex
    2002 / Mannedorf, Switzerland
    photo: ©Harald F. Muller

Both Annette Gigon and Mike Guyer graduated from the Swiss Federal Institute of Technology in Zurich in 1984. From 1985 to 1988, Gigon practiced at Herzog and de Meuron, while Guyer worked at Rem Koolhaas' OMA between 1984 and 1987. In 1989, the two then opened their own firm in a warehouse along the railroad tracks near Zurich Station. At present, their 600-meter-square office is located in a renovated hospital, and Gigon / Guyer, as heirs of the two important European firms they were formerly associated with, are now extremely famous architects.

Gigon / Guyer first came to worldwide attention for the Kirchner Museum in the eastern Swiss city of Davos. The museum, located deep in the mountains at an altitude of 1,500 meters against a backdrop of a conifer forest, is wondrous, and was built to commemorate the work of Davos-born painter Ernst Ludwig Kirchner. Even more wondrous, however, is the fact that despite the snowy region, the building is made of glass. Behind the frosted glass of the exterior wall, though, is actually an exposed reinforced-concrete interior wall. Covering concrete with glass not only improves insulation, but also makes the building shine like a jewel in the pristine light of Davos. But Gigon / Guyer's ingenuous methods don't end there. The building has two floors on ground level and one below. On closer inspection, however, the upper section is equipped with a high sidelight; due to the accumulation of snow in the area, a skylight would have been impossible. On the second floor, the architects created a light room with a height of close to one storey, and as the light shines through the glass floor, it pours down into the first-floor exhibition room.

This natural-lighting system influenced Peter Zumthor's design for the Bergenz Museum, and the glass-covered concrete walls of Gunter Zamp Kelp's Neanderthal Museum. Having established a singular style for museums in Switzerland, Gigon / Guyer further developed the form in their design for the Winterthur Museum. The building, a new wing connected to the original museum, was created as a temporary structure with a prospective service life of ten years, but its sturdy construction seems certain to last much longer.

The first storey houses a parking area, while the exposed reinforced-concrete exhibition space on the second storey stands on slender, round steel columns and square concrete pillars. The exterior wall is surrounded by Profilit glass, with a few centimeters between the two

17 Three Apartment Buildings Susenbergstrasse   2000 / Zurich
    photo: ©Heinrich Helfenstein
18 Residential Complex Broelberg II   2001 / Kilchcerg, Switzerland
    photo: ©Harald F. Muller
19 Kunst-Depot Galerie Henze & Ketterer, Wichtrach   2004 / Wichtrach, Switzerland
    photo: ©Heinrich Helfenstein
20 Historical Villa in Kastanienbaum, Remodelling and Extension   2004 / Kastanienbaum, Switzerland
    photo: ©Lucas Peters
21 Rigihof Restaurant Pavilion, Museum of Transportation Lucerne   2000 / Luzern, Switzerland
    photo: ©Heinrich Helfenstein
22 Auditorium, University of Zurich   2002 / Zurich
    photo: ©Heinrich Helfenstein
23 Espace de l'Art Concret   2003 / Mouans-Sartoux, France
    photo: ©Serge Demailly

photos : Courtesy of the Architect.

materials. Designed for easy ventilation of exhaust fumes, the parking area is bathed in natural light. The reinforced-concrete walls of the second storey are also covered with Profilit glass. However, the light here pours in through a skylight, and as a flat surface wouldn't have been viable because of the snow, the roof is sawtoothed and pitched.

Profilit glass is by no means a new material, but Gigon / Guyer are particularly adept at using readymade materials to create effects that would normally be unthinkable. At the Winterthur, for example, the result is a dazzling, highly transparent exterior wall. A similar method was later used by the pair to produce a chrome exterior wall for the Liner Museum. Gigon / Guyer's third museum, this structure shines with metallic brilliance in the sunlight.

As these examples suggest, Gigon / Guyer's approach to the exterior wall is quite remarkable. Something should also be said about the Kalkriese Archaeological Museum and Park, which makes use of large Corten steel plates. The rusty, archeological color of the steel is a perfect match for the greenery in the surrounding park. Inside the concrete skin of the Oskar Reinhart Collection Museum, on the other hand, is pulverized limestone from the Jura region and copper, causing the surface to gradually change to green.

In other types of Gigon / Guyer buildings, such as the Broelberg Residential Complex , a heat-insulating agent was applied to a brick exterior, which in turn was covered with a beautifully colored layer of stucco. The exterior wall of the Single-Family House comprises a mixture of mineral wool, lime-cement plaster, and concrete tiles. And for Railway Switching Station, a dark brown, iron-oxide pigment was mixed into the concrete, and the facade was given a splendid, rough tone like Colten steel. Wood was used for sections of the facades in the Davos Sports Center, Davos Workshop Building, and the Restaurant Vinikus Expansion, lending the buildings a special demeanor.

Gigon / Guyer might initially seem to share the same concern for the exterior wall as Herzog and de Meuron. But they are clearly more attached to using ordinary materials in an extraordinary way. Gigon / Guyer are currently at work on Prime Tower. The green, high-rise office building will also make use of new materials and will undoubtedly become a new landmark in Zurich.

HEIKKINEN–KOMONEN

Original firm founded as Heikkinen-Komonen-Tiirikainen in 1974, and in 1978, reestablished as Heikkinen-Komonen. Mikko Heikkinen was born in Savonlinna, Finland in 1949. Graduated from the Helsinki University of Technology in 1975. Markku Komonen was born in Lappeenranta, Finland in 1945. Graduated from the Helsinki University of Technology in 1974. Both served as visiting professors at Virginia Polytechnic University in 1992, and currently, teach at the Helsinki University of Technology.

FINLAND

1 Heureka, Finnish Science Center   1988 / Vantaa, Finland
  photo: ©Jussi Tiainen
2 Rovaniemi Airport Terminal   1992 / Rovaniemi, Finland
3 Villa Eila   1995 / Mali, Guinea
  photo: ©Onerva Utriainen

Heikkinen–Komonen

4 European Film College 1993 / Ebeltoft, Denmark
  photo: ©Jussi Tiainen
5 Vuotalo Cultural Center 2000 / Helsinki, Finland
6 Lume Mediacenter 2000 / Helsinki, Finland
  photo: ©Jussi Tiainen
7, 8 School for Chicken Farmers 1999 / Kindia, Guinea

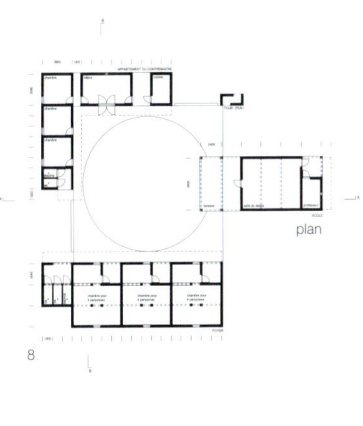

plan

HEIKKINEN-KOMONEN

9 Lappeenranta University of Technology, Phase VII 2004 / Lappeenranta, Finland
10 Juminkeko Center of Carelian Culture 1999 / Kuhmo, Finland
   photo: ©Mikko Averniitty
11 McDonald's Finnish Headquarters 1997 / Helsinki, Finland
   photo: ©Synectics
12 Stakes and Senate Properties Office Building 2002 / Helsinki, Finland

The first time I encountered a work by Heikkinen-Komonen was about ten years ago when I visited the Heureka Finnish Science Center in Vantaa, outside of Helsinki. The varied and complex exterior and the diversity of articulated interior spaces gave each part of the building its own individual identity, and made the overall structure deeply impressive. The science center, the firm's first mature work as professional architects, was designed for a public commission.

Mikko Heikkinen and Markku Komonen's architecture might at first seem to be indicative of the now popular minimalist aesthetic, but it actually has a deep-rooted connection to Finnish modernism and International modernism. More than simple visual imagery, the concept underlying their work is related to amassing and integrating the essence of architecture.

Just as they make reference to contemporary minimalist sculpture and ancient symbolic structures, the architects have adopted elements of pragmatic, vernacular architecture, global geometry, and temporal science. For example, in the Rovaniemi Airport Terminal, a 40-meter-long skylight intersects the space diagonally. It is precisely positioned to correspond to the meridian at the Arctic Circle, and the sunlight that passes through the lens set up on the building's roof projects an analemma, which traces the ellipsoid orbit of the earth. With such high density and contextual referents, the architecture of Heikkinen-Komonen, achieved through a process of distillation and aggregation, integrates programmatic, functional, and technical parameters. To the architects, context is not interpreted as the substantive characteristics that make up a so-called site, but the conceptual circumstances related to the people in a certain place and time. Beneath the concise and understated surface, Heikkinen-Komonen's buildings exhibit an epic scale. Quoting Constantin Brancusi, Komonen says, "The object of art is not brevity, it is the final outcome." This sentiment is also the artistic credo on which the two architects' partnership is founded. True brevity in art is not achieved through elimination, but is rather the result of compression. Heikkinen-Komonen's design vocabulary has unquestionably evolved through their participation in competitions and exhibition designs as well as their early projects. The architects' design strategy makes use of fundamental geometric volumes, which interpenetrate and intersect each other through subtle discrepancies in position, and the

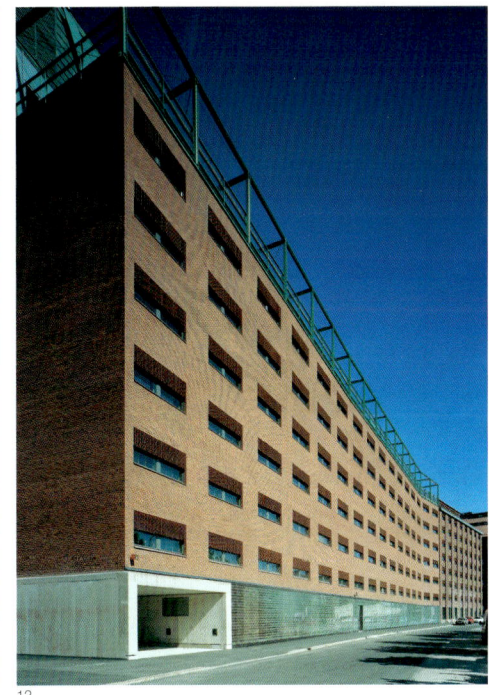

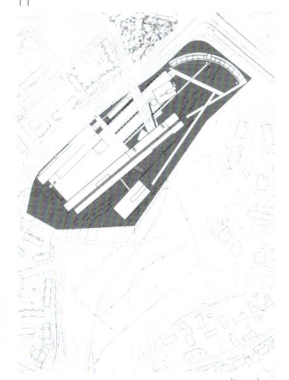

13, 14   Emergency Services College Phase IV   1998 / Kuopio, Finland
15   House Kosketus   2000 / Tuusula, Finland
16   Max Plank Institute of Molecular Cell Biology and Genetics
    2001 / Dresden, Germany
17   Finnish Embassy in the U.S.A. / Washington D.C.
photo: ©Jussi Tiainen

photos : Courtesy of the Architect except ©Synectics

occasional intervention of curved elements. In addition, Heikkinen-Komonen's architecture has an air of high technology, but not of the type that is currently popular. Rather the work is reflective of early pioneers like Pierre Chareau or Jean Prouve, who tended to be more focused on technology than many of their modernist peers. It is also important to note that Heikkinen-Komonen are critical of the machine aesthetic. As in other fields of culture, technological fetishism – a romantic view of things that are mechanical in nature – can be a form of expression as one is developing their architectural philosophy. Ultimately, though, Heikkinen-Komonen have arrived at an anti-romantic stance toward technology. Their pragmatic view of technique, structure, and material is evident in works such as the School for Chicken Farmers, Villa Eila, Elementary School, and the Village Health Center (all in the West African nation of Guinea), the Center of Carelian Culture in Juminkeko, Finland, McDonald's Finnish headquarters, and Phase IV of the Emergency Services College. In Guinea, in particular, local construction methods, techniques and materials (such as clay blocks, wood, and bamboo from the area) were used, and regardless of how refined the technology was, the resulting buildings proved to be highly lyrical architectural expressions.

Both Mikko Heikkinen and Markku Komonen received graduate degrees from the School of Architecture at the Helsinki University of Technology. They opened their own firm in 1974. Originally, a three-partner practice called Heikkinen-Komonen-Tiilikainen, the firm was pared down to the current two in 1978. Since 2000, they have completed such works as the Vuotalo Cultural Center, Lume Mediacenter, House Kosketus, the Stakes and Senate Properties Office Building, and Lappeenranta University of Technology, Phase VII.

Of the group of contemporary Finnish architects who have emerged following the age of great masters from the country such as Alvar Aalto, Aulis Blomstedt, and Reima Pietila, only a handful are known in Japan, with Heikkinen-Komonen and Juha Leiviskä at the top of the list followed by Pekka Helin, Olli Pekka Jokela, and Juhani Pallasmaa. But in terms of their works in foreign countries, including the European Film College and Kolonihaven Architecture Park in Denmark; the Max Planck Institute of Molecular Cell Biology and Genetics in Germany; and the Finnish Embassy in the U.S., Heikkinen-Komonen enjoy an unrivaled reputation internationally.

Herman Hertzberger

THE NETHERLANDS

Born in Amsterdam in 1932. Graduated from the Delft University of Technology in 1958, and established his own firm the same year. From 1959 to 1963, helped edit the magazine _Forum_, with Aldo van Eyck, J.B. Bakema, and others. Began teaching at the Delft University of Technology in 1970. Served as a professor at the University of Geneva from 1986 to 1993. Received the Richard Neutra Award in 1989, and the European Architecture Award (for School Buildings) in 1993. Served as director of the Berlage Institute from 1990 to 1995. Named professor emeritus at the University of Geneva.

1. Waternet Head Office 2005 / Amsterdam
   photo: ©Architectuurstudio Herman Hertzberger
2. Centraal Beheer 1972 / Apeldoorn, The Netherlands
   photo: ©Architectuurstudio Herman Hertzberger
3. Markant Theater 1996 / Uden, The Netherlands
   photo: ©Duccio Malagamba
4. Benelux Merkenburo 1993 / The Hague, The Netherlands
   photo: ©Synectics
5, 6. Chasse Theater 1995 / Breda, The Netherlands
   photo: ©Architectuurstudio Herman Hertzberger
7. Montessori College Oost 2000 / Amsterdam
   photo: ©Duccio Malagamba
8. Office Building 'il Fiore' 2002 / Maastricht, The Netherlands
   photo: ©Architectuurstudio Herman Hertzberger

3

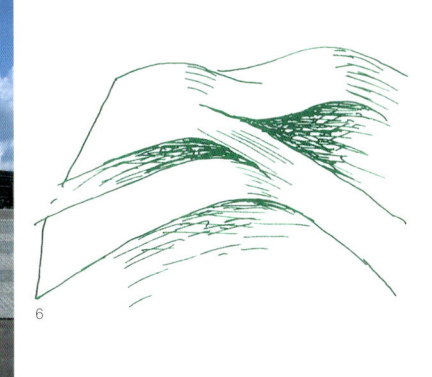

4

5

6

7

8

77

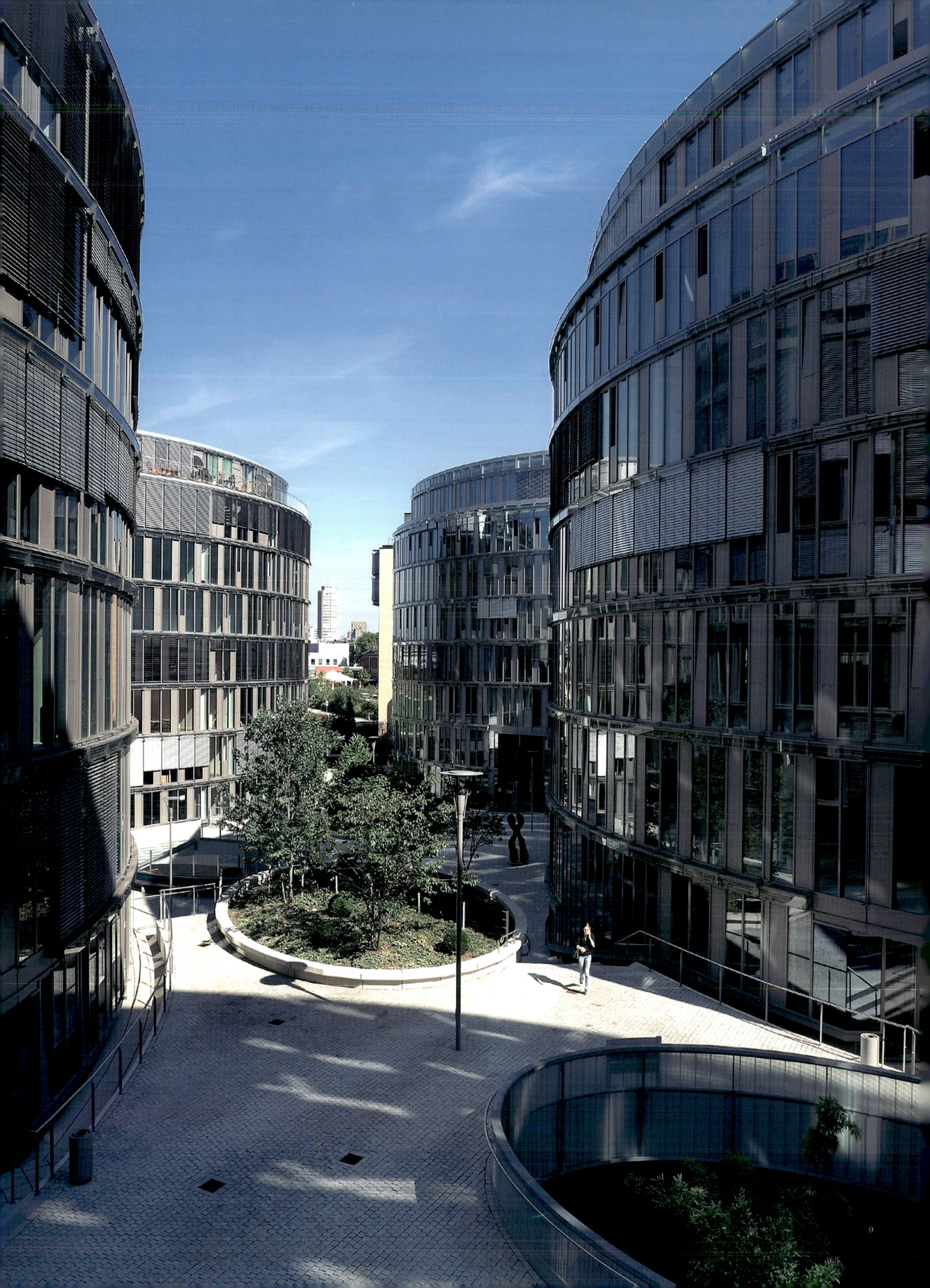

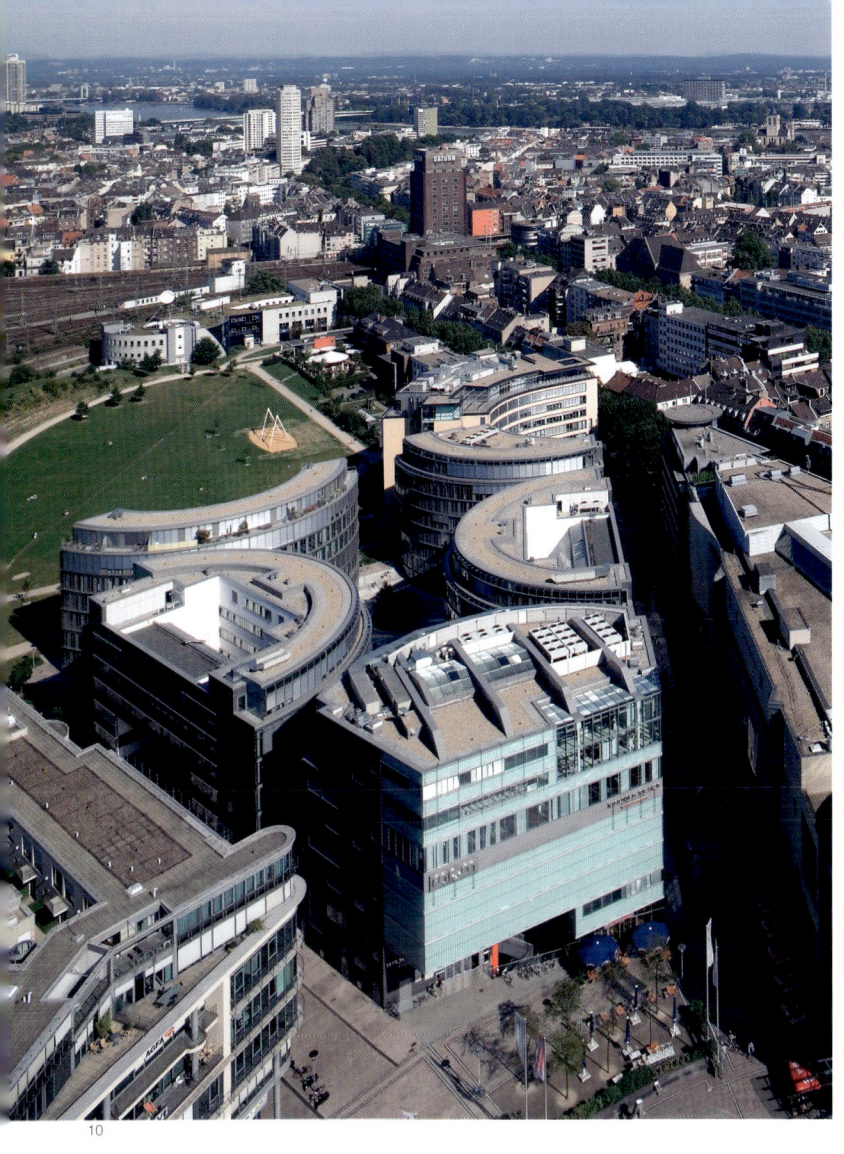

9, 10   Cologne Media Park Office Complex   2004 / Cologne, Germany
        photo: ©Duccio Malagamba
11   Residential Buildings Growing Houses   2002 / Almere, The Netherlands
        photo: ©Architectuurstudio Herman Hertzberger
12   Orpheus Theatre and Conference Center Renovation and Extension
        2004 / Apeldoorn, The Netherlands
        photo: ©Dura Vermeer Bouw Hengelo BV
13   CODA   2004 / Apeldoorn, The Netherlands
        photo: ©Architectuurstudio Herman Hertzberger
14, 15 "De Eilanden" Montessori Primary School   2002 / Amsterdam
        photo: ©Architectuurstudio Herman Hertzberger

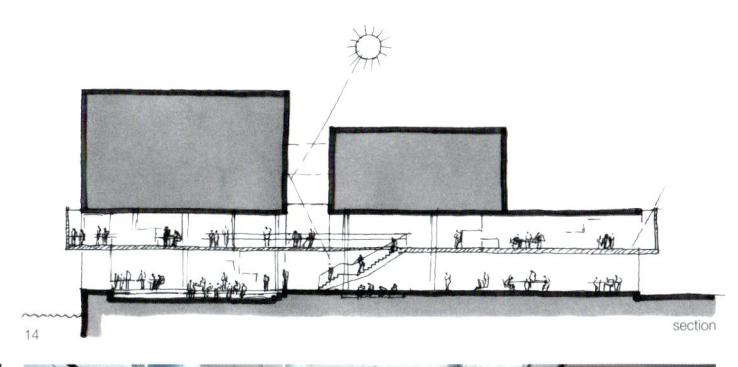

Herman Hertzberger

16 Students' House in Amsterdam   1966 / Amsterdam
   photo: ©Architectuurstudio Herman Hertzberger
17 Verdenburg Music Center   1978 / Utrecht, The Netherlands
   photo: ©Synectics
18 Apollo Schools   1983 / Amsterdam
   photo: ©Ger van der Vlugt
19 Ministry of Social Welfare and Employment   1990 / The Hague, The Netherlands
   photo: ©Aviodrome, The Netherlands

In the late 19th century, neo-Gothic architecture was in the ascendant in Holland, and then in the early 20th century, International modernism began to hold sway. A number of the modernists left their mark on architectural history, including the Amsterdam School, the De Stijl movement, and the De 8 en Opbouw group.
As forefathers of Dutch modernist architecture, one might mention Hendrik Berlage, Michel de Klerk, Jacobus Oud, Jan Duiker, Gerrit Rietveld, W.M. Dudok, and J.B. Bakema. Then following World War II, Aldo van Eyck, who was also involved in Team X, played a central role in establishing Dutch structuralism. With a friend, Herman Hertzberger (born in 1932) was awarded first prize in the Amsterdam Students' House competition during his final year at the Delft University of Technology.

While studying with M. Duintjer, one of Le Corbusier's proteges, around this time, Hertzberger had begun to feel a strong attraction to the latter's architecture, and the influence is quite evident in the prize-winning work.
After graduating from university, Hertzberger became part of the editorial staff at the journal _Forum_. Van Eyck and Bakema were also involved, and Hertzberger learned a great deal from the former in particular. Next, Hertzberger adopted the methods of Dutch structuralism, primarily the use of articulation and clustering, which helped him arrive at new destinations in his own work.
Rather than contrasting public and private spaces, Hertzberger places great importance on creating public spaces that connect articulated private spaces and the continuous and close

territorial relationship between the two. Hertzberger refers to this transformation of public territory into a more private, domestic space as "territorialism."
In Centraal Beheer, one of the architect's early representative works, there is no symbolic, central space. Substituting for the so-called "public space" are passages in the grid that run between each unit in the square office enclosure. By basing the design on a residential metaphor, Hertzberger sets out to domesticate the space while imbuing it with a collective nature.
The fundamental idea behind Centraal Beheer is that the "user is the resident." Basing his work on the concept "buildings are small cities/cities are big buildings" (a quote Van Eyck borrowed from Alberti), Hertzberger arrived at something he calls the "urban interior" ñ or his

20 Dutch Pavilion at the 8th Venice Architecture Biennale
    2002 / Venice
    photo: ©Architectuurstudio Herman Hertzberger
21 Extension to Vanderveen Department Store
    1997 / Assen, The Netherlands
    photo: ©Duccio Malagamba
22 YKK Dormitory & Guesthouse   1998 / Toyama, Japan
    photo: ©Nobuaki Nakagawa
23 RWZI Building / Amsterdam
    photo: ©Johannes Abelings
24 Water-House Torenvalkpad 1998 / Assen, The Netherlands
    photo: ©Architectuurstudio Herman Hertzberger
25 Courtyard Watersnihof (H) and Zwanenhof (C)
    for Residential Building   2004 / Middelburg, The Netherlands
    photo: ©Architectuurstudio Herman Hertzberger
26 Rotterdam Street Residential Buildings   1996 / Rotterdam
    photo: ©AeroC-air
27 Library Breda and Center for Art & Music
    1993 / Breda, The Netherlands
    photo: ©Sybolt Voeten

    photos : Courtesy of the Architect except ©Synectics

interpretation of the ideal living environment. There is no more accurate term for Centraal Beheer than "urban interior."
Due to his extensive use of concrete blocks, Hertzberger's name has nearly become synonymous with the material. Early examples of its use can be seen in the Amsterdam Students' House, Centraal Beheer, Vredenburg Music Center, and the Apollo Schools. In the 1993 Benelux Merkenburo, however, Hertzberger only makes use of a very small number of blocks for the gable walls in each wing.
In fact, there are many glass surfaces and black walls in the Merkenburo, making it one of Hertzberger's more elegant works. Even in the Ministry of Social Welfare and Employment, completed some three years earlier, there is a marked decrease in the use of Hertzberger's beloved concrete and glass blocks, and similarly, there are fewer reinforced-concrete columns, but instead, an increase in the use of steel (I beams).
Although Hertzberger used structuralist techniques for the ministry, this type of methodology is largely missing from subsequent works such as Chasse Theater, Markant Theater, the YKK Dormitory and Guesthouse, Montessori College Oost, the ë il Fioreí Office Building, and the Growing Houses. In his most recent works in particular, Hertzberger's architecture has developed into something extremely sophisticated and refined, as seen in the Orpheus Theatre and Conference Center Renovation and Extension, CODA (Culture Under One Roof Apeldoorn), the Cologne Media Park office complex, the Waternet Head Office, and the Watersniphof (H) and Zwanenhof (C) Courtyard for a Residential Buildings. In the wake of Aldo van Eyck's death, Hertzberger seems to have moved past Dutch structuralism and achieved something altogether new.

Herzog & de Meuron

SWITZERLAND

Firm founded in 1978 by Jacques Herzog and Pierre de Meuron; joined by current partners Harry Gugger in 1991 and Christine Binswanger in 1994. Both Herzog and de Meuron were born in Basel, Switzerland in 1950, and both graduated from the Swiss Federal Institute of Technology. Awarded the Berlin Academy of Arts Prize in 1987, the Andrea Palladio International Prize in 1988, and the German Critics' Prize and the Brunel Prize in 1994. Received the Pritzker Prize in 2001, and RIBA Gold Medal in 2006.

1, 2, 3   de Young Museum   2005 / San Francisco
photo: ©Christian Richters

2   elevation

3   section

Herzog & de Meuron

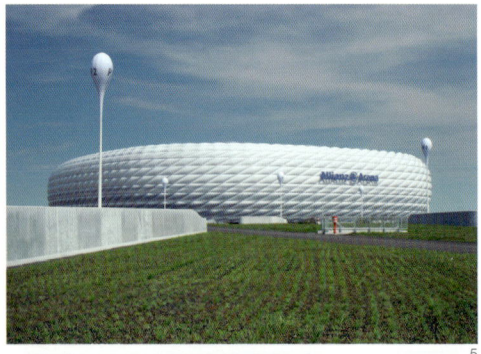

4　PRADA Tokyo　2003 / Tokyo
　photo: ©Synectics
5　Arianz Arena　2005 / Munich
　photo: ©Courtesy of Arianz Arena
6　E,D,E,N, Pavilion　1987 / Rheinfelden, Switzerland
　photo: ©Synectics
7　Social Housing Units on Switzerland Street　2000 / Paris
　photo: ©Synectics
8　Apartment Building along a Party Wall　1988 / Basel, Switzerland
　photo: ©Synectics
9　Schutzenmatt Housing　1993 / Basel, Switzerland
　photo: ©Synectics
10　Signal Box　1995 / Basel, Switzerland
　photo: ©Synectics
11　Pfaffenholz Sports Center　1994 / Basel, Switzerland
　photo: ©Synectics

12 Expansion of the Walker Art Center   2005 / Minneapolis, Minnesota
photo: ©Christian Richters

13 Goetz Gallery   1992 / Munich
photo: ©Synectics

14 Ricola-Europe SA. Production and Storage Building   1993 / Mulhouse-Brunstatt, France
photo: ©Synectics

15 Dominus Winery   1997 / Napa Valley, California
photo: ©Synectics

Herzog & de Meuron

As the world grows ever smaller, Herzog and de Meuron continue to make great leaps forward. The architectural team is active not only in Switzerland, their home country, but also in Germany, England, France, Spain, Italy, Austria, China, Japan, and the U.S. Since they first emerged in the world of architecture, the range of creative expressions has increased considerably due to their influence. Sometimes, their work is opulent, as in Prada Tokyo; other times, it is light and airy, as in Allianz Arena; and still other times, it is weighty, as in the housing complex on the Rue des Suisses in Paris.

Let'look, for example, at the team's design for the de Young Museum. A rectangular parallelepiped with a length of 126 meters, the building is covered with 7,200 sheets of copper. Along with flat panels, there are several other types, including punched and embossed metal sheets, and various combinations of these. The position of each type is designed for a specific part of the building, depending on the direction it faces, and the amount of sunlight and wind it gets. Despite the use of a single material, this varying technique lends a deeply expressive quality to the building. It is just this kind of touch that has exerted a strong impact on architects all over the world.

Both Herzog and de Meuron were born in Basel in 1950, and both of were influenced by Aldo Rossi, who they studied with at the ETH (Swiss Federal Institute of Technology). After graduating, the two set up their own firm in 1978, and began designing buildings in various locations in and around Basel. Herzog and de Meuron, who have stated that "Architecture is the most important cultural expression," have continued to take an experimental approach to creating facades, the single most significant aspect of architectural design.

The Hotel Eden is located on the outskirts of Basel. In the hotel's garden stands the E,D,E,N Pavilion, a four-legged pergola. On closer inspection, one notices that the thin legs spell out the word "Eden." As this example indicates, since early in their career, Herzog and de Meuron have paid close attention to surface design.

Other examples of this focus include the wooden Apartment Building Along a Party Wall, which at first glance resembles a Japanese-style rowhouse; the Schutzenmatt Housing complex, covered with cast-iron doors in an undulating pattern; the wood-wool-board pattern imprinted on glass in the Pfaffenholz Sports Center; the copper panels wrapped around the exterior of Signal Box; the frosted-

16	40 Bond Apertment / New York	
17	Tate Gallery of Modern Art 2000 / London	
	photo: ©Synectics	
18	Library of the Eberswalde Technical School 1999 / Eberswalde, Germany	
	photo: ©Synectics	
19	Shaulager Museum 2003 / Basel, Switzerland	
	photo: ©Synectics	
20	St. Jakob Park Stadium 2002 / Basel, Switzerland	
	photo: ©Synectics	
21, 22	Barcelona Forum 2004 / Barcelona	
	photo: ©Synectics	
23	1987 / Laufen, Switzerland	
	photo: ©Synectics	
24	Ricola Marketing Building 1998 / Laufen, Switzerland	
	photo: ©Synectics	
25	Railway Engine Depot, Auf dem Wolf 1995 / Basel, Switzerland	
	photo: ©Synectics	

glass opening at the Goetz Gallery which changes according to the weather and time; the silk-screened leaf pattern that rises up from the exterior of the Ricola-Europe SA Production and Storage Building; and the fieldstone-packed gabion that covers the Dominus Winery. Herzog and de Meuron came to international attention for their use of a leaf pattern taken from a photograph by Karl Blossfeldt. Working first with artists who had once been involved with Joseph Beuys, the team also began to collaborate with other creative people on architectural design. These included Remy Zaugg and Thomas Ruff. According to them, "Artists have a special familiarity with the surface of a substance, enabling them to access a dimension that is inaccessible to architects." What really catapulted them to international stardom, though, was Herzog and de Meuron's victory in the international competition for the Tate Modern. At the same time, their design for the building earned them the scorn of established architects like Tadao Ando, Renzo Piano, and Rem Koolhaas. In the competition to renovate the Tate, the team took a hint from their earlier work at the Goetz and merely placed a two-storey glass box called a "light beam" on top of the roof, leaving the exterior walls completely untouched. In the architects' view, the striking brick exterior of the original building was exactly what they were after in terms of surface design.

Following the completion of the Tate in 2000, their commissions, exhibiting the same infinite variety of expression, began to pop up all over the world. In the blink of an eye, they created the Rue des Suisses Housing Complex, the Eberswalde Technical School Library, the Schaulager Museum, the St. Jakob Park Stadium, Barcelona Forum, Allianz Arena, the Information, Communication, and Media Center at Brandenburg Technical University, Prada Tokyo, the Walker Art Center and the de Young Museum.

"Architecture has long since stopped emerging from tradition; it now comes from the conceptual or virtual world. This world, based purely on concepts of one's own making, provides the drive for today's architects and the opportunity for architects to express themselves." Through projects currently underway, such as the Beijing Olympic Stadium, the 40 Bond Street Apartments, the Hamburg Concert Hall, and the MoMA Roof Garden, Herzog and de Meuron seem certain to develop further as they set out to create new understandings and expressions in architecture.

HOK/Helmuth Obata Kassabaum

USA

Firm founded by George Hellmuth, Gyo Obata, and George E. Kassabaum in St. Louis in 1955. Today, with an extensive network throughout North and South America, Europe, and Asia, the world's largest architectural office. Following the departure of Hellmuth and the death of Kassabaum, Obata became director of the firm.

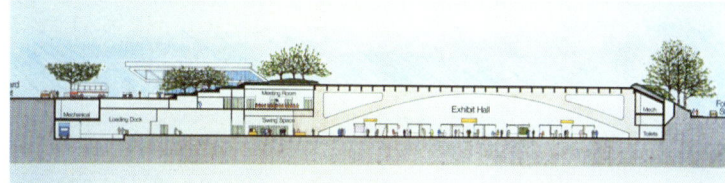

1 Priory Chapel 1962 / St. Louis, Missouri
  photo: ©George Silk
2,3 George R Moscone Convention Center 1981 / San Francisco
  photo: ©Synectics
4 National Air & Space Museum 1976 / Washington D.C.
  photo: ©George Silk
5 EPA Campus 2001 / Reseach Triangle Park, North Carolina
  photo: ©Alan Karchmer

HOK

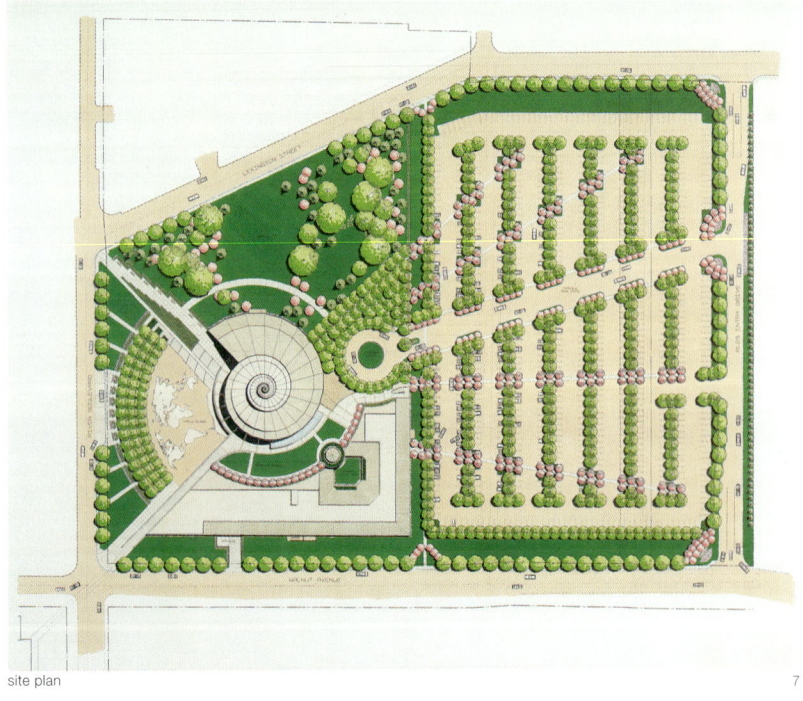

site plan

6, 7	The Conference Center of the Church of Jesus Christ of Latter-Day Saints 1993 / Independence, Missouri
photo: ©Balthazar Korab	11	King Khalid International Airport 1983 / Riyadh, Saudi Arabia
photo: ©Robert Azzi
8	Dallas Galleria 1983 / Dallas, Texas
photo: ©George Cott	12	King Saud University 1984 / Riyadh, Saudi Arabia
photo: ©Robert Azzi
9	Phoenix Municipal Courthouse 1999 / Phoenix, Arizona
photo: ©Nick Merrick, Hedrich-Blessing	13	Ludhiana City Center / Punjab, India
10	Boeing Leadership Center 1999 / St. Louis, Missouri
photo: ©Steve Hall, Hedrich-Blessing	14	Tanmiya Tower / Kuwait City, Kuwait

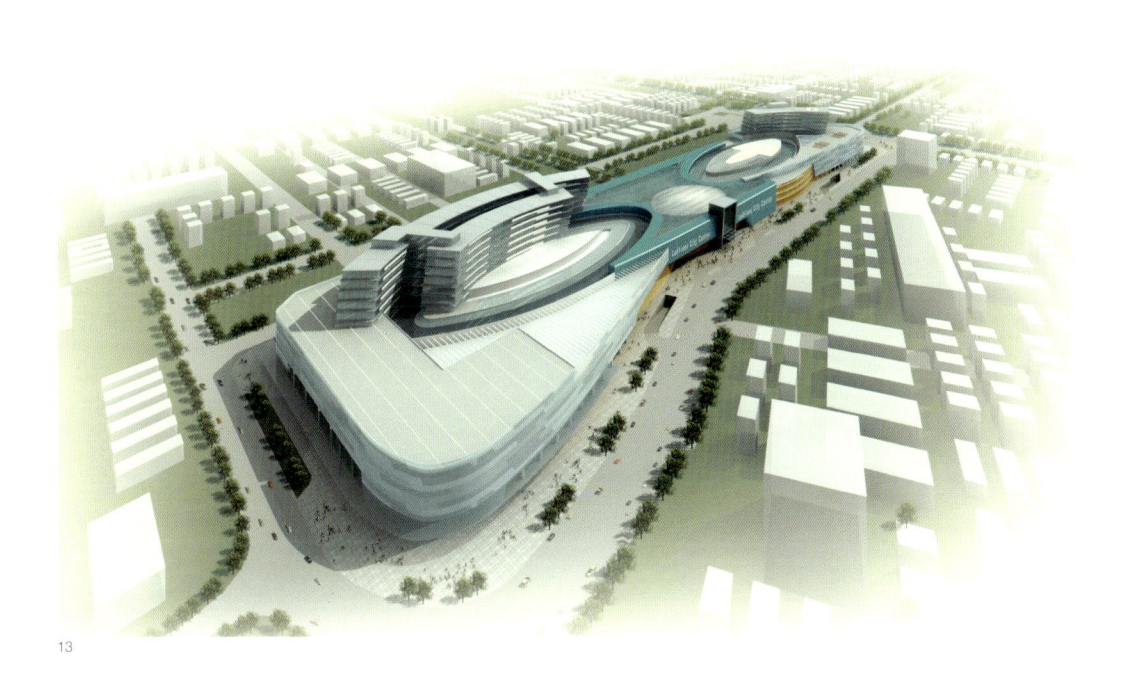

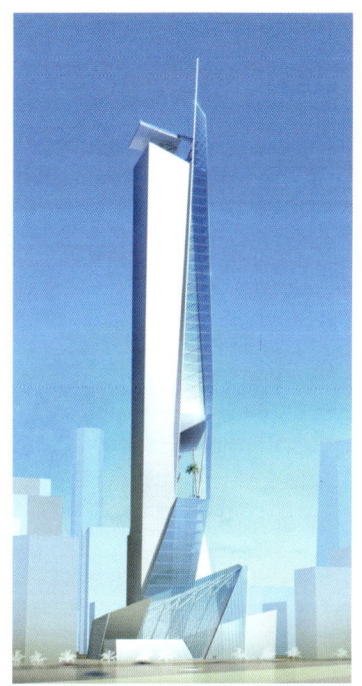

15　St. Louis International Airport East Terminal　1999 / St. Louis, Missouri
　　photo: ©Timothy Hursley
16　The Rehabilitation of St.Louis Union Station　1985 / St. Louis, Missouri
　　photo: ©Bill Mathis
17　New Doha International Airport / Doha, Qatar

Hellmuth Obata Kassabaum (HOK) has its headquarters in St. Louis, Missouri, where interested visitors also have a chance to enjoy the refined beauty of the firm's important early work the Priory Church.
The building's circular plan is a double-layered structure comprising 20 perfect parabolic arches topped off with 20 smaller arches. The white, Felix Candela-like arches resemble pretty flowers in bloom on a 526,000-square-meter hill with a trajectory of rhythmical curves running across a carpet of greenery.
HOK was established by George Hellmuth, Gyo Obata, and George E. Kassabaum in St. Louis in 1955. Today, it is the largest architectural firm in the world. Playing a central role in the practice is Obata, who began his career at Skidmore, Owings, and Merrill (SOM) in Chicago. Steeped in the atmosphere of a city teeming with notable architects, including Louis Sullivan, Frank Lloyd Wright, and Mies van der Rohe, Obata's Chicago influences later became evident in his work.

From Chicago, Obata returned to his hometown of St. Louis. There he began working at Hellmuth, Yamasaki, and Leinweber, known for its thin, shell design of the St. Louis International Airport East Terminal. Working under Minoru Yamasaki as a project architect, the two Japanese-Americans developed a close teacher-student relationship. In 1955, when the firm was dissolved, Obata joined Hellmuth and Kassabaum to establish HOK. Hellmuth left the company in 1978, and since Kassabaum's death in 1982, Obata has headed the firm.

After the founding of HOK, Obata summarized his work by saying, "Architecture is what emerges as a result of a design that is created for a given set of circumstances." This comment shows Obata's emphasis on attitude rather than style. Instead of a consistent and specific type of design, Obata's signature as an architect is related to the actual perception of a place. Expressionistic quirks, strong assertions or arrogance, jokes, and excessive symbolism or monumentalism are rarely found in Obata's work.

As a large-scale renewal project of a historical structure, the Rehabilitation of St. Louis Union Station, one of HOK's most important works, was unusual in the U.S. The plan called for a single, giant complex that would house the old Romanesque station house and train depot together with a shopping mall, luxury hotel, arcade, and a plaza. After its completion, the influence of the project spread to the

18 One Oxford Center 1983 / Pittsburgh, Pennsylvania
    photo: ©HOK
19 Georgia Archives Building 2004 / Morrow, Georgia
    photo: ©Timothy Hursley
20 Avante Center at William R.Harper College 2004 / Palatine, Georgia
    photo: ©Paul Rivera
21 Hong Kong Stadium 1983 / Hong Kong
    photo: ©Kerun Ip
22 King's Library at the British Museum 2003 / London
    photo: ©James Brittain
23 National Air&Space Museum, Steven F.Udvar-Hazy Center 2003 / Chantilly, Virginia
    photo: ©Joseph Romeo

photos : Courtesy of the Architect except ©Synectics

surrounding neighborhood and resulted in improvements to the urban environment. Another of HOK's representative works is the George R. Moscone Convention Center in San Francisco. As an astylar space, the center, built underground, is one of the world's leading exposition sites. The post-tension concrete arches with a span of some 84 meters are simply overwhelming. The roof of the building is an open park, and the building's identity as a convention center is defined by the powerful space frame that forms the canopy.

While most designs are conceived from form, Obata, a proponent of Louis Sullivan's "form-follows-function" ethic, favors function and creates work based on usability. Obata's creative process involves making drawings in his studio, experiencing a three-dimensional area while moving from space to space following a circulation system, and relying on his mind's eye as he continues to develop a design. The interior space that emerges from the process exerts a decisive influence on a building's exterior and final form.

HOK's prowess with complex flowlines is evident in a work such as the National Air and Space Museum in Washington D.C. With an average of approximately 60,000 people per day, traffic in the building is handled with a well-organized flow. This project, however, was redone twice following countless objections to the original design, exhibiting the degree of patience and discipline HOK maintains in executing a project and insuring that it adheres to the original time frame and budget.

In selecting a few examples of the firm's many representative works, I would suggest Priory Chapel, National Air and Space Museum, Moscone Center, Dallas Galleria, the Union Station Rehabilitation, EPA Campus, Phoenix Municipal Courthouse, Boeing Leadership Center, and the Conference Center of the Church of Jesus Christ of Latter-Day Saints. In addition, HOK was commisioned to design King Khalid International Airport, the single largest building site in the world, and King Saud University – both in Saudi Arabia. And through its handling of huge projects in foreign countries, including Ludhiana City Center, Tanmiya Tower, and New Doha International Airport, it is clear that as the world's largest architectural firm, HOK is unchallenged.

Hans Hollein

Austria

Born in Vienna in 1934. Graduated from the Academy of Fine Arts Vienna in 1956. Studied at the Illinois Institute of Technology and completed a postgraduate degree at University of California, Berkeley in 1960. Worked under F. Kaiser. Went independent in 1964. Received the Reynolds Memorial Award in 1966 and 1984, and the Pritzker Prize in 1985. Awarded the Chevalier de l'Ordre National de la Légion d'Honneur in 2003, and the Arnold W. Brunner Memorial Prize in 2004.

1. Retti Candle Shop   1965 / Vienna
   photo: ©Synectics
2. Richard L. Feigen Gallery   1969 / New York
   photo: ©Synectics
3. Abteiberg Museum   1982 / Monchengladbach, Germany
   photo: ©Synectics
4. Haas Haus   1990 / Vienna
   photo: ©Synectics
5. Museum of Modern Art in Frankfurt   1991 / Frankfurt
   photo: ©Synectics
6. Banco Santandal   1993 / Madrid
   photo: ©Synectics
7. Interbank Headquarters   2001 / Lima, Peru
8. Museum of Glass and Ceramics   1978 / Tehran, Iran
   photo: ©Synectics
9, 10. Centrum Bank in Vaduz   2003 / Vaduz, Liechtenstein

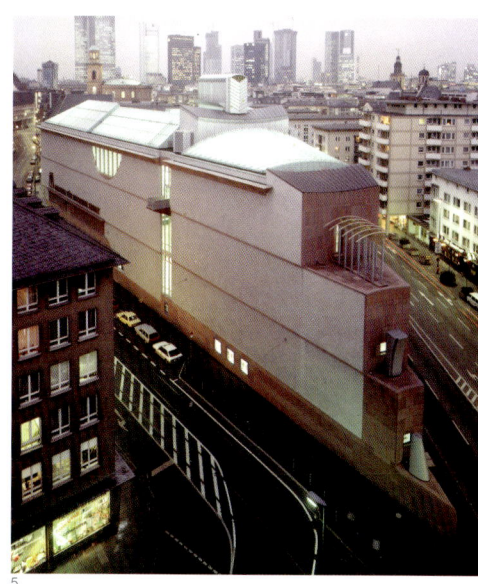

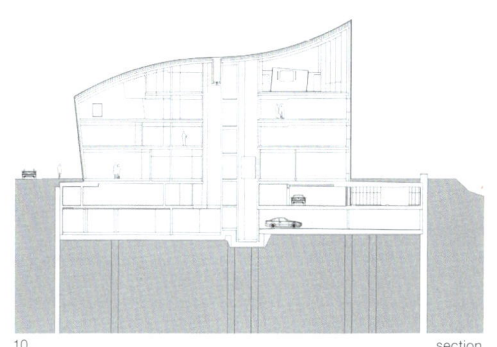

section

95

11, 12 VULCANIA 2002 / Auvergne, France
   13   Exhibition Hall and Museum in St. Polten 2002 / St.Polten, Austria
   14   Schullin Jeweller I 1974 / Vienna
        photo: ©Synectics
   15   Generali / Media-Tower 2001 / Vienna
   16   Austrian Embassy in Berlin 2001 / Berlin
   17   Albertina Museum 2004 / Vienna
   18   Ex-Ospedale / San Giovanni Valdarno, Italy

13

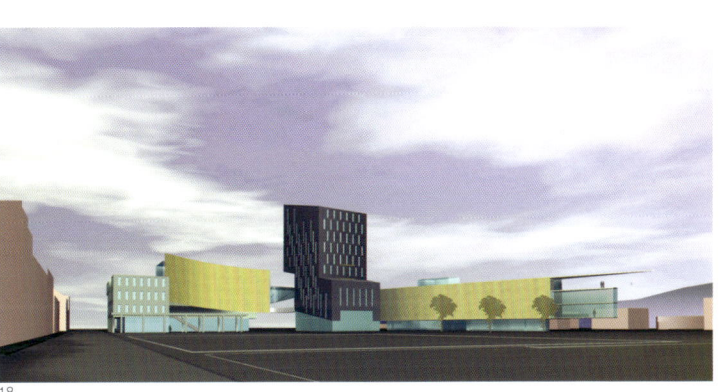

14

15

16

17

18

97

With his debut work still a topic of conversation forty years on, Hans Hollein is not your average architect. The Austrian master's Retti Candle Shop is an extremely unusual example of a world-renowned architect's first building being extant.

A symmetrical space with a width of only 14-square meters, out-of-town visitors are likely to recognize the building immediately without so much as looking at its sign or "speaking facade." And even after all these years, the shiny silver of the aluminum box shows no sign of aging. Considering that Hollein won the Reynolds Memorial Award for the work, it is clear that even as a young architect, he was brimming with ideas.

After this notable beginning, Hollein set about creating an endless array of works. Among the more important are the Richard L. Feigen Gallery, the Museum of Glass and Ceramics, the Museum Abteiberg, the Museum of Modern Art in Frankfurt, the IBA Housing Complex, Haas Haus, Banco Santander, the Exhibition Hall and Museum of Lower Austria in St. Polten, and the Generali Media Tower. I have personally had an opportunity to visit all of these buildings, but after that I found I could no longer keep up with Hollein.

Over his long career, however, Hollein has consistently produced high-quality architecture, including recent examples such as Vulcania (the Vulcano Museum in Auvergne), the Interbank headquarters in Lima, and the Centrum Bank in Vaduz. The originality of Hollein's works in progress is simply astonishing.

It is also unusual to find an architect who is involved in such a diverse range of design work. Along with shops, Hollein has designed museums, schools, banks, apartment buildings, offices, hospitals, and galleries – i.e., numerous architectural typologies. Needless to say, he is also active in urban planning, and along with furniture, has designed exhibitions, installations, and stage sets. In addition, his versatility extends to works of art, as Hollein has shown in various exhibitions including the Venice Biennale. His famous aphorism, "Everything is architecture," epitomizes Hollein's activities.

Why exactly are his interests so varied? No one can really say. Forty years ago, he started his own firm, but rather than pursuing an orderly office system, he decided to base his practice on disorder. An extremely ordered environment can be dull; by comparison, disorder can seem normal and liberating. In Hollein's designs, one finds a two-dimensional quality that combines geometrical forms and natural or irregular

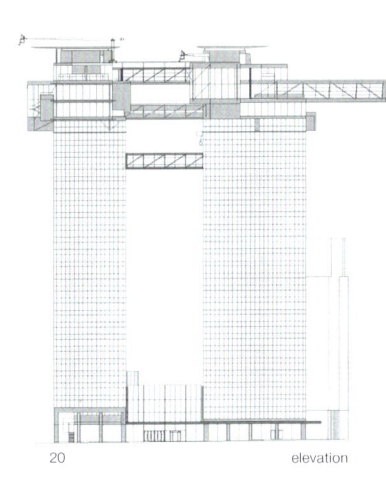

19, 20	PORR Tower / Vienna	23	Saturn Tower 2004 / Vienna
21	Salzburg Museum / Salzburg	24	SEA MIO / Taipei
22	Public School in Donau City 1999 / Vienna		CG: ©Beyer
		25	Gate 2 / Vienna

photos : Courtesy of the Architect except ©Synectics

20 elevation

21

22

23

24

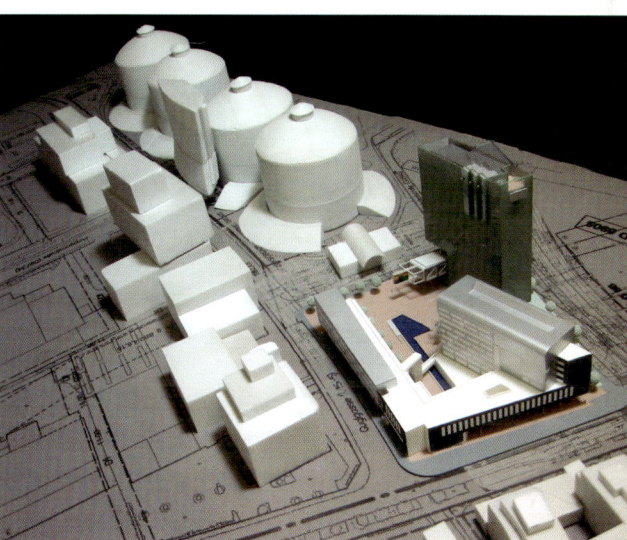

25

shapes. Do these approaches perhaps provide the key to Hollein's ability to express himself so freely in such a diverse way?

Hollein's devout attitude and close connection to history is another difficult thing to explain. Because of it, many people have referred to him as a postmodernist, yet that is not at all his intention. One useful approach to understanding his work is to think of Schullin Jewelry Shop I & II, Austrian Travel Agencies, and Haas Haus as only one genre within a multitude of variations.

At the same time, one can also detect a deconstructionist or structuralist element. Hollein's wide-ranging, "everything-is-architecture" pallet simply contains a wealth of motifs. Although his diversity is widely acknowledged, Hollein's architecture is far too broad in scope to be contained in a single framework like postmodernism or deconstructionism.

An overview of Hollein's recent architecture would include outstanding works such as the Austrian Embassy in Germany and the magnificent Albertina Museum in central Vienna. Their strong presence is created by prominent cantilevered roofs of the type used in Hass Haus. Similarly, the PORR Towers (currently under construction) in Vienna resemble a city floating in mid-air due to the bridge and cantilevers that extend between the two high-rise buildings. A variety of forms are packed into the residential complex Hollein designed in San Giovanni Valdarno, Italy, giving the building the appearance of a real settlement.

Some years ago, the famous piano manufacturer Boesendorfer hired Hollein to design a piano. The press reception for the finished product was held in Tokyo in 1991. Perched on gold legs, the grand piano had a black exterior and a splendid vermilion interior. When provided with exquisite materials, no architect outshines Hollein; he is truly a magician. At the reception, Hollein, tall and clad in his trademark white jacket, stood beside the piano. It was enough to make you think he was the pianist, and as he stood there, he seemed to be thinking to himself, "Everything is architecture."

Helmut Jahn

CANADA

Born in Nuremberg, Germany in 1940. Graduated from the Technische Hochschule in Munich in 1965. In 1967, completed a postgraduate degree at the Illinois Institute of Technology, and in the same year, joined C.F. Murphy Associates. In 1987, became a fellow of the American Institute of Architects, and in 1988, received the R.S. Reynolds Memorial Award. Taught at the Illinois Institute of Technology from 1909 to 1993. In 1994, received the Bundesverdienstkreuz Erster Klasse of the Federal Republic of Germany.

1　IIT Student Housing　2003 / Chicago, Illinois
　Photo: ©Doug Snower
2, 3　Sony Center　2000 / Berlin
　photo: ©Engelhardt/Stellin

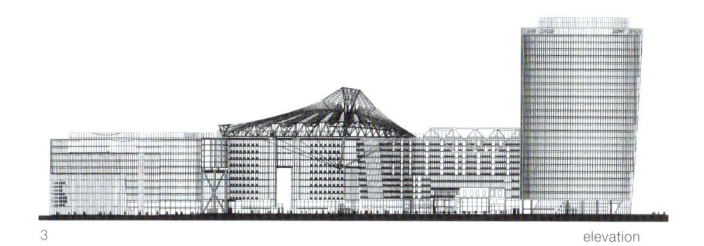

3　　　　　　　　　　　　　　　　elevation

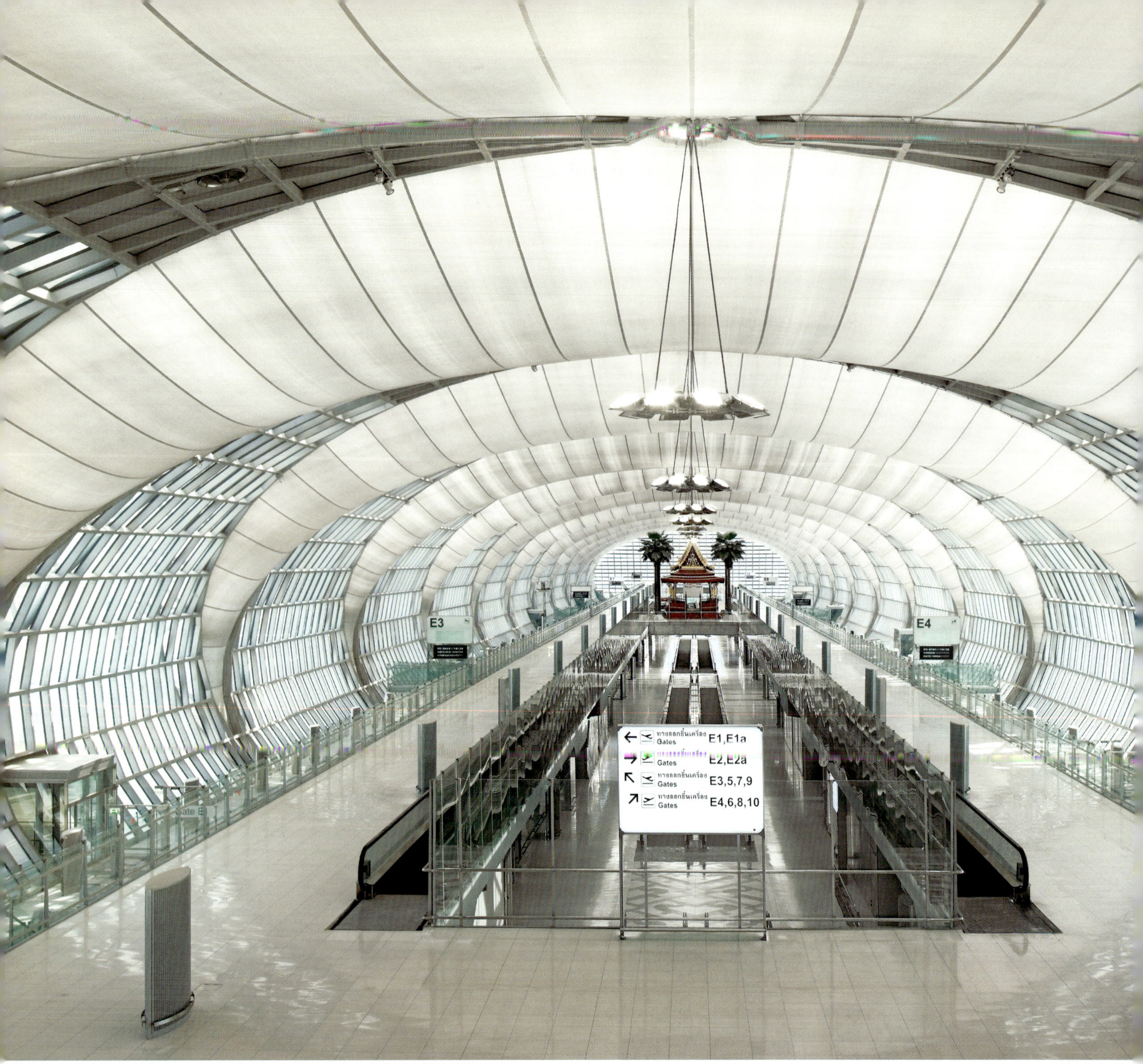
E3
E4
Gates E1,E1a
Gates E2,E2a
Gates E3,5,7,9
Gates E4,6,8,10

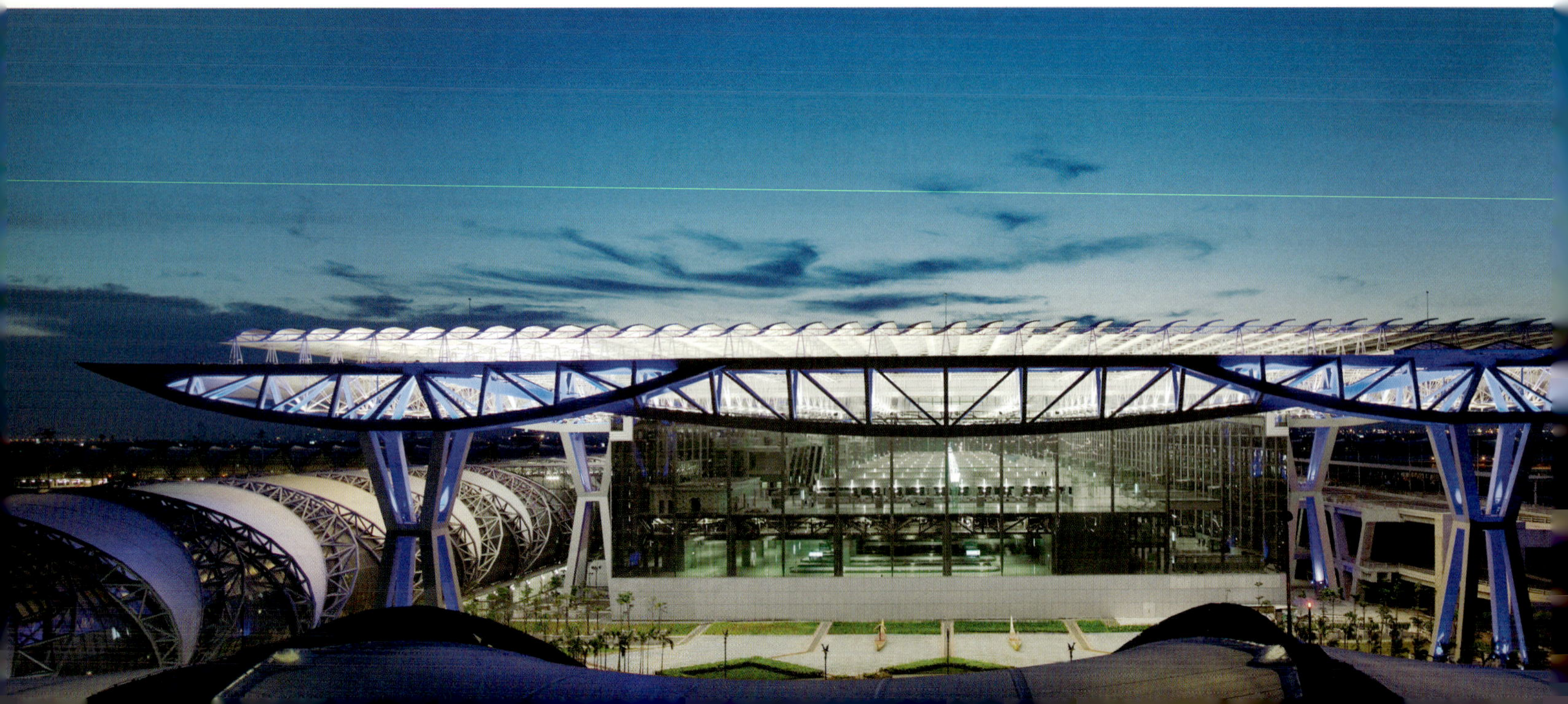

4, 5 Suvarnabhumi International Airport Passenger Terminal Complex   2006 / Bangkok
   photo: ©Rainer Viertlboeck
6, 7 Post Tower   2003 / Bonn
   photo: ©Andreas Keller

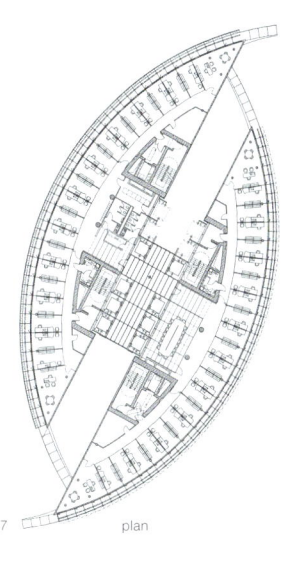

7   plan

103

Helmut Jahn

8 O'hare International Airport United Airlines Terminal 1 Renovation   2004 / Chicago, Illinois
   photo: ©Timothy Hursley
9 James R. Thompson Center   1985 / Chicago, Illinois
   photo: ©Murphy Jahn
10 Shanghai International Expo Center   2001 / Shanghai
   photo: ©Doug Snower
11 Munich Airport Center   1999 / Munich
   photo: ©Engelhardt/Sellin
12 Bayer AG Konzernzentrale   2001 / Leverkusen, Germany
   photo: ©Andreas Keller
13 Tokyo Station Yaesu Redevelopment Project Twin Towers / Tokyo
   photo: ©Steinkamp/Ballogg
14 Kempinski Hotel   1994 / Munich
   photo: ©Hans Ege
15 Cologne/Bonn Airport   2000 / Cologne, Germany
   photo: ©H.G.Esch

Though not as young as he once was, Helmut Jahn is still known as a boy wonder of the American architecture world. After arriving at the Illinois Institute of Technology from Germany in 1966, and working as an assistant to Gene Summers, a pupil of Mies van der Rohe, at C.F. Murphy Associates, Jahn quickly assumed the position of executive vice-president at the firm. In 1982, he was named president. His rapid rise to the top is truly an American success story.

Jahn's own creative activities began in 1974, one year after becoming an executive in the firm, with relatively low-rise works like Kemper Arena. But it wasn't until after becoming CEO of the company that he came into his own as an architect. Beginning with James R. Thompson Center in 1985, and continuing on with Park Avenue Tower in 1986, the United Airlines Terminal One at O'Hare International Airport Renovation in 2004, and One Liberty Place in 1987, the Messeturm in 1991, Kempinski Hotel in 1994, and Sony Center in 2000, most of Jahn's work has been grand-scale architecture.

It is simply astounding that, though American, an atelier-style operation like Murphy / Jahn, has come as it has grown to oversee such large-scale architectural projects. By comparison, one might look at the work of Cesar Pelli. Both architects are skilled at designing high-rise buildings, but both also create their share of low-rise works. Pelli, however, often uses heavy materials such as brick in his low rises, while in recent years, Jahn has adopted throughly high-tech materials like glass and metal.

Jahn's success after taking over the reins at C.F. Murphy lies in his skillful fusion of creative design and organizational professionalism. This methodology alone distinguishes him from more widely known design studios and corporate architects.

Jahn's works also display a diverse range of architectural typology. His various projects, which include high-rise buildings, airport masterplans, freight transport facilities, urban planning, and low-rise commercial complexes, are filled with an abundance of interactive ideas and can also be intellectually stimulating, as Jahn takes on another type of architecture. To ensure thoroughness in his methodology, Jahn looks over each of the firm's projects himself. This is clear from his famous sketches, which are completely covered with his writing.

In recent years, Jahn has often used the term "archi-neering," a composite form of architecture and engineering. "Beginning in the

16 Highlight Munich Business Towers   2003 / Munich
   photo: ©Rainer Viertlboeck
17 Messeturm   1991 / Frankfurt
   photo: ©Roland Halbe
18 Neues Kranzler Eck   2000 / Berlin
   photo: ©Christian Gahl
19 Park Avenue Tower   1987 / New York
   photo: ©Synectics
20 Kaufhof Galerria   2001 / Chemnitz, Germany
   photo: ©Roland Halbe
21 One Liberty Place   1987 / Philadelphia, Pennsylvania
   photo: ©Lawrence S. Williams
22 European Union Headquarters   1998 / Brussels, Belgium
   photo: ©Hisao Suzuki

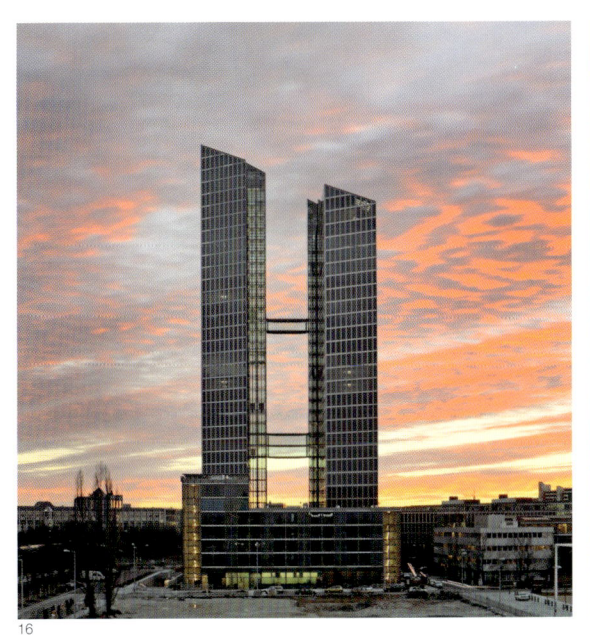

photos : Courtesy of the Architect except ©Synectics

21st century, architecture will be created using elements which transform its essence though new technology. By including photosynthetic, photovoltaic, and photochromatic operations in the skin of a building, we will be able to synthesize energy. This will become viable through a change in the relationship between architect and engineer."
Jahn also suggests that through "archi-neering," the advent of a new type of optical building will become a reality. Among Jahn's completed works, Post Tower comes closest to attaining this goal. Comprised of a 162-meter tower and a low-rise building, the latter's roof is made of steel grid-mesh. Each of the grids is equipped with an environmentally adaptive cell that includes a optical battery.
The cells have brought us one step closer to a future with the optical building skins that Jahn has predicted. Among the high-performance features offered by the technology are: 1. variable optical transparency; 2. external heat absorption; 3. internal heat absorption; 4. solar energy absorption; 5. variable ventilation; and 6. acoustic absorption.
Many of Jahn's works are in Germany, including Neues Kranzler Eck, Cologne/Bonn Airport, Munich Airport Center, Kempinski Hotel, Bayer AG Konzernzentrale, Kaufhof Galeria, and the Highlight Munich Business Towers. Among his completed designs in other countries are the IIT Student Housing Complex in Chicago, Shanghai International Expo Center, and the European Union Headquarters in Brussels. And at last, he has also recently arrived in Japan by winning a design competition for the Yaesu Redevelopment Project to build Twin Towers at Tokyo Station.

Dani Karavan

ISRAEL

Born in Tel Aviv, Israel in 1930. From 1943 to 1949, studied art with Avni, Steimatsky, and Ardon. Then, studied at Academia delle Belle Arti in Florence in 1956 and 1957. Designed stage sets for dance and theatre groups from 1960 to 1973. Awarded the Israel Prize in 1977. In 1992, received the UNESCO Miro Medal and in 1994, the UNESCO Picasso Medal. Awarded the Silver Medal for Plastic Arts of the French Academy of Architecture in 1994, and in 1998, the Praemium Imperiale Award for Architecture. Active throughout the world, including Japan, Karavan is one of the foremost environmental sculptors.

1 Kikar Levana   1988 / Tel Aviv, Israel
2 Illustration by Karavan
3 Negev Monument   1968 / Beersheva, Israel
4 Jerusalem, City of Peace   1976 / Venice, Italy

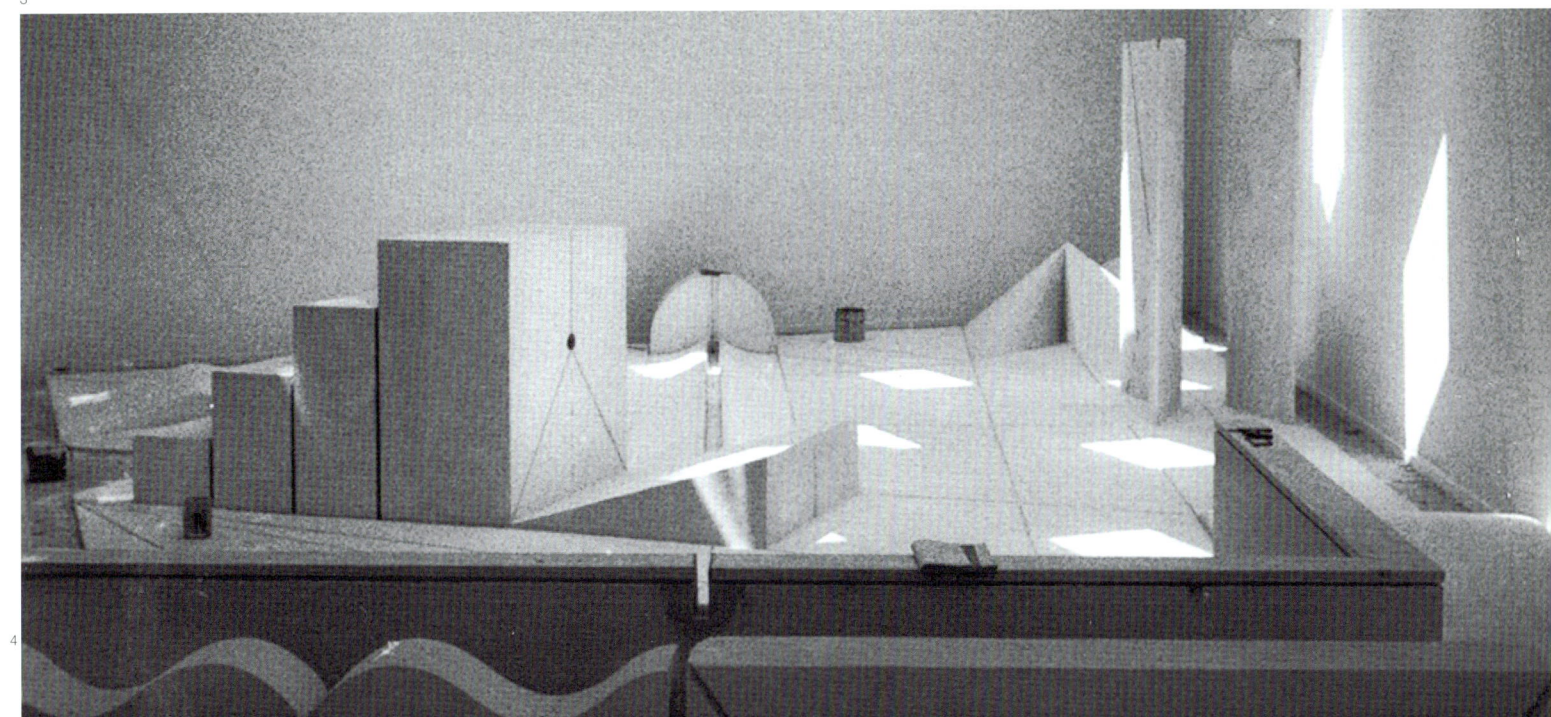

Dani Karavan

5 Axe Majeur 1980 / Cergy-Pontoise, France
6 Ma'alot 1986 / Cologne, Germany
7 Grundgesetz 49 2002 / Berlin
8 Bereshit 2000 / Kagoshima, Japan

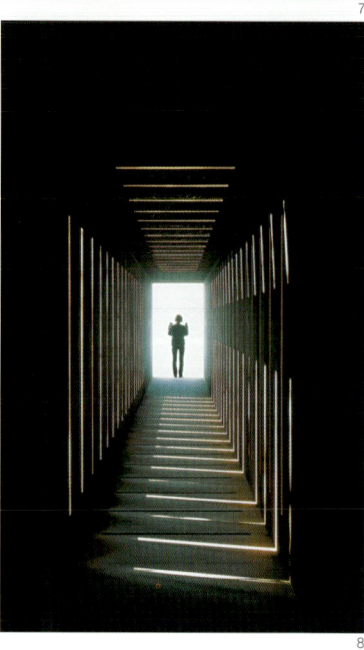

9 Place for the Communication Center of Credit Suisse 1995 / Zurich, Switzerland
10, 11 Way of the Hidden Garden 1999 / Sapporo, Japan
12 Passages-Homage to Walter Benjamin 1994 / Port Bou, Spain

photos : Courtesy of the Architect

perspective drawing

13 Two Enviroments for Peace   1978 / Florence, Italy
14 Way of Light   1988 / Soeul
15 Square of Tolerance-Homage to Yitzhak Rabin   1996 / Paris
16 Garden of Memories   1999 / Duisburg, Germany
17 Homage to the Prisoners of the Camp Gurs   1994 / Gurs, France
18 Dialogue   1989 / Duisburg, Germany

In July 1990, on the way back to Japan from Europe, I made a stop in Tel Aviv. I had an appointment to meet the architect Zvi Hecker, who asked if I'd like to meet an interesting sculptor and took me to a park in the city. After climbing a grassy knoll, we came to a rectangular lot with a number of white, geometrical objects such as a pyramid, hemisphere, tower, tiered mass, and a cylinder, which combined were an example of high art. In a little while, a man of small stature appeared wearing a hunting cap. When Hecker introduced him, I realized that this was none other than Dani Karavan, the designer of this chalk-white, environmental sculpture called "Kikar Levana."

At the time, Karavan was already active internationally as an environmental sculptor, but unaware of that, I was simply left with the impression that for an artist he made incredibly architectural sculptures. Like a work of architecture, "Kikar Levana" is a sculpture that allows the viewer to spatially experience its interior.

In 1968, some 20 years earlier, Karavan had created his first environmental sculpture, "Negev Monument." It was through this site-specific work that Karavan discovered his creative vocabulary, production method, and theoretical base.

Since the beginning of the 20th century, when Constantin Brancusi broke from the classical sculptural vocabulary which had been developed by Auguste Rodin in the previous century, artists such as Alberto Giacometti and Isamu Noguchi devoted themselves to the creation of new sculptural spaces and definitions.

Starting out in the performing arts in 1960, Karavan followed in these artists' footsteps. However, what makes Karavan's work completely different from his three predecessors is that rather than producing objects that can be installed in any space, Karavan creates site-specific works – i.e., environmental sculptures – which are directly related to the topology and context of the lot.

"Negev Monument," the prototype for Karavan's environmental sculptures, was begun in 1963 and completed in 1968, but Le Corbusier's chapel at Ronchamp, which had been built some years previous, had made an indelible impression on the young Karavan. Often called Le Corbusier's sole sculptural work, the chapel aims to fuse architecture with sculpture, and its strong commitment to the surrounding environment and lot exerted a

19　Way of Peace　1996 / Nitzana, Israel
20　Mimaamakim　1997 / Gelsenkirchen, Germany
21　Way of Human Rights　1993 / Nuremberg, Germany

photos : Courtesy of the Architect

strong influence on Karavan's first work. Karavan was also friendly with Noguchi. He mentions that Noguchi was Brancusi's student, and that Le Corbusier paid frequent visits to Brancusi. In Karavan's Monument, it's possible to detect Brancusi's influence as filtered through Le Corbusier and Noguchi.

Take, for example, Brancusi's "Endless Column" in Targu Jiu, Romania, the sculptor's homeland. By adopting this concept and shifting it, Karavan created a horizontal axis that stretched for several kilometers. Along the axis, he placed a few environmental objects. "Axe Majeur," outside of Paris in Cergy Pontoise, is an urban axis that runs for a length of three kilometers and includes twelve detention points. This is an example of how Karavan developed Brancusi's ideas on an urban scale. After getting his start with Negev Monument, Karavan produced "Jerusalem, City of Peace," for the 1976 Venice Biennale. The minimalist space, made of white concrete, was an environmental sculpture which allowed visitors to experience its upper section and interior. Following this work, Karavan began to enjoy international stardom.

Soon after came representative works around the world including "Kikar Levana," "Two Environments for Peace," "Ma'alot," "Way of Light," "Way of Human Rights," "Passages – Homage to Walter Benjamin," and "Square of Tolerance – Homage to Yitzhak Rabin." At the turn of the 21st century, Karavan completed works in Germany and Japan. The two German works are "Grundgesetz 49" and "Garden of Memories," which Norman Foster asked Karavan to create for a space in Duisburg. In Japan, Karavan created "Bereshit" for the Kirishima Art Forest in Kagoshima Prefecture. As these examples demonstrate, Karavan's work is borderless. His environmental sculpture is an exploration of figurative memory that stretches from the deserts to the cities, and on to the parks, hills, forests, plains, lakes, and seas.

Kim Young-Sub

SOUTH KOREA

Born in Mokpo, Korea in 1950. Graduated from Sungkyunkwan University in 1974. Established Kim Young-Sub and Kunchook-Moonhwa Architect Associates in 1982. Received the Grand Prize in the Korean Institute of Architects Award in 1988, and the Korean Architectural Culture Award in 1992, 1993, 1996, and 1997. Received the Grand Prize in the Korean Environmental Design and Architecture Award in 1995 and 1999, and the Seventh Kim Swoo-Geun Award in 1996. In 2000, received the Fifth Catholic Church Arts Award, and participated in the Asia Design Forum East Wind 2000.

plan

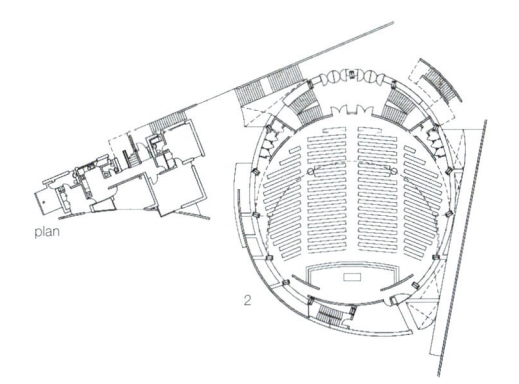

1, 2 Resurrection Catholic Church 1997 / Gyeonggi-do, Korea
3 Chungang Catholic Church 2000 / Gyeonggi-do, Korea
4 Balan Catholic Church 1999 / Gyeonggi-do, Korea

KIM YOUNG-SUB

5 Joong-Ang Catholic Church   2003 / Gyeonggi-do, Korea
6 Chodang Catholic Church   1999 / Kangneung City, Korea
7 Cheongyang Catholic Church   1999 / Chungcheongnam-do, Korea

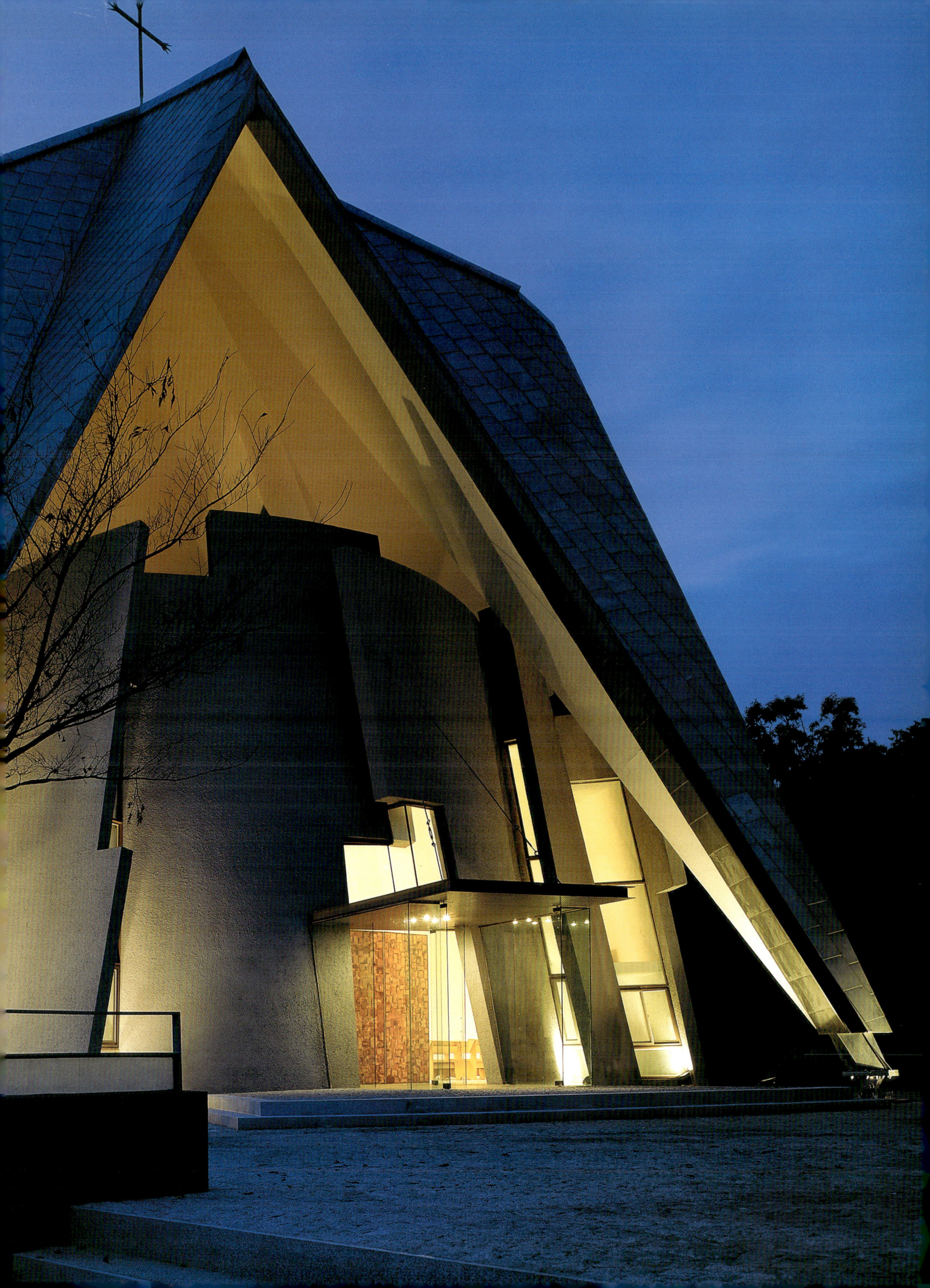

Kim Young-Sub

8 Restaurant Bamboo House   1995 / Seoul
9 Dong-il Women Laborer's Welfare Center and Nursery   1996 / Pusan, Korea
10 Myunghweewon Rehabilitation Center for the Handicapped   1997 / Gyeonggi-do, Korea
11 Catholic University Library and Lecture Hall   1995 / Seoul

In the final year of the 20th century at "East Wind 2000," a forum on architecture held in Tokyo, Kim Young-Sub warned that it was necessary for the city of the next century to be "environmentally sustainable, culturally variable, and ecologically stable."
For a ten-year period in the 1970s and 80s, Kim says that he was perfectly satisfied living with his wife and children in an approximately 80-square-meter apartment. But as his three children grew older, he decided to create Kim Young-Sub House by renovating a traditional _hanok_. For Kim, this house, with its quiet courtyard and natural surroundings, seemed to be an illustration of the future. Thus, his proposal for the city must have evolved out of his experience of living in a traditional Korean house.
Not long after, Kim became a proponent and practitioner of the preservation and renovation of _hanok_. Being incredibly thorough in his approach, Kim's interest in the field has never waned, giving some indication of his perfectionism as a craftsman who followed through until he became a professional.
Another example is the large quantity of records Kim has amassed as part of his long-term interest in music. He is apparently knowledgeable enough on the topic to serve as a commentator on FM radio, and deliver lectures on university-level music and art history. On top of all this, Kim is conversant in several languages, including Latin, and once held an exhibition called "Buildings Seen Through an Old Lens," featuring pictures he had taken with an old folding camera. He is an accomplished figure in a wide range of different fields.

Kim's other area of distinction is his mastery of Catholic church architecture. His work is exemplified by the presence of both skill and integrity, qualities which are a necessity for a good architect. Each of Kim's designs present aspects for particular problems, and like his interest in a wide range of subjects, his buildings suggest the workings of a diverse morphological imagination. In this respect, there is a clear difference between Kim and architects with a single theory and approach.
In visiting the churches which Kim has created, one detects a tenacious will in determining the form. One also senses Kim's zeal to produce a new tradition to complement the history of Korean church architecture. The succession of churches Kim has produced are clearly a series of experiments.
In his works, Kim has eliminated the customary

12, 13	House for Kim Young-Sub 1997 / Seoul	18	Korea Life Insurance, Suji Training Center & Master Plan 1998 / Gyeonggi-do, Korea
14	Ikchunggak & Crystal House 1997 / Seoul	19	Shenyang Children Activity Center / Competition
15	J-Residence 1992 / Pusan, Korea	20	Sanghyowon Botanical Garden / Jeju-do, Korea
16	Kookmin Books 2004 / Gyeonggi-do, Korea	21	Yongmoon Youth Retreat Camp 1996 / Gyeonggi-do, Korea
17	Nanam Publishing House 2003 / Gyeonggi-do, Korea	22	Seoul Performing Art Center

photos : Courtesy of the Architect

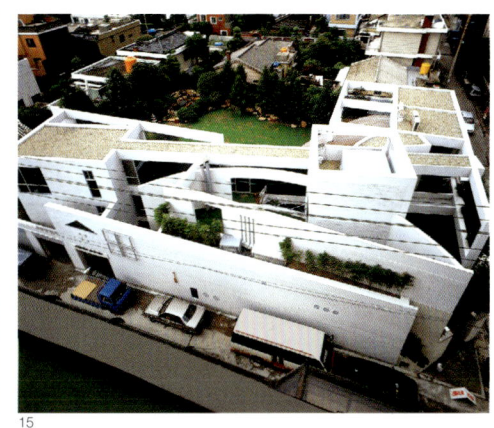

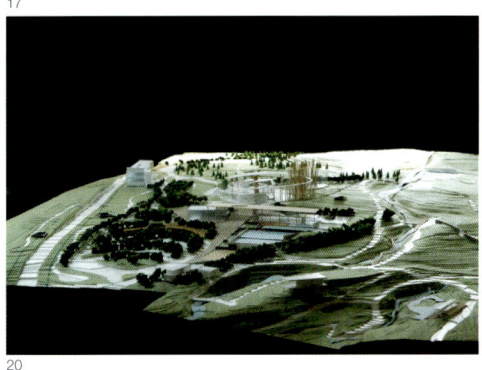

notions of church architecture and old symbolic forms. In lieu of that, he has introduced contemporary architectural grammar based on a translation of the Bible. His insatiable hunger for innovation is embodied in the large, dynamic chapel space imbued with a volume that soars toward the heavens at Chungang Catholic Church. In another example, the oval form tinged with a hint of roundness at the Resurrection Catholic Church creates a womblike space filled with a gentle aspect. For Balan Catholic Church, Kim evolved a distinctive form as an interpretation of the roof and style of a traditional building, while his Cheongyang Catholic Church is unique for a sculptural object that serves to emphasize the visual symbolism. Other outstanding religious works by the architect include Chodang Catholic Church and Joong-Ang Catholic Church.

Examples of Kim's other architectural typologies are the Korea Life Insurance Suji Training Center, Bamboo House Restaurant, the Dong-il Women Laborers' Welfare Center and Nursery, Myunghweewon Rehabilitation Center for the Handicapped, Yongmoon Youth Retreat Camp, and the Catholic University Library and Lecture Hall. Here, one senses obvious references to the brick buildings Louis Kahn designed on the Indian subcontinent. Referencing respected predecessors is one of Kim's primary design methods. In some cases, the references are explicit, while in others, they are implicit. In Ikchunggak and Crystal House, Kim defines the space by directly alluding to Kurt Schwitters' "Merzbau." In his writing on the practice, it is clear that Kim is a very sincere architect.

Kim has said, "Architecture is a translation of the intentions of an era into a space." Will Kim, whose reception of the Korea Architecture Culture Award was well-deserved, now be able to transform himself into one of South Korea's few international designers? Only time will tell.

Josef Paul Kleihues

Germany

Born in Rheine/Westfalen, Germany in 1933. Studied at Stuttgart Technical University from 1955 to 1957, and at Berlin Technical University from 1957 to 1959. Received a scholarship to Ecole Nationale Supérieure des Beaux Arts in 1960. Established his own firm in 1962. Taught at the University of Dortmund from 1973 to 1994. Appointed professor at the Dusseldorf Art Academy in 1994. Served as director of the International Building Exhibition (IBA). Died in August 2004.

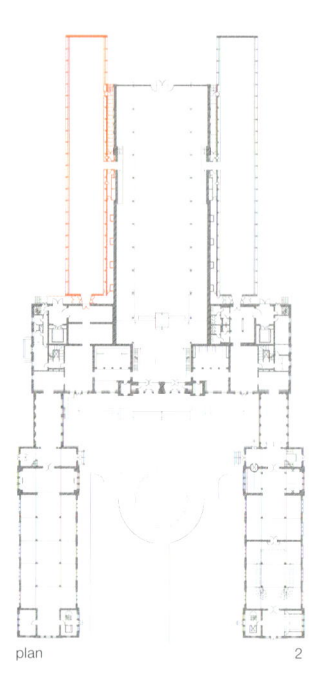

1, 2   Museum of Contemporary Art, Berlin   1996 / Berlin
3   Triangle   1996 / Berlin
photo: ©Synectics
4, 5   Museum of Pre- and Early History   1986 / Frankfurt
photo: ©Synectics

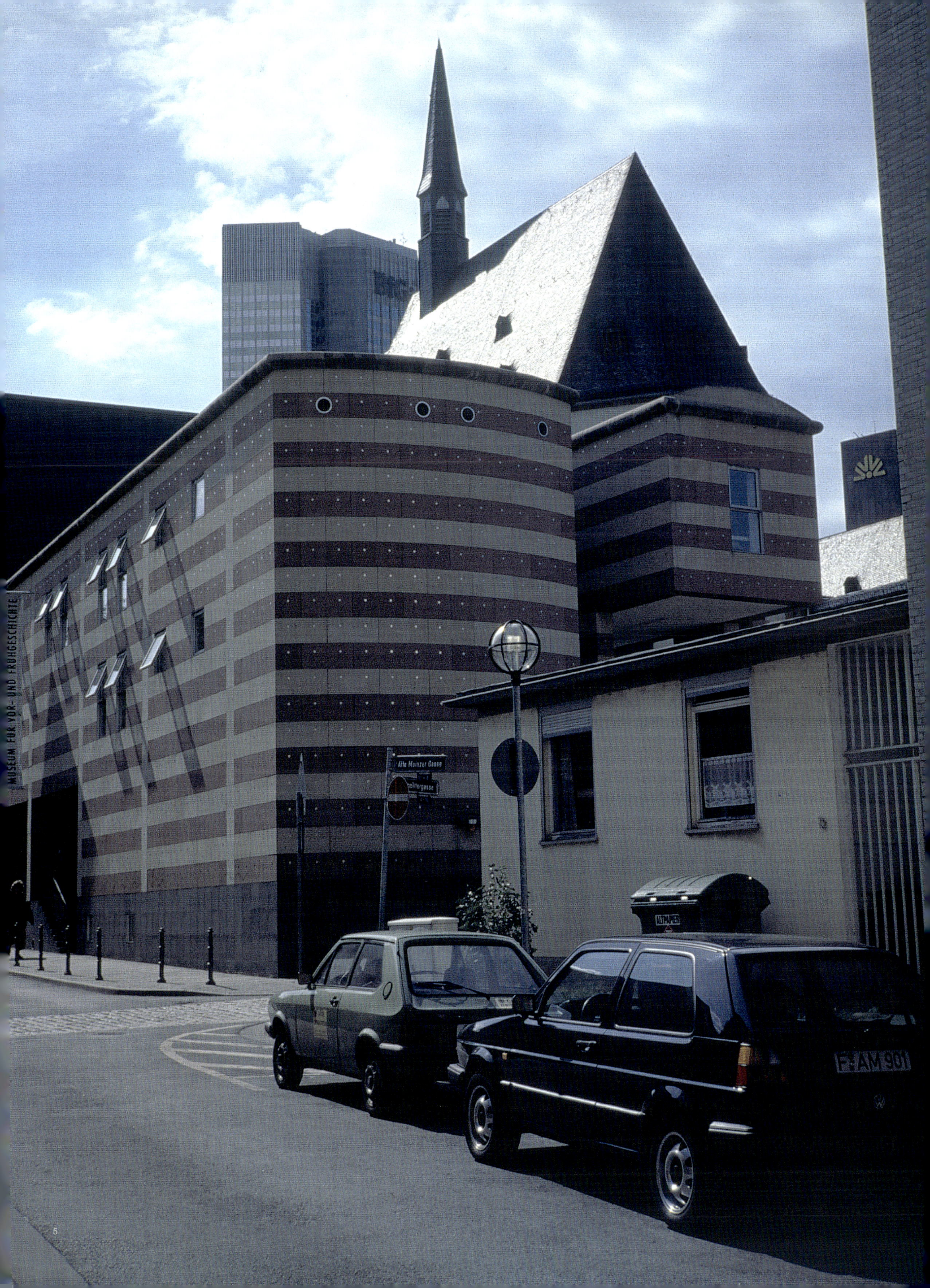

5

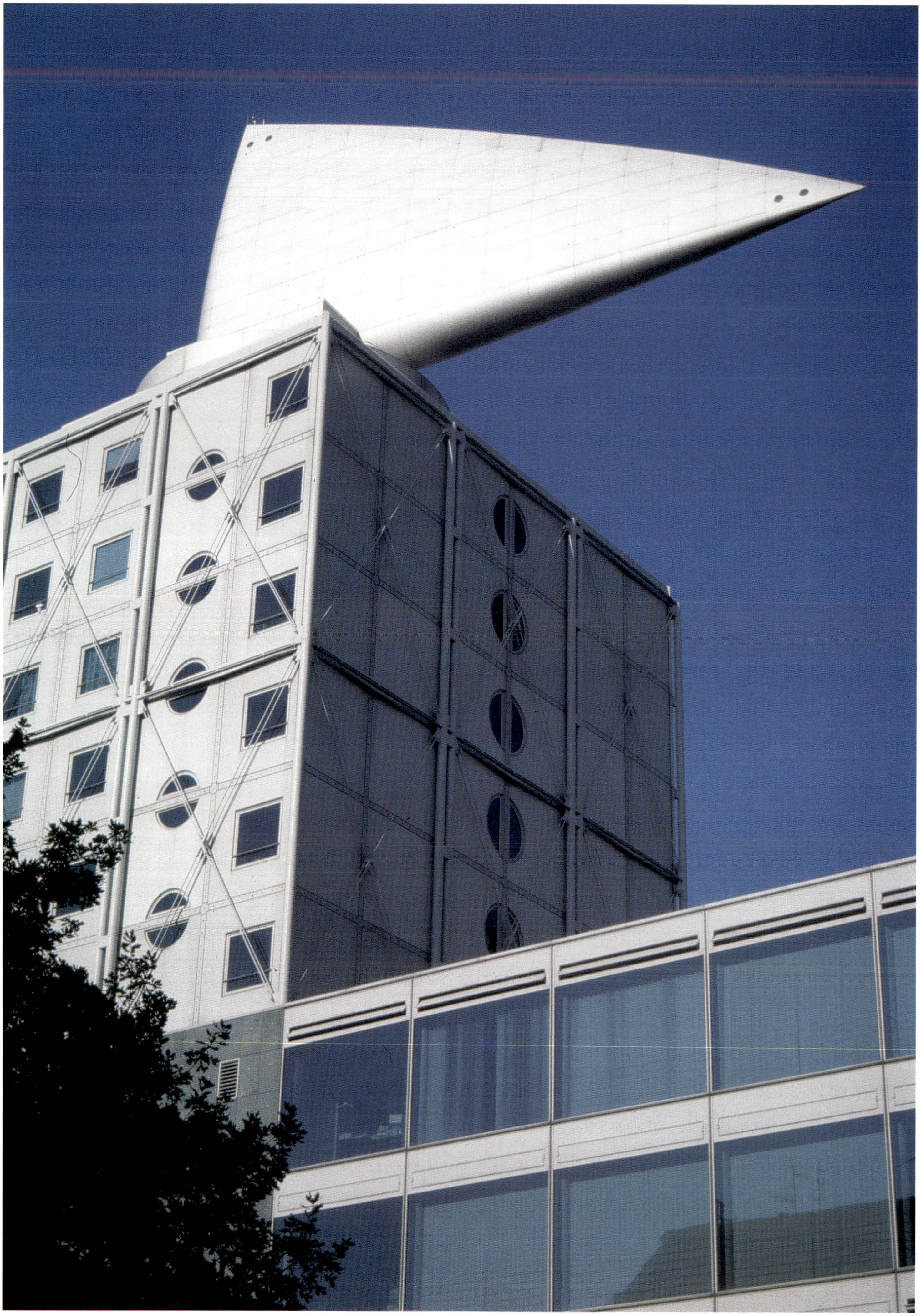

6

plan

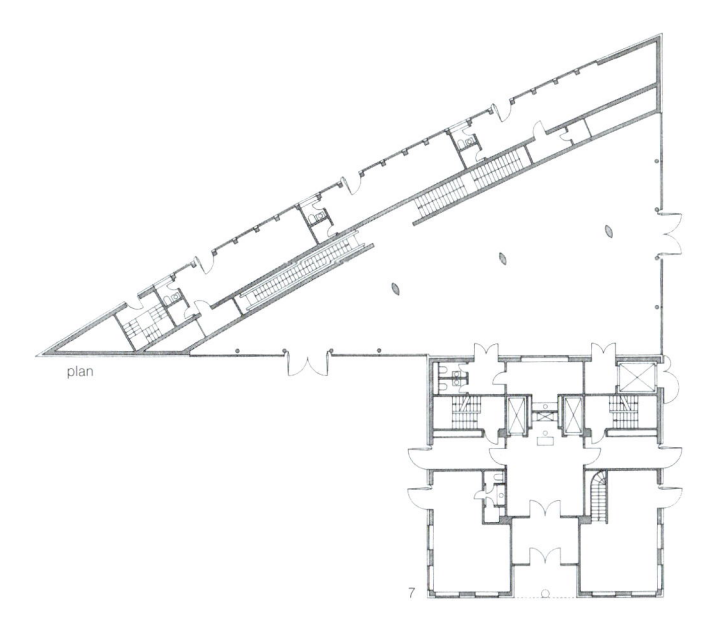

6, 7   Kant Triangle   1994 / Berlin
       photo: ©Synectics

8   Europolis / Competition

9   Kornwestheim City Gallery   1989 / Kornwestheim, Germany

10   Museum of Contemporary Art, Chicago   1996 / Chicago
       photo: ©Synectics

11, 12 Park Lenne / Competition

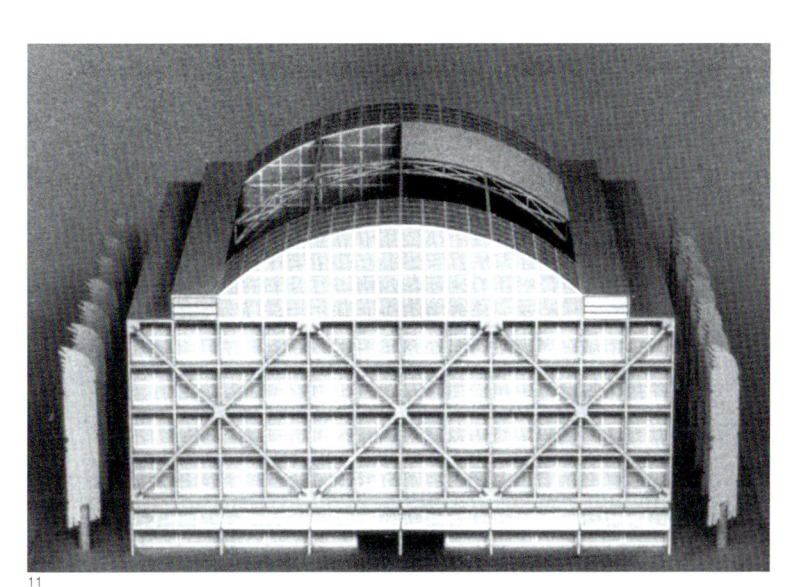

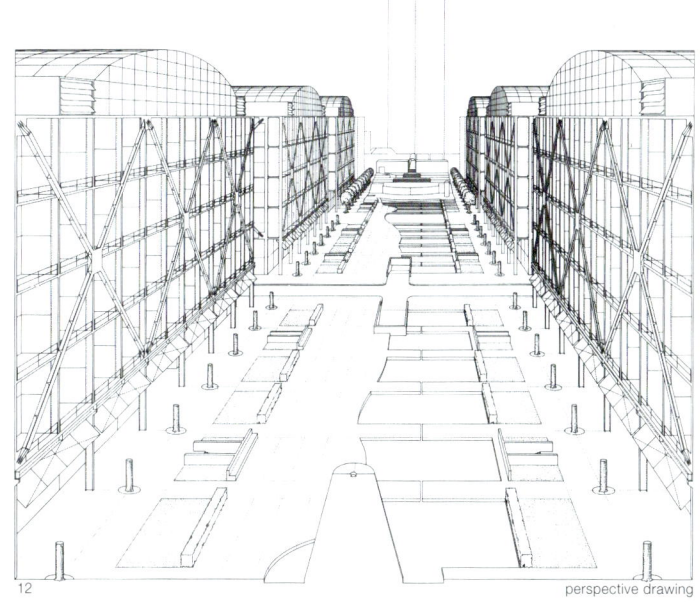

perspective drawing

121

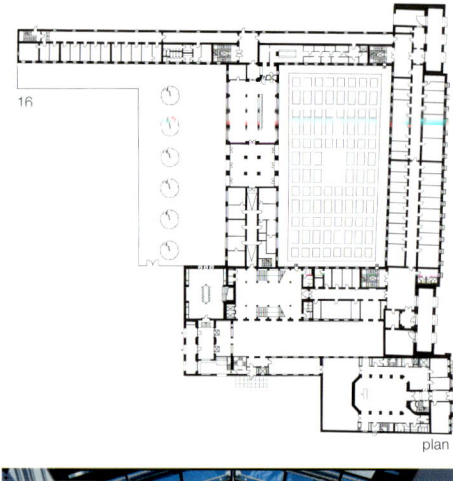

Josef Paul Kleihues

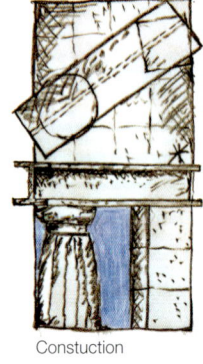

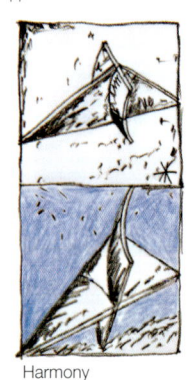

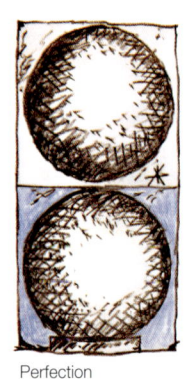

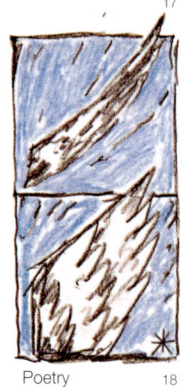

Geometry | Constuction | Harmony | Perfection | Function | Utopia | Poetry

Between the 1980s and the turn of the 21st century, urban redevelopment projects were undertaken in a number of large European cities. Among these were the Grand Projet in Paris, the Docklands redevelopment in London, and the International Building Exhibition (IBA) in Berlin. Due to the reunification of East and West Germany, there was an especially great rush to build in Berlin.

An army of architects, including 100 German and 50 foreign teams, amassed in the city, but the guiding light of German architecture was Josef Paul Kleihues. In his capacity as director of the IBA from 1979 to 1987, Kleihues enacted a policy of "critical reconstruction," and succeeded in transforming Berlin from a city that had not yet fully recovered from the ravages of war to a center of outstanding architecture. Despite the decidedly major role he played, Kleihues' modesty only allowed him to receive a few IBA design commissions. One of these was the Museum of Contemporary Art, Berlin. An example of Kleihues' neat and clean brand of neo-rationalism, the museum is a highly impressive structure. The work, a renovated train station, somehow reflects the building's history, and serves as a striking crystallization of "poetic rationalism," one of the concepts advocated by Kleihues.

The master of German classical architecture, Karl Friedrich Schinkel, speaking of a failed design attempt, once said, "I quickly realized my error in conceiving a fundamentally flawed image. I had created the overall concept of the architectural work in a literal way by merely focusing on the lesser objectives and the building's construction. Yet, a completed work of architecture must contain two essential elements – history and poetry." Kleihues' "poetic rationalism" is an attempt to do just that. Schinkel's comment is a warning that architecture which is determined solely by rationalism results in airless, rigid buildings. In an essay called "Noro lim, noro lim, Asfaloth!", published in _Dortmunder Architektur_ (No. 15), Kleihues quotes the philosopher Friedrich Schelling: "...the incomprehensible basis of reality, that which cannot be transposed to reason, try as you may." Kleihues mentions that inherent in the term "poetic rationalism," which he uses in reference to his work, is Schelling's "incomprehensible basis" and Wittgenstein's "expressive impossibility."

The Prehistory and Early History Museum is located in the historic heart of Frankfurt. Due

13, 14 Berlin Cleansing Department   1978 / Berlin
    15 Hospital Berlin-Neukolln   1986 / Berlin
16, 17 Federal Ministry of Labour and Social Affairs   2001 / Berlin
    18 The 7 Colums of Architecture
    19 Hotel Maritim   2005 / Berlin   (Jan Kleihues)
    20 Capital Museum of Beijing / Competition
    21 Hotel Concorde   2005 / Berlin   (Jan Kleihues)

photos: Courtesy of the Architect except ©Synectics

to Kleihues' skillful integration of ancient church history and a touch of Viennese modern architecture, the building, a renovated and expanded Carmelite monastery, is imbued with poetry. The striped, sandstone exterior walls create a special atmosphere topped off with the architect's unique use of rivets. This design, probably inspired by a similar rivet feature in Otto Wagner's Post Office Savings Bank, led the way to Kornwestheim City Gallery, Kant Triangle, Triangle Building, and the Chicago Museum of Contemporary Art, and became part of Kleihues' architectural language.

Taking advantage of the momentum he had gained from his urban planning work with the IBA, Kleihues entered and won competitions such as the Tiergarten Urban Planning Project and the Lenne Park Residential Project. Also in Berlin, he was commissioned to design the Berlin Cleansing Department, Berlin-Neukolln Hospital, and the Federal Ministry of Labour and Social Affairs building.

Kleihues' friend John Hejduk explains, "He dealt with social problems through architecture. With his hospitals, he treated people's bodies and with his museums, he treated people's minds."

Born in Rheine, Westphalia in 1933, Kleishues received an elite education, studying at Stuttgart Polytechnic and the Technical University of Berlin, and then going on to the École des Beaux-Arts in Paris. After graduation, he joined Peter Poelzig's (son of the architect Hans Poelzig) architectural firm. And from 1973 to 1994, he taught at the University of Dortmund. Kleihues died in August 2004 at the age of 71. Now when one visits Berlin and sees the gigantic sail turning on the roof of the Kant Triangle, one can't help but imagine that the man himself is watching over future generations of IBA architecture.

At present, Kleihues' architectural firm is overseen by his son, Jan. Continuing his father's hard work under the name Kleihues and Kleihues, Jan's recent works include the Hotel Concorde and Hotel Maritim.

KPF/Kohn Pedersen Fox

USA

Firm founded by Eugene Kohn, William Pederson, and Sheldon Fox in 1976. After Fox died in 2006, Kohn became chairman of the practice, and Pederson the principal design partner. With more than 400 employees, involved in design projects in over 30 cities around the world. In addition to the Arnold W. Brunner Memorial Prize in 1985, has received over 200 awards. Pederson was born in St. Paul, Minnesota in 1938. Graduated from the University of Minnesota in 1961, and completed a postgraduate degree at MIT in 1963. In 1965, awarded the Rome Prize.

1. 2 Bishopsgate Tower / London

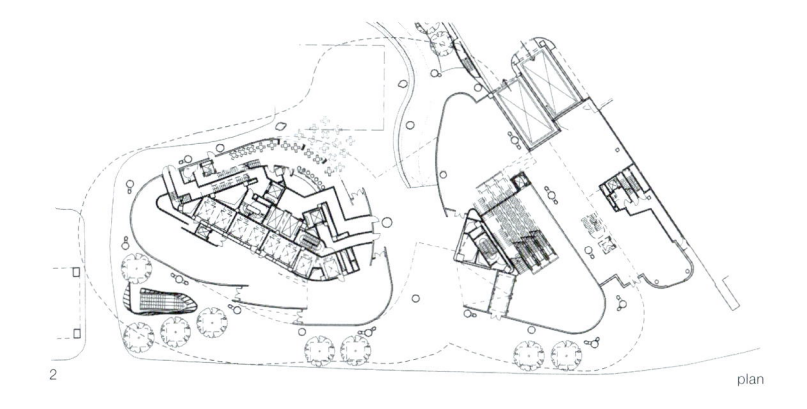

2 plan

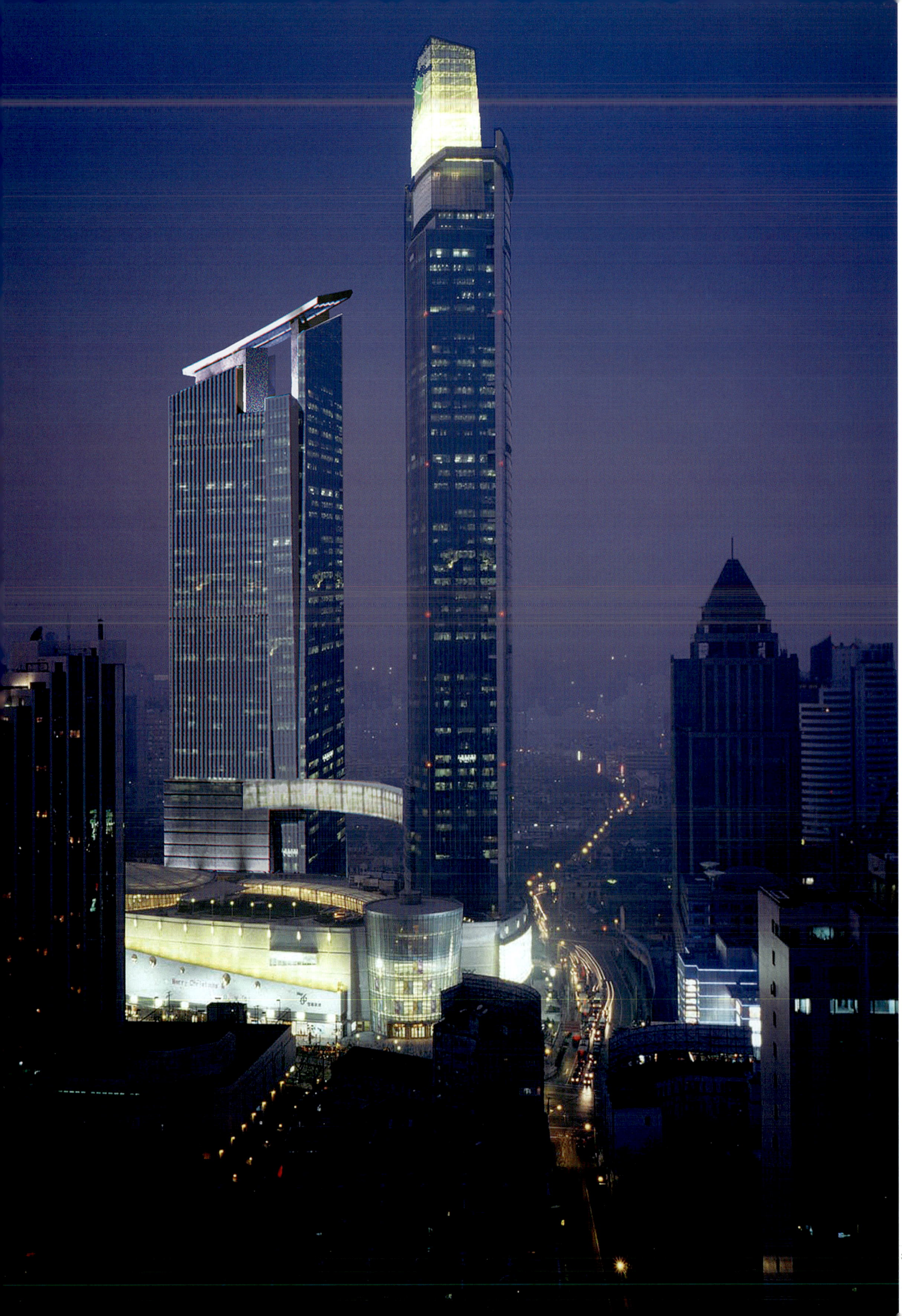

3 Plaza 66   2002 / Shanghai
   photo: ©John Butlin
4 Rodin Museum   1998 / Seoul
   photo: ©Timothy Hursley
5 Roppongi Hills   2003 / Tokyo
   photo: ©Synectics
6 Merrill Lynch Japan Headquarters   2004 / Tokyo

7, 8 Gannett /USA Today Headquarters   2001 / Mclean, Virginia
      photo: ©Michael Dersin
9   DG Bank Headquarters   1993 / Frankfurt
      photo: ©Dennis Gilbert
10, 11 IBM Corporate Headquarters   1997 / Armonk, New York
        photo: ©Peter Aaron/ESTO

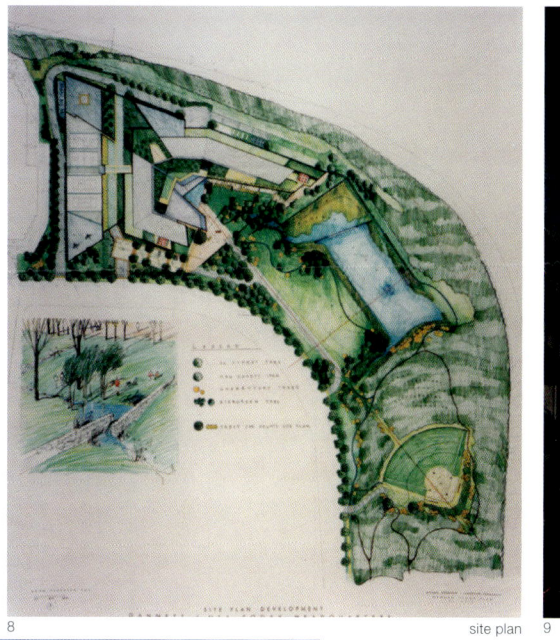

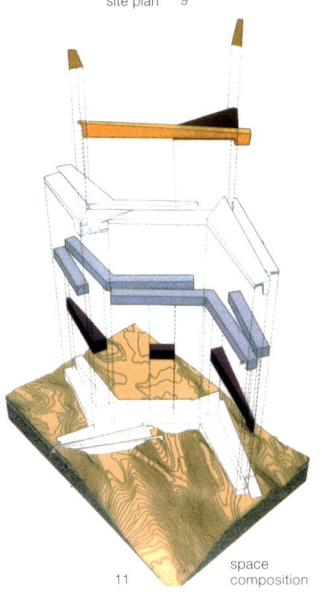

site plan

space composition

12 333 Wacker Drive 1993 / Chicago, Illinois
photo: ©Barbara Karant
13 Shanghai World Financial Center / Shanghai

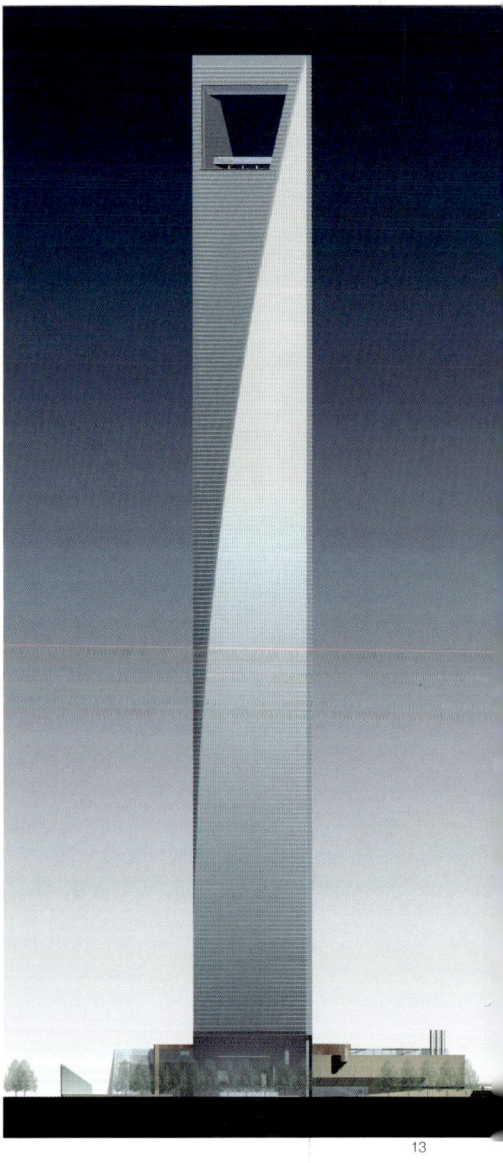

As they grow bigger, the names of many American architecture firms become longer acronyms for their founders' names. SOM, HOK, DMJM, CRSS, and RTKL are all large and well-established companies that are known around the world. It was about 30 years ago that a newcomer called KPF (Kohn, Pedersen, Fox) arrived and rapidly made great strides in the field.

The trio of principals behind KPF are Eugene Kohn, William Pedersen, and the late Sheldon Fox. All three left positions at John Carl Warnecke and Associates in 1976, and following the sudden growth of their own firm, now employ a staff of over 400 people. While the firm is small compared to other super high-rise designers like the gigantic SOM and HOK, KPF have something of an advantage due to the high-profile nature of their work.

Though there are numerous super high-rise buildings throughout the U.S., few could be called memorable or notable works. With the beauty of its rounded walls, however, the early KPF work, 333 Wacker Drive, is unrivaled and retains a sense of freshness. Having also made inroads in East Asia, KPF designed the Rodin Museum in Seoul, and Roppongi Hills and the Merrill Lynch Japan Headquarters in Tokyo, and is currently moving forward with the 492-meter-high Shanghai World Financial Center to solidify its position in the region. From these examples, it is clear that despite its size, KPF is truly one of the most powerful firms in the world.

Thirty years after it was founded, the management of KPF, which had by this point become one of the largest architecture firms, had already entered its second generation. Fox, the oldest of the three principals, left the firm in 2006 at the age of 67. Pederson, who at 59 was the youngest of the three and had been the chief designer since the firm began, now took hold of the reins.

Born in Minneapolis in 1938, Pederson graduated from the University of Minnesota in 1961. He went on to do graduate work at MIT in 1963. In 1965, he was awarded the Rome Prize, and studied at the American Academy in Rome for two years. Before helping to found KPF, he worked for Pietro Belluschi (1963) and Eduardo Catalino (1965), as an assistant to I.M. Pei (1967-71), and finally, served as vice president at John Carl Warnecke and Associates (1971-76).

The successful development of KPF over the firm's first 30 years was deeply rooted in a design philosophy that relied on collaboration and dialogue. Not only was this process

14 Philadelphia International Airport   2003 / Pennsylvania, Philadelphia
15 Baruch College New Academic Complex   2002 / New York
    photo: ©Michael Moran
16 International Commerce Center / Hong Kong
17 World Trade Center Extension   2004 / Amsterdam
    photo: ©H.G.Esch
18 Suyoung Bay Landmark Tower
19 First Hawaiian Center   1996 / Honolulu
    photo: ©Timothy Hursley

20 Procter & Gamble World Headquarters   1985 / Cincinnati, Ohio
    photo: ©Jock Pottle
21 Endesa Headquarters   2003 / Madrid
    photo: ©H.G.Esch
22 900 N Michigan   1989 / Chicago, Illinois
    photo: ©Jock Pottle/ESTO
23 The World Bank Headquarters   1996 / Washington D.C.
    photo: ©Timothy Hursley

photos : Courtesy of the Architect except ©Synectics

employed within the firm, but a free exchange of ideas with the client was also strongly emphasized. Using this unique approach, which the firm refers to as the "comparative process," KPF ensures that all of the client's needs and desires are satisfied while moving forward with each aspect of the project. The idea is not to make suggestions that will be greeted with approval or disapproval, but rather to present questions and answers that will aid in the creation of a more perfect work.

The "comparative process" is not limited to interaction with the client. It also extends to adapting buildings to the environment. Each of KPF's works has its own individual character, yet in terms of form, tireless efforts are made to create a dialogue between the building and its surroundings.

Having completed a long succession of huge projects including the DG Bank Headquarters, the World Bank Headquarters, the IBM Corporate Headquarters, the New Academic Complex at Baruch College, the Gannett /USA Today Headquarters, Plaza 66, and Philadelphia International Airport, KPF has grown to be an architectural team with a strong commitment to commercialism and a close working relationship with developers. At present, the firm is continuing work on the Suyoung Bay Landmark Tower, Bishopsgate Tower, and the International Commerce Center in Hong Kong. It isn't for nothing that developers and company heads agree to the faintly post-modern flavor and not overly minimal style of a building like the Procter & Gamble World Headquarters. KPF's works, which integrate easily interpreted elements into a single cohesive structure, have their foundation in the motto, "A whole is superior to a collection of parts." And striking a balance between internal needs and external possibilities while making maximum use of a given space is undoubtedly KPF's forte.

C.Y. Lee

TAIWAN

Born in Guangdong, China in 1938. Graduated from the School of Architecture at National Cheng Kung University in 1961. Completed a postgraduate degree in architecture at Princeton University in 1966. In 1970 and 1971, worked at China Urban Development Project. Served as vice-president at William L. Pereira and Associates in 1976 and 1977. In 1978, established his own firm, C.Y. Lee and Partners. In 1995, selected as one of the most outstanding architects in Taiwan by the Taiwanese Ministry of the Interior. In 2002, awarded a gold medal by _Architect Magazine_.

photo: ©Hsiao-Shin Huang

1, 2, 3　Taipei 101　2004 / Taipei

photo: ©Synectics
photo: ©Synectics

132

4

5

6

4　Grand 50 Tower　1992 / Koahsing, Taiwan
5　Shanghai Bund Guangming Tower / Shanghai
6　Fangyuan Mansion　2001 / Shenyang, China

7　Tuntex Tower　1998 / Koahsing, Taiwan
8　Chungtai Zen Temple　1998 / Puli, Taiwan
9, 10　Guangdong Tobacco Tower / Competition

7

9

8

10

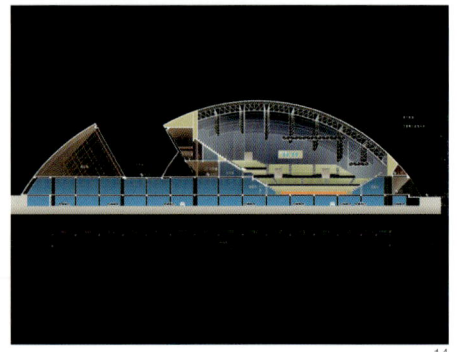

With the completion of Taipei 101 as the world's largest tower, outstripping Malaysia's Petronas Twin Towers, C.Y. Lee established his reputation as one of Taiwan's most internationally famous architects.

Born in Guangdong in 1938, Lee graduated from the architectural department at National Cheng Kung University in 1961. He completed a Master's degree in Architecture at Princeton University in 1966, and then went to work at the Department of Housing and Urban Development in Boston. He then continued his training both in Taiwan and China, and became vice-president at the American firm William L. Pereira and Associates in 1976. The excellent architectural training Lee received in the U.S. was instrumental in helping him develop an international career. In 1978, at the age of 40, he founded his own firm, C.Y. Lee and Partners, in Taiwan.

Taipei 101 was the largest engineering project in the history of building construction in Taiwan. The super high rise, with a total of 101 stories and a height of 508 meters, is knotted like a stalk of bamboo and its distinctive form is a clear departure from the superflat designs that are currently so common in international-style architecture.

The shaft-like building is made up of eight-storey segments – this is connected to the Chinese belief that eight is a lucky number. It's immediately obvious from the exterior of Taipei 101 that the form is Asian. But what made a globally active architect like Lee avoid an international style for the skyscraper?

"As globalization continues, the world's architecture has come to be increasingly generic. Primitive and individualistic expressions are falling away in every region. Each of the world's cities should develop its own unique cultural identity. In this way, architecture will be able to express a globalization that is rich in diversity."

As a result, Lee's work of the last 20 or so years is deeply rooted in Asian culture, makes full use of modern technology, and reflects the aesthetic concepts and singular structure of Asian society. Thus, Lee has successfully created a "New Oriental Architecture."

Lee's philosophy is based on macro, universal ideas that are mindful of Asian values, but includes concepts that are aligned with trends in world architecture. Further, even in large-scale works like Taipei 101 and the Tung Wang Palace Housing, built on an expansive lot, Lee's architecture acts as a bridge connecting Asia's refined cultural spirit from the past to the

11 Shanghai Bund Parcel 204 / Shanghai
12 Ta – An Public Housing 1987 / Taipei
13, 14 Xiamen Gymnasium / Xiamen, China
15 Tung Wang Palace Housing 1987 / Taipei
16, 17 Marine Prospect Garden Housing 1994 / Taipei
18 Hung Kuo Office Headquarters 1989 / Taipei
19 Mount Emei Golden Top Temple Planning / Sichuan, China
20 Xian Faman Temple / Xian, China
21 Renovation of the Building Facades on Zhong Shan Road / Shanghai

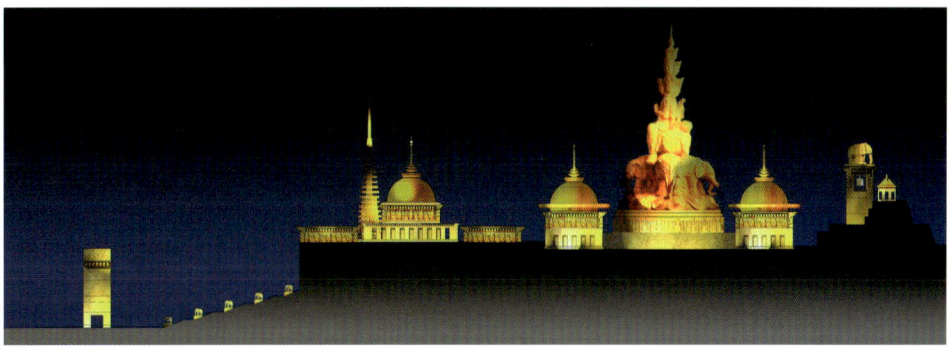

photos : Courtesy of the Architect

present. As a result, Lee's highly respected expressions have helped introduce Eastern culture on the global stage.

As one might expect for a Taiwanese architect, the scale of many of Lee's works is large. For example, the Tuntex Sky Tower is a landmark skyscraper with a total of 85 stories. A huge tunnel runs below the center of the tower, which stands between two base-platforms. Lee's design references the principles of ancient Chinese terrestrial fortune-telling as well as various climatic conditions, topographies, and aesthetics.

The Hung Kuo Headquarters is imbued with curves that suggest the traditional Chinese lotus, while the large candilever is reminiscent of the roofs in old Chinese architecture. The Chungtai Zen Temple was created as a sacred space to respond to the demands of the present by altering the form of the 1,000-year-old temple. The design of the Grand 50 Tower alludes to the Chinese pagoda and a Chinese-style garden parapet. Unlike a sharp Western-style spire, above the segmented shaft, the structure seems to be spreading its arms wide and supporting the heavens.

Works like the Fangyuan Mansion, the Marine Prospect Garden House, and the Ta-an Public Housing are a few of the many outstanding examples of Lee's "New Oriental Architecture." Like the evolution of the universe, Lee's buildings are based on a unified architectural philosophy, and with his free-spirited approach to design, he has developed a diverse and organic body of work.

From his stand-alone buildings to his urban designs, Lee's various creations all have integrity and convey a special type of originality. Lee uses architecture as a bridge that shifts between time and space, and with an integrated form of creation, dredges up the spirit of the Chinese culture and projects these elements into the future.

In an interview I conducted with Lee in Taipei last December, he said, "Well, in the end I am very fond of large-scale buildings." There's no question about that. Lee's firm is currently working on huge projects such as the Xiamen Gymnasium, the Shanghai Bund Parcel 204, the Shanghai Bund Guangming Tower, and the Guangdong Tobacco Tower.

Imre Makovecz

HUNGARY

Born in Hungary in 1935. Graduated from the Technical University of Budapest in 1959. From 1959 to 1962, worked at the Buvati design studio. From 1962 to 1977, built up practical experience. From 1977 to 1981, worked at the Pilis Forestry Association. From 1981 to 1991, served as principal at Makona Associated Architects. In 1987, named honorary fellow of the AIA. In 1991, renamed his firm Makona Architectural Studio. In 1992, received honorary fellowship from the Royal Incorporation of Architects in Scotland. In 1997, awarded the L'Academie d'Architecture Gold Medal, and in 1998, an honorary fellowship from the RIBA.

1 Sarospatak Cultural Center 1983 / Sarospatak, Hungary
2,3 Visegrad Forest Educational Center 1987 / Visegrad, Hungary
4 Mako Theater 1998 / Mako, Hungary
photo: ©Szanto Tamas

Imre Makovecz

5, 6, 7   Paks Roman Catholic Church   1991 / Paks, Hungary
8   Eger Swimming Pool   2000 / Eger, Hungary
9   Large Auditorium at Peter Pazmany Catholic University   2001 / Piliscsaba, Hungary
photo: ©ZSITVA
10   Farkasret Funeral Chapel   1977 / Budapest, Hungary

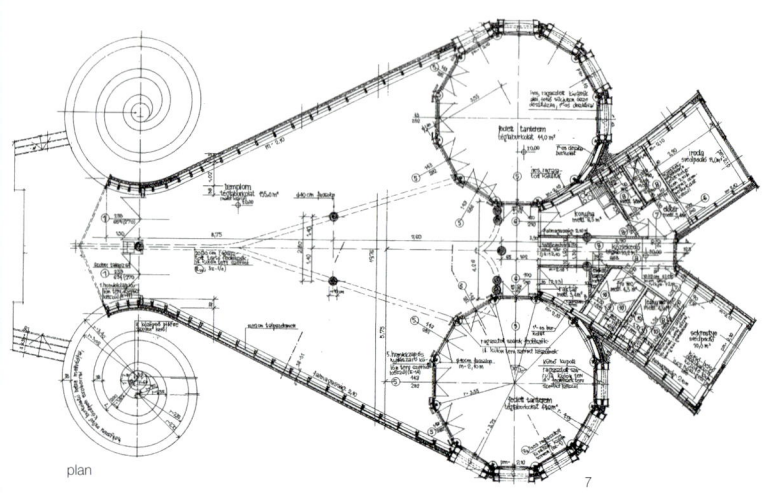

plan

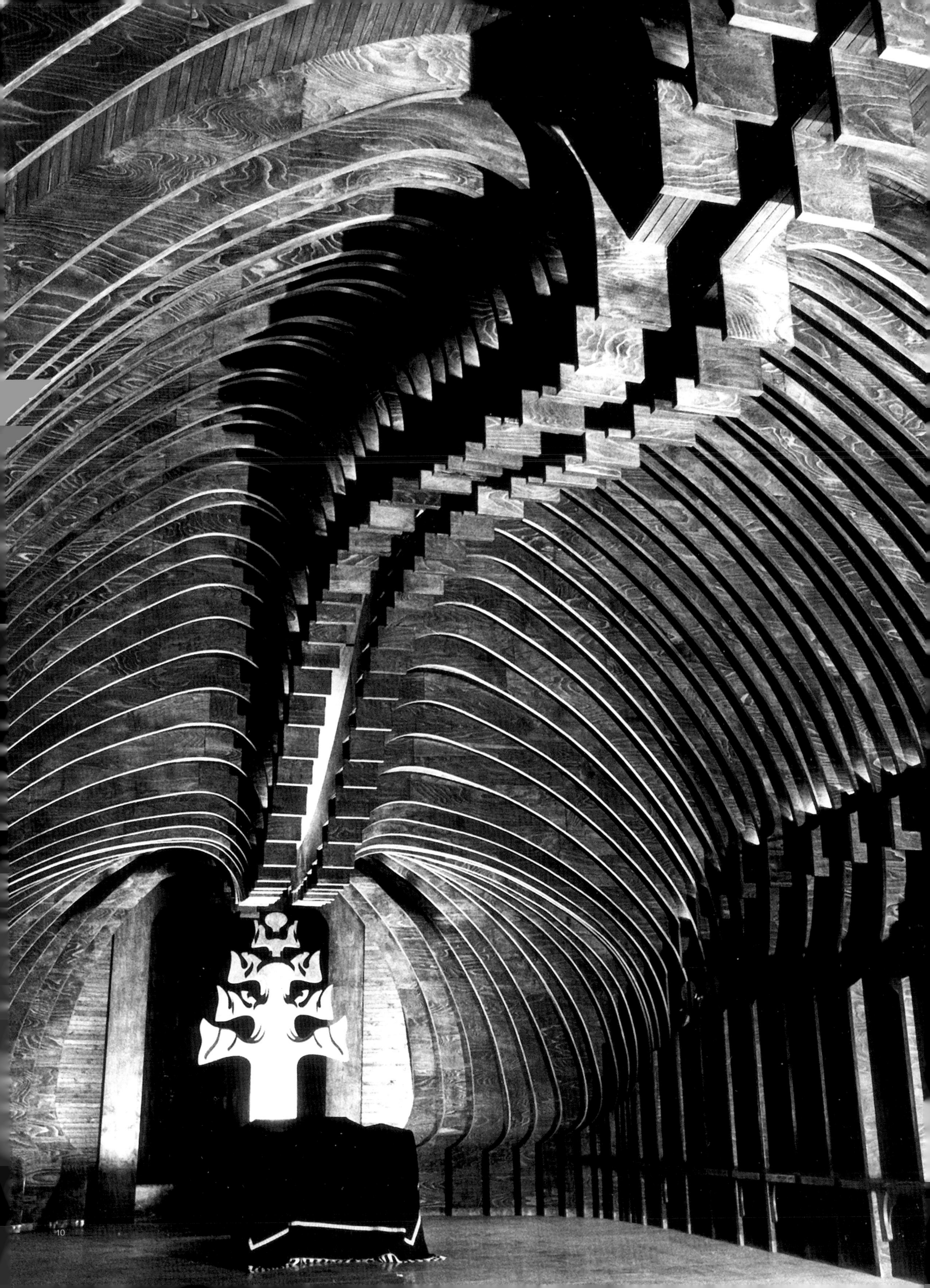

Imre Makovecz

Hungary's most representative contemporary architect, Imre Makovecz, is also one of the country's few internationally renowned designers.
In a far east Asian country such as Japan, the information about architecture in a far eastern European country like Hungary is very minimal. Aside from contemporary designers, my own knowledge of Hungarian architecture is also sadly lacking, and essentially limited to the noted National Romanticist Lechner Ödön. Under the circumstances, Makovecz has proved to be a great success.
Born in Budapest in 1935, Makovecz was the son of a carpenter. In 1959, he graduated from the Technical University of Budapest, and went on to develop his skills as an architect during a stint with an urban development studio called Buvati in Budapest. After this, he also worked for design studios such as Szövterv (the Architectural Planning Office of the National Agricultural Collective), VÁTI (the Hungarian National Urban Planning Office), and the Pilis Forestry Association, creating an especially large body of work at the latter.
Important works such as the Farkasret Funeral Chapel, Mogyoro-hegy Restaurant, Dobogoko Ski Lodge, Tokaj Meeting Pavilion, Visegrad Forest Educational Center, and the Sarospatak Cultural Center were all created before he struck out on his own in 1983.
When viewed from the perspective of current trends in contemporary architecture, Makovecz's works display a decidedly maverick quality. But he can also be placed within the context of what the American critic Kenneth Frampton called "critical regionalism," a term used in reference to architects working on the periphery of Europe.
Makovecz's highly distinctive work was initially subjected to harsh criticism for its supposedly heretical nature. Yet, the original basis for Makovecz's buildings was Hungarian folk arts, as he was part of the generation that was greatly influenced by this movement in Hungarian dance, music, handicrafts, and architecture which was promoted by the musicians Bela Bartok and Zoltán Kodály in the 1930s.
The Tokaj Meeting Pavilion, completed in 1979, was part of an art colony, where a large number of ethnologists, teachers, and students assembled. As they discussed an educational program, they also planned a group project to build the structure. Makovecz played a leading role by providing a design for the building, and his career continued to evolve in this manner as a platform for folk arts.

11 Baks Village Community Center   1988 / Baks, Hungary
12, 13 Szigetvar Cultural Center   1988 / Szigetvar, Hungary
14 Mogyoro-hegy Restaurant   1979 / Visegrad, Hungary
15 Siofok Lutheran Church   1990 / Siofok, Hungary
16 Dobogoko Ski Lodge   1979 / Dobogoko, Hungary
17 Tokaj Meeting Pavilion   1979 / Tokaj, Hungary
18 Szazhalombatta Roman Catholic Church   1996 / Szazhalombatta, Hungary
19, 20 Budapest Catholic Church Budapest / Hungary
21 Lendva Theater   1991 / Lendva, Slovenia

photos : Courtesy of the Architect

The work, which inspired the new trend of organic Hungarian architecture, was not, however, influenced solely by domestic folk arts. While on the one hand, Makovecz was greatly influenced by the anthroposophical ideas of Rudolf Steiner, he was also enamored of architects such as the American master of organic design Frank Lloyd Wright, and others with work in a similar vein such as Bruce Goff and Herb Greene.

In addition, there is an mistakable influence of animism and Eastern mythological elements derived from the ancient Celts and pre-Christian Magyar culture in Makovecz's architecture. In other words, his intellectual sources are not rooted solely in Hungarian tradition and culture, but lie in the more universal aspects of various foreign cultures. The most pronounced characteristic of Makovecz' buildings is the roof. In most of his early works, he made use of the indigenous Hungarian domed-roof design that is constructed out of bent wood and known as "hajlek." But following the last building of this kind, the Visegrad Forest Educational Center, at the age of 48, Makovecz went independent and began to exhibit subtle changes in style.

Even in the Siofok Lutheran Church and the Paks Roman Catholic Church, which inevitably owe something to the Gothic style of religious architecture, and the later commissioned works Szigetva Cultural Center and the Szazhalombatta Roman Catholic Church, there are groups of towers that seem to have some Magyar symbolism. The Mako Theater, however, features a universal form that is a blend of four small towers and a dome-shaped main roof.

In subsequent low-rise works, such as the Eger Swimming Pool and the Large Auditorium at Peter Pazmany Catholic University, Makovecz also makes use of the "hajlek" style, but features like the skylight in the auditorium clearly have no relationship to Magyar culture. While Makovecz's architecture reflects an underlying sense of ancient cultural traditions and folk arts, he continually seems to be moving forward with work that boasts a more consciously global perspective.

Mecanoo

THE NETHERLANDS

Firm founded by an architectural planning group in Rotterdam in 1984. Formed after five friends won a housing complex competition, but of the original members only Francine Houben remains. Born in Sittard, the Netherlands in 1955, she graduated from Delft University of Technology in 1984. Currently, teaches at the same university. From the Maaskant Prize for Young Architects in 1984 to the Dutch Building Prize in 2003, the firm has received numerous awards.

1   Kruisplein Housing   1985 / Rotterdam
2   Boompjes Restaurant   1990 / Rotterdam
    photo: ©Synectics
3   Herdenkingsplein Housing   1994 / Maastricht, The Netherlands
    photo: ©Synectics
4, 5   Lausanne Learning Center / Competition

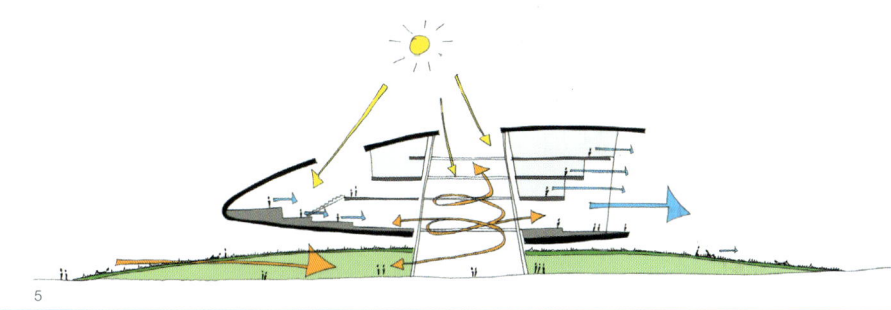

6

7 8

144

6 'La Llotja' Theater & Congress Center / Lleida, Spain
7 Library for the Delft University of Technology   1998 / Delft, The Netherlands
   photo: ©Synectics
8 St. Laurence Cemetery Chapel   2001 / Rotterdam
   photo: ©Christian Richers
9, 10 National Heritage Museum   2000 / Arnhem, The Netherlands
   photo: ©Christian Richers

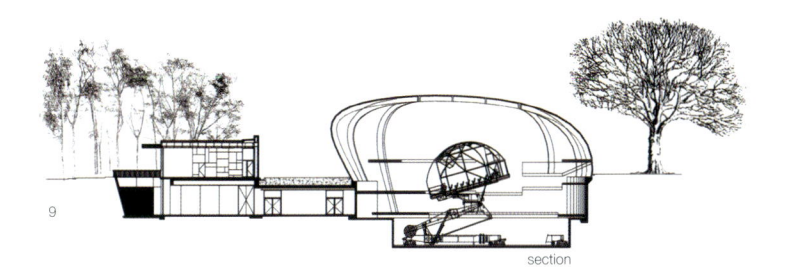

9 section

10

Mecanoo

11 Campus Masterplan for the Delft University of Technology 2001-02Design / Delft, The Netherlands
12 Courthouse in Trento / Trento, Italy
13, 14 Philips Business Innovation Center 2006 / Nijmegen, The Netherlands
photo: ©Christian Richers
15 Canadaplein Cultural Center 2000 / Alkmaar, The Netherlands
photo: ©Christian Richers
16 Faculty of Management and Economics at Utrecht University 1995 / Utrecht
photo: ©Synectics
17 Montevideo 2005 / Rotterdam
CG: ©DPI Animation House
18 Digital Port Rotterdam 2004 / Rotterdam
19 Nieuw Terbregge 2000 / Rotterdam
photo: ©Christian Richers

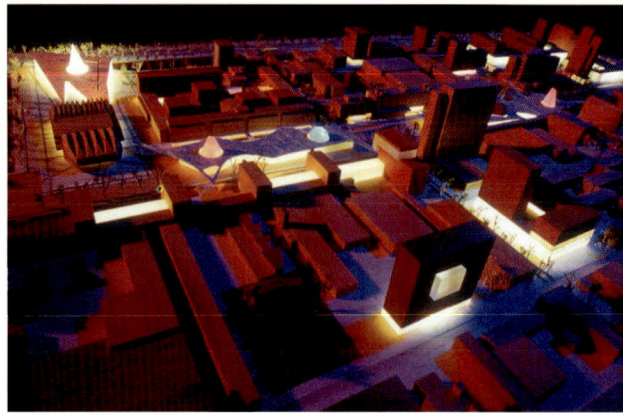

The members of the Mecanoo group were still students when they won the Kruisplein Housing Complex competition (1982-85). Their design activities had begun in 1981 when five friends who were all employees of the Rotterdam Public Works Agency decided to form a group. After that, they all entered the Delft University of Technology and following graduation, in 1984, founded Mecanoo. At the time, they were all around 28, which brought them notice as a "super-young" group.

The original founding members comprised Francine Houben, Roelf Steenhuis, Erick van Egeraat, Henk Döll, and Chris de Weijer. Steenhuis left the group in 1989 and Egeraat left in 1995. This led the other male members of the group, Weijer and Doll, to leave as well. Although many expected that Mecanoo would disband completely at this point, Houben, the last remaining original member, swiftly carried on.

Perhaps because the group's members had been immersed in Dutch modernism in university or because they were used to the rigid architectural environment at the Public Works Agency, Mecanno's early style was steeped in the modernist tradition. It is common for emerging architects, particularly in their handling of public buildings, to display a strong sense of traditionalism. In this respect, Mecanoo was no different.

But in Mecanoo's recent designs, the firm seems to have entered an entirely new age. It might seem obvious considering that 20 years have passed, but in terms of diversity, Mecanoo is unrivaled in the Dutch architecture world. The exterior of the Herdenkingsplein Housing Complex in Maastricht, for example, is covered with wood paneling, lending the building a relaxed, nostalgic air. In an era when exteriors are almost unanimously glass or concrete, the skillful use of wood has become one of Mecanoo's trademarks.

Other Mecanoo works using wood include the ceiling and eaves of the Boompjes Restaurant (no longer extant), the exterior walls of the courtyard building and auditorium in the Faculty of Management and Economics at Utrecht University, and in a slightly altered form, the wickerwork-style facade made of thin planks of wood at the Canadaplein Cultural Center. The interior of the St. Marya of the Angels Chapel at St. Lawrence Cemetery is another variation on this theme.

Moreover, the thatched roof (greenery) at the Delft University of Technology Library is another crucial example. When the university

20 Palace Justice in Cordoba / Cordoba, Spain
21 MOdAM 1985 / Milan, Italy
22 Officers Hotel De Citadel 2004 / The Hague, The Netherlands
photo: ©Christian Richers

photos : Courtesy of the Architect except ©Synectics

approached Mecanoo about the project, it asked that rather than focusing on the building itself, the group view the work as a public space for students to gather. Mecanno responded with a slanted, thatched roof. Explaining its decision, the group said, "Holland is trying to increase its land through reclamation projects. The library was designed as a metaphor for a polder [reclaimed area] with pasture grass growing out of it." Many students can now be seen collecting and grazing on this plain.
In a recent work, the National Heritage Museum, the oval-shaped auditorium appears to be entirely covered with steel plates, but while the main building is made of glass, a complex brick wall creates a different impression. Though similar to the experimental use of brick seen in Koetalo (Experimental House), the noted architect Alvar Aalto's personal summer house, Mecanoo's work is more ambitious, making use of brick of all types and realizing a number of unique details.
The work illustrates how Mecanoo splendidly combines various materials and forms, the selection of which creates a vivid contrast between different parts of the building.
Contrasts are visible everywhere – open/closed, hard/soft, inward/outward – and the materials also include warm elements such as wood, bamboo, and copper and cool, modern elements such as glass, steel, and concrete. This gives the exterior a rich and familiar expression.
Mecanoo's motto holds that the aesthetics of architecture lie in contrast.
At present, some 65 people make up the Mecanoo staff, and of the 300 projects the firm has been involved with so far, approximately 100 have been completed. Currently underway are a variety of large projects with spectacular designs such as the Learning Center in Lausanne, Switzerland, the La Llotja Theater and Congress Center in Spain, the Philips Business Innovation Center in The Netherlands, and a masterplan for the campus at Delft University of Technology. Mecanoo's attempts to draw out the potential inherent in the space, form, and material in each of these situations will undoubtedly lead to work of even greater depth.

Richard Meier

USA

Born in Newark, New Jersey in 1934. Graduated from Cornell University. After working at Davis, Brody and Wisniewski, traveled extensively in Europe. After returning to the U.S., worked at Skidmore, Owings and Merrill, and Marcel Breuer's firm. Established his own firm in New York in 1963. Has taught at Cooper Union, Yale University, Harvard University, and UCLA. Among the many awards received are the Pritzker Prize in 1984, a Royal Gold Medal from the RIBA in 1989, and an AIA Gold Medal and the Praemium Imperiale Award for Architecture in 1997.

1, 2　High Museum of Art　1983 / Atlanta, Georgia
　　　photo: ©Masaki Sakuramoto
　3　Ulm Exhibition and Assembly Hall　1993 / Ulm, Germany
　　　photo: ©Synectics

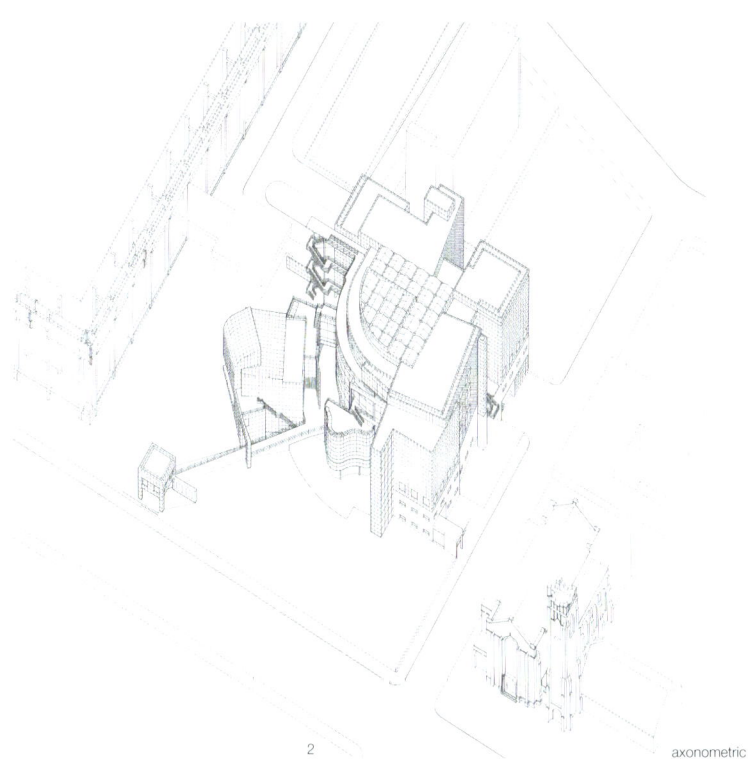

2　　　　　　　　　　　　　　　　　　　　axonometric

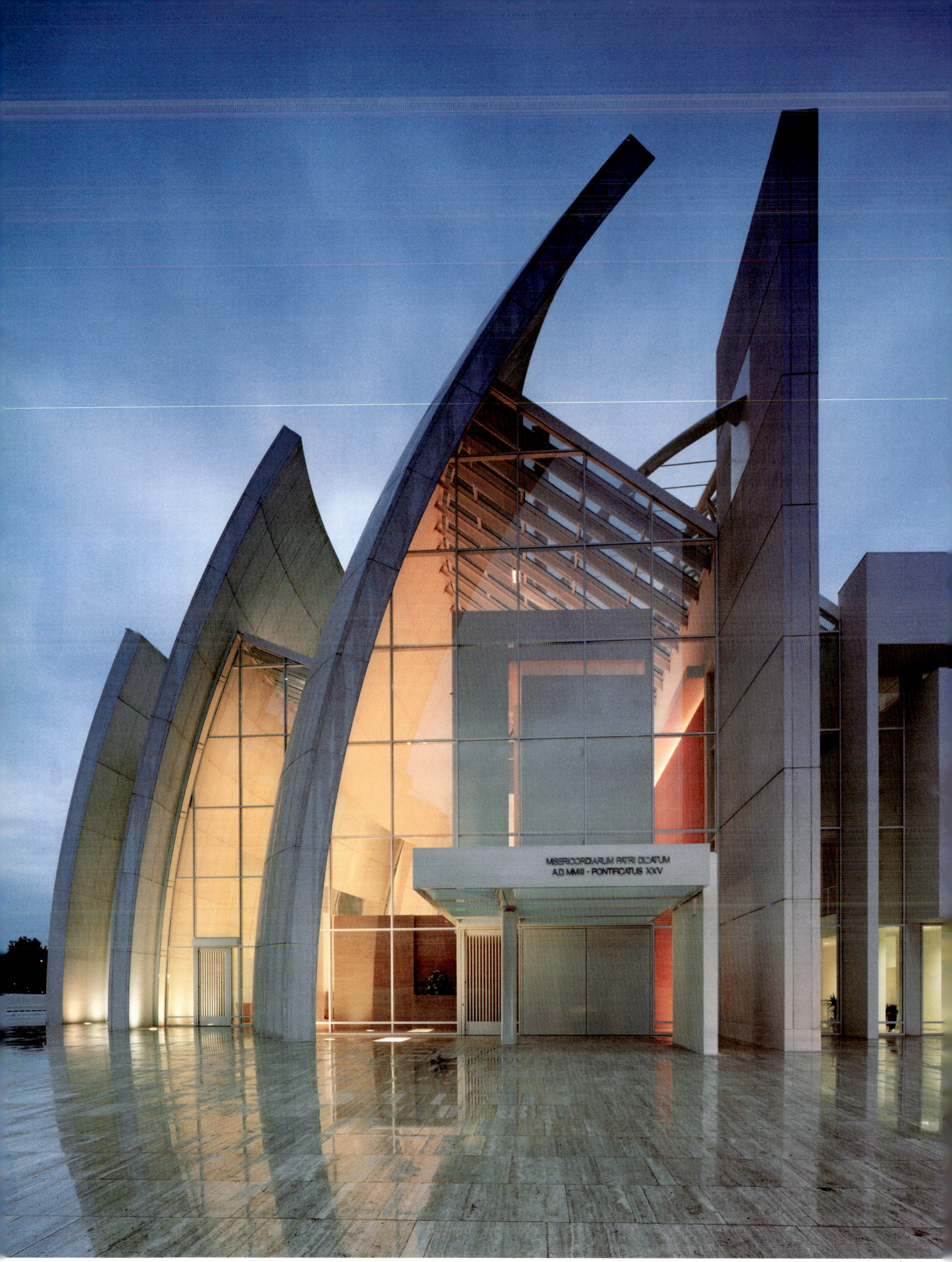

4

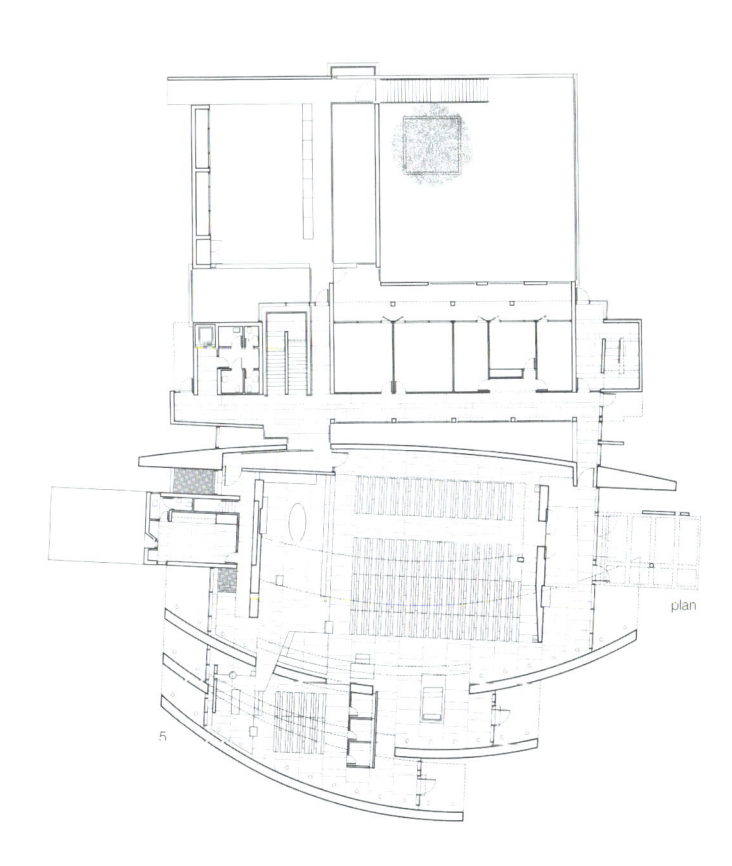

4, 5	Jubilee Church 2003 / Roma	10	Canal + Headquarters 1992 / Paris
	photo: ©Alan Karchmer / ESTO		photo: ©Synectics
6	Rachofsky Art Museum 1996 / Dallas, Texas	11	The Getty Center 1997 / Los Angeles
	photo: ©Synectics		photo: ©Synectics
7	Athenium 1979 / New Harmony, Indiana	12	The Hague City Hall and Central Library 1995 / The Hague, The Netherlands
	photo: ©Sakuramoto		photo: ©Synectics
8	Barcelona Museum of Contemporary Art 1995 / Barcelona, Spain	13	Burda Collection Museum 2004 / Baden-Baden, Germany
	photo: ©Synectics		
9	Frankfurt Museum for Applied Arts 1985 / Frankfurt, Germany		
	photo: ©Synectics		

RICHARD MEIER

14 Museum of Television & Radio 1996 / Beverly Hills, California
photo: ©Synectics
15 Beach House / Miami, Florida
16 Hartford Seminary 1981 / Hartford, Connecticut
photo: ©Synectics
17 Cornell University Life Science Technology Building / Ithaca, New York

The Rachofsky Art Museum, located in the suburbs of Dallas, is one of Richard Meier's masterpieces. The work, by this magician of white structures, is unrivaled in its beauty. I have visited about a dozen of Meier's buildings, but the Rachofsky House is in a class of its own. Originally a private residence, the owners, who are art collectors, later opened the house as a museum. Lying silent and still with a long, horizontal white body, beguiling in its immaculate state, the building stands across an expansive lawn, which has an artwork partially buried in the ground. The right side of the building (as seen from the front) is equipped with a glass staircase, and outside it, stands a large tree with finely shaped branches. The pull between the tree and the building is magnificent enough to be felt whether one is inside or outside. It isn't easy to see private homes that have been designed by famous architects. This is the only Meier residence that I have managed to see. Among his other works, I have visited the Frankfurt Museum for Applied Arts, the Barcelona Museum of Contemporary Art, the Athenium, Canal+ Headquarters, the Getty Center, the City Hall and Central Library in The Hague, the Sandra Day O'Connor United States Courthouse, and Jubilee Church. From this list alone, one can see how many large-scale projects Meier has designed. Meier is able to attract such first-rate clients for the simple reason that he always makes a strong showing in competitions.

There is no one else in Meier's family tree with a background in architecture or art. While still in high school, however, he began to read architecture books, and create models. In Japan, it is often said that Kenzo Tange's National Gymnasium for the Tokyo Olympics and his other inspirational works must have been a big factor in helping many students decide their course in life. But it would seem as if Meier was born with an architecture gene, as he has taken to the work so naturally.

While working his way through Cornell University, Meier has said he was deeply impressed by the famous architects he encountered as lecturers at the school. These included Frank Lloyd Wright, who was extremely popular at the time, R. Buckminster Fuller, and Paul Rudolph. After graduation, Meier found a job at the Davis, Brody and Wisniewski firm, and then set out on a trip to Europe. Ever since university, he had had an interest in Le Corbusier, so meeting the Swiss architect in Paris and having a chance to visit his white buildings was a deeply significant

18 Right wing   165 Charles Street Apartments   2005 / New York
photo: ©Meier&Partners
Two left wings   173 / 176 Perry Street Condominium Towers   2002 / New York
photo: ©Meier&Partners
19 Restaurant 66   2003 / New York
photo: ©Gong Dong
20 Gagosian Gallery   1995 / Beverly Hills, California
photo: ©Gagosian Gallery
21 Office and Retail Building   1998 / Basel, Switzerland
photo: ©Synectics
22 Sandra Day O'Connor United States Courthouse   2000 / Phoenix, Arizona
photo: ©Synectics

photos : Courtesy of the Architect except ©Synectics, ©Gagosian Gallery and ©Esto

22

experience for him. Upon returning from this six-month trip, Meier found jobs at Skidmore, Owings and Merrill, and Marcel Breuer before starting his own practice. While working for Breuer, Meier completed his first work, the Lambert Beach House on Fire Island.
Even in Japan, it's a well-known fact that Peter Eisenman is Meier's cousin. Eisenman, known as quite a powerhouse, proposed a conference for young architects which in time led to the emergence of the "New York Five," a group consisting of Michael Graves, Charles Gwathmey, and John Hejduk in addition to Eisenman and Meier. In later years, membership in the group served as an effective advertisement, as each of the five went on to become prominent figures in their own right. Among Meier's works, Smith House might be mentioned as one of the most important early buildings. With the turn in its exterior staircase, the tall, white residence, which looks onto Long Island Sound, alludes to Le Corbusier's Villa Garches. In a similar way, Meier was clearly influenced by Breuer in his design for the Lambert Beach House.
The presence of other masters of modern architecture can also be detected in his work. The House for Mr. and Mrs. Jerome Meier is a single-story structure, but the elevation surface makes conscious reference to Wright's Falling Water. The Olivetti Training Center Prototype is a carbon copy of the W-shaped design of Alvar Aalto's Baker House. Moreover, the rotunda of one of Meier's representative works, the High Museum of Art, resembles Wright's Guggenheim Museum. To Meier, the vocabulary of noted modern architects is a means of strengthening his designs.
The long, white slope which allows visitors to enjoy an "architectural walk" at Le Corbusier's Villa Savoye has also been brought to life at a number of Meier works, including the Burda Collection Museum, the Museum of Television and Radio, the Frankfurt Museum for Applied Arts, and the Barcelona Museum of Contemporary Art. Unlike other architects, ever since Smith House, Meier has maintained a consistent style. His concise and transparent, chalk-white spaces have the ability to uplift the human spirit, brimming as they do with a sense of cleanliness and the sublime. These qualities in Meier's work are eternal. And it is this unchanging style that attracts clients who are in charge of large-scale architecture projects. It is also the reason why, at 49, Meier became the youngest person to ever receive the Pritzker Prize.

Enric Miralles Benedetta Tagliabue

SPAIN

Enric Miralles was born in Barcelona in 1955. Graduated from the School of Architecture of Barcelona (ETSAB) in 1978. Received a Fulbright Scholarship to study at Columbia University in 1980 and 1981. Served as director of the firm Enric Miralles and Carme Pinos from 1983 to 1990. Invited to occupy the Tange Kenzo Chair at the Harvard Graduate School of Design in 1992. Established a new practice, Enric Miralles and Benedetta Tagliabue, in 1993. Died of illness in 2000. Posthumously awarded the Gold Medal by the Catalan Council of Architects in 2002. Benedetta Tagliabue was born in Milan in 1963, and graduated from the University Iuav of Venice in 1989.

site plan

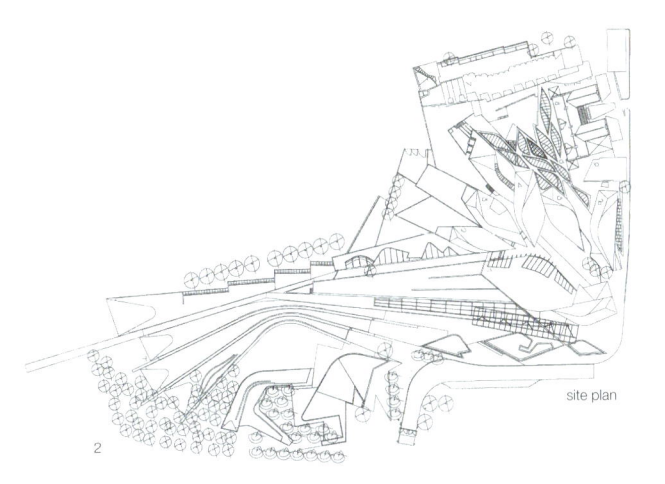

1, 2, 3 New Scottish Parliament 2004 / Edinburgh, Scotland
photo: ©Christian Richers

4 Takaoka Station Pavilion 1993 / Toyama, Japan
photo: ©Synectics

5, 6	Utrecht City Hall 1999 / Utrecht, The Netherlands photo: ©Synectics
7	Hamburg Music School 2000 / Hamburg, Germany photo: ©Duccio Malagamba
8, 9, 10	Diagonal Mar Park 2002 / Barcelona photo: ©Synectics
11	Unazuki Meditation Pavilion 1993 / Toyama, Japan photo: ©Synectics

12, 13 Vigo University Campus   1999 / Vigo, Spain
    photo: ©Duccio Malagamba
14 Igualada Cemetery   1995 / Barcelona
15 Olympic Archery Pavilions   1991 / Barcelona
    photo: ©Duccio Malagamba

In Toyama Prefecture, there is a spa town called Unazuki. Atop a bridge over a river that runs through the town stands a steel monument with a twisted form that recalls the famous creature from the film _Alien_. The Unazaki Meditation Pavilion was the late Enric Miralles' debut work in Japan, and was part of the architect Arata Isozaki's "Face of the Town" project. Miralles was also involved in creating the Takaoka Station Pavilion, a tangled set of steel lines that look similar to an avant-garde art work and cover the upper part of the station entrance. Miralles' knowledge of a deep-rooted strain of pantheism in Western culture informed his architectural career. Aspects of this pantheism can be detected in his use of artificial elements from nature. For example, he would often fill the void space in a train or public building with wood or steel trees. Among the numerous works using this technique are the two in Toyama as well as Roofs in Parets del Valles, Rambla in Reus, Roofs in the Avenida Icaria, and Diagonal Mar Park.

Enric Miralles was probably the most cutting-edge and avant-garde designer of all contemporary Spanish architects. And perhaps the most representative of Miralles' many representative buildings is the New Scottish Parliament, which with its tangled, deconstructed exterior and assembly hall is masterful due to the breath of fresh air it brings to the traditionally very conservative architectural typology of legislative buildings. Utrecht City Hall in the Netherlands was also a rather serious government building, but by maintaining the quality of the structure's original monumental facade, standing on a canal bank, Miralles' renovation of the building took into consideration the history and environment of the area while adding an element of deconstruction. By deepening the building's close connection to the plaza behind it, Miralles also helped reappraise the neo-classical interior design.

Miralles' plan for the Hamburg Music School, which incorporated the trees already standing on the lot, was also marvelous. The concave exterior, which faces an inner courtyard where a group of large trees stands, is covered with colorful vertical stripes in a design that is at once deconstructivist and recalls a sort of female beauty. The Santa Caterina Market rehabilitation also possesses these qualities. The roof is covered with ceramic tiles in 61 different and very brilliant colors that take their inspiration from the bright hues of fruits and vegetables that one might find at the market.

16, 17 Rehabilitation of Santa Caterina Market   2005 / Barcelona
18 National Center for Rhythmic Gymnastics   1993 / Alicante, Spain
19 Borneo Sporenburg Housing Complex   2000 / Amsterdam
    photo: ©Lourdes Jansana
20 Gas Natural New Headquarters   2005 / Barcelona
    photo: ©Synectics
21 Palafolls Public Library / Palafolls, Spain
22 University of Architecture in Venezia / Venezia
    photo: ©Lourdes Jansana

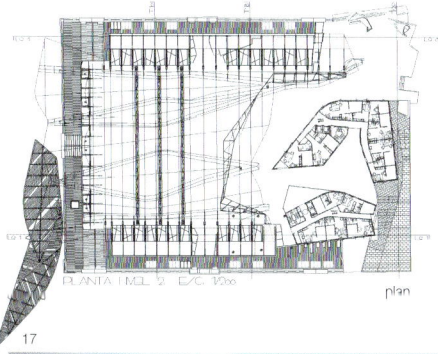

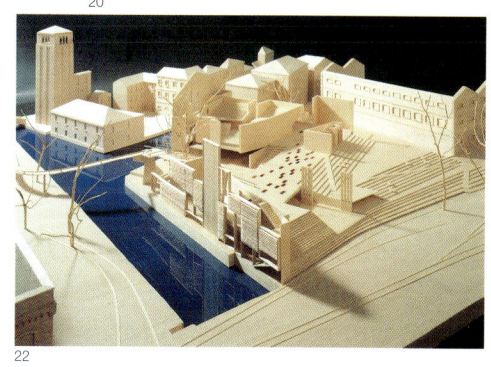

Miralles retained the original three-section gabled roof of the old market building and created a colorful work by preserving the radius of the wave-shaped structure.

As one might expect, the entrance facade, which faces the road, includes a collection of structural columns comprised of Miralles' trademark steel trees in small bushy groups – another deconstructivist expression. The interior is a large and expansive space with long steel beams supporting the wave-shaped roof. Miralles' random positioning of the groups of columns, each set of which includes several parts, gives the design a refreshing air.

Prior to the current Santa Caterina Market, there was another market with the same name on the lot, and prior to that a monastery, so the site is imbued with three generations of historical change. Miralles retained the original gate from the monastery, followed the basic framework of the old market, and fused everything together with a new covering. Miralles, who once said, "Buildings can be used over and over to create good architectural solutions," used the theory of dialectic "incorporation" to produce excellent spaces with a fusion of new and old buildings. Miralles took an early interest in the incorporation method, as can be seen in works such as La Llauna School, Igualada Cemetery, and the Boarding School in Morella. The Santa Caterina Market rehabilitation encouraged a new interpretation of environmental changes and the environment itself, and made use of Miralles' ultimate concept: "infinite integration."

Initially, Miralles collaborated with his first wife Carme Pinos on completed works like the Olympic Archery Pavilion, the National Center for Rhythmic Gymnastics, Igualada Cemetery, and the Boarding School in Morella. Then he joined forces with Benedetta Tagliabue, who became his partner and second wife, to create countless important works before succumbing to illness in 2000. Following his death, Tagliabue has taken over and completed projects Miralles started such as the Borneo Sporenburg Housing Complex, the New Scottish Parliament, Santa Caterina Market, Diagonal Mar Park, the Gas Natural New Headquarters, the Vigo University Campus, and is currently working on Palafolls Public Library and the University Institute of Architecture of Venice (I.U.A.V.).

MVRDV

THE NETHERLANDS

Firm founded in 1991 by Winy Maas (born in 1959), Jacob van Rijs (born in 1964), and Nathalie de Vries (born in 1965). All three principals studied at the Delft University of Technology, and prior to starting their own practice, Maas and van Rijs worked at OMA, while de Vries was part of Mecanoo. One of the most representative young, Dutch design groups.

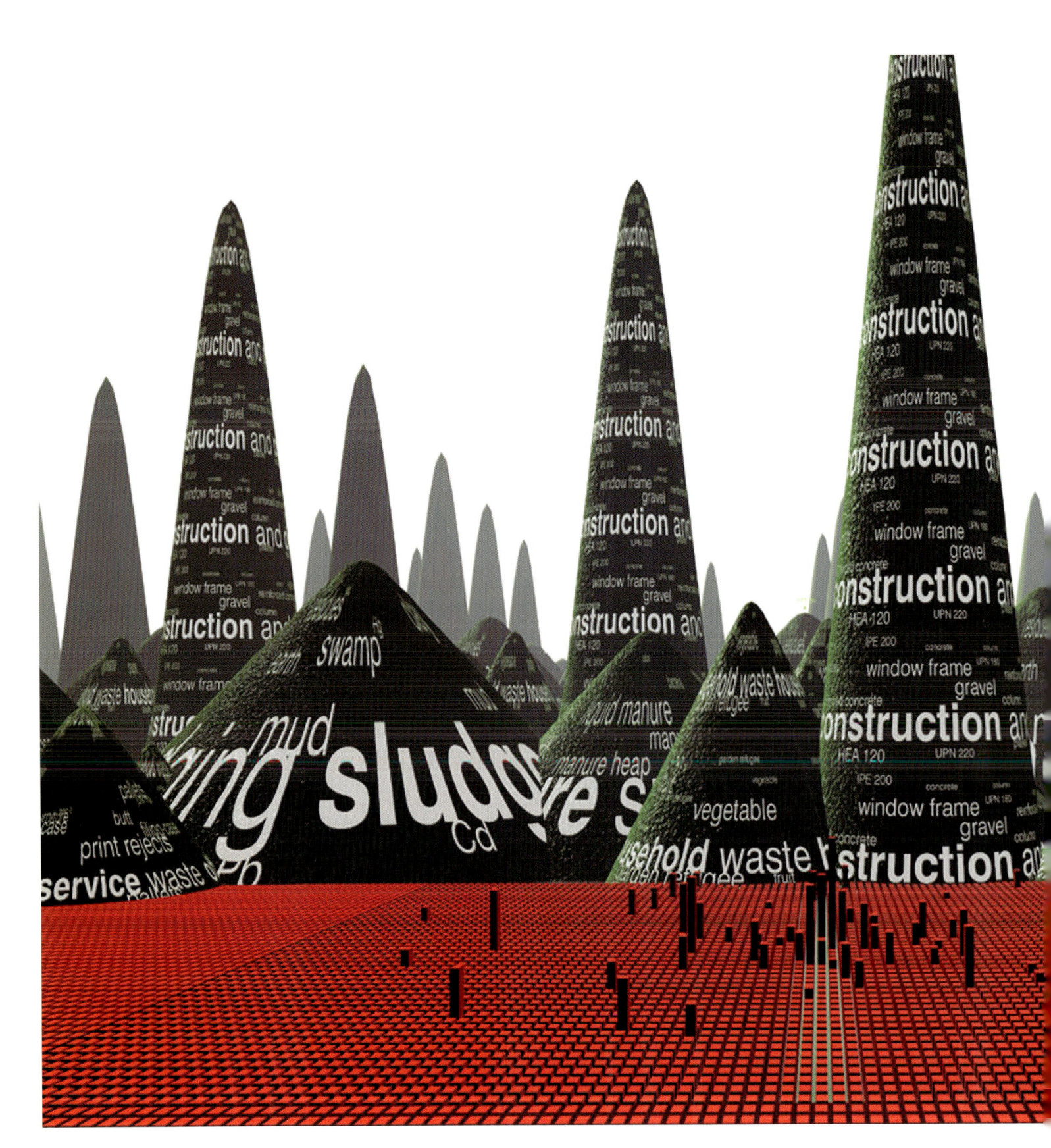

1	Meta City / Datatown
2	Villa VPRO 1997 / Hilversum, The Netherlands photo: ©Synectics
3, 4	100 WoZoCo 1997 / Amsterdam photo: ©Synectics
5	Les Halles

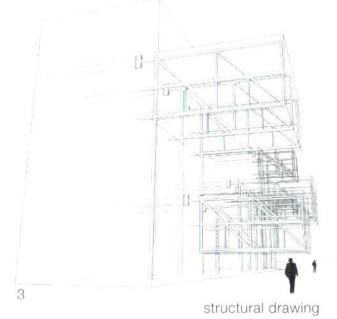

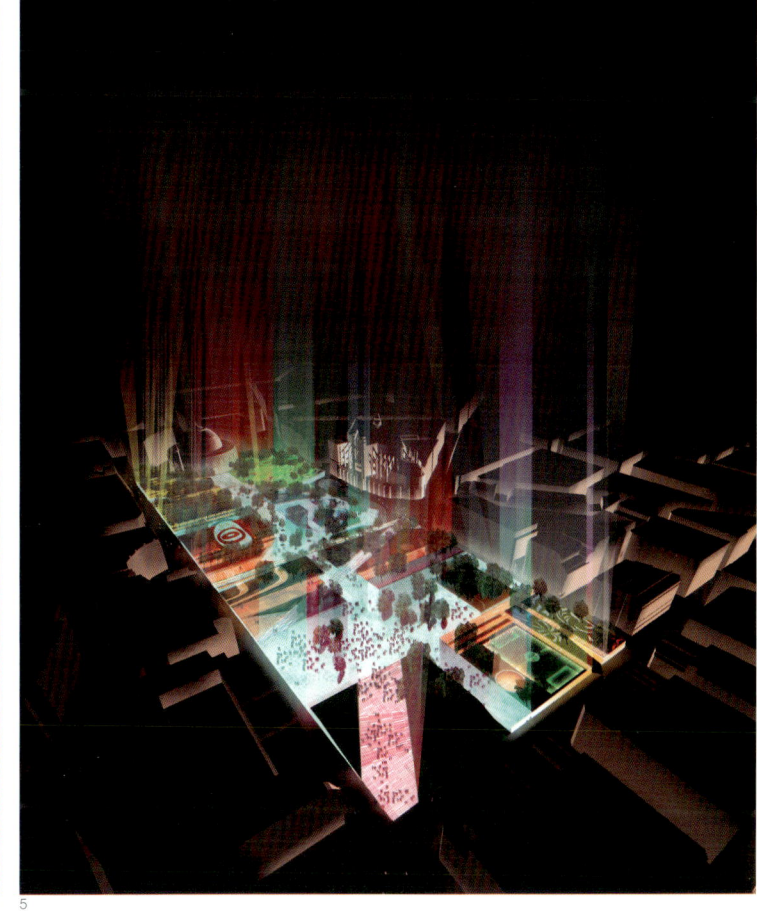

structural drawing

161

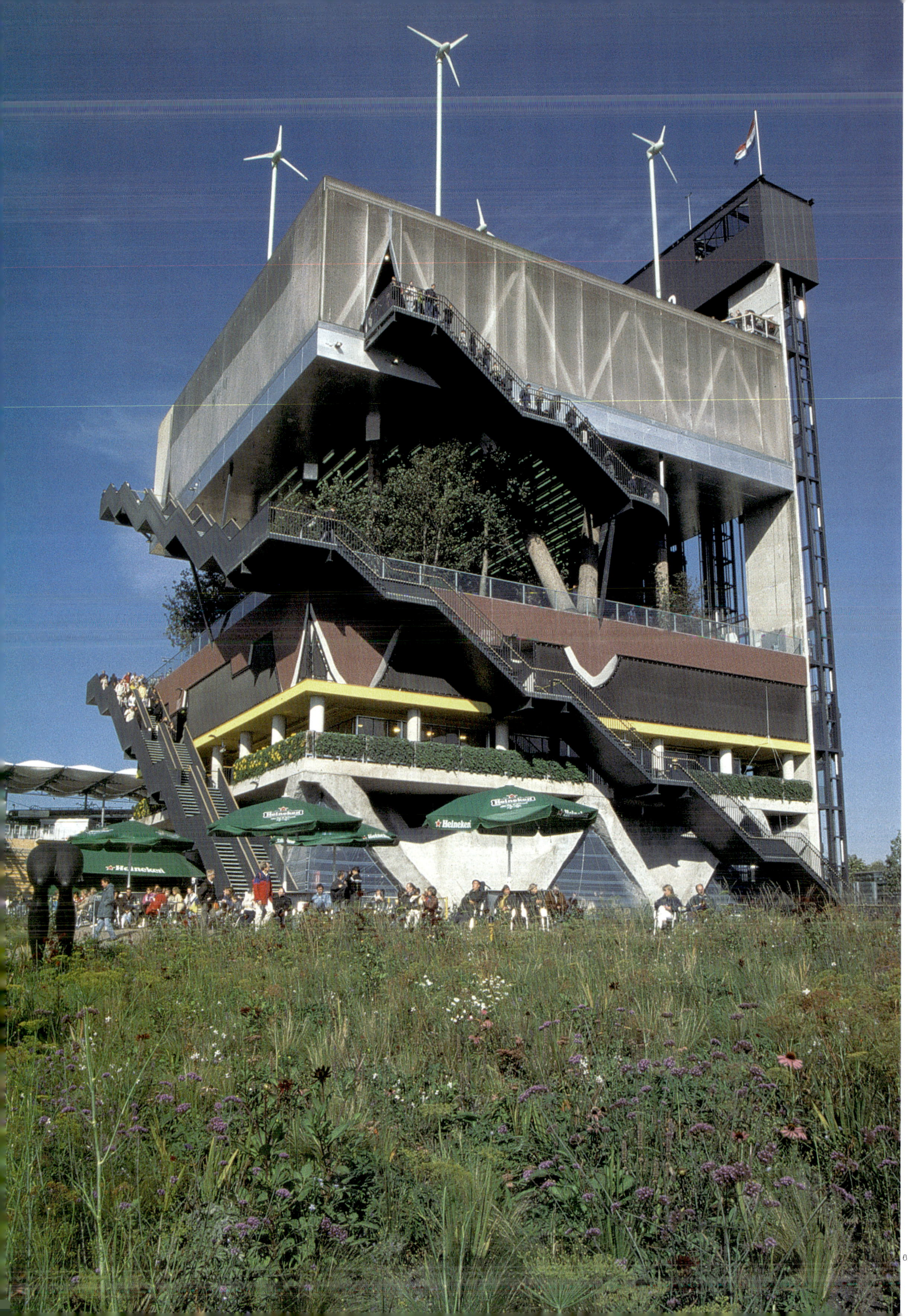
Heineken

6, 7   Hannover Expo 2000 Dutch Pavilion   2000 / Hannover, Germany
       photo: ©Synectics
8   NYC2012
9   Pig City

10   Parkrand Building
11   Branbant Library

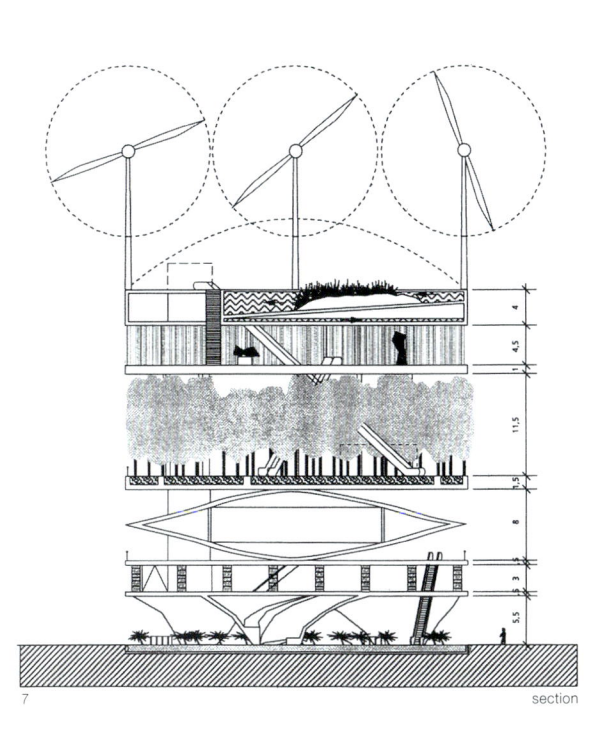

section

163

MVRDV

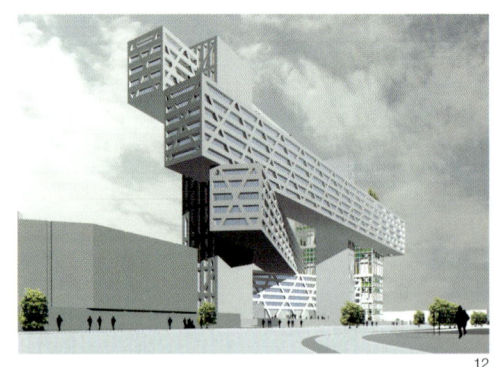

12 EPO Office

13 Silodam   2002 / Amsterdam
photo: ©Synectics

14 Hageneiland Housing   2001 / Ypenburg, The Netherlands
photo: ©Synectics

15 Mirador   2004 / Madrid
photo: ©Synectics

16 Borneo Sporenburg Houses   1999·2000 / Amsterdam
photo: ©Synectics

17 Container City

18 Liuzhou Housing

19 Frosilos Housing   2005 / Copenhagen

20 New Orleans Project

21 Matsudai Cultural Village Museum   2003 / Niigata, Japan
photo: ©Synectics

22 Omotesando Project

photos : Courtesy of the Architect except ©Synectics

MVRDV, a group of young, cutting-edge, Dutch architects, first received international recognition when WoZoCo, a 100-apartment complex for the elderly, was completed in the Western Garden section of Amsterdam. The 11.3-meter cantilevers jutting out from the north facade of the building were simply breathtaking.

At around the same time, the group completed Villa VPRO in Hilversum. The floor inside the work displayed an extraordinary interior landscape using a prominent three-dimensional design. In addition, the exterior facade captured widespread attention for its cross-sectional form in which the warped floor slab was gradually altered to become the ceiling slab. MVRDV focuses on the high density of contemporary cities and architecture using a "datascape," or accumulation and analysis of a vast and complex body of data, which forms the basis of the group's designs. A case in point is a work like Meta city/Data town.

Some 1,477 people would live in Meta city/Data town, a theoretical town based solely on a huge amount of high-density data. This number is four times Holland's actual per-square-kilometer population density, and represents a level of overcrowding equivalent to relocating the entire population of the US to a single city. The tremendous amount of garbage and waste generated by the self-sufficient Meta city/Data town would be collected in heaps the size of a super high-rise building. The image of these gigantic conical towers of garbage is quite stunning. Inherent in MVRDV's studies and projects depicting urban density are a host of similarly phenomenal ideas.

The weaving towers in the vanishing NYC2012 project represent nighttime in the high-density urban center of New York, while also depicting a stunning urbanscape, the likes of which have never been seen. In addition, Pig City, a mass-production plan designed to deal with the lack of land in Holland, a major exporter of pork, is fascinating as a unique urban landscape in which piggeries are stacked vertically to form high-rise buildings. MVRDV's optimistic projects are rooted in the following idea: "Architects have the power to change society. Therefore, it is vitally important for us to devise models for change."

Of MVRDV's three founding members, two, Winy Maas and Jacob van Rijs, were formerly associated with OMA; the third, Nathalie de Vries, once belonged to Mecanoo. In his book _Delirious New York_, OMA's Rem Koolhaas introduces the idea of urban high-density as

"the culture of high density," and I suspect that this theory exerted a certain amount of influence on Maas and van Rijs.
Along with the aforementioned Meta city/Data town, NYC2012, and Pig City, MVRDV's unfinished works that reflect the high-density concept include the Parkrand Building, with its "openair living"; Brabant Library, a cylindrical, high rise with a train line passing through it; Container City, a collection of 3,500 shipping containers; Les Halles, a high-density underground city; and EPO Office, a daring design for a structure that floats in midair. All of these are notable not only for the group's application of the high-density concept but for the originality of the idea.
Among MVRDV's completed works which are distinguished for their use of the high-density concept are housing complexes such as Silodam, Borneo Sporenburg, Hageneiland, Mirador, and Frosilos.
As all of this suggests, MVRDV proceeds simultaneously with a number of different projects, both actual and theoretical, without making any clear distinction between the two. In many instances, there are clients and advisors involved in the theoretical projects. And it isn't uncommon for the firm to go back and forth from a theoretical work like Berlin Void to actual ones like Silodam and the Dutch Pavilion at Expo 2000, and then shift back to one of the group's theoretical Stacking Projects.
One constant in MVRDV's work is the idea of "artificial ecology." The Dutch Pavilion was a mini-ecosystem with a vertically arranged mass of nature – a method which once again seems very valid in Holland. The Liuzhou Housing Complex in China is also an artificial ecology combining residences with nature in mountains known for their limestone quarries, and the New Orleans Project calls for buildings to be buried inside hills.
The group's Matsudai Cultural Village Museum has just been completed in Japan. And there are some magnificent proposals among MVRDV's entries to competitions such as the Pinault Museum in Paris, and the Eyebeam Institute in New York. The Omotesando Project (now under construction), it won't be long before the group's innovative designs pervade the world.

Neutelings Riedijk

THE NETHERLANDS

Firm founded by Willem Jan Neutelings and Michiel Riedijk in 1997. Neutelings was born in the Netherlands in 1959. Studied at the Delft University of Technology from 1977 to 1986. Worked at OMA from 1981 to 1986. Established offices in Rotterdam and Antwerp. Riedijk was born in the Netherlands in 1964. Studied at the Delft University of Technology from 1983 to 1989. From 1989 to 1996, worked at both Neutelings' and J.D. Bokkoring's firm.

1 Lakeside Housing 'The Sphinxes' 2003 / Huizen, The Netherlands
  photo: ©Jeroen Musch
2 Bruges Concert Hall / Competition
3 Almere Theater and School of Arts / Competition

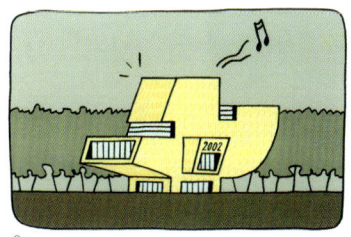

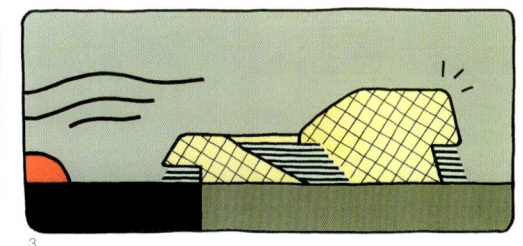

4, 5	Utrecht University Minnaert Building 1997 / Utrecht, The Netherlands photo: ©Synectics
6	Maastricht Fire Station 1999 / Maastricht, The Netherlands photo: ©Christian Richters
7	Roads and Waterworks Support Center 1998 / Harlingen, The Netherlands photo: ©Christian Richters
8	Shipping & Transport College 2005 / Rotterdam photo: ©Jeroen Musch
9	IJ-Tower 1998 / Amsterdam photo: ©Synectics
10	Mullerpier Apartment Block 3 2003 / Rotterdam photo: ©Jeroen Musch
11	Mullerpier Apartment Block 7 2006 / Rotterdam photo: ©Jeroen Musch

8

9

10

11

12, 13   Breda Fire Station   1999 / Breda, The Netherlands
         photo: ©Christian Richters
14   Veenman Printers Building   1997 / Ede, The Netherlands
         photo: ©Christian Richters
15   The New Complex for the Ministries of Justice and Internal Affairs in The Hague / Competition
16   ABN AMRO Bank Headquarters / Competition

It was the subject of much discussion at the time. The building looked as if gigantic worms were crawling across the exterior wall. The unusual appearance of Neutelings Riedijk's Minnaert Building caused quite a stir. Attracted by all the attention, I also paid a visit to the building, which stands in one corner toward the rear of the University of Utrecht.

The "big worms" on the outside of the building are actually the various ducts that would ordinarily be buried within the walls. Apparently not all of them are real; some are just a part of the design. What is more surprising, however, is that hidden behind the motif is a clever, sustainable-design apparatus that is highly functional.

The building, a research facility, is also unprecedented in that rain falls over a large pond that was constructed inside the second-floor hall. The rain falls from high sidelights which are positioned above the pond. During the summer in particular, this interior rain works to cool down the air inside. And since the water is recycled from the pond, the cooling sensation is just as effective on sunny, hot days. Willem Jan Neutelings and Michiel Riedijk, the firm's principals, often use cartoons to express their work. Not merely sketches or drawings, but actual comical touches. The Bruges Concert Hall, for example, includes a series of musical notes dancing across the upper part of the building. On the Almere Theater and School of Arts, the sun is beginning to rise above the sea, and as the Breda Fire Station stands watch over the streets, the moon shines down and a night breeze blows through the air. This sort of humorous illustration is both a good way of expressing a building's character and an enjoyable detail.

With the exception of the Minnaert Building, most of Neutelings Riedijk's works remain relatively unknown outside of Holland. IJ-Tower, which stands in Amsterdam's Eastern Harbor district, is an expressive landmark with a white exterior wall, sections of which are gouged out and painted reddish-brown. Strewn across the exterior wall of the Veenman Printers Building are letters of the alphabet. The Dutch Roads and Waterworks Support Center is distinguished by its low, slanting exterior wall. These are a few of the architects' best known and most representative works.

All four make use of various exterior walls and manipulations of form. Neutelings Riedijk's other works share a common design vocabulary, and can be grouped accordingly. One group consists of housing complexes and office

17   Antwerp Youth Hostel / Competition
18   Tilburg Row House   1996 / Tilburg, The Netherlands
        photo: ©Synectics
19   Casino in Utrecht / Utrecht, the Netherlands
20   Hotel & Shopping Center in Paris / Paris
21   Grand Egyptian Museum / Competition
22   Moscow City Hall / Competition
23   European Central Bank / Competition

   photos : Courtesy of the Architect except ©Synectics

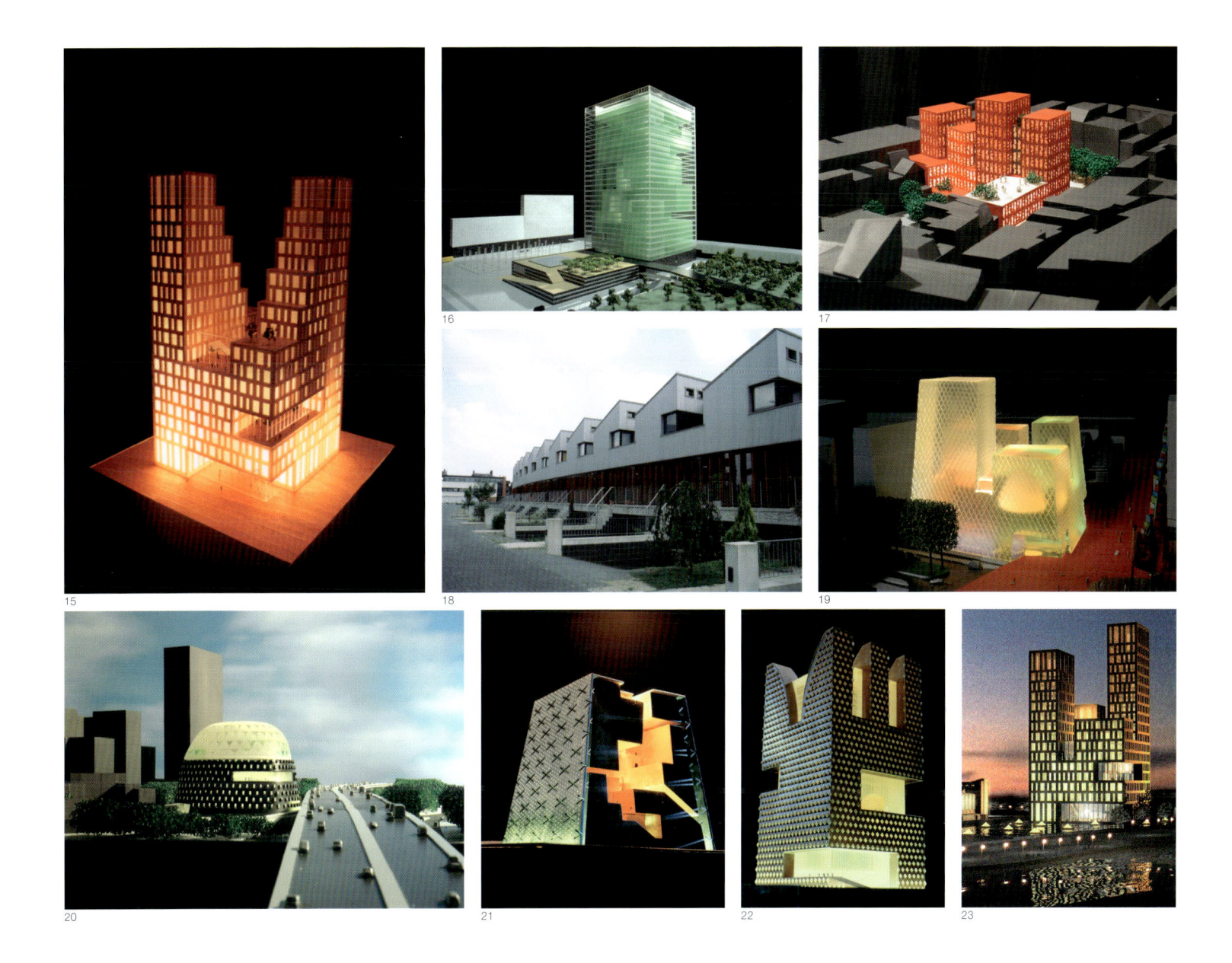

buildings with cantilevers and protruding upper levels, and smart, pent roofs. In this category, one might include "The Sphinxes" Lakeside Housing Complex, the Shipping and Transport College, the Mullerpier Apartment Blocks 3 and 7, and Breda Fire Station. Each of the buildings is distinctive enough to be almost immediately identifiable as a Neutelings Riedijk work.
Another distinctive element of the architects' vocabulary is a varied inner facade that is produced through the use of an exterior wall with an erect, rectangular mass and a scooped-out interior. Examples of this style include the New Ministries of Justice and Internal Affairs in The Hague, the Grand Egyptian Museum, the Antwerp Youth Hostel, Moscow City Hall, the ABN AMRO Bank Headquarters, and the European Central Bank.

One more element is the use of organic lines, which is representative of Neutelings Riedijk's futuristic works such as the Hotel and Shopping Center in Paris, the Casino in Utrecht, Casino in Knokke, the Almere Theater and School of Arts, and the Bruges Concert Hall.
In their work, Neutelings Riedijk use a heterodox methodology based on a design credo of "laziness." According to Neutelings, in a paper called "On laziness, recycling, sculptural mathematics and ingenuity," "As one of the Seven Deadly Sins, sloth is the most useful to the architect. Diligence and ambition are a dangerous combination, but laziness and ambition create a good balance, and produce a good result. This is because covering up one's laziness requires ingenuity. In our work, we go to great lengths to apply laziness to our design method." The architects also claim that the

most effective use of laziness is to talk a client out of a commission. It is this laziness that Neutelings Riedijk suggest has led to a decrease in useless architectural design and unneeded construction.

NOX

THE NETHERLANDS

Lars Spuybroek was born in Rotterdam in 1959, and graduated from the Delft University of Technology. Established NOX in Rotterdam in the early 90s, and began researching the relationship between architecture and computers. Received the Mart Stam Incentive Award in 1991, and the Iakov Chernikhov Prize in 1997. Since 2002, has held a tenured professorship at the University of Kassel where he runs the CAD/Digital Design Techniques Department.

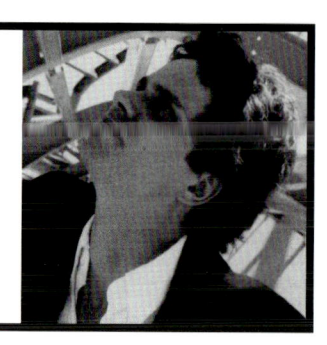

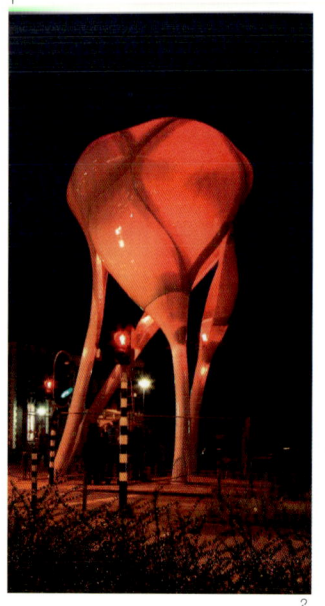

1 Dutch H2O EXPO 1997 / Neeltje Jans, The Netherlands
2, 3 D-Tower 2003 / Doetinchem, The Netherlands
4 V2-mediaLab 1998 / Rotterdam
5 Popular Music Center CRMA
6 Son-O-House 2003 / Son en Breugel, The Netherlands
7 European Central Bank / Competition
8 Metz Pompidou Center / Competition

9

9, 10, 11　Maison Folie　2003 / Lille, France
　　12　Beach Hotel and Boulevard in Noordwij
　　13　Blow Out　1997 / Neeltje Jans, The Netherlands
　　14　Soft Office
　　15　Galerie der Forschung

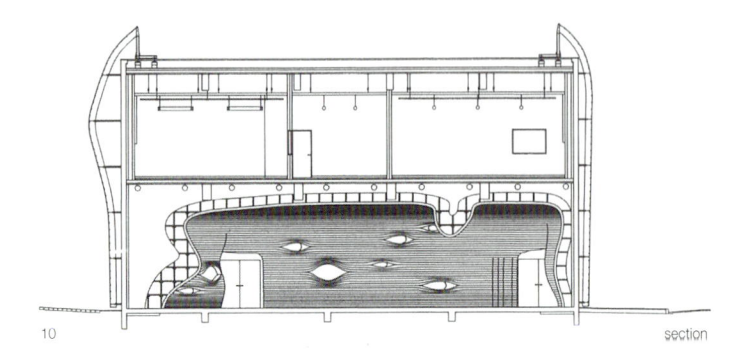

10　　　　　　　　　　　　　　　　　　　section

1/4

11

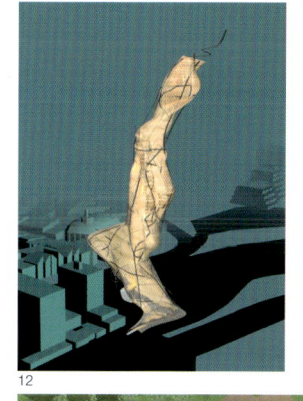

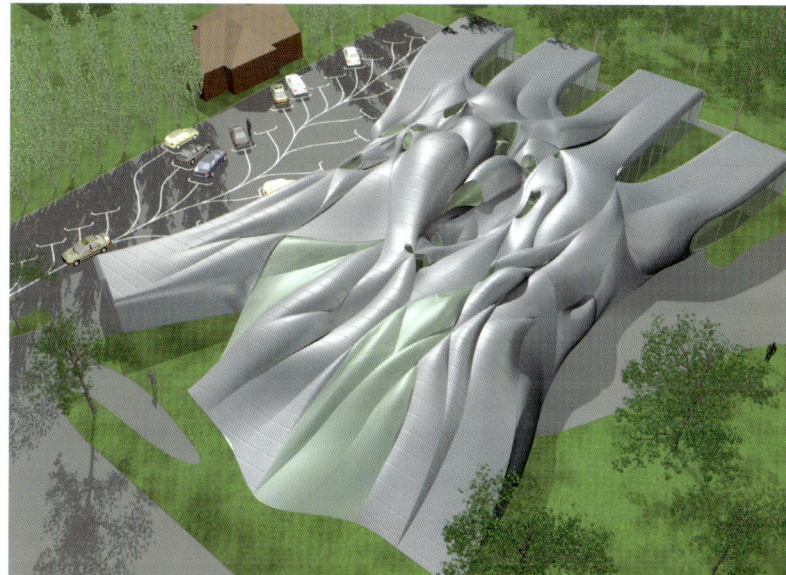

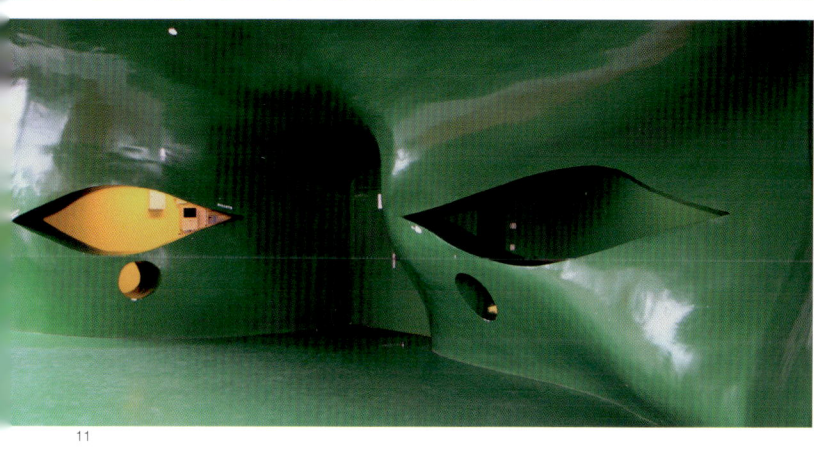

12
13

14

15

175

NOX

NOX's debut work, Dutch H2O EXPO, was quite controversial when it was unveiled in 1997. Located in the province of Zeeland in southwestern Holland, it is a strange building that resembles a shiny silver worm or slug crawling across the ground. In terms of function, the work is a rather formal exhibition space concerned with transportation, public works, and water management. Based on the concept of integrating the environment with the human body and technology, the displays focus on the life cycle of water.

However, the space itself is slanted without a level floor in sight, and the building, with its unified floor, walls, and ceiling, is like the inside of a body. The entire interior is organized with a single fresh and fluid design. Buildings, such as this one, that reference liquid geometry and the fluid concentration of substances are known as "fluid architecture," and are created with the kind of multimedia technology that NOX is so adept at using. Following this work, NOX began to produce organic buildings that were just plain weird if not actually eerie.

D-Tower is a light tower that stands on a street corner with a form that bulges out above four legs and looks like part of a living organism. The color of the light changes constantly and the tower has become a symbol of the city. Other completed NOX works include Maison Folie, Son-O-House, and V2-mediaLab. The first was a renovation of an old industrial building in the French city of Lille. Using a mesh skin, the firm added an organic coating to the exterior wall. Son-O-House is a public artwork that is both house and sound installation in Son en Breugel, and V2-mediaLab is a renovation project for a Rotterdam-based company called V2. Most of NOX's works have curved walls that appear fluid and organic, and many of the firm's unfinished projects are even more audacious and powerful. At the top of the list is NOX's New World Trade Center Proposal, in which the firm calls for several, slightly flattened snakelike super high-rise towers to be erected at Ground Zero.

NOX's entry for the European Central Bank competition, held by the Frankfurt-based corporation, envisioned a host of large and small buildings in a cluster with parabolic curves. The opening to the buildings was a round window. The firm's design for Popular Music Center CRMA facility in Nancy, France, won second prize. It was an organic form that recalled a lump of meat that had been cut into thin slices.

16 New World Trade Center Proposal
17 Interactive Public Art Work for the City of Flims
18 Jalisco State Public Library / Competition
19 Jeongok Prehistory Museum / Competition
20 ParisBRAIN
21 French H2O EXPO / Paris, French
22 Quartier de L'enfant / Competition
23 Seoul Opera House
24 Venus & Herkules / Competition
25 wetGRID 1999-2000 / Nantes, France

photos : Courtesy of the Architect

NOX's proposal for the Metz Pompidou Center competition, which was ultimately won by Shigeru Ban, called for a huge, white lump that resembled a large mountain with a crack-like opening.
Soft Office, currently under construction, is as the name suggests, an office space covered with a soft coating. Its appearance is distinguished by an uncountable collection of walls. The facility in Warwickshire, England will be an interactive office for a TV production company that includes shops and a gymnasium.
Lars Spuybroek, the principal of NOX, began researching the relationship between architecture and the media, in particular computers, in the early 90s. He has published a magazine called _NOX_ (later, _Forum_), produced a video called _Soft City_, and created interactive electronic artworks such as "Soft Site," "edit Spline," and "deep Surface." His architectural work began to be realized in the late 90s.
Spuybroek, who has said that diagramming is the most important technical innovation in architectural design of the last 15 years, predicts that the movement toward metadesign in the fields of graphic design and industrial design will continue.
Spuybroek makes use of a variety of diagramming methods, including flexigrams, haptograms, kinetograms, and biograms. Yet, he is never satisfied with any single method. Each type of diagramming is not fixed, nor is it the sole means of problem resolution. As they are related to each other, by connecting all of them to one system, it is possible change everything with one parameter.
He himself uses diagramming with a flexible interactive system. Sketching is something Spuybroek never does; instead, he constructs a computer-generated machine. "Virtual integral" systems are a kind of matrix that allow each relationship to be easily adjusted. After all of the data has been input and processed, an algorithmic solution can be quickly found. Will NOX's use of convenient machinery help expand its architectural possibilities?

O'Donnell + Tuomey

IRELAND

In 1976, Sheila O'Donnell and John Tuomey graduated from the School of Architecture of University College Dublin. In 1988, they established their own practice. Named fellows of the RIAI (Royal Institute of the Architects of Ireland) in 1994. In addition to lecturing at University College Dublin, they have worked as critics in the U.K. and U.S., and widely published and exhibited. In 1986 and 1987, received the American Institute of Architects (AAI) Award, and in 1988, 1990, and 1992, the AAI Downes Medal.

1, 2   Blackwood Golf Club   1994 / Co.Down, Nothern Ireland

2 elevation

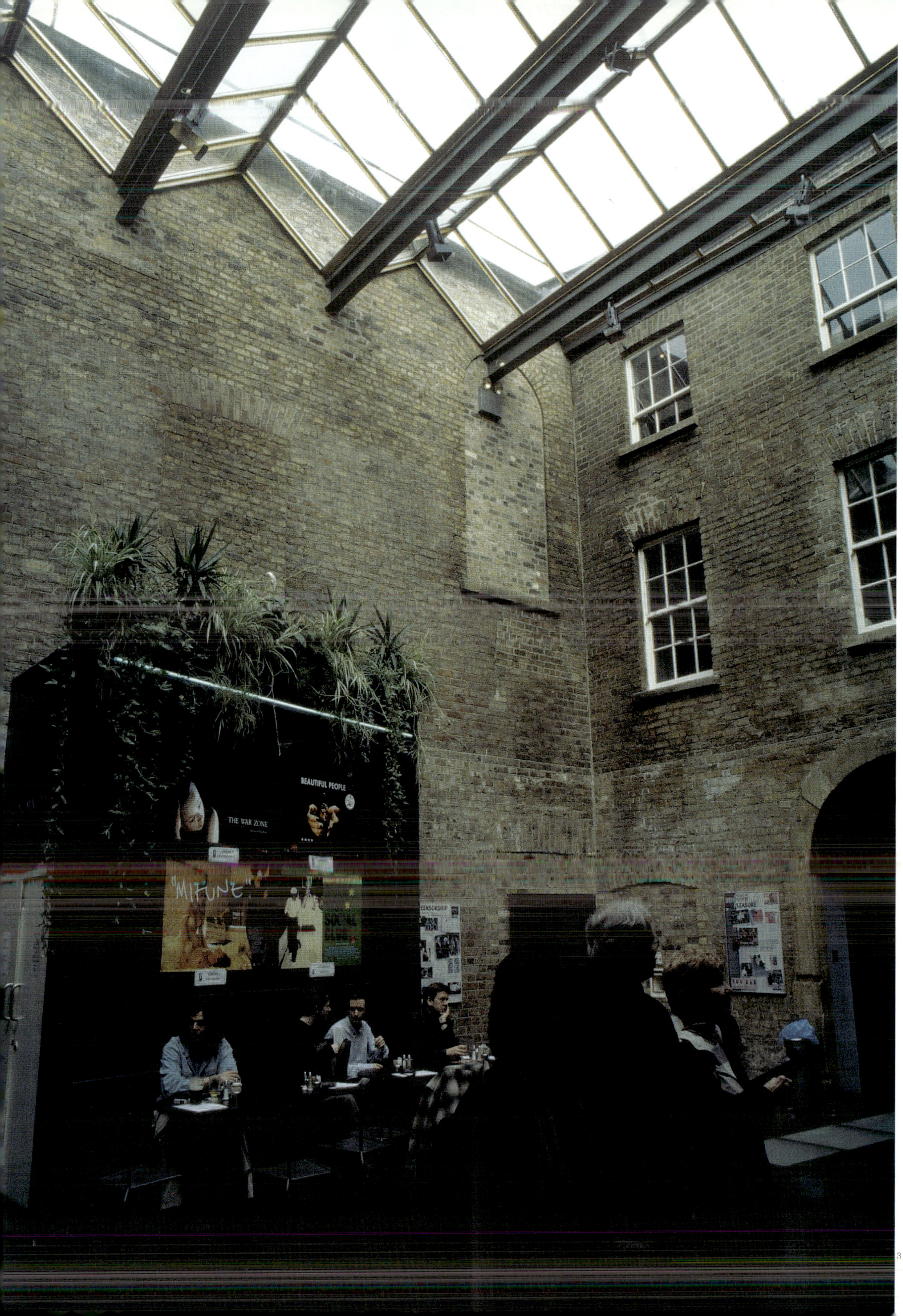
BEAUTIFUL PEOPLE
THE WAR ZONE
"MIFUNE"
CENSORSHIP

3, 4, 5   Irish Film Center   1992 / Dublin, Ireland
          photo: ©Synectics
6, 7   Photography Gallery   1996 / Dublin, Ireland
          photo: ©Synectics
8   National Photography Archive   1996 / Dublin, Ireland
          photo: ©Synectics
9   Hudson House   1998 / Co.Meath, Ireland
10   Irish Pavilion   1992 / Dublin, Ireland
11   Letterfrack Furniture College   2001 / Co.Galway, Ireland

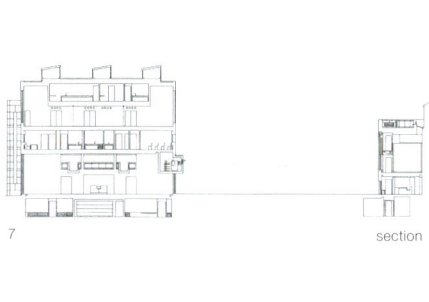

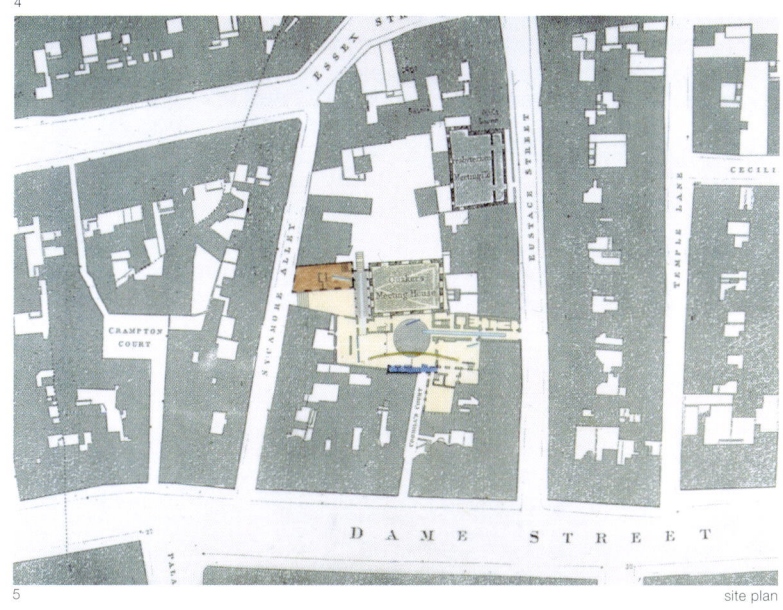

section

site plan

12 Lewis Glucksman Gallery
2004 / Cork, Ireland
photo: ©Dennis Gilbert

13, 14 Ranelagh Multi Denominational School
1998 / Dublin, Ireland
photo: ©Synthesis

I first became interested in the architecture of Sheila O'Donnell and John Tuomey after seeing an article on their Irish Film Center in a magazine. That was also the first time I felt attracted to Irish architecture in general. Because the film center, originally an old Quaker meeting house, was in a remote section of the city, the narrow paths that led from three nearby streets gave the site a secretive air after the lengthy approach. There was something indescribably charming about the ancient brick wall in the courtyard, which was covered with a skylight.

The old, bright courtyard served as an oasis not only for films fans, but nearby residents as well, and offered a chance for travelers and businessmen to allay their fatigue. In the meeting-house square, I came upon the Photography Gallery and National Photography Archive, which had also been designed by O'Donnell Tuomey. In fair weather, a film projected from the archive can be seen on the screen that obstructs a large window in the gallery, and all of a sudden the square is transformed into a movie Theater. Though different in scale and circumstance, the approach to this scenographic city is similar to the "urban room" of St. Mark's Square in Venice.

Temple Bar Square is located in the heart of Dublin. In 1991, an architectural competition was staged to redesign the surrounding area. Group 91, a collection of young architects comprising eight teams, was the overall winner, but O'Donnell Tuomey were also among the designers involved. One reason they were allowed to produce the three aforementioned works, despite the way they intervened so spectacularly with the city, was the architects' respectful attitude toward the scale and texture of the already existing urban fabric. Further, while they exhibited a free form of expression as architects, O'Donnell Tuomey maintained a sense of contextual suitability.

Hailed for defining a new type of Dublin architecture, O'Donnell Tuomey were also labeled "Irish rationalists" by former AA director Alvin Boyarski. This was after the two had graduated from Univeristy College in Dublin, relocated to London, and had begun collaborating with James Stirling. Later, coming into contact with the works of the Italian rationalist architect Aldo Rossi would prove extremely beneficial to the pair.

Rossi's works taught O'Donnell Tuomey the true poetic value and strength of architecture. After returning to Ireland, they sensed a link

15 Cherry Orchard Primary School   2006 / Co.Dublin, Ireland
    photo: ©Dennis Gilbert
16 Galbally Social Housing   2002 / Co.Limerick, Ireland
    photo: ©Ros Kavanagh
17 Lyric Theater / Belfast, Ireland
18 Sean O'casey Community Center / Dublin, Ireland
19 Ranelagh Multi Denominational School Extension / Dublin, Ireland
20 Ormond Quay / Competition
21 Timberyard Social Housing / Dublin, Ireland
22 Lincoln Arts Theater / Competition
23 Howth House   2003 / Co.Dublin, Ireland
    photo: ©Dennis Gilbert
24 Center for Research into Infectious Diseases at University College Dublin   2003 / Dublin, Ireland
    photo: ©Dennis Gilbert

photos : Courtesy of the Architect except ©Synectics

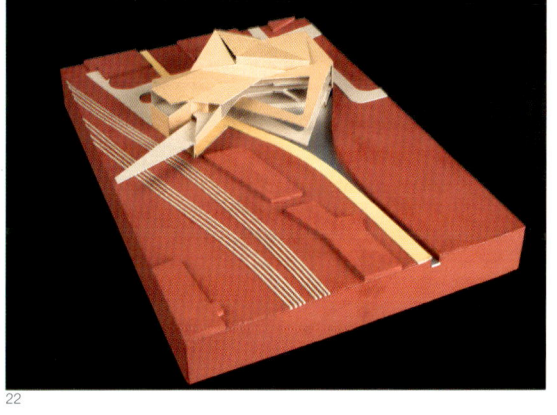

between Italian rationalism and traditional Irish building methods, and traveled around looking at domestic architecture. As a result, they found that compared to English architecture, the Irish variety was simpler and more primordial, and as an object, created a stronger contrast with the landscape. Modeled on a vernacular Irish hut, the Irish Pavilion, produced to coincide with the opening of the Irish Museum of Modern Art (renovated by Shay Cleary) was designed by the architects. The work resembled a hay barn from the Irish countryside and was instrumental in launching their career.

In addition to the three mentioned above, O'Donnell Tuomey have created gifted works such as the Blackwood Golf Club, Hudson House, Ranelagh Multi-Denominational School, Letterfrack Furniture College, the Center for Research into Infectious Diseases at University College Dublin, Lewis Glucksman Gallery, and the Galbally Social Housing. Moreover, many of these works have received awards from the RIAI (Royal Institute of the Architects of Ireland) and the RIBA (Royal Institute of British Architects). Of these, the Ranelagh school is a particularly outstanding work, which has received the AAI Downes Medal and RIAI Award, and was nominated for the Mies van der Rohe Award and the Stirling Prize.

After I paid my initial visit some years ago to see the film center and photography gallery, I also made a trip to the Ranelagh school. The building, which stands at an intersection in a quiet residential area, was cloaked in a roadside exterior wall made of recycled bricks that was marked by its dramatic contours. The gentle, wooden exterior wall on the playground side of the building was bathed in sunlight, creating an unexplainably pleasant atmosphere. Deep eaves, long hallways, wooden sashes, and furniture ñ I found myself carried way by an aromatic illusion of the wooden fragrance found in old, Japanese elementary schools. On the way back, I stopped to have a chat with the architects at their office. The quiet, leisurely space gave me the strong sensation that this was the birthplace of O Donnell Tuomey's rational, vernacular works. At present, along with winning the international competition for the Lyric Theater, the firm is at work on Sean O'Casey Community Center, Timberyard Social Housing, and the Ranelagh Multi-Denominational School Extension.

GUSTAV PEICHL

AUSTRIA

Born in Vienna in 1928. Graduated from the Academy of Fine Arts, Vienna in 1954. Began drawing cartoons under the pen-name "Ironimus" in 1954. Established his own architectural firm in 1955. Named professor of the Master School at the Academy of Fine Arts, Vienna from 1973 to 1996, and the dean at the same institution from 1987 to 1988. Received the Reynolds Memorial Award in 1975, and the Mies van der Rohe Award in 1986.

1. German Art and Exhibition Hall 1992 / Bonn
   photo: ©Richard Bryant
2. Gustav Peichl - Haus
   photo: ©Hanlo
3. Millennium Tower 1999 / Vienna
   photo: ©Monika Nicolic

Illustration of Himself

3

GUSTAV PEICHL

4 Karikatur Museum   2001 / Krems, Austria
   photo: ©Martin Wawra
5 KITA-Kindergarden   1999 / Berlin
6 Messe Wien   2003 / Vienna
   photo: ©Gisela Erlacher
7 ORF Station in St. Polten   1994 / St. Polten, Austria
8 EVN Forum   1993 / Maria Enzersdolf, Austria
9 Phosphate Elimination Plant, Berlin-Tegel   1985 / Berlin
   photo: ©Synectics
10. 11. 12 Austria Tower

10 plan

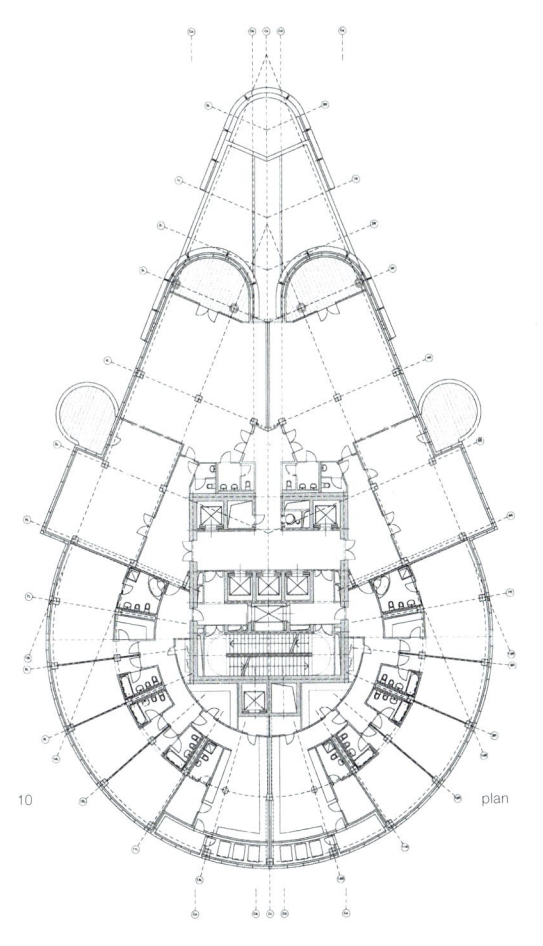

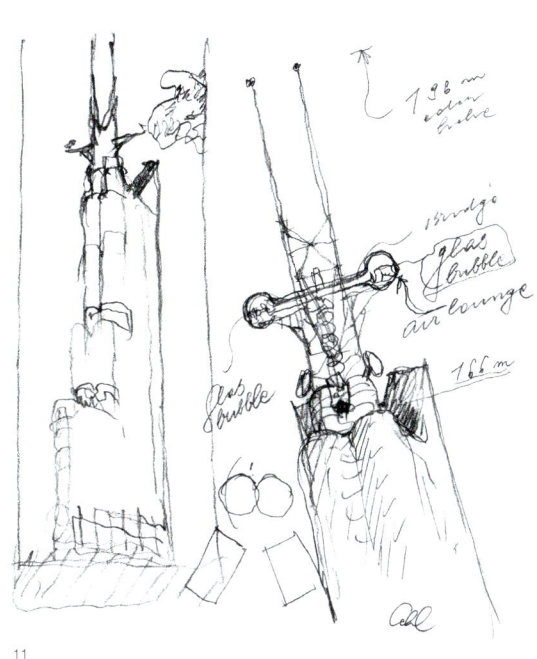

11

12

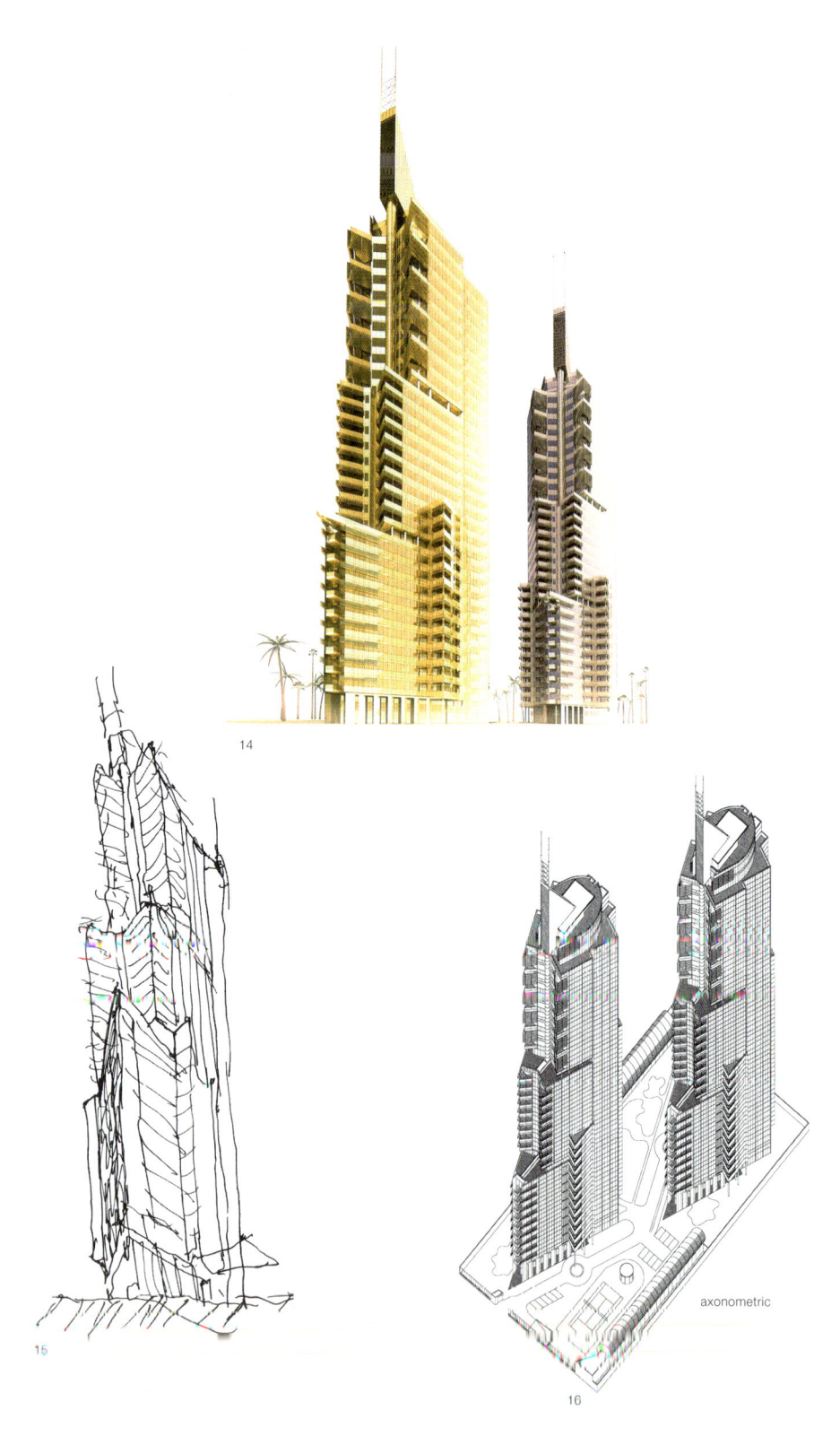

13   Alte Donau Tower   1998 / Vienna
     photo: ©Anna Blau

Eccentricity defines some architects. As one of the leading architects in Austria, Gustav Peichl is involved in numerous projects both domestically and in Germany. He has received the Mies van der Rohe Award, the Berlin Architecture Prize, the Reynolds Prize, and the Austrian Architecture Award, and despite being in his 70s, Peichl is still very active. But he has another side – that's what makes him eccentric. In some quarters, he is renowned as an architect, while in others, he is more popular as a political cartoonist. Peichl is as good at changing jobs as Arsene Lupin. He has been drawing satirical political cartoons for a number of Austrian newspapers, including the _Wiener Zeitung_, for some ten years. His pen-name, Ironimus, means "satirist" or "ironist." Though his work may not be known all over Europe, he is recognized as one of the greatest political cartoonists in Austria.

Naturally, political cartoons are filled with humor, and perhaps because of this, there is also an element of humor in Peichl's recent architecture. For example, in the design he came up with for the German Art and Exhibition Hall in Bonn, Germany, he played an interesting trick. In the upper section of the entrance gate, Peichl cut the beam in the center and left it as a slit. For the facade that faces the courtyard, he used rippled glass with a curved surface.

Or in Peichl's EVN Forum, the light cupola (a group of skylights), which is integrated into the roof, the colors and shapes create a comical effect. But the Karikatumuseum in Krems, completed in 2001, is perhaps the best example. The museum, devoted to cartoons, is a perfect showcase for Peichl. The design of the building's skylight is structured in a random sawtooth pattern that resembles the Alpine peaks, and the facade is fitted out with two windows and red rectangles that recall a human face, giving the structure an anthropomorphic character. The semi-circular shape of the Gustav Peichl Haus and the breast shape of KITA-Kindergarten are two more instances of the architect's humor.

From all of these examples, one might get the impression that Peichl's work is limited to comical architecture, but this is not at all the case. One need only look at the architect's early work, which is decidedly mechanical and functional. Also among Peichl's designs are the EFA Radio Satellite Station in Aflenz as well as the Austrian Broadcasting Stations in Linz, Salzburg, Innsbruck, Dornbirn, Graz, Eisenstadt, and Sankt Polten. As Peichl was

17 Neues Haus 2001 / Munich
    photo: ©Gisela Erlacher
18, 19 Toscanahof 2004 / Vienna
    photo: ©Anna Blau
20 Erzherzog Karl Stadt Apartment 1999 / Vienna
    photo: ©Gisela Erlacher
21 Rehearsal Stage of the Burgtheater 1993 / Vienna
    photo: ©Gisela Erlacher

    photos : Courtesy of the Architect except ©Synectics

commissioned to design a total of seven public architecture projects with the same function, it is clear that his work is well-liked.
Of these works, the most recent, the broadcast station in Sankt Polten, is incomparably high-tech. The square building makes use of a symmetrical design, one of Peichl's favorite motifs, while the exterior is covered with shiny, silver aluminum panels. All over the exterior walls are metallic louvers, giving the work a cohesive function and design which doesn't betray a hint of the humorous touches mentioned above. Another representative work of Peichl's industrial architecture is the Phosphate Elimination Plant in Berlin-Tegel. Peichl is also one of Austria's most prominent designers of high-rise buildings. Among his works are the Austria Tower, Mirage Tower (part of the same development as Austria Tower), and Millennium Tower, which was completed in 1999 and is quickly becoming another important work in the Peichl canon. With a height of 202 meters, it is the tallest tower in Austria. In addition to a large number of offices, 400 apartments and 50 shops are housed within the 100,000 square-meter building. The tower, based on the concept of making a "city within the city," has attracted many tenants and visitors, and become hugely successful. As part of the Holzmeister tradition, Peichl is in practice one of the few Austrian architects who embodies "rational modernism." Nevertheless, it is clear that he is perfectly comfortable with two types of architectural typologies – those which are rich in humor and wit, and industrial architecture with a very obvious function.
Moreover, between 1973 and 1996, Peichl also took on a third job as a lecturer at the Academy of Fine Arts, Vienna. Now, however, he has returned to a two-pronged attack (architect and cartoonist), and begun to engage in collaborations with Rudolf Weber. The first of these, the Alte Donau Tower, has a cylindrical form with four apartments on each floor. The exterior wall, with bright blue stripes running from top to bottom, exudes a sense of fun. Other recent Peichl works include Messe Wien and Toscanahof.

Cesar Pelli

USA

Born in Tucuman, Argentina in 1926. After graduating from the University of Tucuman in 1949, completed a postgraduate degree at the University of Illinois. From 1954 to 1964, worked at Eero Saarinen's firm. From 1964 to 1968, worked at DMJM. During a period as design partner at Gruen Associates, from 1968 to 1976, won numerous competitions. In 1977, became dean of the School of Architecture at Yale University, and established his own firm, Cesar Pelli and Associates. Received AIA Gold Medal in 1995. Currently, his firm is known as Pelli, Clarke, Pelli Architects, and has completed many projects in Japan and elsewhere.

2 plan

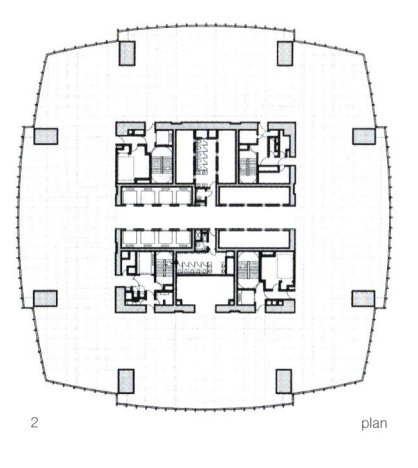

1, 2 International Finace Center 2004 / Hong Kong
photo: ©Tim Griffith / Esto

Cesar Pelli

3 Seahawk Hotel & Resort   1995 / Fukuoka, Japan
   photo: ©Synectics
4 NTT Shinjuku Headquarters Building   1995 / Tokyo
   photo: ©Synectics
5 Kurayoshi Park Square   2001 / Tottori, Japan
6 Atago Green Hills   2001 / Tokyo
   photo: ©Synectics
7 Nakanoshima Mitsui Building   2002 / Osaka, Japan
8 National Museum of Art   2004 / Osaka, Japan
9 World Financial Center   1987 / New York
   photo: ©Synectics
10, 11 Petronas Towers   1997 / Kuala Lumpur, Malaysia
   photo: ©Synectics

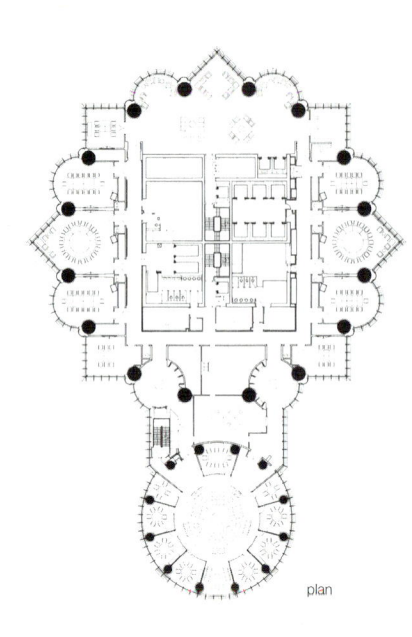

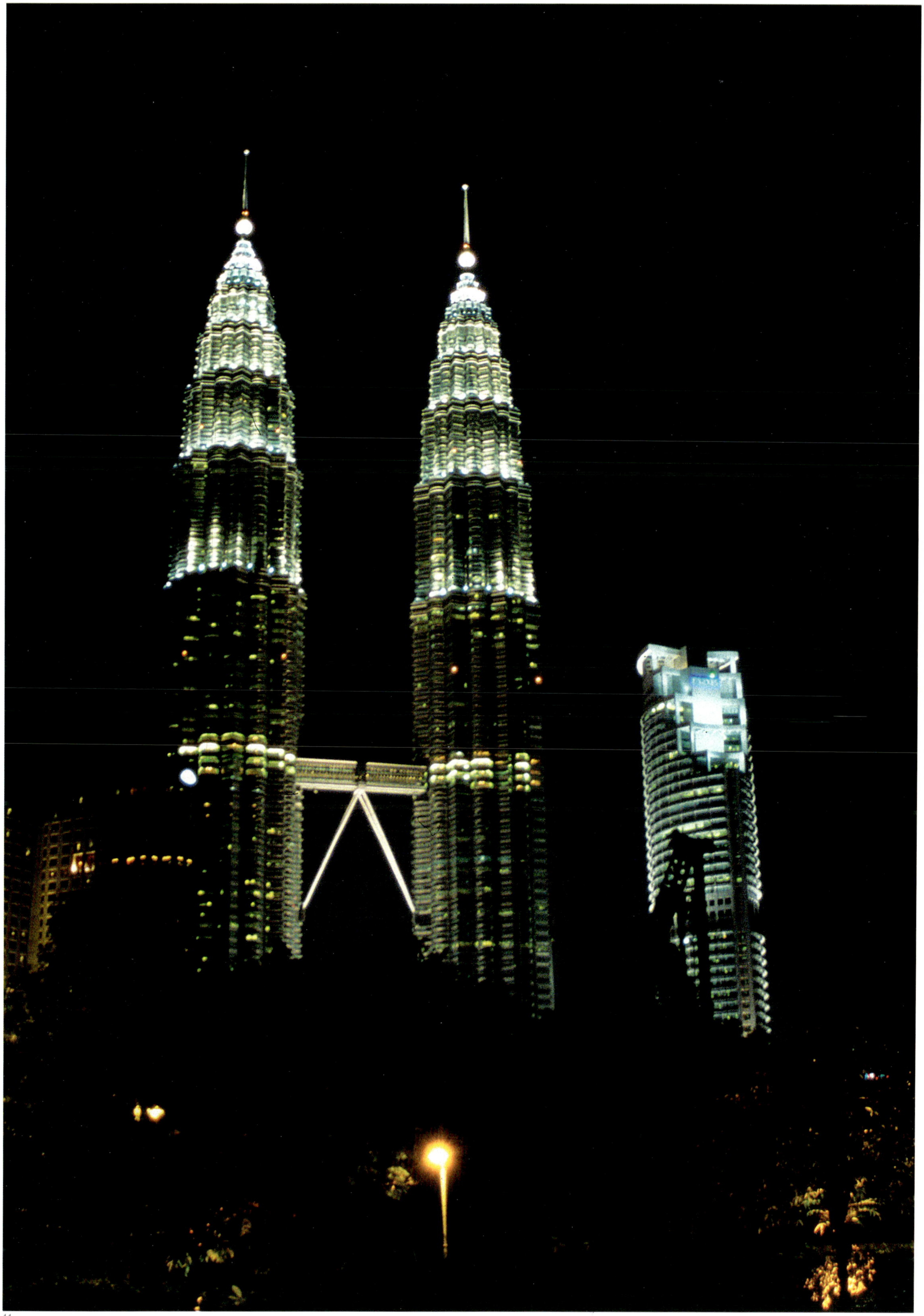

11

12, 13	Pacific Design Center 1975 / Los Angeles, California
photo: ©Synectics	18	Kyushu University New Campus Masterplan 2005 / Fukuoka, Japan	
14	Cira Center 2005 / Philadelphia, Pennsylvania	19	MoMA Tower 1984 / New York
photo: ©Synectics	
15	Aronoff Center for the Arts 1995 / Minneapolis, Minnesota
photo: ©J.Miles Wolf	20	Rice University Herring Hall 1984 / Houston, Texas
photo: ©Synectics	
16	Torre Bank Boston 2000 / Buenos Aires, Argentina
photo: ©Carlos Pelli	21	UW Physics and Astronomy Wings 1994 / Seattle, Washington
photo: ©Timothy Hursley	
17	Passenger Terminal 2, Tokyo International Airport (Haneda) 2004 / Tokyo	22	Lerner Research Institute 1999 / Cleveland, Ohio	

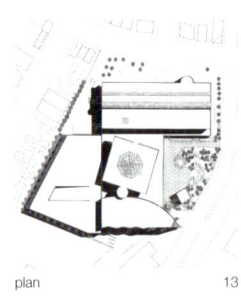

Compared to Europe, it is still fairly unusual for a foreign architect to establish a presence in a far eastern, island-nation like Japan. Cesar Pelli, however, has made great inroads in this area.

In recent years, he has been involved with some truly outstanding projects in Japan. His work includes the Sea Hawk Hotel and Resort, the NTT Shinjuku Headquarters Building, Kurayoshi Park Square, Atago Green Hills, and in the last few years, the Nakanoshima Mitsui Building, the National Museum of Art, Passenger Terminal 2 at Tokyo International Airport (Haneda), and the Kyushu University New Campus Masterplan.

In my research, I was astounded to find that a foreign firm such as Pelli's has been active in so many different projects in a single country, despite the economic downturn in Japan and the fact that countless domestic design firms find themselves with an excess of time on their hands. I'm left with the impression that Pelli is very good at business, and that most of these projects were successful due to his strong competition entries and proposals. When one sees how active the firm is in the U.S., where Pelli is based, as well as other countries, it is clear that he is involved in an extremely large number of projects.

Ninety people work at Pelli's American headquarters, while his Japan office has a staff of 35. If Hellmuth, Obata, and Kassabaum (HOK) is the top American firm in terms of size, then Pelli is about number 50, which for an atelier-style firm is really rather large. But the key to Pelli's success in Japan lies in his unwavering alliance with Jun Mitsui, head of Cesar Pelli Japan and former senior associate at the U.S. branch. In fact, the overall design for all of Pelli's projects in Japan is conducted at the Japanese branch of his firm.

Despite the size of the firm, Pelli is a force to be reckoned with in competitions. His first work in Japan, the U.S. Embassy in Japan, was won during Pelli's partnership with Gruen Associates, and during the same era, he won competitions for the U.N. City Project in Vienna and the Pacific Design Center. Next, Pelli was involved in super high-rise projects such as MoMA Tower, the World Financial Center, and Carnegie Hall Tower.

In his designs, Pelli has gone to great lengths to eliminate morphological preconceptions, saying that architecture should respond to the residents of a place. It is his belief that good architecture is created by integrating the special characteristics of each project including

23 Carnegie Hall Tower 1990 / New York
photo: ©Synectics
24 Owens Corning World Headquarters 1996 / Toledo, Ohio
photo: ©Timothy Hursley
25 Minneapolis Central Library 2006 / Minneapolis, Minnesota
26 Crile Clinic Building 1984 / Cleveland, Ohio
photo: ©Timothy Hursley
27 Wells Fargo Center 1989 / Minneapolis, Minnesota
photo: ©Steven Bergerson

photos : Courtesy of the Architect except ©Synectics

location, construction technique, and objective. This approach has been turned into a concrete design strategy called "design on response" at Cesar Pelli Japan. As Mitsui says, "More than the architectural design itself, each era demands a fertile and safe street or urban space created by a number of buildings. In thinking of architecture, one thinks of the city, and in thinking of the city, one thinks of people's comfort, and in thinking of people, one wants to make even more attractive architecture."
This fundamental concept forms the backbone for the firm's competition strategy.
The Petronas Twin Towers, which when they were completed in 1997 reigned as the tallest towers in the world, is another competition work that was won on the basis of this concept. The consummate practitioner, Pelli has completed a number of other large-scale projects in recent years, including the Owens Corning World Headquarters, Aronoff Center for the Arts, Wells Fargo Center, Torre Bank Boston, and the International Finance Center the tallest building in Hong Kong. He also designed Cira Center, and the Minneapolis Central Library.
Cesar Pelli was born in Tucuman, Argentina, and graduated from the University of Tucuman. After immigrating to the U.S. in 1952 and attending the University of Illinois, he worked for Eero Saarinen's firm for ten years, and was in charge of famous projects such as the TWA Terminal Building. Next, as noted above, he joined Gruen Associates. Although there are other famous Argentinean architects such as Emilio Ambasz, and the married team Diana Agrest and Mario Gandelsonas, Cesar Pelli is unquestionably the top foreign-born designer in the American architecture world and an international superstar.

Dominique Perrault

FRANCE

Born in Clermont-Ferrand, France in 1953. Graduated from University No. 6 in 1978 and from Ecole Nationale des Ponts et Chaussees in 1979. Completed a post-graduate degree at Ecole des Hautes Etudes en Sciences Sociales in 1980. From 1980 to 1982, worked at the offices of Martin van Trek, Rune Dotteionde and Antoine Grumbach. Established his own firm in 1981. Worked at the Institute of Urban Development in France from 1982 to 1984. Awarded the Grand Prix National de l'Architecture in 1993, and the Mies van der Rohe Award in 1997.

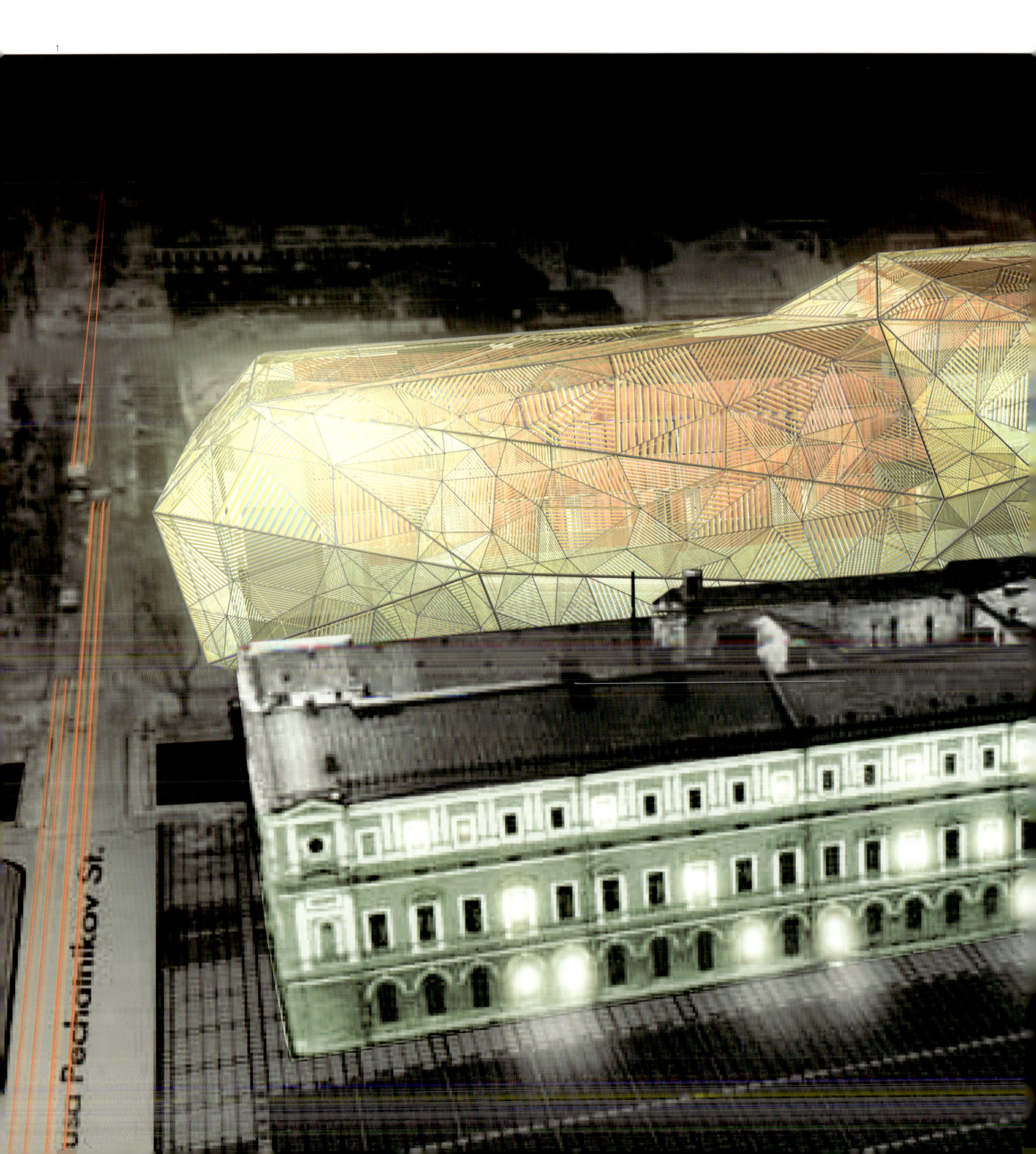

1, 2 Theater Mariinsky / St. Petersburg, Russia

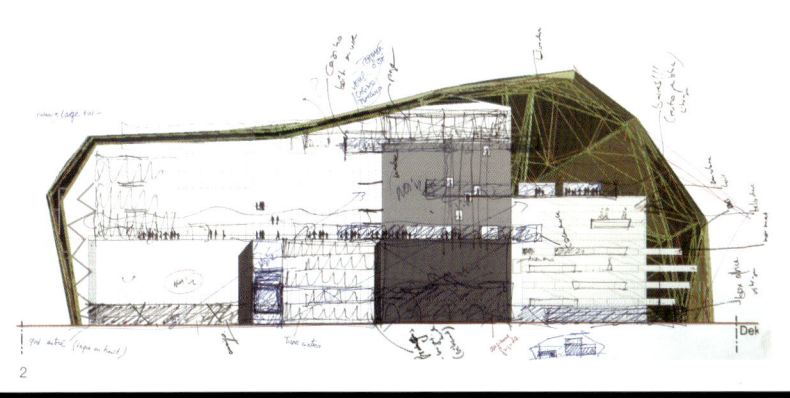

DOMINIQUE PERRAULT

3   Olympic Velodrome and Swimming Pool   1997 / Berlin
    photo: ©Synectics
4   French National Library   1995 / Paris
    photo: ©Synectics
5   KANSAI-KAN of the National Diet Library / Competition
    photo: ©Georges Fessy
6   ESIEE   1987 / Paris
    photo: ©Deidi Von Schaewen
7   Venissieux Central Mediatheque   2001 / Lyon, France
    photo: ©Georges Fessy
8   Aplix Factory   1999 / Le Cellier-sur-Loire, France
    photo: ©Georges Fessy
9   Innsbruck Town Hall   2002 / Innsbruck, Austria
10 Olympic Tennis Center / Madrid
11 Habitat Sky Hotel / Barcelona
12 Extension to the Zurich Landesmuseum / Competition
13 Development Project for Las Teresitas Seafront / Tenerife, Spain

14 Court of Justice of the European Communities / Luxembourg
15 Villa One 1995 / Britanny, France
16 Hotel Industriel Berlier 1990 / Paris
    photo: ©Synectics
17 SAGEP 1993 / Ivry-sur-Seine, France
    photo: ©Michel Denance
18 3* and 4* Hotels / Milan
19 Butterfly Pavilion 2006 / Niigata, Japan
20 Leon Convention Center / Leon, Spain
21 Vienna Sky Tower / Vienna
22 Ewha Woman's University Campus Center / Seoul
23 Piazza Garibaldi / Naples, Italy

photos : Courtesy of the Architect except ©Synectics

The mid-career designer Dominique Perrault is best known for winning the French National Library Competition at the age of 36, and rocketing onto the international scene as the darling of French architecture. Then, after the huge Olympic Velodrome and Swimming Pool project also fell to him, Perrault showed that he had the qualifications to take on two challenging international competitions at once. This made his reputation as a global superstar. The two projects, with their massive citylike scale, serve as excellent examples of the relationship between Perrault's architecture, based on his personal design philosophy, and nature. Perrault's preoccupation with nature approaches land art, and to preserve traces of an overall landscape, including its trees, water, and land, he has devised the technique of making a building vanish by submerging it in its surroundings.

For the French National Library, this meant burying the bulk of the gigantic, 400-meter-long building and leaving only the towers at each of the building's four corners visible. Moreover, Perrault inserted an inner courtyard filled with untamed greenery that is off-limits to people, with the idea that like a garden in a monastery, patrons would be able to immerse themselves in meditation and books as they made their way around the perimeter. The Olympic Velodrome and Swimming Pool too were created by submerging two pure geometric shapes, the circle of the velodrome (cycling track) and the rectangle of the pool, and leaving absolutely no trace of the building above ground. The only thing visible is 400 apple trees planted in the park.

Perrault also used this elimination concept in a slightly different form in his plan for the Kansai-kan of the National Diet Library in Japan. In this design, an artificial landscape was created by chopping down a hill and completely exposing a valley for the site, which made Perrault feel that he had to somehow preserve the natural landscape. To reproduce it, he restored one part of the hill and creating a garden. In the center of the site, he once again buried the library and positioned only the roof above ground, as if it were some high-tech, optical machine. He used similar methods for remarkable works such as Galician Cultural City and Villa One.

It is clear from these examples that Dominique Perrault is an architect with a tremendous respect for the landscape. How did he arrive at this? While working on an earlier design for the ESIEE, an engineering school located outside Paris in Marne-la-Vallee, Perrault first began to take notice of nature. Rather than standing the facade of the huge, white, 300-meter-long building upright, Perrault devised a slanted roof that sloped toward the surface of the ground. He apparently first conceived of "architecture within a landscape" by placing the structure lower to the ground as he attempted to create this massive building in an expanse of nature.

Perrault has been known to remark, "Form is not the problem of architecture." And in fact, much of his work is based on simple squares, rectangles or combinations of the two. Whether the Hotel Industriel Berlier, where Perrault's office was located, Aplix Factory, the SAGEP water treatment plant, the Technical Book Center, Venissieux Central Mediatheque, or M-Preis Supermarket, there is absolutely no sign of any toying with the form. To Perrault, form is the result of process. Another unmistakable characteristic of his work is the use of a yin/yang sort of Japanese dualism. The subterranean French National Library certainly exists, but at the same time seems to express a contradictory state of absence. This paradoxical schema also underlies the huge natural void (read: Imperial Palace) that occupies the heart of the megalopolis of Tokyo.

Defining the entire environment that surrounds him as a natural space, Perrault believes that creating an office in the middle of a city (i.e., nature), is a marvelous way to get energy from all the noise and hubbub. At completing the Innsbruck Town Hall, he is now at work on the Olympic Tennis Center, the Court of Justice of the European Communities, the Habitat Sky Hotel in Barcelona, an extension to the Zürich Landesmuseum, and the Las Teresitas Seafront development project on Tenerife. He has also won competitions for the Mariinsky Theatre in St. Petersburg and Ewha Women's University Campus Center in South Korea, the Vienna Sky Tower, and Three- and Four-Star Hotel in Milan. Perrault also recently completed his first work in Japan, a noh stage called the Butterfly Pavilion. It is clearly a very busy time for him.

Ricardo Porro

FRANCE

Born in Cuba in 1925. After graduating from the University of Havana, studied at the Sorbonne and the Institute of Urban Development in France. Then studied briefly in Venice. Returned to Cuba from 1949 to 1954, where he designed several villas. To escape the revolution, he took asylum in Caracas and taught at the Central University of Venezuela. From 1966 to 1992, taught at numerous schools in France and opened his own firm in Paris.

1

1, 2, 3 School of Plastic Arts 1964 / Havana, Cuba

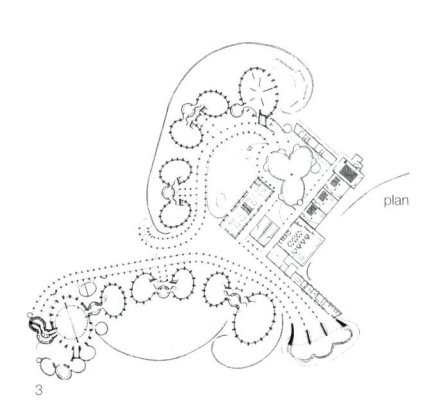

Ricardo Porro

plan

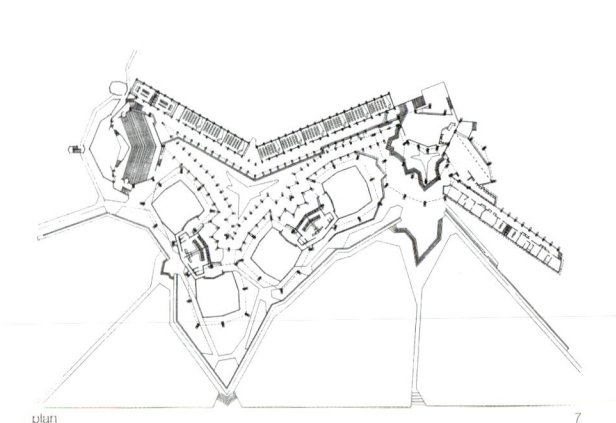

204

4   Villa Armenteros   1950 / Havana, Cuba
5   Sculpture of Mouths / Liechtenstein
6   Office & Art Center   1975 / Liechtenstein
7, 8, 9   School of Modern Dance   1964 / Havana, Cuba
10   College de Cergy-le-Haut   1997 / Cergy-le-Haut, France
11   30 Residential Dwellings in Stains   1991 / Stains, France

12 College Elsa Triolet   1990 / Saint-Denis, France
13, 14 Dwellings in La Courneuve   1995 / La Courneuve, France
15 College Fabien   1993 / Montreuil, France
16 Barracs of the Republican Security Force in Velizy   1991 / Paris

17 Police Headquarter in Plaisir   2006 / Plaisir, France
18 Psychiatric Hospital in Meulan les Mureaux / Meulan les Mureaux, France
19 Students Dwellings in Cergy Pontoise   1994 / Cergy Pontoise, France
20 Restaurant & Hotel, Technical High School in Rouen   2004 / Rouen, France

photos : Courtesy of the Architect

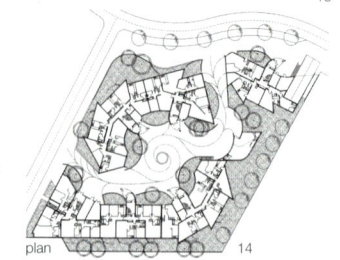

After studying architecture at the University of Havana, Ricardo Porro went to France, where he studied at the Sorbonne and the Institute of Urban Development. Then for a brief period, he studied in Venice. Between 1949 and 1954, Porro returned to Cuba, where he designed his first architectural work, Villa Armenteros. He was 24 and had consciously invoked the spirit of Mies van der Rohe. Then, to avoid getting caught up in the impending revolution, Porro took refuge in Caracas. There, he became involved in the Banco Obrero Housing Project and accepted a teaching post at the Central University of Venezuela.

As the revolution began to die down, Porro returned to Havana, and embarked on a full-fledged career as an architect. He organized a construction project for an art school in Cuba Cabana, and designed the Schools of Plastic Arts and Modern Dance there himself. The buildings are still considered to be some of Porro's most important works.

The School of Plastic Arts, completed when Porro was 38, is the largest work of his career. It was based on the image of a small city. The overall plan comprised an organic structure resembling the female reproductive system. Porro readily admits that the design is erotic in nature: "The building represents Mother Earth, or the act of making love to a woman. The studio represents a woman's breasts, and I positioned a sculpture of a papaya, which in Cuba is a female symbol, in the center of the square. Like thanatos, eros is one of the keys to the human psyche."

The brick domes and vaults at the school are also meant to resemble biological organs. With long corridors that correspond to pipes and rooms that correspond to organs, the interior of the building seems like a womb. The integration of structures such as the studio wing, with its organic curves, and the office wing, with its straight lines, make the work seem both pleasant and stoic. This is in part because of the work's androgynous nature; it is a hybrid form that encompasses both positive and negative, and male and female elements. The School of Modern Dance, completed during the same period on the same site, is the embodiment of a city or town. The placement and form of the school, which represents the early romanticism of the Cuban Revolution, seems to be communicating something. Rather than the biological form used in the School of Plastic Arts, the work has an informal, planar shape similar to a pair of glasses. To Porro, this design symbolized the drastic changes that the

17

18 19 20

Cuban people had gone through in the revolution. Like a pair of fragmented glasses, the studio consists of two spaces and with its centripetal design, the work exudes energy.
In 1960, after completing these two works, Porro moved to France. From then until 1992, he served as an instructor at a variety of different schools. In the meantime, he became a sculptor, and also developed his skills as a painter. This led him to regularly include his own sculptures and paintings in his architectural works. For example, in 1975, Porro added "Sculpture of Mouths," depicting a strange human form, to the Office and Art Center, his first European work. And in the courtyard of the School of Plastic Arts in Havana, he created the aforementioned papaya sculpture as a symbol of the female sexual organ.
In 1986, Porro began working with the architect Renaud de la Noue, and together the two designed 30 Residential Dwellings in Stains as well as the square on the site. From this point on, Porro suddenly became more and more active in France. Among his works were College de Cergy-le-Haut, which referenced the traditional French castle Ch_teaux de la Loire; College Elsa Triolet, which made use of a dove motif; and the La Courneuve Dwellings, notable for its sidewalls, which resemble human ears. In addition, Porro designed College Fabien, a hermaphroditic example of architecture that combined both male and female components, and the Barracks of the Republican Security Force in Velizy, which was inspired by Paulo Uccello's painting "The Battle of San Romano." One after another, all over France in particular, Porro produced organic and androgynous architectural masterworks. With his experiences in Cuba as a foundation, he had become especially deft at designing schools, hence the large number of educational facilities.
Born into a wealthy family and a fervent reader since childhood, Porro came to love Plato, Dante, Thomas Mann, Martin Heidegger and Marcel Proust in his later years. In architecture, he was hugely influenced by Michelangelo, Borromini, Frank Lloyd Wright, and Erik Gunnar Asplund. From his Cuban period, when he deviated from the logic of modern architecture, to his contemporary work, which has been called heretical for its mixture of expressionistic, epicurean, organic, and hermaphroditic elements, Porro has consistently received acclaim for his idiosyncratic exteriors and the stark contrast created by his rich, warm interiors.

Miguel Angel Roca

ARGENTINA

Born in Cordoba, Argentina in 1940. From 1959 to 1965, studied architecture and urban planning at the National University of Cordoba. After completing a postgraduate degree at the University of Pennsylvania, worked under Louis Kahn in 1967 and 1968. Awarded the Gold Medal by the World Biennale of Architecture (Bulgaria) in 1985. Received the Grand Prix at the Buenos Aires International Biennale in 1991. Served as dean of the School of Architecture, Urban Planning and Design at the National University of Cordoba.

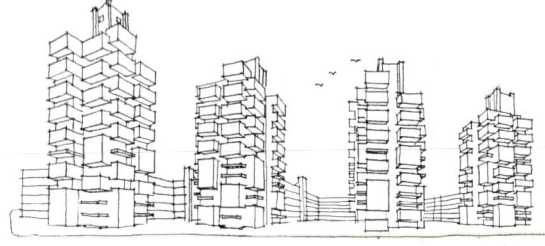

1, 2 Santo Domingo Housing Complex
      1975 / Cordoba, Argentina
3 Plaza de Armas   1981 / Cordoba, Argentina
4 Uruguay Central District Council   1991 / La Paz, Bolivia
5 CPC Route 20   1999 / Cordoba, Argentina
6 School of Arts at the National University of Cordoba
   2001 / Cordoba, Argentina

MIGUEL ANGEL ROCA

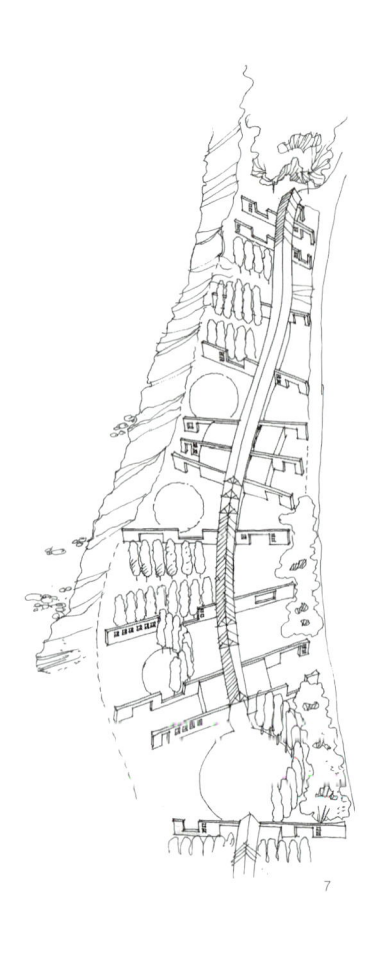

7, 8   La Florida Park   1990 / La Paz, Bolivia
9   Faculty of Law at the National University of Cordoba   2001 / Cordoba, Argentina

10　Cordoba Office Center　1993 / Cordoba, Argentina
11　Post-graduate School of Economics
　　at the National University of Cordoba　2001 / Cordoba, Argentina
12　Paseo De Las Artes Cultural Center　1979 / Cordoba, Argentina
13　Italia Plaza　1980 / Cordoba, Argentina
14　Claustrorum at the National University of Cordoba
　　1998 / Cordoba, Argentina
15　House at Calamuchita　2004 / Cordoba, Argentina
16　Renovation for Corrientes Street
　　2006 / Buenos Aires, Argentina

I have a clear memory from about 20 years ago of something I saw in a foreign architecture magazine. In a square abutting a classical building was a series of white lines depicting a structure in an elevation view. This was Plaza de Armas, a work by the Argentinean architect Miguel Angel Roca.

In later years, I would occasionally spot other works by Roca conveyed from the other side of the globe in a magazine. They were the type of works it was impossible to forget. Partly, this was because the only information about South American architects that made it to Japan was connected to the Brazilian master Oscar Niemeyer.

Born in Cordoba, Roca is an internationally active architect who represents not only Argentina but the whole of South America. Since opening his own firm in 1970, he has been involved in over 150 projects. Roca has worked in La Paz, the capital of neighboring Bolivia, and as far away as South Africa, Morocco, Hong Kong, and Singapore. Fervently involved in educational activities, Roca has taught in Brazil, the U.S., France, Italy as well as Argentina.

Roca's works make use of many different architectural typologies. Among his representative buildings are the Santo Domingo Housing Complex, Plaza de Armas, the Uruguay Central District Council, La Florida Park, CPC Monsenor Pablo Cabrera, the Cordoba Office Center, CPC Route 20, and the Faculty of Law, the School of Arts, the Claustrorum, and the Post-graduate School of Economics at the National University of Cordoba. What distinguishes his works is the element of urban planning that is also present in Plaza de Armas.

Many years ago, the plaza was used as a parking lot. By drawing the outline of the cathedral that stands beside the square, Roca made people on their way to the city aware of the site's cultural and historical importance. He also drove the cars out and returned the square to pedestrians. In the case of Cordoba's Paseo de las Artes Cultural Center, a 19th-century district for working-class residents was set to be destroyed, but Roca decided to preserve several of the dwellings and wall surfaces, and revived the area by creating a small park and a culture center.

Fundamentally, Roca's manner of intervening in a city is, as these projects illustrate, to revitalize an area by inserting "urban fragments." Like Le Corbusier's plans for Rio de Janeiro and Algiers, Roca avoids total urban

17　Spain Plaza　1969 / Cordoba, Argentina
18　CPC Monsenor Pablo Cabrera　1999 / Cordoba, Argentina
19　Underground Passage between Two Museums in Cordoba　2006 / Cordoba, Argentina

photos : Courtesy of the Architect.

planning involving the construction of a new city in place of an already existing one. Moreover, in works like Spain Plaza and Italia Plaza, Roca, a student of Louis Kahn, achieved a special charm by filling the sites with swinging, heavy geometrical objects of the kind that Kahn used in his non-residential works.
La Florida Park, in La Paz, is one of Roca's most poetic and moving works. On a long, thin site along a river stands a roofed colonnade that undulates like a snake. Intersecting it at many points are reinforced concrete walls, which create a wondrous and tension-filled urban space as ambiguous fragments arranged in a line.
The surfaces of the numerous walls are painted brilliant colors that resemble those of _awayo_, the traditional Indio belts worn by women. They are also similar to the pink wall surfaces used by Luis Barragan in San Cristobal, and the two works both have large wall openings. Barragan once wrote, "The garden is poetic, mysterious, enchanting, serene, and enjoyable." In the shade of the trees that is cast across the colorful, Latin-style walls in the park, one detects the "spatial poetry" that underlies Barragan's work.
Miguel Angel Roca was a precocious child born to a Cordoba architect. Except for an interest in drawing, the young Roca showed no inclinations toward architecture. But he went on to do post-graduate work at the University of Pennsylvania with Louis Kahn, and later worked at Kahn's firm. Roca sees architecture as something that is much more than a simple method of aesthetic expression and serves as a sociopolitical medium that provides physical shelter and structures an environment. In addition to the poetic flavor of his work, one finds political overtones. As a result, some have come to refer to Roca's work as "poetic-political" architecture.
Along with the recently completed House at Calamuchita, at the end of 2005, Roca finished large, urban works such as Underground Museum Passage in Cordoba and Renovation for Corrientes Street.

Aldo Rossi

ITALY

Born in Milan in 1931. Graduated from Politecnico di Milano in 1959, and opened his own firm the same year. Taught at the University Iuav of Venice and Politecnico di Milano. Member of the editorial board at the architectural journal _Casabella Continuita_ from 1961 to 1964. Beginning in 1971, taught for several years in Switzerland. Became a professor at University Iuav of Venice in 1975. Awarded the Pritzker Prize in 1990. Died in a car accident in 1997.

1 Bonnefanten Museum 1994 / Maastricht, The Netherlands
  photo: ©Synectics
2 Renovation & Extension of the School in Broni 1970 / Broni, Italy
3 Fagano Olona School 1972 / Varese, Italy
4 Hotel il Palazzo 1989 / Fukuoka, Japan
  photo: ©Synectics
5 San Cataldo Cemetery 1984 / Modena, Italy
  photo: ©Synectics

ALDO ROSSI

6 Teatro del Mondo   1980 / Venice
7 Carlo Felice Theater   1990 / Genova, Italy
8 Tower Shopping Center   1985 / Parma, Italy
9, 10 Casa Aurora   1987 / Turin, Italy
11 Ambiente Showroom   1991 / Tokyo
    photo: ©Synectics
12 Asaba Design Office   1991 / Tokyo
    photo: ©Synectics
13, 14 Mojiko Hotel   1998 / Fukuoka, Japan
15, 16 Celebration Building   1996 / Orlando, Florida

8

9

10

11

12

13

14

15

16

217

Aldo Rossi

17, 18 Scholastic Building   2001 / New York
19 ABC Building   2000 / Burbank, California
photo: ©Synectics
20 Gallaratese Housing   1970 / Milan, italy
21 Pocono Pine House   1989 / Mount Pocono, Pennsylvania

On November 28, 1989, an opening reception was held at the Hotel Il Palazzo, Aldo Rossi's masterwork in Fukuoka. Dubbed the "hotel that never sleeps," the magnificent Palazzo captured the attention of people all around the world. Inside the hotel, there was a bar designed by Rossi and Shiro Kuramata, Gaetano Pesce, and Ettore Sottsass, which made it easy to see why no one was getting any sleep. That night, Rossi himself was behind the bar, pouring out glasses of his favorite _sake_ for architects and journalists from around the country. I was also fortunate to be there. That night Rossi seemed to shine with a special brilliance – and that was just as it should have been. Compared to his works of the past, with their rather paltry materials, splendid things had been used to create this building, and with input from a host of first-rate designers, the hotel was brimming with examples of great design. The facade, constructed of red, round travertine columns and a blue-green, copper platband, has a hardened, taciturn expression. There is a silence here similar to that in de Chirico's metaphysical paintings which express the gloom of the city. This empty, desolate atmosphere that is such a special part of Rossi's works can be traced back to early works such as the renovation of a school in Broni and another school project in Fagano Olona. But where does the atmosphere come from?

In 1971, Rossi was involved in a car accident that completely changed his life. Having come face-to-face with death, he began to see the city as a huge encampment for the living and the cemetery as a city of the dead. The concept for San Cataldo Cemetery, which Rossi developed during his stay in the hospital, was recognized as the most outstanding entry in the competition. Projected onto this necropolis was Rossi's own sense of anxiety and fear of death.

Born the son of a Milan bicycle manufacturer in 1931, Rossi studied architecture and film at the Polytechnic University of Milan. In time, his compulsive attraction to film shifted to architecture, and his interest in theater grew stronger. Rossi once reminisced, "In my architecture lies an unending fascination with the theater." In 1979, Rossi designed the Teatro del Mondo for the Venice Biennale. The small wooden building with a seating capacity of 250 is a "floating theater" located in one of Venice's canals. Explaining the work, Rossi said, "This is a place where architecture ends and a world of imagination begins." Following this work, Rossi designed the Carlo Felice Theatre in Genoa. By applying the motif of a

22 Vassiviere Art Center   1991 / Bess-et-Saint-Anastasise, France
    photo: ©Jaques Hoepffer / Courtesy of the Art Center
23 IBA Housing at Wilhelmstrasse   1984 / Berlin
    photo: ©Synectics
24 IBA Housing at Thomas Dehler Strasse   1986 / Berlin
    photo: ©Synectics
25 Sandro Pertini Monument   1988 / Milan
    photo: ©Synectics
26 IBA Housing at Schutzenstrasse   1999 / Berlin
    photo: ©Synectics
27 Wohnanlage La Villette   1991 / Paris
    photo: ©Synectics
28 Fontivegge Directional & Commercial Center   1988 / Perugia, Italy

photos : Courtesy of Morris Adjmi except ©Synectics and ©Jaques Hoepffer

town square to the interior, Rossi arrived at an excellent work which, in his familiar style, established a close link with the city.

Rossi's work is called "analogical architecture." For example, he sometimes referred to a painting of Venice by the 18th-century Italian painter Canaletto which hangs in the National Gallery in Parma. In the painting one finds further references to three works by Palladio: "Design for the Rialto Bridge," "Basilica," and "Palazzo Chiericati." The subjects of the latter two are Vicenza rather than Venice. Therefore, Rossi explained, the city in the picture is an analogy for Venice, and this is what inspired his analogical architecture.

The foundations of Rossi's analogical architecture are the old barn, corridor, factory, silo, and warehouse that slumbered in the depths of his memory. These surreal and plain forms that seem to have been frozen in time served as an analogy for the rational architecture of the Gallaratese Housing Complex. The conjoined walls and columns and the long corridors give the building a terse, metaphysical air.

In the 80s, Rossi began work on a housing complex as part of the International Building Exposition (IBA) in Berlin, and at the same time, in Italy, he developed large works such as the Centro Torri Shopping Center and Casa Aurora. Following the completion of the Il Palazzo, Rossi also created a series of works in Japan. These eight buildings include the Ambiente Showroom, Asaba Design Office, and Mojiko Hotel. He also pursued a successful collaboration with the noted Japanese designer Shigeru Uchida.

In 1990, Rossi was awarded the Pritzker Prize, which is considered to be the Nobel Prize of the architecture world. Next, he expanded his activities around the globe. In particular, Rossi's many works in the U.S., including the Celebration Building, the Pocono Pines House, the ABC Building, and the Scholastic Building. In addition, as seen in works such as the Bonnefanten Museum in Holland and the Center for Contemporary Art in Vassiviere in France, Rossi's work became elegant and beautiful.

However, in 1997, Rossi was again involved in a car accident. This time the man whose life had been so greatly altered by a crash lost his life. I still have fond memories of drinking _sake_ with him at Il Palazzo, and appearing on TV together at the Rossi exhibition in Ginza. His death at 66 occurred far too soon and left many sad people behind as the master architect flitted across the skies of Lombardia.

Roto Architects

USA

Firm founded by Michael Rotondi, who was born in Los Angeles in 1949. Graduated from the Southern California Institute of Architecture (SCI-Arc) in 1973, and has taught at the same institution since 1976. In 1975, established Morphosis with Thom Mayne. The two continued their partnership until 1991, when Rotondi founded Roto Architects. In addition to being one of the "founder-students" of SCI-Arc, also served as director of the school for ten years from 1987 to 1997.

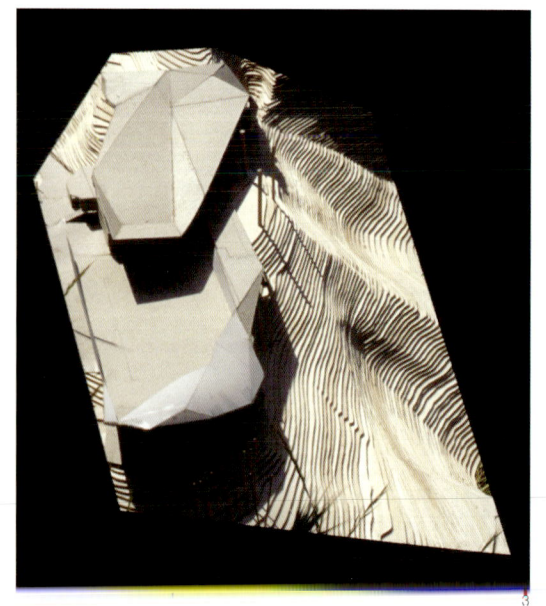

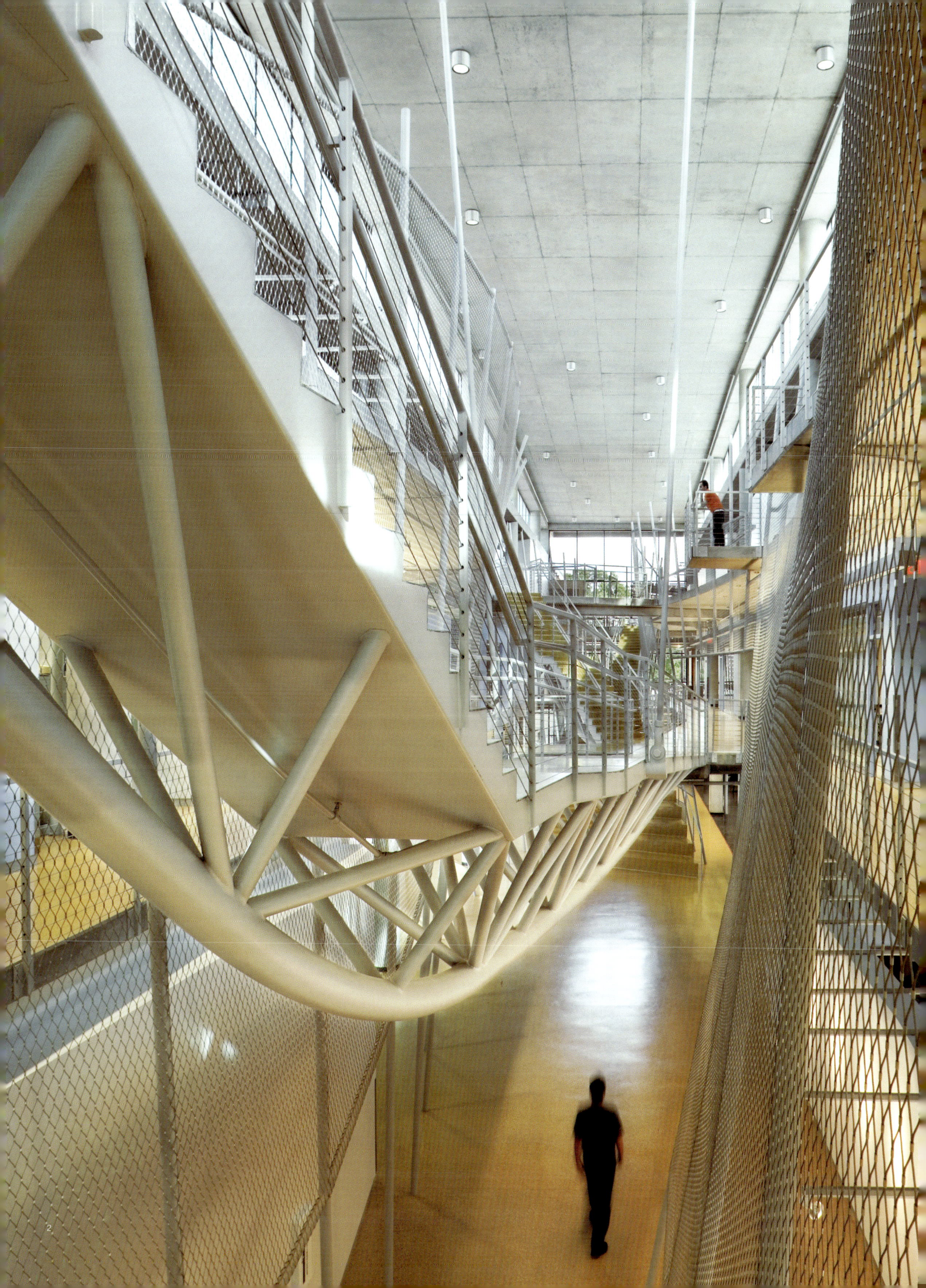

2

Roto Architects

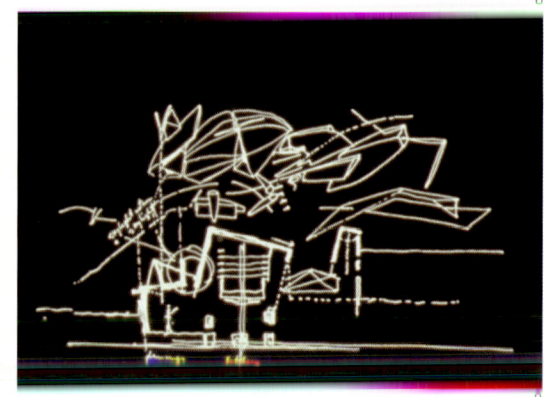

11

1, 2 Architecture and Art Building at Prairie View A&M
     University   2005 / Prairie View, Texas
3, 4 Oak Pass House
  5 Warehouse C   1999 / Nagasaki, Japan
  6 Restaurant Nicola   1993 / Los Angeles
  7 Carlson Reges House   1998 / Los Angeles
8, 9 New Jersey House
     1996 / Barnerdsville, New Jersey
 10 Sinte Gleska University
     1999 / Antelope, South Dakota
11, 12 Dorland Mountain Arts Colony
     1994 / Temecula, California

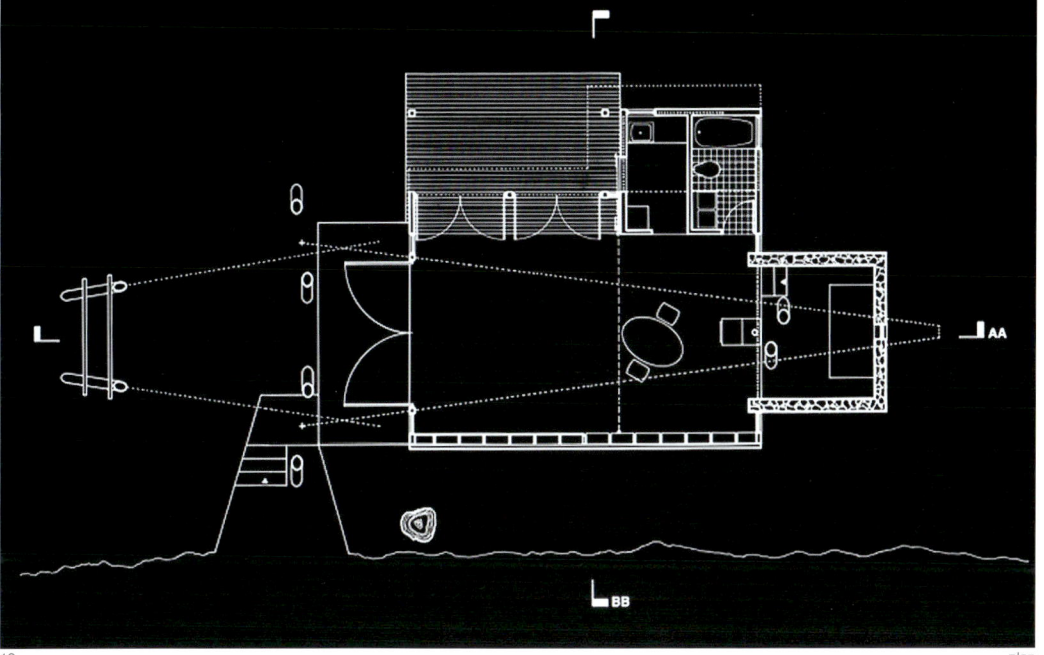

12

plan

223

ROTO ARCHITECTS

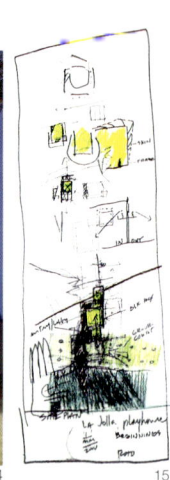

13	Cliffside House
14, 15	La Jolla Playhouse at UCSD 2005 / La Jolla, California
16	Miracle Manor Retreat 1998 / Desert Hot Springs, California
17	Pacoima Neighborhood City Hall / Pacoima, California
18	Forest Refuge
19	Hollywood Orange / Hollywood
20	Vogt Industrial Commons
21	100,000 Stupas / Santa Cruz, California
22	Stillpoints Exhibition (SCI-Arc) 2004 / Los Angels

photos : Courtesy of the Architect.

Against the bleak urban landscape of the harbor facilities, a stone causing many ripples in the design world was tossed into the bay. At a Mitsubishi Heavy Industries warehouse in Nagasaki Port, a topology called Warehouse C was created by Michael Rotondi as his debut work in Japan.

On the roof of the Warehouse, a traditional garden, open to the public, was covered with a large, lightweight sunshade made of Teflon and enclosed in a steel frame that resembled a ship's sail. The dynamic form added a bright spot to the shipyard.

The huge, confounding orange orb bobbing over the roof only strengthened the image. It was also interesting that when the orange ball suddenly appeared in one's field of view as one walked through the city, it created a sense of displacement. The interior of the orb was used as an event space.

Rotondi, who originally formed a partnership with Thom Mayne called Morphosis, founded his own office, Roto Architects, in 1991. During the Morphosis era, Rotondi was accustomed to working with the mass media, but he says he is now more hesitant to show his works. His interest lies in environmental issues, scientific paradigms, and participatory design. The design process favored by Rotondi and his partner Clark Stevens comprises analysis and hypotesis, the intuitive selecting and combining of possibilities, and a certain amount of trial and error.

In the architects' office, there is a very average CAD station, and a segmented, dissected revolving model, and only five meters away, a meeting table covered with a wide roll of paper. There are management diagrams, sectional site plans, capacity plans, construction sketches, and telephone messages strewn across the tabletop.

This long table is the office diary as well as its laboratory and playground. It is from here that spaces are configured and structures are shaped. In other words, design at Roto Architects is practiced through meticulous surveys and research, and various graphic representations of data.

The simple but elegant tent-based interior design Rotondi produced for Nicola Restaurant not long after leaving Morphosis was a topic of much conversation. And his design vocabulary took shape in the 1996 work, New Jersey House. For this large villa, built on an Arcadian lot in the Eastern U.S. state, Rotondi made use of fragmentation, a technique at which he is very adept.

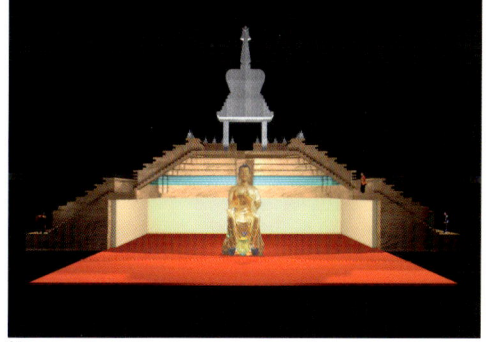

The building, structured in nearly pavilion-like sections, was meticulously handcrafted out of materials like natural stone, plaster, fir, and lead-coated steel plates. By disconnecting and dividing the space, natural light bathes the interior, creating a variety of volumes and surface layers.

Roto Architects is housed in a renovated brewery. The private residence of the building's owner, Carlson-Reges House (also designed by the firm) also creates a sense of dépaysement. It looks as if Mad Max had visited Pierre Chareau's Glass House. The intricate, vertigo-inducing space is truly a sight to see with an assemblage of objets trouvés. Similarly, the Dorland Mountain Arts Colony, located in the mountains west of Palm Springs, was cobbled together out of an artful bricolage of objets trouvés and natural materials found nearby and unified in a rough-tech style similar to that of Eric Owen Moss. It is a primitive hut designed and constructed by the firm. Among Roto Architects' other works (completed and uncompleted) in California are Oak Pass House, Cliffside House, and the La Jolla Playhouse at UC San Diego.

In 1993, the firm began jointly designing Sinte Gleska University, the oldest Native American college, located in Todd County, South Dakota, with the local Lakota people. For this project the architects brought to life the traditional teaching of the tribal elders – i.e., "a system of movement and breath – there is an interdependence of all things, which are fundamentally connected, in Heaven and on Earth." The work is an excellent example of Rotondi's skillful use of participatory design. The Architecture and Art Building at Prairie View, part of A&M University, is the firm's greatest recent work, while Miracle Manor Retreat is another notable completed building, and others such as the Hollywood Orange and Pacoima Neighborhood City Hall are currently underway.

Sauerbruch Hutton

GERMANY

Firm founded by Matthias Sauerbruch and Louisa Hutton in 1989. Sauerbruch was born in Germany in 1955, and graduated from the Universität der Künste and the AA School of Architecture in 1984. Taught at Berlin Technical University from 1995 to 2001. Hutton was born in England in 1957, and graduated from Bristol University in 1980, and the AA School in 1985.

1 N House   1999 / London
   photo: ©Bitter+Bredt
2 H House   1995 / London
   photo: ©Bitter+Bredt

4 Photonikzentrum   1998 / Berlin
   photo: ©Bitter+Bredt
5, 6 GSW Headquarters   1999 / Berlin
   photo: ©Annette Kisling

6
plan

7, 8 Federal Agency for the Environment 2005 / Dessau, Germany photo: ©Jan Bitter	11 Zumzobel Staff 1999 / Berlin photo: ©Bitter+Bredt
9 Experimental Factory in Magdeburg 2001 / Magdeburg, Germany photo: ©Gerrit Engel	12 Pharmacological Research Laboratories in Biberach 2002 / Biberach, Germany photo: ©Jan Bitter
10 Hennigsdorf Town Hall 2003 / Hennigsdorf, Germany photo: ©Bitter+Bredt	13 The British Council in Germany 2000 / Berlin photo: ©Bitter+Bredt

7 8

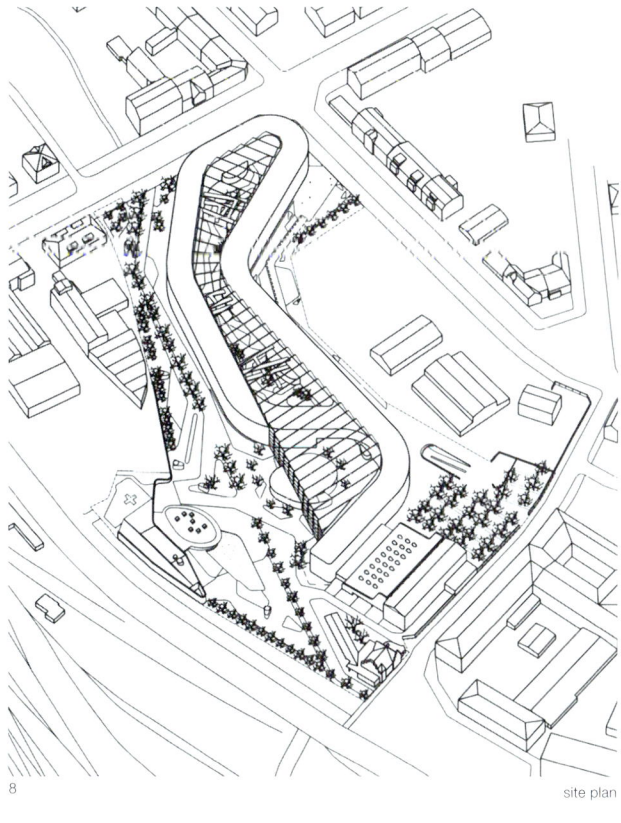

site plan

11 12 13

229

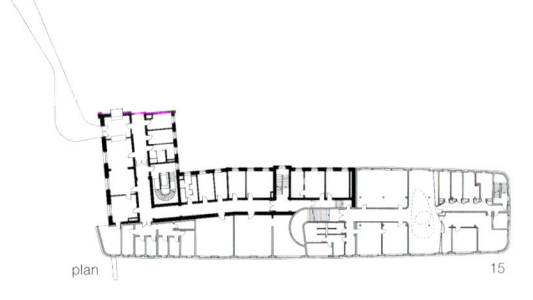

14, 15 Berlin Fire & Police Station for the Government District   2004 / Berlin
photo: ©Bitter+Bredt

16 Offices for the KfW Banking Group / Frankfurt
photo: ©Lepkowski Studios

17 Museum for the Brandhorst Collection / Munich, Germany
photo: ©Lepkowski Studios

18 High-Bay Warehouse for Sedus   2003 / Dogern, Germany
photo: ©Jan Bitter

19 Jessop West Building at Sheffield University / Sheffield, UK
photo: ©Lepkowski Studios

20 ADAC Headquarters / Munich, Germany
photo: ©Simone Rosenberg

photos : Courtesy of the Architect

Friedrichstrasse runs north-south through northeastern Berlin. It is an avenue that is lined with works by renowned architects, including Jean Nouvel, I.M. Pei, Oswald Mathias Ungers, Philip Johnson, Rem Koolhaas, and Peter Eisenman.
In addition, in the area around Kochstrasse, which cuts across Friedrichstrasse from east to west, there are many other works by noted designers such as Vittorio Gregotti, Aldo Rossi, Raimund Abraham, and John Hejduk. Looking east from this intersection, a fairly high red and orange building with a slightly curved facade stands majestically near the next intersection. This is the GSW Headquarters, a noted work by Sauerbruch Hutton.
Matthias Sauerbruch and Louisa Hutton met while they were both studying at the AA School. For five years after graduation, they taught at the school, and Sauerbruch worked with Elia Zenghelis, while Hutton was associated with Alison and Peter Smithson. The couple then relocated to Berlin, as the city seemed to be speeding headlong into the future.
During their time in London, the pair were primarily involved in the renovation of private residences such as N House, H House, and L House, but to heighten the effect of their work, they added strong colors. Whether Sauerbruch Hutton's use of color is part of the actual architecture or a visual presentation, the technique has the potential to change a given set of conditions and transform a space without actually altering its physical dimensions.
In Berlin at the time, Aldo Rossi's concept of "critical reconstruction" was being applied to "urban architecture." This called for the identification of the city's culture based on the memory of its buildings, in other words, by maintaining a set of typological circumstances, it was suggested that architecture which was based primarily on the traditions of Berlin could be created.
The first work Sauerbruch Hutton designed in Berlin was the Photonikzentrum. With an amoeba-like, free-curving plan, the building consists of two glass-covered wings. What immediately catches the eye are the colorful venetian blinds inside, which strongly assert the presence of the building despite its rather low height.
The pair's second work in Berlin, the GSW Headquarters, was even more extraordinary. For this expansion project, Sauerbruch Hutton broadened the curved, wide facade, which faced west, to seemingly conceal the

preexisting structure. Made entirely of glass, the facade comprises a double wall with a one-meter wide airspace. In addition, by equipping the airspace with vertical louvers, the surface can be changed to appear red, pink, orange, ocher or white. And because each room has its own louvers, the facade is all the more attractive for its daily variations.

Sauerbruch says, "We discovered that a space could be visually expanded through the use of color." Although the physical limitations of the lot couldn't be altered, the use of various tones and hues made it possible to express depth and movement in a space. Like the masters of color, El Lissitzky and Josef Albers, the pair ultimately use color to create a kind of emotional expression that is similar to music.

Among Sauerbruch Hutton's other works are the Experimental Factory in Magdeburg, enveloped in a striped curtain of color that runs from the building's exterior walls to its roof; the British Council in Germany, with its colorful patterned ceiling; the Zumtobel Staff Lighting Showroom, also in Berlin, where light plays off the bluish interior; the Pharmacological Research Laboratories in Biberach, and the Berlin Fire and Police Station for the Government District with their colorful exterior walls; Hennigsdorf Town Hall, notable for the circular design of its upper section; the High-Bay Warehouse for Sedus Stoll, with its rectangular elevation covered with a colorful mosaic; and the Federal Environmental Agency in Dessau which boasts a long, curved, snakelike form.

Projects by Sauerbruch Hutton that are currently underway are the Museum for the Brandhorst Collection, the KfW Banking Group Headquarters, the Jessop West Building at Sheffield University, and the ADAC Headquarters. All of these works are sure to be subjects of conversation once they are completed.

SCHMIDT HAMMER LASSEN

DENMARK

Established in 1986, the firm's five principals include Morten Schmidt (born in 1956, graduated from the Aarhus School of Architecture in 1982), Kim Holst Jensen (born in 1964, graduated from the Aarhus School of Architecture in 1991), John Foldbjerg Lassen (born in 1953, graduated from the Aarhus School of Architecture in 1983), Bjarne Hammer (born in 1955, graduated from the Aarhus School of Architecture in 1982), and Morten Holm (born in 1968, graduated from the Aarhus School of Architecture in 1994).

1 Performers House / Sikleborg, Denmark
2 Amazon Court / Prague, Czech
3 Thor Heyerdahl College / Larvik, Norway
4 Aberdeen University Library / Aberdeen, UK
5, 6 Aarhus Museum of Modern Art (ARoS)   2004 / Aarhus, Denmark

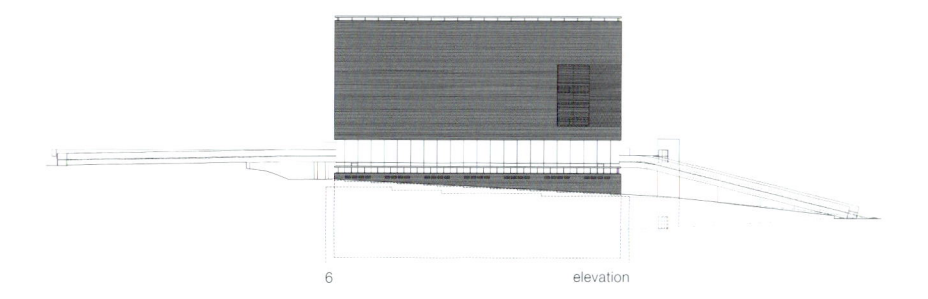

6   elevation

axonometric projection

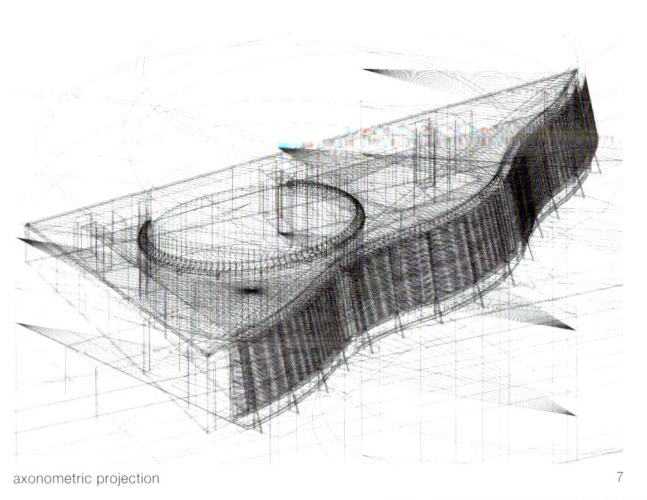

10 axonometric projection

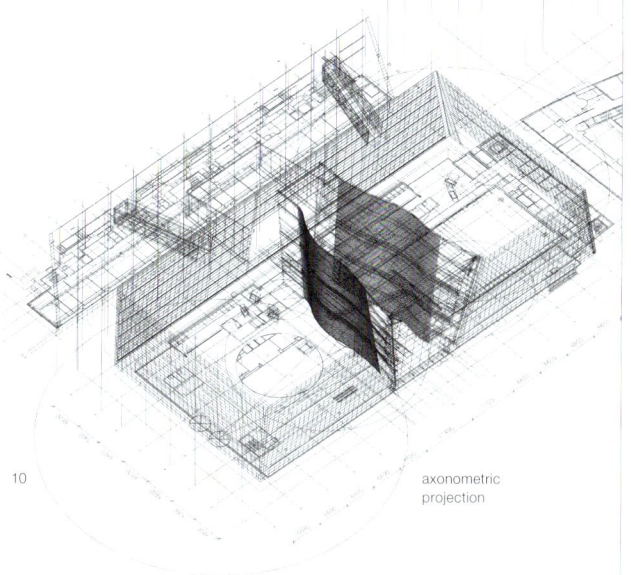

13

7, 8   Culture Center   1997 / Nukk, Greenland
9, 10 The Danish Royal Library   1999 / Copenhagen
11   Cathedral of Northern Lights / Alta, Norway
12   Halmstad Library   2006 / Halmstad, Sweden
photo: ©Adam Mork
13   FLAKES

Schmidt Hammer Lassen (SHL) arrived on the international architecture scene just as the 20th century was on the way out, with the important 1999 work, The Danish Royal Library. Until then, the firm was almost completely unknown in Japan. Most of the architects' work is in fact in their home country, Denmark, but in 1997, SHL completed its first major foreign project, the Culture Center in Greenland. After that, the firm went completely international, clenching a number of foreign competitions including the Cathedral of Northern Lights in Norway, Halmstad Library in Sweden, and Strasbourg Library in France. In Finland, the firm also developed FLAKES, a colorful and transparent, fiberglass stacking chair, for the Piiroinen furniture company. The architects then began targeting the U.S. and Japan.

The Royal Library, which brought SHL almost immediate international attention, is a shiny, black mass that stands next to the Sydhavnen Canal in the Slotsholmen district of Copenhagen. Dubbed the "Black Diamond," the building, covered in Nero Zimbabwe, a type of granite from South Africa, has a sharp image. The building's interior offers an excellent example of one of SHL's design characteristics. The massive atrium is a dynamic space created by the curved walls on each floor and the long travelator. The firm went on to use a similar technique for the Aarhus Museum of Modern Art (ARoS), completed in 2004. Standing atop a grassy expanse, ARoS is a red cube with a white interior. The volume of red bricks used for the building is approximately 50 meters by 50 meters by 50 meters. Its simple exterior is common in SHL's work. But as with the interior of The Royal Library, an astounding space awaits inside. In the huge chalk atrium, with its large curved surfaces, an ascending spiral slope creates a beautiful and vibrant architectural aesthetic. This is the second important feature of SHL's work. While attempting to solve functional, practical, and financial problems with its work, SHL also strives to create work that is somehow daring and challenging. And the atrium in the library, sandwiched between curved walls, and the spiral slope in ARoS are exactly that. The Nykredit New Headquarters, completed in 2001, also drew attention for its exceptional design, featuring a box-shaped conference hall which floats in the seven-level breezeway of the atrium by means of a suspension system. Often emerging victorious at competitions, SHL has many projects lined up for the future.

14 Nykredit New Headquarters 2001 / Copenhagen
15 Testrup Folk High School 1999 / Marslet, Denmark
16 Culture Island in Middelfart 2005 / Middelfart, Denmark
    photo: ©Thomas Molvig
17 Sparekassen Ostjylland 2005 / Hammel, Denmark
    photo: ©Thomas Molvig
18 The Frigate Jylland 2005 / Ebeltoft, Denmark
    photo: ©Frigate Erik
19 Residential Scheme in Jelling / Jelling, Denmark

photos : Courtesy of the Architect

Scheduled for completion in 2007 is the Performers House in Denmark; in 2008, the Amazon Court in the Czech Republic; in 2009, Thor Heyerdahl College in Norway; and in 2011, Aberdeen University Library in Scotland. From this list, it's clear that the firm's outstanding brand of design has been recognized throughout Europe.

Perhaps the key to the high-quality work SHL has created lies in the excellent organizational structure of the firm. In addition to SHL's specialty in building design, the firm includes four separate divisions which support its architectural projects: a special project division, a furniture and fittings division, a landscape design division, and a graphic design (communications) division.

Founded in 1986 by Morten Schmidt, Bjarne Hammer, and John Lassen, some 20 years later, SHL has grown into one of the largest architectural firms in Denmark, with a staff of over 100 people. Following the later addition of Kim Holst Jensen, and more recently Morten Holm, the firm now operates on a five-partner structure. And despite his long career with SHL, at 52, Lassen is still a young man. After graduating form the Architecture School at the University of Aarhus, the founding members set up SHL's main office in Aarhus and a branch in Copenhagen. The architects, whose modus operandi calls for assembling a good team to create design, say, "Architecture today is extremely complicated and it's very difficult for only one architect to see to the design, engineering and management of a project. To realize quality architecture, a team of strong individuals is necessary. What's most important is how well these individuals can join forces to make a solid collaborative unit." This knowing outlook ranks with Renzo Piano's admirable observation, "The creation of architecture isn't the result of the efforts of a single person, but the gift of teamwork."

SNOHETTA

NORWAY

Firm founded in Oslo in 1987. Current principals are Craig Dykers (born in Frankfurt in 1961; American nationality), who graduated from the University of Texas in 1985, and Kjetil Thorsen (born in Norway in 1958), who graduated from the Technical University of Graz in 1985. Snohetta is both an architecture and a landscape architecture firm.

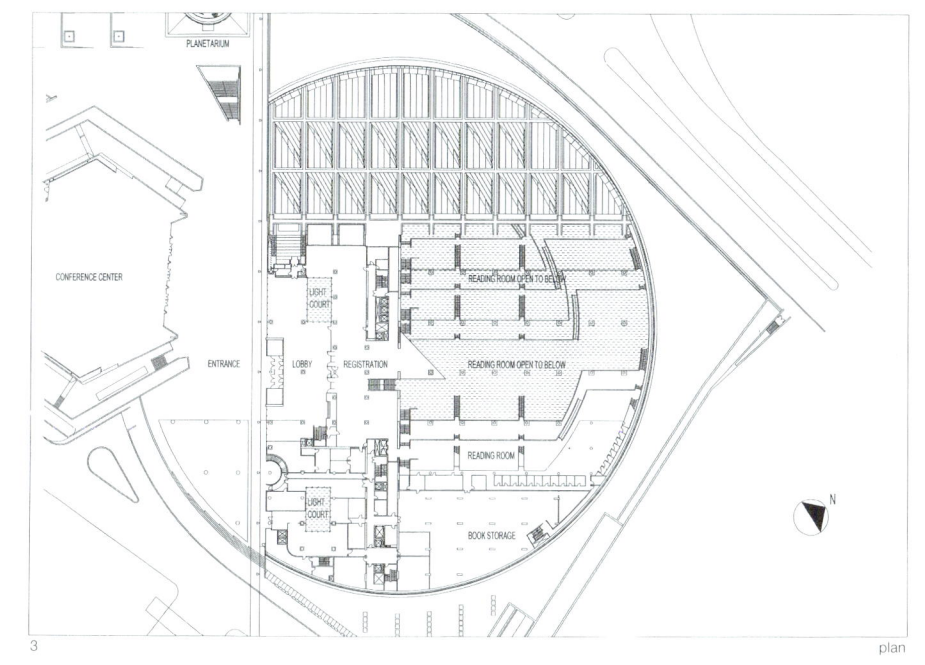

1 KHIB-National Academy of the Arts in Bergen / Bergen, Norway
2, 3 Alexandria Library   2002 / Alexandria, Egypt
photo: ©Gerald Zugman

Snohetta

4　New National Opera House / Oslo, Norway
5　Hamar Town Hall　2001 / Hamar, Norway
　　photo: ©Damian Heinisch
6　Institute for Neurobiologie in Marseilles　2003 / Marseilles, France

7　Olafia Urban Plaza　1998 / Oslo, Norway
8　Karmoy Fishing Museum　1998 / Karmoy, Norway
　　photo: ©Arfo
9　Lillehammer Olympic Art Museum　1993 / Lillehammer, Norway
　　photo: ©Arfo
10, 11　The Royal Norwegian Embassy in Berlin　1999 / Berlin
　　photo: ©Arfo

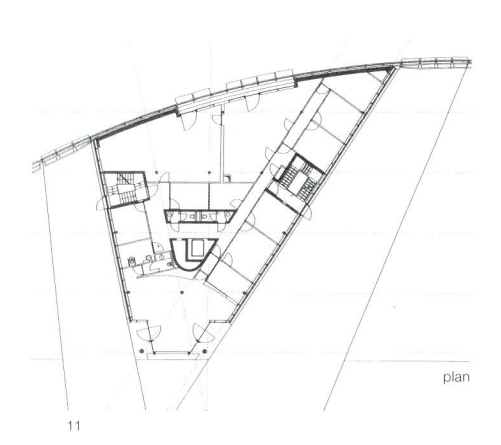

plan

In November 1994, I paid a visit to the Snohetta offices in the dead of winter in the frozen city of Oslo. I decided to go then because it seemed as if the Alexandria Library, a commission the firm won in a 1989 competition, was near completion. But contrary to my expectations, it was daunting to think that construction would so on be starting.

On the way out, I was given a pamphlet about the firm titled "Arkitektguiden Snohetta." On the cover was a photograph of a geometrical construction made out of folded paper like origamic architecture in the palm of a person's hand. This proposal for the Nara Convention Hall was selected as one of the five best entries in the design competition. The architectural form, created by folding and bending a piece of paper that was identical in shape to the lot, was a typical Snohetta design, a mental operation that was based on the landscape of the proposed site.

The firm also entered the competition for the Kansai branch of the National Diet Library. The highly-acclaimed design was based on a clear-cut planar structure that was divided vertically into six sections to form a unique space. This was integrated with a roof design that comprised glass slits as well as complex twists. Having entered two competitions in Japan, Snohetta seems to have a special interest in the country. The fact that one of the judges in the Alexandria Library competition was Fumihiko Maki may also have something to do with it.

Snohetta was formed in 1987 as an architecture collective consisting of people from many different countries. At present, the firm is overseen by Craig Dykers and Kjetil Thorsen. The group's name is derived from a celestial, snow-capped mountain that is located in Norway. Rather than simply focusing on architectural design, a number of the group's members specialize in landscape architecture. According to company data from several years ago, 31 of Snohetta's 52 workers are architects, nine landscape architects, and five interior designers (the remaining seven are office workers). Clearly, Snohetta places great importance on landscape design.

One good example is Sonja Henie Plaza in the center of Oslo. The square serves as a transportation nexus while also existing as an independent architectural element in the middle of a cluster of buildings. The retaining walls on the ramps have a colorful appearance and the landscape design exudes an exciting

12	Arnes Street Rehabilitation 2001 / Arnes, Norway
13	Sonja Henie Plaza 1989 / Oslo, Norway
	photo: ©Synectics
14	Turner Center 2005 / Margate, UK
15	Toyen Culture Park 1994 / Oslo, Norway
16	Bjornson's Garden 1996 / Oslo, Norway
	photo: ©Snohetta
17	Nara Convention Hall / Competition
18	WTC Cultural Center / New York
19	Artesia 2002 / Oslo, Norway
	photo: ©Damian Heinisch
20	Morild Lighting Design 2002 / Skien, Norway

photos : Courtesy of the Architect except ©Synectics

atmosphere. Other examples of the group's landscape design include Toyen Culture Park, Bjornson's Garden, the Arnes Street Rehabilitation, and Olafia Urban Plaza. In addition, Snohetta managed to take a program to integrate doctors, patients, treatments, and a hospital into one community and turn it into a comprehensive landscape at the New Oslo Municipal Hospital. Here the architecture becomes the landscape, and the landscape becomes the architecture.
Snohetta beat out a number of other strong contenders in the international competition for Alexandria Library, one of the group's most important works and one which brought it worldwide fame. Fourteen years in the making, the library is the largest facility of its type in the Middle East and is imbued with a wealth of architecture, history, culture, and landscape.

Built by Ptolemy I in 295 BC, it was originally the largest library in the world, housing a collection of 500,000 books that represented the wisdom of Greco-Roman culture. As a base for Mediterranean culture, it is said that the venerable library was used by noted figures such as Euclid and Archimedes.
The new building features a diagonally-cut cylinder with a diameter of 160 meters which extends 32 meters above the ground and twelve meters below it, and a lowered fifth facade (ceiling). These were extracted from the ancient ground level and exposed to act as a symbol of knowledge passing into the future. The slanted glass ceiling, covered with a grid pattern, functions as a skylight and window, incorporating Alexandria's vivid blue sea into the work.
In the time that it took Snohetta to complete

the building, the firm also finished the Lillehammer Olympic Art Museum, Karmoy Fishing Museum, the Royal Norwegian Embassy in Berlin, Hamar Town Hall, and the Institute for Neurobiology in Marseilles. In 2005, Snohetta also went on to complete the Turner Center in England. This work is a unique structure which stands near a historic bridge and is situated on the water's edge.
In 2008, Snohetta is set to create a beautiful New National Opera House on a manmade plateau floating in the sea along Oslo's coastline. At almost the same time, the firm will be working on the WTC Culture Center in New York, and in 2009, the National Academy of the Arts in Bergen is also scheduled to be completed.

Paolo Soleri

ITALY/USA

Born in Turin, Italy in 1919. Completed a doctorate at Politecnico di Torino in 1946. Worked under Frank Lloyd Wright in 1947. Established the non-profit, educational organization the Cosanti Foundation in 1956. Received the American Institute of Architects' Gold Medal for Craftsmanship in 1963. In 1981, awarded the Gold Medal by the World Biennale of Architecture, and in 2000, the Leone d'oro by the Venice Architecture Biennale.

1

1, 2, 3   Arcosanti   1970– / Cordes Junction, Arizona

2   photo: ©Ivan Pintar

3   photo: ©Jeffrey Manta

photo: ©Cosanti Foundation

245

Paolo Soleri

4   Dome House   1949 / Cave Creek, Arizona
    photo: ©Cosanti Foundation
5   Solimene Ceramics Factory   1953 / Vietri sul Mare, Italy
    photo: ©Robert Vignoli
6   Paolo Soleri Theater   1966 / Santa Fe, New Mexico
    photo: ©Cosanti Foundation

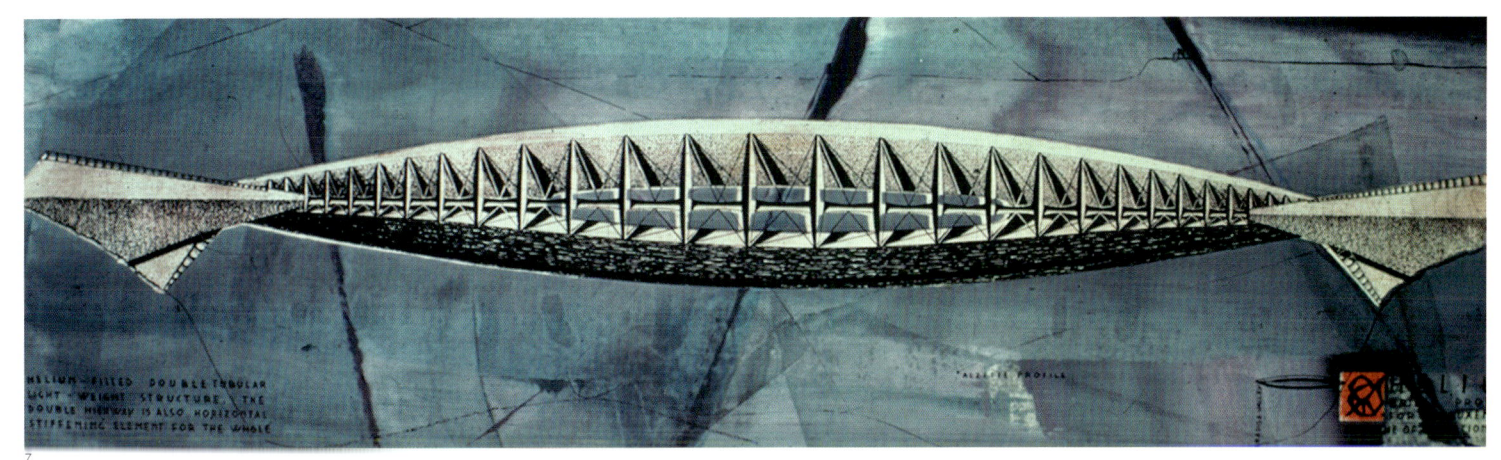

7   Double Tubular Bridge
    photo: ©Ivan Pintar
8   Levitation Bridge
    photo: ©Ivan Pintar
9   Interior Design for Arizona University Cancer Center Chapel
    1986 / Tucson, Arizona
    photo: ©Cosanti Foundation
10 Beast Bridge
    photo: ©Ivan Pintar
11 Pumpkin Apse & Barrel Vault(Cosanti)   1971 / Cordes Junction, Arizona
    photo: ©Jeffrey Manta
12, 13 Ceramics Studio(Cosanti)   1958 / Pradaise Valley, Arizona
    photo: ©Jeffrey Manta   photo: ©Cosanti Foundation

Paolo Soleri

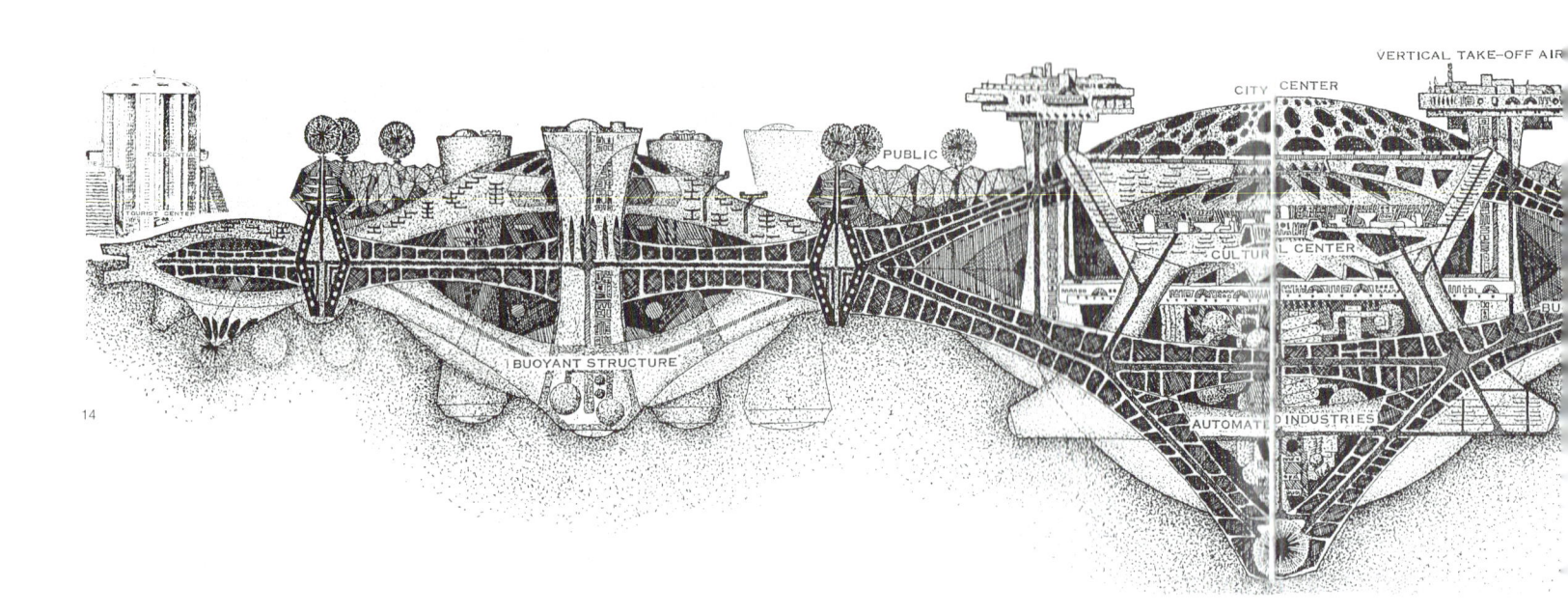

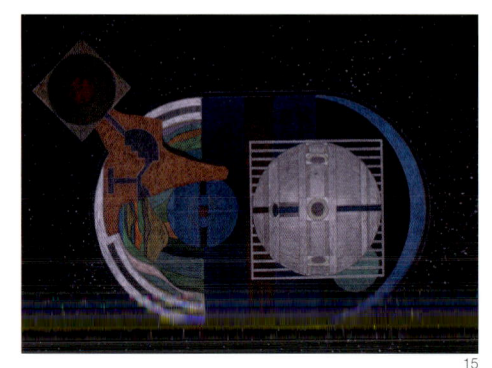

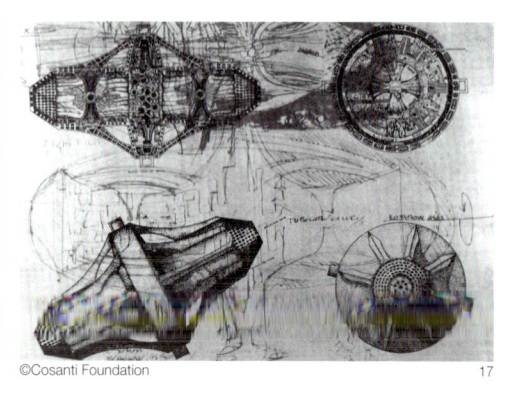

In mid-October 1994, after arriving at Phoenix Airport, I continued on another two hours by car into the expanse of desert that surrounds the American city. Eventually, Arcosanti, built along the edge of some large cliffs, came into view.

Paolo Soleri, hoping to establish a utopian city in the middle of the desert, began building Arcosanti in 1970, and today, some thirty years later, it is still under construction. Like Gaudi's Temple de la Sagrada Família, the project has proceeded at a slow pace. Two immediate concerns connected to the city's future are a lack of funding and Soleri's advanced age. The concept behind the city, designed for 5,000 people, was based on an experience from Soleri's childhood. Soleri's father was an Italian alpinist, and on his days off, he would take young Paolo on trips to the Alps. Despite his youth, Soleri sensed a clear difference between the sordid nature of the city and the pristine beauty of the mountains. As a result, he decided he would like to offer others an opportunity to enjoy the wonders of nature on a site not too distant from the city.

Soleri's concept of the compact city was based on "Arcology," a fusion of architecture and ecology. The land immediately surrounding the city would be used for concentrated farming, while the majority of the remaining area would be left untouched. The "Arcology" concept was intended for very small cities. By walking only a few minutes, residents of the city would find themselves in the middle of a vast wilderness.

In Soleri's concept, this type of artificial habitat, developed through technology, was an organic body that stood in contraposition to nature. He referred to this special type of topography, when properly incorporated into the environment, as "neo-nature."

Soleri's design method was a form of American humanism based on his studies with Frank Lloyd Wright. In other words, Soleri is part of an environmentological tradition which stretches from Horace Greenough to R. Buckminster Fuller. Soleri's conviction that architecture and ecology must move forward at the same pace was first expressed concretely in the Arcosanti project, but there were ample indications of the direction he would take in his first work, Dome House.

Built in the middle of the desert in Cave Creek, Arizona, the work was executed in the most minimal manner. Dome House's bioclimatic design, meant to correspond with the local environment, appears to consist

14 Novanoah I
15, 16 Space for Peace
   photo: ©Scott Riley
17 Asteromo
   photo: ©Cosanti Foundation
18, 19 Hexahedron
   photo: ©Ivan Pintar
20, 21 SOLARE: Lean Linear City / China
   photo: ©Cosanti Foundation
22 Sundial Bridge for Scottsdale Canal / Scottsdale, Arizona
   photo: ©Cosanti Foundation

photos: Courtesy of the Architect

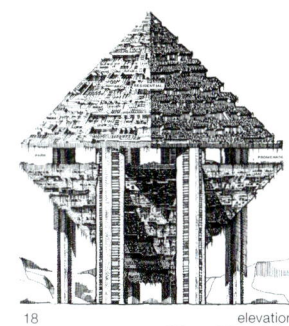

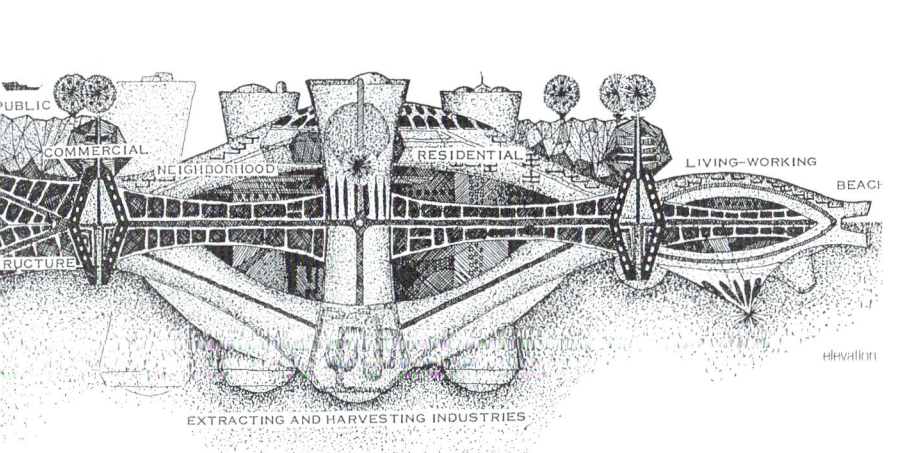

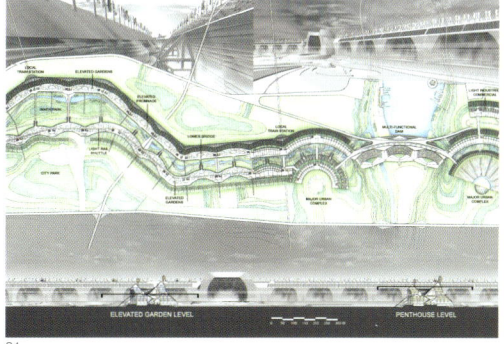

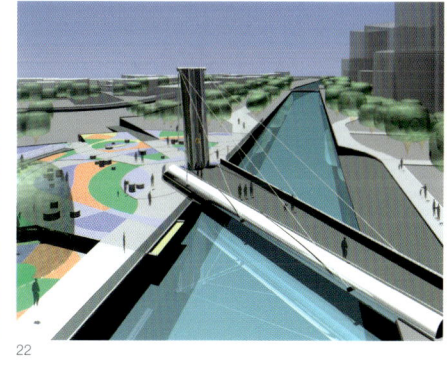

merely of a circular glass dome on a narrow sliver of land, but the rest of the structure can be found underground.

With Dome House, Soleri was making reference to the large underground areas known as "kiva" that are used by the Pueblo Indians for religious rites. The work also exhibits the strong influence of the circular designs that Wright developed for public architecture in his later years.

After returning to Italy in the early 1950s, Soleri built a house-cum-studio in Salerno. Though it was destroyed in a flood in 1954, Soleri also designed the nearby Solimene Ceramics Factory around the same time. The exterior walls, which include a number of ceramic vases, resemble the skin of an armadillo. The center of the empty interior and the positioning of the flow line on the border between the exterior and interior space are elements of the fundamental Arcology layout.

In 1956, Soleri established the Cosanti Foundation, and began designing a variety of buildings for it. The experimental structures, created from a mixture of silt from the bed of the Salt River and concrete, were situated on a lot in Paradise Valley. Using the same method, he completed the Paolo Soleri Theater in Santa Fe, New Mexico in 1966 by pouring concrete directly into the ground.

Because he was so singly devoted to Arcosanti, Soleri was not a particularly prolific architect. But in addition to bridges such as Double Tubular Bridge, Levitation Bridge and Beast Bridge, he designed the Ceramics Studio, Pumpkin Apse and the Barrel Vault at Arcosanti. He also completed the interior design for the University of Arizona Cancer Center Chapel in Tucson.

Among Soleri's unfinished works are many proposals for huge city-sized projects such as the fantastic, floating Novanoah I; Space for Peace; Hexahedron, a vertical Arcology project for 170,000 residents; Asteromo, a space Arcology designed to revolve around the earth and house a population of 70,000; a small city of 5,000 to 10,000 people constructed around the planet; and Solare: A Lean Linear City, a proposal for China. Construction on Arcosanti, the sole work of this type to be realized, continues in the Arizona desert with no end in sight.

SOM/Skidmore, Owings & Merrill

USA

Firmed founded by Louis Skidmore and Nathaniel Owings in 1936. In 1939, became Skidmore, Owings and Merrill. Offices in Chicago, New York, Washington D.C., San Francisco, Los Angeles, London, Hong Kong, and Sao Paulo. Has received over 800 awards. As an organizational design firm, SOM has also produced such noted architects as Gordon Bunshaft, Walter Netsch, and David Childs.

1

1, 2   Freedom Tower / New York

SOM

3 Sears Tower 1974 / Chicago, Illinois
 photo: ©Timothy Hursley
4 John Hancock Center 1970 / Chicago, Illinois
 photo: ©Timothy Hursley
5, 6 Jin Mao Tower 1999 / Shanghai
 photo: ©Hedrich-Blessing
7, 8 Burj Dobai Tower / Dobai, United Arab Emirates

5

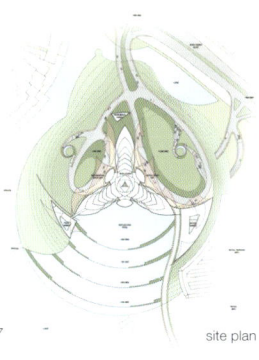

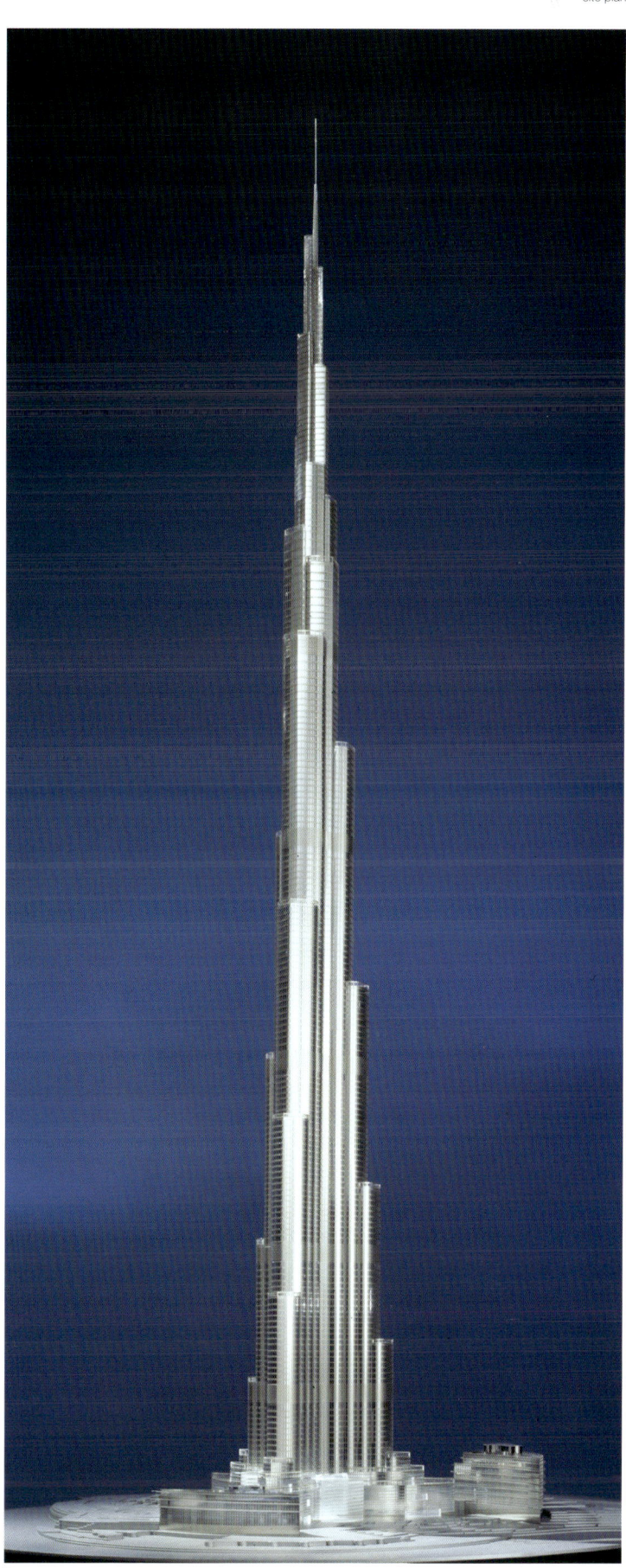

7 site plan

6

8

253

9, 10	US Air Force Academy Chapel 1963 / Colorado Spring, Colorado
photo: ©Hedrich-Blessing	15	Washington Mall 1976 / Washington D.C.
11	Beinecke Rare Book & Manuscript Library 1963 / New Heaven, Connecticut
photo: ©Synectics	16	Greenwich Academy Upper School 2002 / Greenwich, Connecticut
photo: ©Robert Polidori
12	Hirshhorn Museum & Sculpture Garden 1974 / Washington D.C.
photo: ©Synectics	17	Skyscraper Museum 2004 / New York
photo: ©Robert Polidori
13	Lever House 1952 / New York
photo: ©Florian Holzherr	18	Oakland Cathedral / Oakland, California
14	Jeddah Airport 1982 / Jeddah, Saudi Arabia
photo: ©Jay Langlois	19	Broadgate Development 1992 / London
photo: ©Hedrich-Blessing
		20	Chase Manhattan Bank Tower & Plaza 1960 / New York
photo: ©Synectics

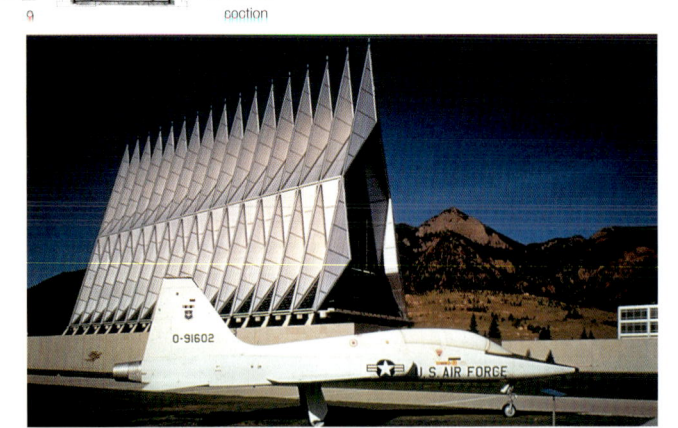

The major American architecture firm Skidmore, Owings, and Merrill is an international corporation with offices in New York, Chicago, Washington D.C., San Francisco, Los Angeles, London, Shanghai, and Hong Kong. It's so large in fact that today only rarely does one come across the names of any of the firm's partners. Yet, star architects like Gordon Bunshaft at the New York office, Walter Netsch, Myron Goldsmith, and Bruce Graham in Chicago, and Edward Bassett in San Francisco, all of whom were responsible for countless important works, are still remembered as the face of SOM.

Today's SOM is based not on high-profile architects, however, but on the theories of Nathaniel A. Owings, one of the firm's founders who viewed the partners as individual architects at each office like a variety of branches growing out of one large tree trunk. Established in 1936, SOM was at one time the largest architectural firm in the world (today, the largest is HOK), and is still considered to be the foremost global firm in terms of sophisticated design and technical quality. As proof, one need only note the proportionately high number of architectural masterpieces in the 20th and 21st century that were created by SOM. There is, for example, the Sears Tower, the tallest building in the U.S.; Lever House, the prototype of the 20th-century office building; the Beinecke Rare Book & Manuscript Library, with its special aesthetic of natural light filtered through onyx; the Marine Midland Bank, famous for its exquisite pairing with a red sculpture by Isamu Noguchi; the U.S. Air Force Academy Chapel, with a sharp, geometric shape that has made it renowned as a work of religious architecture; and the John Hancock Center, a slim, super high rise of beautiful crystal. The classic works of SOM are enough to trigger a never-ending episode of architectural nostalgia.

Since the firm was formed, SOM has completed over 10,000 projects in more than 50 countries around the world, including works of architecture, interior design, and urban planning. The first Architecture Firm Award, the American Institute of Architects' (AIA) most prestigious honor to be conferred on companies, was presented to SOM in 1962. SOM is also the only firm to receive the award twice, having been honored once again in 1996. With more than 900 awards, SOM has attained a higher standing than any other American design office.

With its main office on Wall Street, SOM is

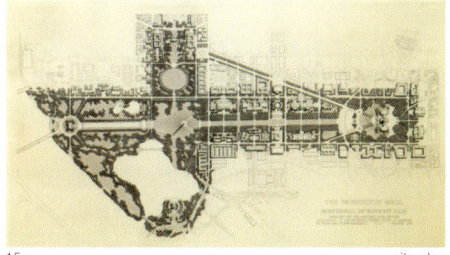

21	Marin Midland Bank 1967 / New York photo: ©Synectics	
22	Worldwide Plaza 1989 / New York photo: ©Synectics	
23	Time Warner Center 2003 / New York photo: ©Synectics	
24	Former Pepsi Cola Building 1960 / New York photo: ©Synectics	
25	San Francisco International Airport 2001 / San Francisco photo: ©Timothy Hursley	

photos : Courtesy of the Architect except ©Synectics

playing a core role in the project to revitalize New York's downtown. World Trade Center Tower 1, also known as Freedom Tower, is one of the firm's more high-profile works. It will stand at Ground Zero. At the time of completion, it will be the tallest building in the world, and rejuvenate the New York skyline. SOM is also at work on the new 7 World Trade Center. Currently under construction, the building is expected to receive LEED's (Leadership in Energy and Environmental Design) silver certification.

In addition, SOM designed the Skyscraper Museum in nearby Battery Park City. Though small in scale, the work will surely make an important contribution to development in Lower Manhattan. Among SOM's many projects, this work is particularly significant for its use of well-known visual artists. Seven World Trade Center will also include a large-scale work by the famed artist Jenny Holzer, and currently, discussions are underway about the possibility of integrating art into the top floor of Freedom Tower.

Among SOM's recent representative works are many that have enlivened the pages of architecture magazines around the world, including Jin Mao Tower, San Francisco International Airport, Greenwich Academy Upper School, and Time Warner Center. Especially important among these is Time Warner Center, located on Columbus Circle, as it demonstrates that SOM is still leaving its mark on the New York skyline in the 21st century.

Even more important are SOM's future projects, including Burj Dubai Tower in Dubai, Freedom Tower in New York, and Oakland Cathedral in California. Freedom Tower is of special interest, as it will outstrip the Petronas Towers in Malaysia (452 meters), the Shanghai World Financial Center (492 meters), and Taipei 101 (508 meters) as the tallest building in the world. But since this record is set to be broken by the firm itself with the Burj Dubai Tower (over 800 meters), it looks as if SOM alone leads the world in the race to rise to greater heights.

Studio Granda

ICELAND

Firm founded in 1987 by Margret Hardardottir, who was born in Reykjavik, Iceland in 1959, and graduated from Edinburgh University in 1981 and the AA School in 1984. Steve Christer, who was born in England in 1960 and graduated from the University of Newcastle upon tyne in 1981 and the AA School in 1984. Became internationally recognized after winning the Supreme Court of Iceland and Reykjavik City Hall competitions.

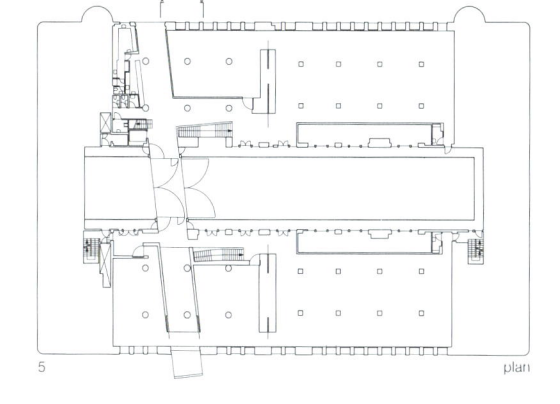

1 Reykjavik City Hall   1992 / Reykjavik, Iceland
   photo: ©Synectics
2 Hrolfsskalavor Residence   2006 / Reykjavik, Iceland
   photo: ©Sigurgeir Sigurjonsson
3 Lindakirkja Church, Chapel and Congregational Hall / Competition
4, 5 Reykjavik Art Museum   2000 / Reykjavik, Iceland
   photo: ©Sigurgeir Sigurjonsson

Studio Granda

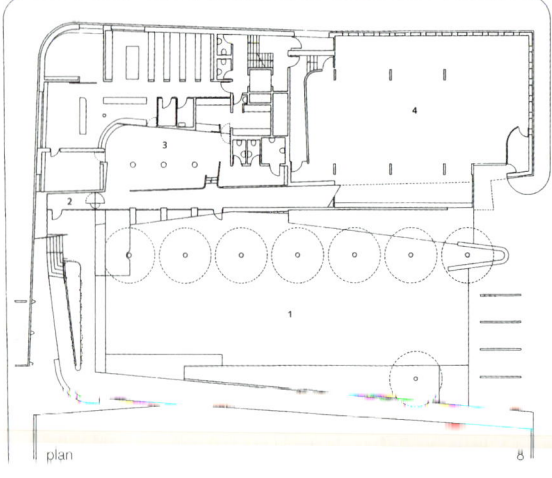

plan

6, 7, 8 Supreme Court of Iceland   1996 / Reykjavik, Iceland
           photo: ©Sigurgeir Sigurjonsson
     9 Student and Research Center for the University of Iceland / Competition
    10 Hofdabakka Highway Interchange   1995 / Reykjavik, Iceland
           photo: ©Sigurgeir Sigurjonsson
    11 Kringlumyra Footbridge   1995 / Reykjavik, Iceland
           photo: ©Sigurgeir Sigurjonsson

Studio Granda

12 Coastal Apartments in Stokkseyri / Stokkseyri, Iceland
13 Kringlan Shopping Mall Car Park
2004 / Reykjavik, Iceland
photo: ©Sigurgeir Sigurjonsson
14, 15 Aktion Poliphile 1992 / Wiesbaden, Germany
16 Stekkjarbakki Highway Interchange 2004 / Reykjavik, Iceland
photo: ©Sigurgeir Sigurjonsson
17 Three Footbridges over Hringbraut & Njardagata
2006 / Reykjavik, Iceland
photo: ©Sigurgeir Sigurjonsson
18 Skeidarvogs Highway Interchange 1999 / Reykjavik, Iceland
photo: ©Sigurgeir Sigurjonsson

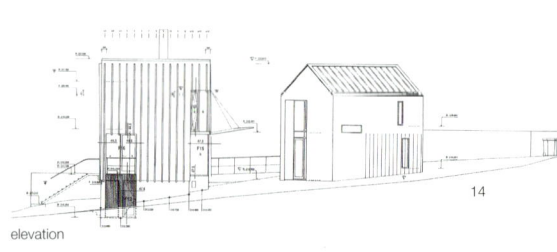

The landscape of Iceland is unbelievably varied, from desolate glacial expanses to lava fields and low-lying arable land. And because it is located right above the spot where the North American and European Plates meet, earthquakes and volcanic eruptions are frequent, and change is perennial.

According to Margret Hardardottir and Steve Christer, the directors of the internationally-active, Icelandic firm Studio Granda, it is extremely challenging to practice architecture in such an unforgiving environment. Hardardottir and Christer first met at London's AA School; they married after graduation in 1984. Following their first work, a one-car garage, the couple won the 1987 Reykjavik City Hall competition, and with this commission, established their own firm the same year. As one of Studio Granda's representative works, the city hall project brought Hardardottir and Christer international acclaim. I first came across them in a magazine article on the project. The structure, standing in one of the most remote parts of the world, is aesthetically brilliant, with a pregnant arc reflected on the surface of a lake in this lonely northern land.

When I actually visited Iceland a few years later, I was surprised at what I found. Along with the beautiful city hall, the firm had developed countless innovative designs. Among these was a building that was partly covered in moss. Half of the building was located within a lake, and the roofscape consisted of a geometrical complex. Hardardottir and Christer suggested that it was truly remarkable that they have been able to receive approval for such challenging proposals. They explained, "The four-and-a-half years it took to construct this unique building seemed both long and short. At school, there was never any time to analyze and prepare our ideas. What we actually did involved eliminating unnecessary ideas, and boiling the plan down until we were left with the most essential elements."

Having become involved with a large-scale project like the City Hall commission just three years after graduation, the proposal included some unreasonable aspects. Fortunately, however, Studio Granda continues to shine. In 1993, the architects won a competition for the Supreme Court of Iceland. It's virtually impossible for a young architect to create the sole example of a country's architectural typology, so this project was especially important.

The court building, which stands on a hill in the center of Reykjavik, has a subdued

19 Bifrost Business School Extension, Cafe and Quadrangle 2002 / Nordurdalur, Iceland photo: ©Sigurgeir Sigurjonsson	23 Skrudas Residence 2004 / Gardabaer, Iceland photo: ©Sigurgeir Sigurjonsson
20 Student Accommodation & Research Wing at Bifrost Business School 2005 / Nordurdalur, Iceland photo: ©Sigurgeir Sigurjonsson	24 Valhalla Summer Residence 2003 / Reykjavik, Iceland photo: ©Sigurgeir Sigurjonsson
21 Laugalaekjarskoli Secondary School Extension 2004 / Reykjavik, Iceland photo: ©Sigurgeir Sigurjonsson	25 Vogaskoli Secondary School Extension / Competition
	26 Gufunes Churchyard Service Building / Competition
22 Skefjar Office 2003 / Reykjavik, Iceland photo: ©Sigurgeir Sigurjonsson	27 Bookcover Design by Studio Granda

photos : Courtesy of the Architect except ©Synectics

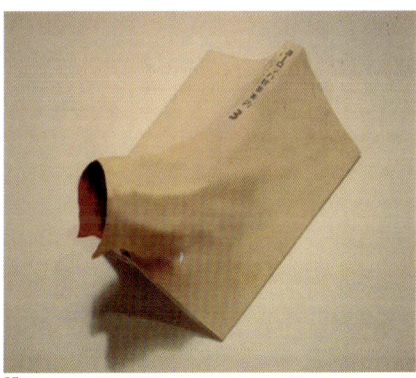

appearance created by the blue-green copper sheets and volcanic basalt that cover it. Looking up the hill from the avenue below, the blue-green shade of the exterior walls gives the structure a symbolic air. The entrance, reflective perhaps of the national character, is small and in no way monumental. Inside, one is suddenly faced with a salon-like lobby. Before taking a tour of the building, I felt somewhat nervous to be visiting the "supreme court," but an employee in the lobby simply said, "Please feel free to go and look around upstairs." It seemed like a very welcoming courthouse.

The firm continues to be blessed with luck. Studio Granda's proposal for the Reykjavik Art Museum was an overwhelming success. Renovating an old dockside building, the unique concept called for the courtyard to be used as an exhibition space. With metal sheets covering the walls, the interior looks sleek and somewhat futuristic. The entrance canopy on the building's exterior is upturned, and the understated renovation style preserves the memory of a drawbridge that stood among the piers many years ago.

With three large public projects under their belt, HardardÛttir and Christer define architecture this way: "Architecture is nothing more than the job of discovering ways to represent the world we live in. To achieve this, we must imbue our work with our emotions and attitudes, regardless of how boring, irrational, intuitive or intellectual they are, and give them a physical form. This is an essential part of reflecting the truth of human existence through architectural creation."

In addition to the large projects, the firm is currently working on the Hrolfsskalavor Residence, the Lindakirkja Church, the Chapel and Congregational Hall, the Coastal Apartments in Stokkseyri, and the Student and Research Center at the University of Iceland. Among Studio Granda's completed works are many related to the urban infrastructure and engineering. These six projects include the Hofdabakka Highway Interchange, Kringlumyra Footbridge, Kringlan Shopping Mall Car Park, the Skeidarvogs Highway and Stekkjarbakki Highway Interchanges, and three footbridges in Hringbraut and Njardagata.

For a Belgian book cover competition, Christer took my book _Europe: The Contemporary Architecture Guide_ (Toto Publishing, 1998) as his model. The work, depicting a glove, is filled with a gentle Scandinavian wit and is one of my favorites.

SZYSZKOWITZ – KOWALSKI

AUSTRIA

Michael Szyszkowitz was born in Graz, Austria in 1944, and graduated from Graz University of Technology in 1971. Karla Kowalski was born in Beuthen, Poland in 1941, and graduated from the Darmstadt Technical University in 1968 followed by postgraduate study at AA School of Architecture in 1968 and 1969. She has taught at Stuttgart Technical University since 1988. Both worked at Gunter Behnisch's firm (Szyszkowitz from 1970; Kowalski from 1969) and both participated in the Munich Olympics project until 1971. The two began working as a team in 1973, and established their own firm in 1978.

1 Institute for Biochemistry and Biotechnology, Technical University of Graz   2000 / Graz, Austria
2, 3   House H   1993 / Bad Mergentheim, Germany
4   IBA Emscher Park Housing Estate   1997 / Gelsenkirchen, Germany

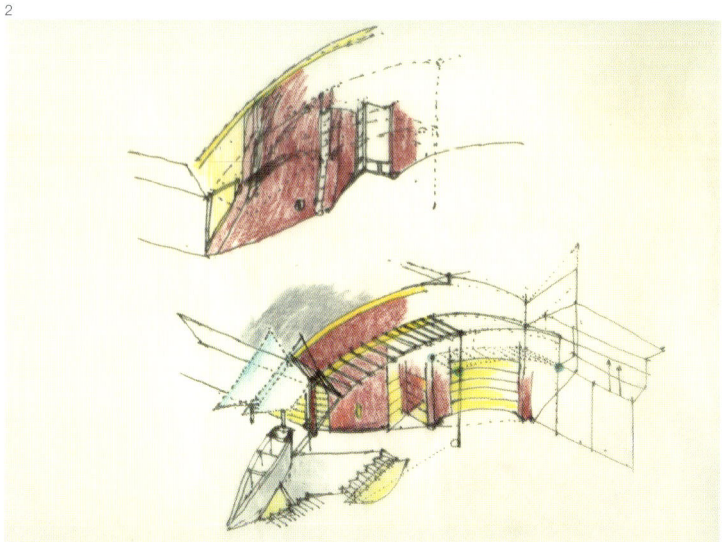

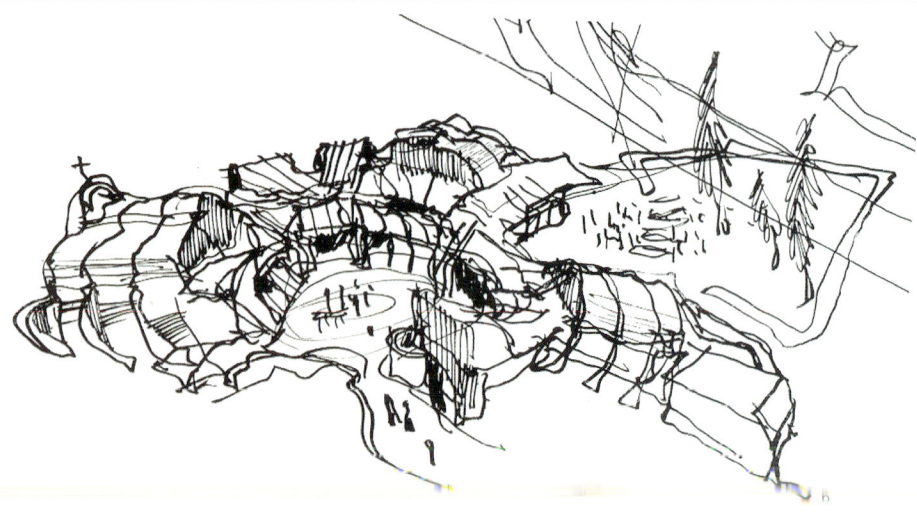

SZYSZKOWITZ – KOWALSKI

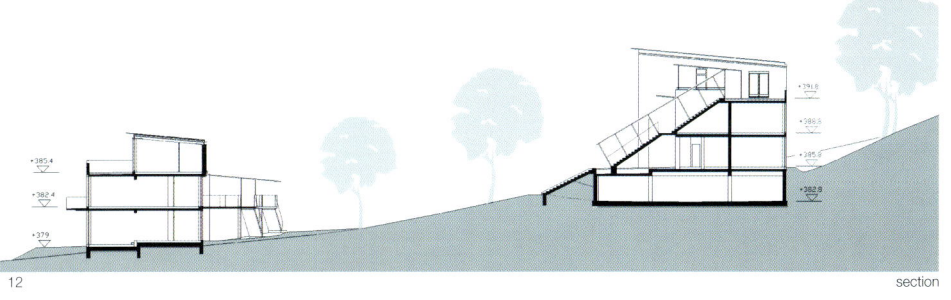

5, 6   Catholic Parish Center Graz-Ragnitz   1987 / Graz-Ragnitz, Austria
7   Kastner+Ohler Department Store Extension   1994 / Graz, Austria
8   Primary School+Day-Nursery Langobardenstrasse / Vienna
9   House W   1974 / Graz, Austria
10   St. Ulrich Cultural Center   2000 / Greith, Austria
11, 12   Schiessstatte Housing Estate   1999 / Graz, Austria
13   Kastner+Ohler Underground Parking   2003 / Graz, Austria
   photo: ©Angelo Kaunat

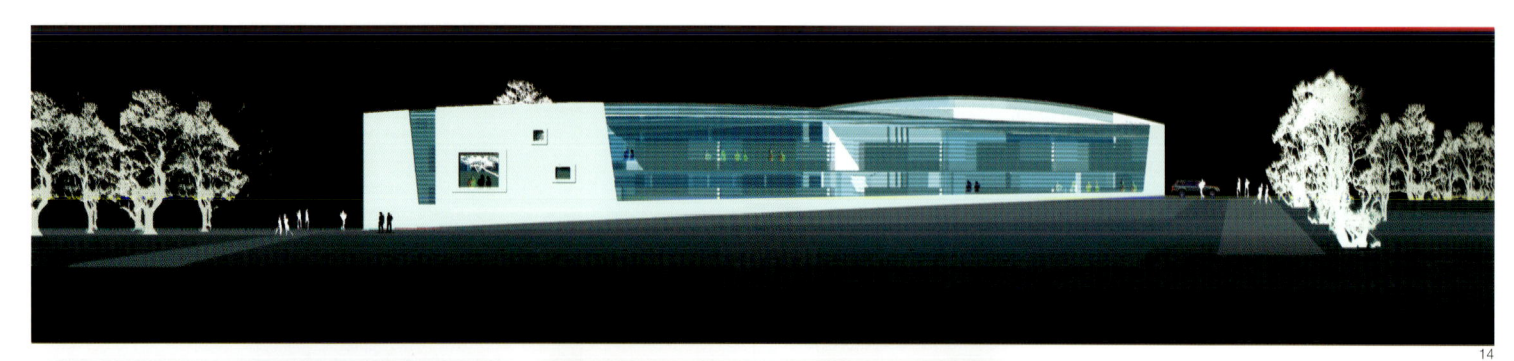

Szyszkowitz - Kowalski

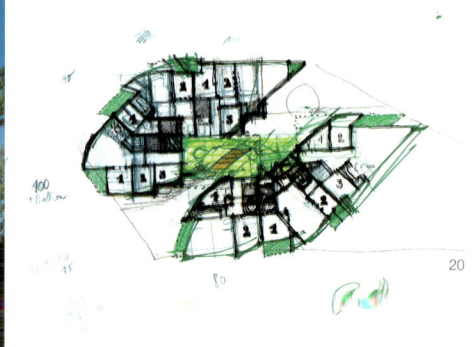

Along with Gunther Domenig, Michael Szyszkowitz and Karla Kowalski are the chief proponents of the new Graz architecture. Graz is the capital of Steiermark, a state in southeast Austria which has long had a reputation for defying the country's architectural conventions. And Szyszkowitz - Kowalski's style is a prime example.

The singular nature of their work is immediately recognizable. Known for their biomorphic designs, Szyszkowitz - Kowalski's buildings are highly suggestive of other forms. With an undeniably organic appearance, the works display aspects of both anthropomorphism and anthroposophy.

These latter tendencies are particularly apparent in the Institute for Biochemistry and Biotechnology at Graz University of Technology, and the Catholic Parish Center Graz-Raggnitz, while the biomorphic aspects of Szyszkowitz - Kowalski's work are evident in private residences such as House W, House H, and House K, which resemble insects. By stating, "The interpretation of space and time is fundamental to architectural expression," Szyszkowitz - Kowalski attempt to add a contemporary element to a historical perspective. Also present in their work is a personal viewpoint, as every type of creative activity is, after all, rooted in the individual. In that sense, Szyszkowitz - Kowalski's architecture shoulders the substantial weight of historical and traditional localism.

The firm's works express an architectural structure that is defined by sophisticated and pure forms. Yet due to their complexity, it is quite difficult to convey the nature of Szyszkowitz - Kowalski's work in words. In contemporary terms, their organic, expressionist, and anthroposophical architecture might well be categorized as deconstructivist, the style that evolved out of post-structuralism. But even prior to this, Szyszkowitz - Kowalski's work often displayed biomorphic aspects, and in terms of form, material, and color, it seems to follow in the footsteps of the rich, baroque architecture of the Steiermark region.

One of the most visible tendencies in the architects' recent work is their engagement with the environment. The main theme of the IBA Emscher Park Housing Estate is the surrounding landscape and open areas, as suggested by the garden (square) adjacent to the complex and the space around each housing facility.

The quadrangular square, used as an "external

14 High School Project Wolkersdorf
15 Center of Studies, Technical University of Graz   2000 / Graz, Austria
16, 17 Project Ruhr GmbH / Competition
18, 19, 20 Office and Health Center by the City Park   2006 / Nuremberg, Germany
21 House K   1996 / Graz, Austria
22 The Headquarters of the Steiermarkische Sparkasse Bank   2006 / Graz, Austria
photo: ©Angelo Kaunat

residence," functions as a public thoroughfare as well as a playground, while the open space, called "earth living," functions as a private garden with multiple uses.

The Study Center at the Graz University of Technology also has an environmental orientation. The inner courtyard, open only on the west side, has a unique atmosphere. Above the grass-covered ground is a rope stretching between the two opposing buildings as part of a plan to cultivate the growth of ivy, which will eventually serve as a "green roof" to cover the courtyard. This will, it is hoped, encourage students to gather in the plant-rich space.

As Szyszkowitz - Kowalski's works have become somewhat more focused on environmental concerns, the appearance of biomorphic forms in their has decreased. This is apparent not only in the IBA Emscher Park Estate and the Graz University Study Center, but also in the Schiesstatte Housing Estate, St. Ulrich Cultural Center, and the Kastner and Ohler Department Underground Parking. Yet, their minutely segmented, intricately intertwined facade, the foundation of biomorphic design, is still alive and well, and is the most quickly identifiable feature of Szyszkowitz - Kowalski's design. In addition, the freewheeling nature and deconstructivist tinge of their past works has disappeared somewhat, and the distinct and eye-opening facades in works such as the Wolkersdorf School Project are startling to anyone familiar with the architects' older output.

Szyszkowitz - Kowalski are partners both in architecture and in life. Szyszkowitz was educated at the Graz University of Technology, while Kowalski graduated from the Technical University in Darmstadt. Both worked under the German architect Gunter Behnisch, and helped design the 1972 Munich Olympic Park. And Behnisch's freestyle technique of handling form is certainly apparent in Szyszkowitz - Kowalski's architecture.

After establishing their own firm in Graz in 1978, Szyszkowitz - Kowalski have continued to work as professor-architects, both teaching and practicing. They now represent the world-famous Graz style.

TEN Arquitectos

MEXICO

Firm founded in Mexico City by Enrique Norten and Bernardo Gómez-Pimienta in 1985. At present, Gomez-Pimienta has his own practice, while Norten continues as head of the firm. Norten was born in in Mexico City in 1954. Studied at Universidad Iberoamericana, and completed a postgraduate degree at Cornell University in 1980. In 1998, TEN Arquitectos received the first Mies van der Rohe Prize for Latin American Architecture.

1. Hotel Habita   2000 / Mexico City
   photo: ©Luis Gordoa
2. Televisa Mixed Use Building   1995 / Colonia Doctores, Mexico
   photo: ©Luis Gordoa, Armando Hashimoto
3. National School of Theater   1994 / Tlalpan, Mexico
   photo: ©Luis Gordoa
4. JVC Convention and Exhibition Center / Jalisco, Mexico
5, 6. Educare Sports Facilities   2001 / Jalisco, Mexico
   photo: ©Jaime Navarro
7. Lincoln East / Miami, Florida

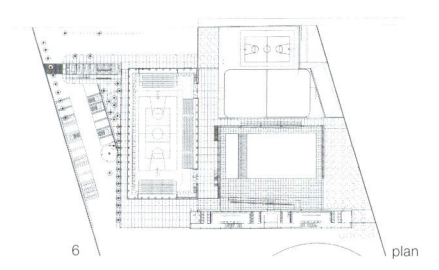

270

8   Visual and Performing Arts Library in Brooklin / New York
9   Harlem Park / New York
10 Brickell Plaza / Miami, Florida
11 Moda in Casa   1993 / Mexico City
    photo: ©Luis Gordoa
12 Princeton Parking Garage   2000 / Princeton, New Jersey
    photo: ©Paul Warchol
13 Espana Park Residential Building   2001 / Mexico City

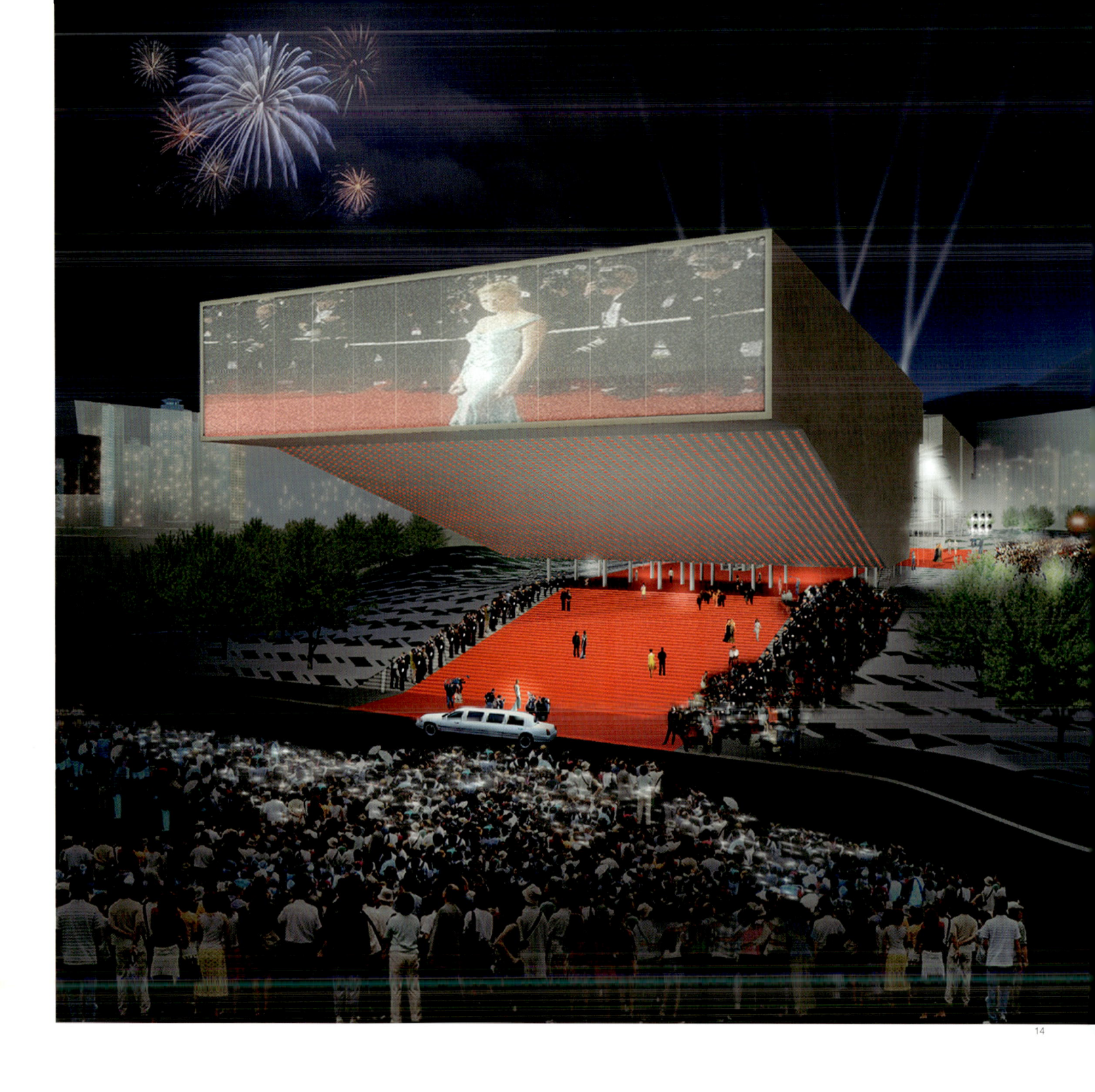

The first time I visited Mexico in 1991, the only contemporary Mexican architect known in Japan was Ricardo Legorreta, who had been influenced by Luis Barragan. When I visited again in 1995, I went to see Legorreta's Art City. In one corner of the site I also found TEN Arquitectos' National School of Theater. Initially, the cylinders with their elliptical sections reminded me of Renzo Piano's Kansai International Airport terminal. Seeing the work's shiny metallic exterior, which went far beyond Mexican modernism, made me realize that there was a lot more going in the country than I had first thought.

Enrique Norten, the principal of TEN Arquitectos, carried out design projects with his friend Bernardo Gomez-Pimienta, and the language of their contemporary form of modernism has developed in many unexpected ways in the Latin Climate.

The cylinders at the theater school were further evolved for the Mixed-Use Building for Televisa, which earned TEN Arquitectos the first Mies van der Rohe Award in Latin America in 1998. The committee explained its choice by saying, "With comprehensive solutions to complex problems, special consideration for urban planning, and innovative technological and morphological approaches, the firm has resolved precise urban situations with unique propositions."

While fusing a modern architectural vocabulary with the traditional culture and environment of Mexico, TEN Arquitectos has reinvented the modernist ethos. Instead of burying unsolved issues in historical memories, the architects explore the contradictions inherent in the complicated process of advancing Mexican modernism.

Hotel Habita, one of the firm's representative works, is perhaps the best recent example of TEN Arquitectos' contemporary-modern style. Located in a business district, the building is covered with a translucent, glass skin that gives the renovated hotel an elegant, superflat look. Covering buildings with translucent glass is currently all the rage, and with its extremely urbanistic appearance, the work accentuates the surrounding streetscape.

Similarly, the prism in the gymnasium, with frosted-glass lining the upper section of its walls, at the Educare Sports Facilities in Guadalajara is utterly urban. In addition, at the bottom, the walls are equipped with high-tech, metallic panels that open and close automatically according to changes in the climate, including sunshine, temperature, rain

14 Pusan Cinema Complex / Competition
15 Guadalajara Guggenheim Museum / Guadalajara, Mexico
16 HOUSE RR 1997 / Mexico City
    photo: ©Luis Gordoa
17 HOUSE LE 1995 / Colonia Condesa, Mexico
    photo: ©Luis Gordoa, Armando Hashimoto
18 Chopo Museum Renovation / Mexico City
19 HOUSE C 2004 / Mexico City
    photo: ©Luis Gordoa

photos : Courtesy of the Architect

and wind. Further, attached to the side of the building is a long, pool wing, the south side of which is made completely of glass blocks. At night, the interior light serves also to illuminate the soccer pitch next to the building.

In all of the important TEN Arquitectos works mentioned above, one finds a gorgeously urban quality without a touch of Mexican color. The firm's aesthetic sense isn't founded on a Mexican master-architect like Barragan, but neither does it owe anything to Mexican vernacularism. After both Norten and Gomez-Pimienta graduated from Universidad Iberoamericana, the former went on to do a Master's at Cornell University while the latter attended Columbia. And in TEN Arquitectos' work, there is an unmistakable influence of the American urban environment. (Incidentally, Gomez-Pimienta has left the firm and currently has his own practice.)

Yet, while TEN Arquitectos' works might seem to have cast aside any Mexican flavor, the characteristics of North America's most populous city are clearly present. In Mexico, buildings such as the Espana Park Residential Building, Moda in Casa, the City Express Reforma Hotel, and the JVC Convention and Exhibition Center are responses to the overwhelming complexity of the city, and on the other hand, continue to add sophistication to the urban fabric.

In the climate of change and conflict that currently exists, TEN Arquitectos acts as a bridge between national borders, and urban, architectural, and landscape design, and their critical activities help synthesize a variety of differences.

Currently, the firm is becoming even more active internationally. Along with completed works like Princeton Parking Garage in the U.S., Norten is moving ahead with the Lincoln East, the Brickell Plaza, the James Hotel, Hotel Budapest, Harlem Park, and the Visual and Performing Arts Library in Brooklyn. And through its involvement in competitions such as the Weston Performing Arts Center, the Guggenheim Museum in Guadalajara, the Busan Cinema Complex, and the Free Library of Philadelphia, TEN Arquitectos looks set to expand even further around the world.

UN Studio

THE NETHERLANDS

Ben van Berkel was born in Utrecht, the Netherlands in 1957. Graduated from the Rietveld Academy in Amsterdam in 1982, and from the AA School of Architecture in 1987. In 1987 and 1988, worked under Santiago Calatrava. In 1988, established the Van Berkel and Bos Architectuurbureau with Caroline Bos. Bos was born in Rotterdam in 1959, and studied art history at Birkbeck College at the University of London.

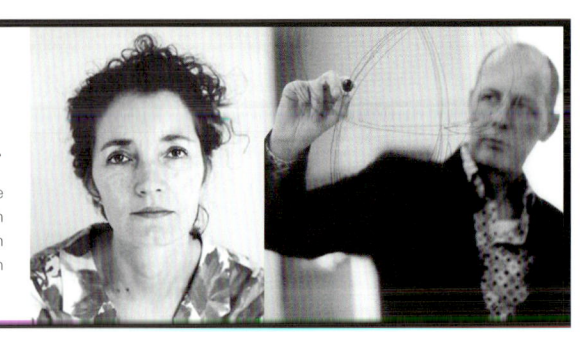

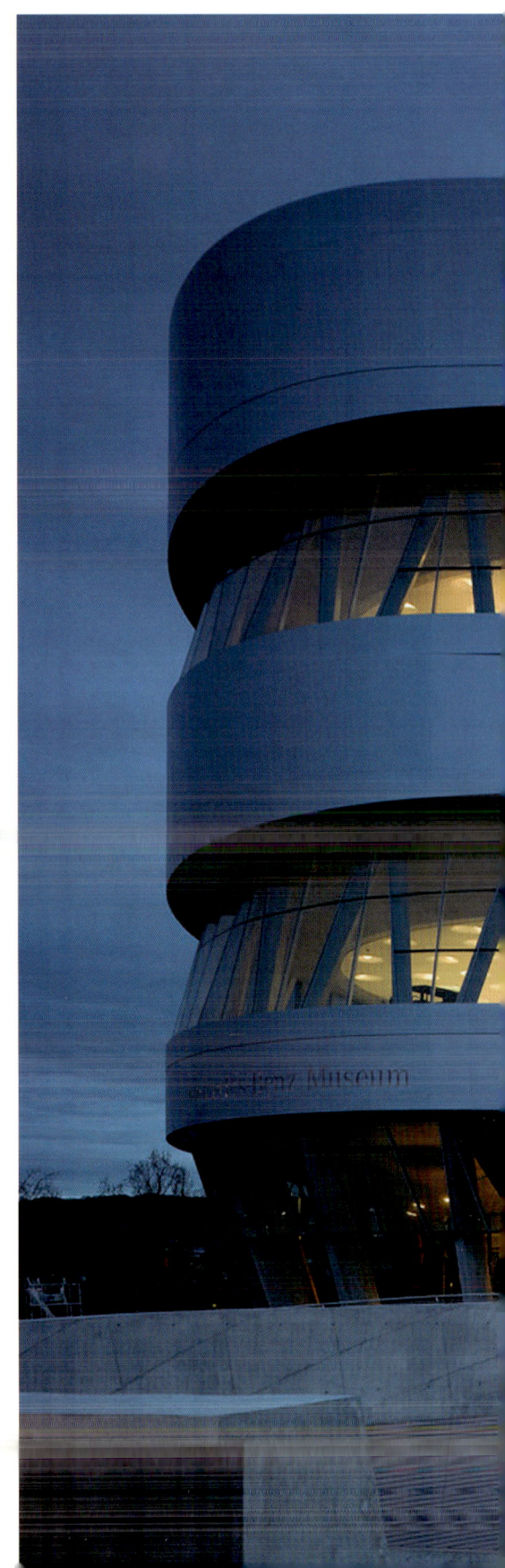

1. Karbouw Office 1992 / Amersfoort, The Netherlands
2. Moebius House 1998 / Het Gooi, The Netherlands
3. Piet Hein Tunnel 1997 / Amsterdam
   photo: ©Synectics
4. Arnhem Central / Arnhem, The Netherlands
5, 6. Mercedes-Benz Museum 2006 / Stuttgart, Germany
   photo: ©Christian Richters

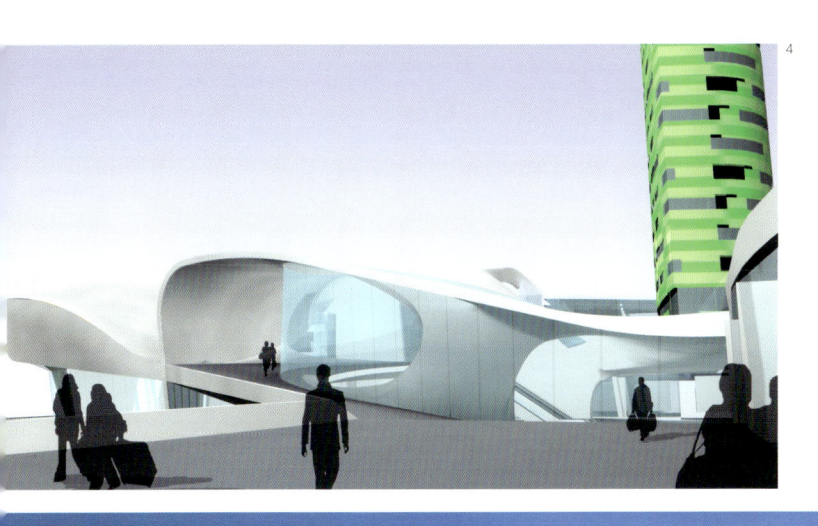

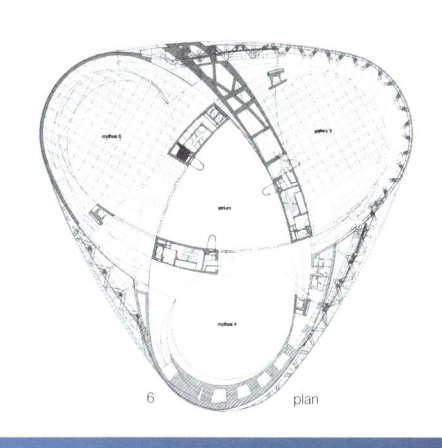

4

6 plan

5

UN Studio

7 Electrical Substation   2002 / Innsbruck, Austria
8 Erasmus Bridge   1996 / Rotterdam
9 Prince Claus Bridge   2003 / Utrecht, The Netherlands
10 Townhall and Theater Ijsselstein   2000 / Ijsselstein, The Netherlands
   photo: ©Synectics
11 Het Valkhof Museum   1999 / Nijmegen, The Netherlands
   photo: ©Synectics
12 Akron Art Museum / Akron, Ohio
13 Living Tomorrow   2003 / Amsterdam
   photo: ©Synectics
14 NMR Facility   2000 / Utrecht, The Netherlands
   photo: ©Synectics

15 REMU Electricity Substation   1993 / Amersfoort, The Netherlands
   photo: ©Synectics
16 Carnegie Science Center
17, 18 Office "La Defense"   2004 / Almere, The Netherlands
   photo: ©Christian Richters
19 Galleria Hall West   2004 / Seoul
   photo: ©Christian Richters

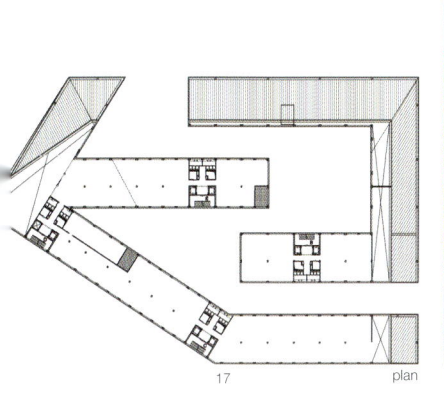

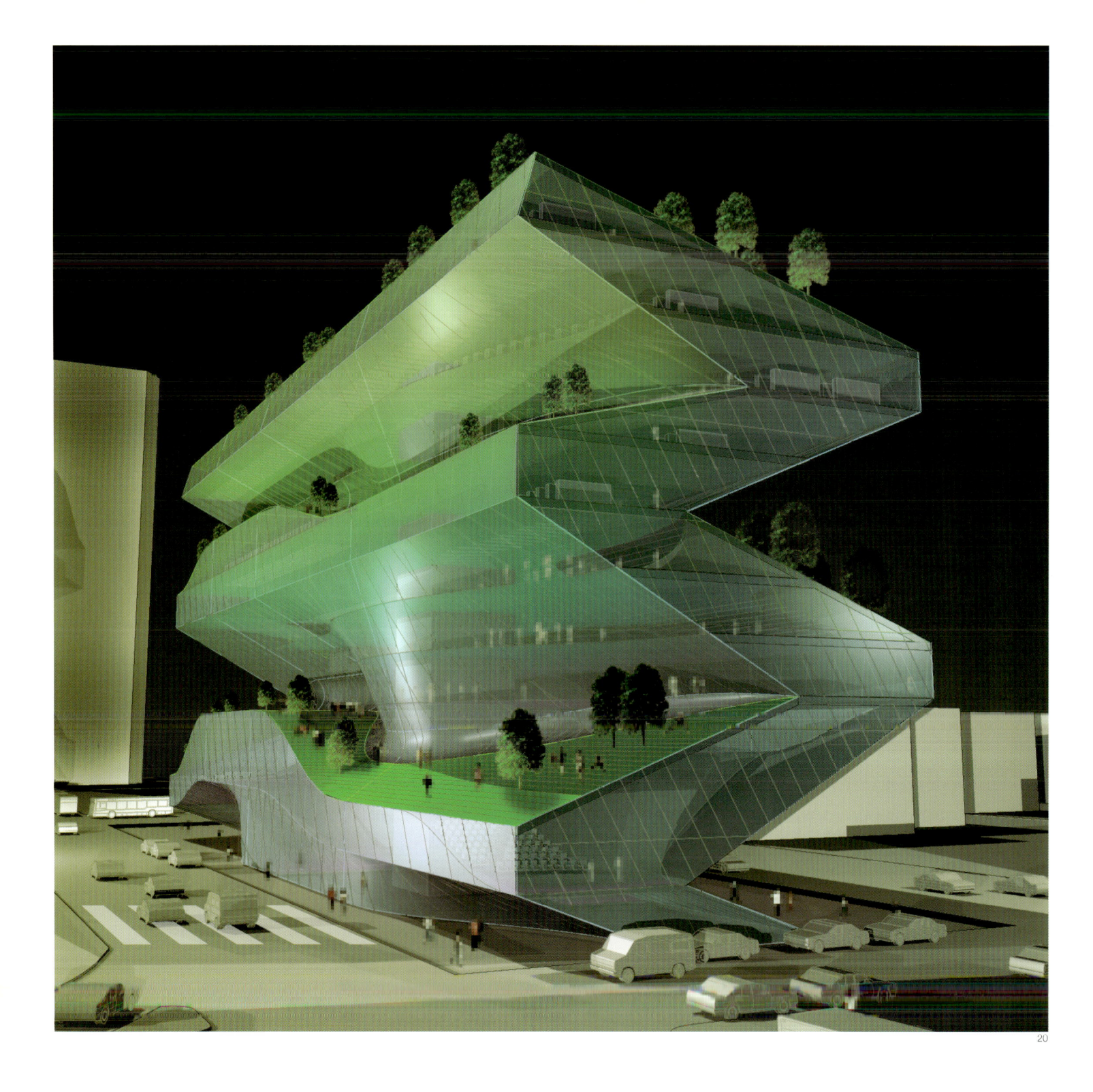

Born in 1957, the architect Ben van Berkel, one of the founders of UN Studio, is only 50. After studying at Rietveld Academy in Amsterdam, he continued his education at the AA School of Architecture in London, where he earned his diploma in 1987. While at AA, he studied with Zaha Hadid, and after graduating, received practical experience working for Santiago Calatrava. Van Berkel is clearly very international.

The flowing lines in van Berkel's Karbouw Office Building and Moebius House, and the "off-center" or "distorted" aspects in the REMU Electricity Substation and Bridge Master's House recall Hadid's designs, while the dynamic structural engineering of Erasmus Bridge and Prince Claus Bridge reflect Calatrava's influence.

Van Berkel has combined Hadid's deconstructivism and Calatrava's structural expressionism, skillfully applying each as the situation demands, but there is more to his work than this: Van Berkel provides us with a preview of what an architect should be in the 21st century and beyond.

In van Berkel's view, an architect should be a fashion designer who designs the future. The architect's workplace will also take on a new structure, that of a limitless virtual studio. The network-oriented profession of the past will go from being a cooperative activity involving a client, investor, user, and technical consultant to also include a design engineer, financier, executive, process specialist, designer, and stylist. The new architectural network studio will be a hybrid consisting of a club, atelier, laboratory, and automobile factory that cultivates "plug-in professionalism."

In the past, van Berkel's work was limited to his homeland of Holland, but in recent years, he has become increasingly active abroad. Distancing himself from the national style that defines the work of the majority of Dutch architects, van Berkel has created unique works with an international perspective. As he spent his early years in training abroad, van Berkel depends on foreign culture for much of his inspiration.

There is another reason for his unique approach. Unlike many young Dutch architects, van Berkel didn't get his start in design with government-sponsored housing complexes. The first buildings he worked on were instead related to civil engineering and public infrastructure – the kind of project your average architect would never even consider. Due to this influence, van Berkel's work

20 Newer Orleans Mediatheque
21 Theater Agora / Lelystad, The Netherlands
22 Te Papa Museum Extension / Wellington, New Zealand
23 Mahler 4 Office Towers
24 Battersea Weave Offfice Building / London
25 Exhibition for "Summer of LOVE" 2005 / Frankfurt
26 Park and Rijn Towers 2005 / Arnhem, The Netherlands
27 Hotel Castell 2004 / Zuoz, The Netherlands

photos : Courtesy of the Architect except ©Synectics

contains a technical aspect similar to that of an engineer or urban planner and a sense of pragmatism.
Rather than seeing these projects as monuments, van Berkel takes an ethical approach to infrastructure. Before the aforementioned REMU project, van Berkel made similar works such as the Erasmus Bridge, Piet Hein Tunnel, Arnhem Central, NMR Facility, Electrical Substation (in Innsbruck), and the Prince Claus Bridge. Which is to say, van Berkel has a special talent for imbuing cliched industrial objects such as bridges, power stations, and manufacturing plants with a morphological, spatial identity.
Moreover, in avoiding static monuments, van Berkel's design style, which is based on networks, transport, motion, energy, and flow, has exerted a huge influence on architects who are involved with architectural forms of the past. Van Berkel calls his method, which includes this type of dynamic element, "mobile force."
In addition, van Berkel has completed a number of cultural facilities that supersede genre, such as the Het Valkhof Museum, the Townhall and Theater in Ijsselstein, Living Tomorrow, the La Defense office building, Galleria Hall West, and the Mercedes-Benz Museum. Among his unfinished projects are Carnegie Science Center, Theater Agora, the Akron Art Museum, the Newer Orleans Mediatheque, the Te Papa Museum Extension, Mahler 4 Office Towers, and the Battersea Weave Office Building. With a resume that includes a stint as visiting professor at Columbia University, guest critic at Harvard University, and unit master at AA along with a reputation as a polemicist, he is second only to Rem Koolhaas as Holland's most internationally recognized architect.

Erick van Egeraat

The Netherlands

Born in Amsterdam in 1956. Helped found the group Mecanoo in 1983, and graduated from the Delft University of Technology in 1984. Left Mecanoo in 1995, and established his own firm in Rotterdam. At present, maintains additional offices in Budapest, London, and Prague.

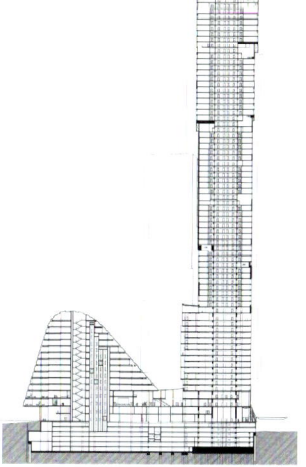

1 ING Head Office 2004 / Budapest
2, 3 Capital City / Moscow

section

Erick van Egeraat

4 Inholland University 2000 / Rotterdam	9 Main Building and Auditorium, University of Leipzig / Augustusplatz, Germany
5 Alphen aan den Rijn City Hall 2002 / Alphen aan den Rijn, The Netherlands	10 Russian Avant-Garde Residential Complex / Moscow
6 Crawford Municipal Art Gallery 2000 / Cork, Ireland	11 Mahler 4 Office Tower / Amsterdam
7 Royal Netherlands Embassy in Poland 2004 / Warsaw	12 Natural History Museum Rotterdam 1996 / Rotterdam photo: ©Synectics
8 Luxury Housing Mauritskade 2002 / Amsterdam	13, 14 Kroyers Plads Housing Complex / Copenhagen

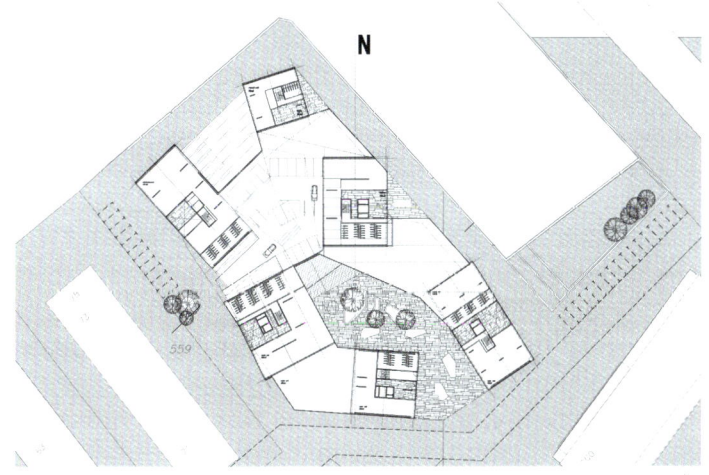

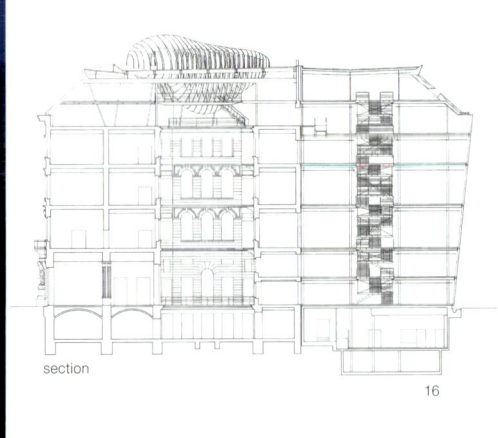

Erick van Egeraat started his career as one of the founding members of a young Dutch architecture group called Mecanoo. After leaving the group in 1995, Egeraat established his own firm in Rotterdam called Erick van Egeraat Associated Architects (EEA). As of 2005, after ten years of steady growth, the firm had offices in London, Prague, and Budapest, and had turned into a major practice employing a staff of some 100 people. What is especially notable about the firm is its success in Eastern Europe.
Capital City (or Gorod Stolits) is a huge project that includes office and residential spaces, and a retail area. The structure consists of two low rises, a cone-shaped dome, and two super high rises, one 49-stories-tall and the other 61-stories.
The low-rise section houses a shopping and entertainment area, with more retail outlets in the mid-rise section and a combination of offices and residences on the higher levels of the structure. The most surprising thing about the work is the cutting-edge architectural expression used for all three buildings. To make the two super high-rise buildings appear less massive, van Egeraat altered the position of the diagonal axis line to make it look slightly off-center. The upper part of the facades also have a number of overhanging sections and varying levels, and through van Egeraat's use of a combination of horizontal, vertical, and square openings, he succeeded in creating a powerful expression, which includes a strong element of movement. Movement of this type can often be found in van Egeraat's work.
In Budapest, van Egeraat designed the ING Bank and the NNI Hungary offices, and the ING Head Office. He renovated and expanded the original 19th-century building, covered the courtyard with a glass roof, and created a boardroom which resembles a whale. The unique whalelike structure is especially interesting for its strong sense of movement. The facade of the building is segmented into countless vertical stripes, which look as if they're undulating. Because this undulating effect adds dynamism to the work, it is called a "moving facade." Similarly, the cantilevers at the edges of the raised Alphen aan den Rijn City Hall make it look like some kind of animal raising its head. Moreover, the comical appearance of Popstage Mezz in Breda, which according to one's perspective resembles a seal clothed in metalic sheets, is truly amusing. Despite the growth of his firm, van Egeraat still feels the need to be personally involved in the

15, 16   ING Bank and NN Hungary Offices
         1994 / Budapest

17, 18   Brewinc College / Doetinchem, The Netherlands

19, 20   Popstage Mezz
         2002 / Breda, The Netherlands

21   School for Fashion and Graphic Industry Utrecht
      1997 / Utrecht, The Netherlands
      photo: ©Synectics

22   Deak Palace Renovation   2004 / Budapest
      photo: ©Christian Richters

photos : Courtesy of the Architect except
©Synectics and ©Christian Richters

---

decision-making process for every project. All of the fundamental ideas for EEA projects are his, and emerge out of his own sketches. He is constantly searching for a design that will define the character of a building. For this reason, his initial sketches are quickly realized as distinct ideas which relate directly to the final result. A case in point is the Kroyers Plads Housing Complex in Copenhagen. The buildings which originally stood on the lot, situated on a canal, were equipped with massive, gabled roofs. Van Egeraat took the basic structure of six floors and a roof, and expanded it into six floors topped by a ten-floor roof. The collection of six, 16-floor buildings with roofs like steeply inclined towers, make an attractive sight, resembling a small, waterside town straight out of a fairy tale. Van Egeraat refers to his work as "sensual architecture." Rather than being founded solely on rational or functional concepts, he tends to rely more on their opposite – namely, sensual ideas. Van Egeraat's designs, which are acute responses to a set of given conditions or environments, are informed by an emotional viewpoint.

Unlike the current tendency toward architectural symmetry and order, van Egeraat has intentionally incorporated asymmetry and disharmony without any negative connotations. This has greatly enriched his work, as seen in the Crawford Municipal Art Gallery, the Royal Netherlands Embassy in Poland, the Luxury Housing Mauritskade, the Mahler 4 Office Tower, the Russian Avant-Garde Residential Complex, the Main Building and Auditorium at the University of Leipzig, and Brewinc College. On the other hand, some of the architect's works are notable for their simple ornamentation. These include Inholland University, the School for Fashion and Graphic Industry Utrecht, the Natural History Museum Rotterdam and the Deak Palace Renovation project.

In addition, the contraposition which van Egeraat has deliberately employed is reminiscent of the inversion or reversal found in mannerism or baroque architecture. This developed into a system of personal expression wherein human sensitivity is reintroduced into architecture through soft but abstract forms without resorting to "historicist" nostalgia and revivalism. Many EEA works exhibit a strong contemporary sense of architecture achieved through the fusion of sensual charms. Erick van Egeraat is doing nothing less than changing the face of the Eastern European urbanscape.

VSBA / Robert Venturi and Denise Scott Brown

USA

Firm founded by Robert Venturi and Denise Scott Brown in 1967. Venturi was born in Philadelphia in 1925, and graduated from Princeton University in 1950. Worked under Eero Saarinen. Awarded the Pritzker Prize in 1991. Scott Brown was born in Nkana, Zambia in 1931. Completed a postgraduate degree in urban planning and a doctorate degree in architecture at University of Pennsylvania. Received the Vilcek Preize in 2007.

1 The Biomedical & Biological Sciences Research Building at the University of Kentucky   2005 / Lexington, Kentucky
  photo: ©Matt Wargo
2 Seattle Art Museum   1991 / Seattle, Washington
  photo: ©Synectics
3, 4 National Gallery Sainsbury Wing   1991 / London
  photo: ©Synectics

perspective drawing

VSBA

5   Vanna Venturi House   1964 / Chestnut Hill, Pennsylvania

6   Guild House   1966 / Philadelphia, Pennsylvania
photo: ©William Watkins

7, 8   Gordon Wu Hall, Princeton University   1983 / Princeton, New Jersey
photo: ©Synectics

9   Lewis Thomas Laboratory, Princeton University   1983 / Princeton, New Jersey
photo: ©Synectics

10   Fisher and Bendheim Hall, Princeton University   1989 / Princeton, New Jersey

11   Frist Campus Center, Princeton University   2000 / Princeton, New Jersey
photo: ©Matt Wargo

12   Clinical Research Building, Pennsylvania University   1991 / Philadelphia, Pennsylvania

13   Parelman Quadrangle, Pennsylvania University   2000 / Philadelphia, Pennsylvania

14   UCLA Gonda Neuroscience and Genetics Research Center   1998 / Los Angels
photo: ©Matt Wargo

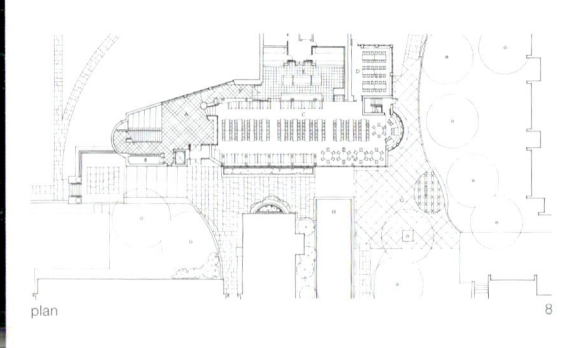

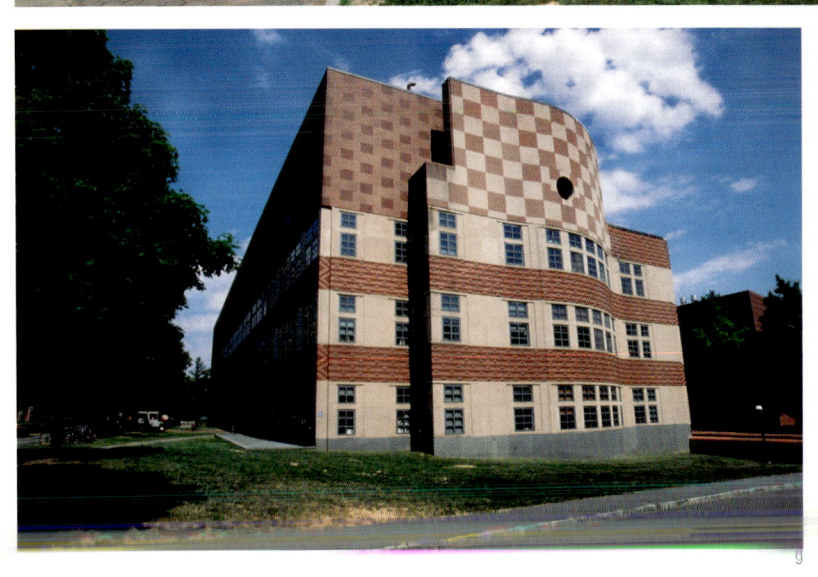

11

12

13

14

289

VSBA

15 Allen Memorial Art Museum   1976 / Oberlin, Ohio
16 San Diego Museum of Contemporary Art La Jolla Wing   1996 / La Jolla, California
17 Institute for Scientific Information Corporate Headquarters   1979 / Philadelphia, Pennsylvania
18 Franklin Court   1976 / Philadelphia, Pennsylvania
19 Freedom Plaza   1980 / Washington D.C.
20 Dixwell Fire Station   1974 / New Heaven, Connecticut

Half a century has passed since the publication of _Complexity and Contradiction in Architecture_ (1966), Robert Venturi's first book, which clearly laid out his anti-modernist position. In contrast to the simplification favored by modernism, Venturi proposed "complexity and contradiction," and rather than purification, he suggested the post-modern method of "blending." His antithesis to modernism has been translated into 18 languages and exerted a tremendous impact on architects all over the world.

Making his debut with Vanna Venturi House, in the early 60s, Venturi practiced a brand of architecture that distorted preexisting forms of culture and design. This initial work, based on the theme of contradiction, was completed in 1964. In 1966, he designed Guild House. At around the same time, Venturi was working on the rough draft of _Complexity and Contradiction in Architecture_, for which Vanna Venturi House in particular served as a model.

Born in Philadelphia, Venturi completed both an undergraduate and graduate degree with honors at Princeton University. After being awarded the Rome Prize, he worked under Eero Saarinen, and taught at the University of Pennsylvania and Yale. Over the years, Venturi has served as a lecturer, critic, committee member, and trustee at the University of Delaware, Harvard University, the University of Virginia, Oberlin University, Rice University, UCLA, UC Santa Barbara, and the American Academy in Rome. As a result, Venturi's firm, VSBA (Venturi, Scott Brown and Associates) has received a large number of commissions from universities.

At his alma mater alone, Venturi has been extremely prolific, completing a total of eight projects. Along with works that signaled the rise of post-modernism like Gordon Wu Hall, Lewis Thomas Laboratory, and Fisher and Bendheim Halls, there is the recently completed Frist Campus Center. The open and functional facade(called a "window wall") on the south side of the center is a modern-day masterpiece, which exhibits none of the vestiges of post-modernism.

Other outstanding examples of Venturi's post-modernist architecture can be found on campuses such as the Clinical Research Building and Perelman Quadrangle at the University of Pennsylvania, and the Gonda (Goldschmied) Neuroscience & Genetics Research Center and MacDonald Medical Research Laboratories at UCLA.

21 The Anlyan Center Medical for Research and Education at Yale University   2003 / New Haven, Connecticut
    photo: ©Matt Wargo
22 Palmer Drive Development at the University of Michigan   2005 / Ann Arbor, Michigan
    photo: ©Matt Wargo
23 Lehigh Valley Hospital   2005 / Bethlehem, Pennsylvania
    photo: ©Lehigh Valley Health System
24 Toulouse Provincial Capitol Building   1999 / Toulouse, France
    photo: ©Matt Wargo
25 Dalian Road Development / Competition

    photos : Courtesy of the Architect except ©Synectics

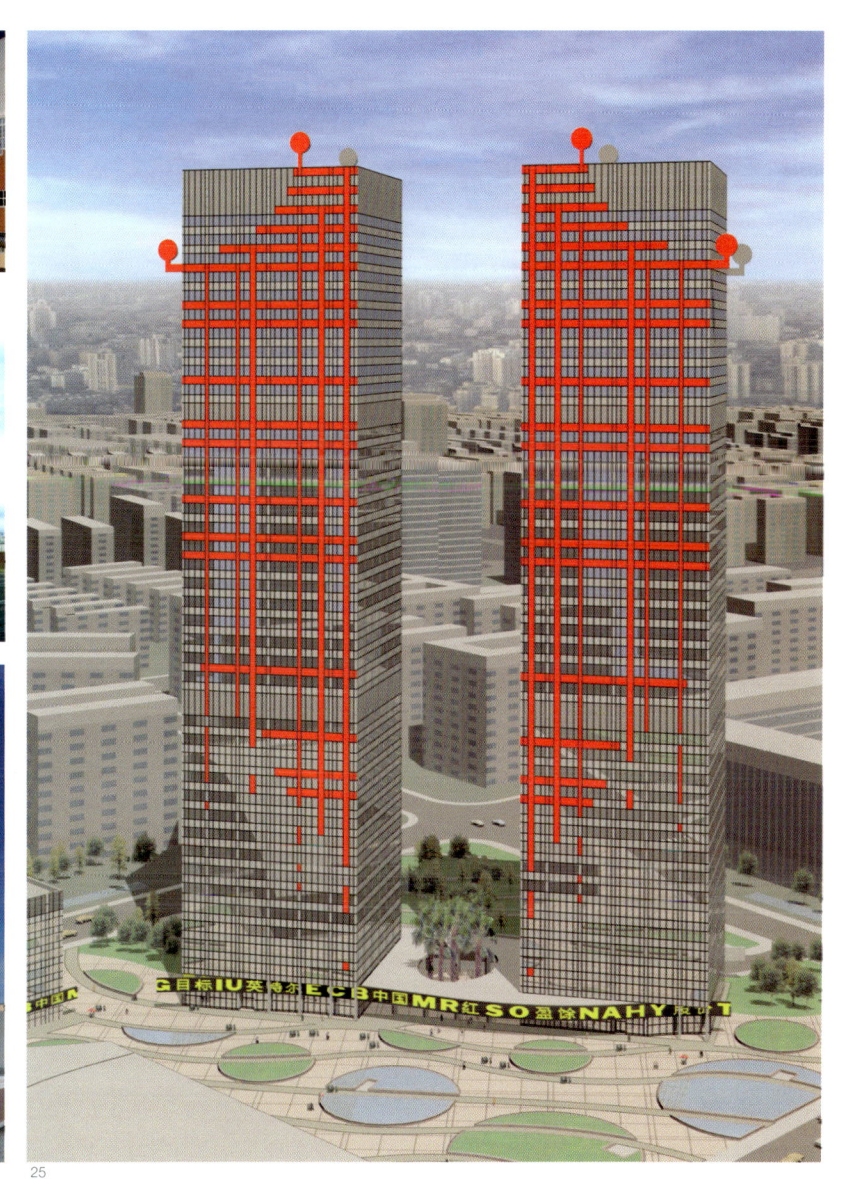

VSBA has also produced many excellent museums, including the Sainsbury Wing of the National Gallery Sainsbury Wing in London and the Seattle Art Museum – two more post-modern masterpieces. The "Mickey Mouse columns" at the Allen Memorial Art Museum, a "decorated shed" in Venturian terms, are famous symbols of post-modernism. A renovation of an older facility, the chalk-white La Jolla Wing of the San Diego Museum of Contemporary Art cuts an elegant figure along the coast in Southern California. There are also world-renowned works such as the Institute for Scientific Information, a prime example of a "decorated shed"; Franklin Court and Freedom Plaza, both of which hold strong memories of the past; and Dixwell Fire Station, symbolized by its lettered sign.

In 1990, Venturi accompanied his wife, the urban designer Denise Scott Brown, on a trip to Japan. In an interview I conducted with him, I remarked, "When it comes to postmodern architecture, Japanese architects are constantly reminded of your works and writings from the 1960s." Venturi unexpectedly shot back with a rejoinder, "It is unfortunate that we are connected to the today's post-modernism because the course that post-modernism has taken deviates greatly from what we originally set out to do."

As a lover of genuine post-modernism, this master of design who has been instrumental in the movement, also conveyed his image of the city of Tokyo with this comment, "...an aesthetic of fertility seems to take precedence over an aesthetic of neatness and orderliness. A living organism in the process of growth is inevitably faced with 'complexity and contradiction.' Contradiction is one part of growing, and growth is proof that the organism is alive. The unification of Paris is unquestionably beautiful, but it doesn't excite me quite as much as Tokyo." With his view of "complexity and contradiction" intact, Venturi left the city with the words, "Learning from Tokyo."

Even into the 21st century, Venturi has continued his long run of success with works like the Anlyan Center for Medical Research and Education at Yale University, the Biomedical Biological Science Research Building at the University of Kentucky, the Palmer Drive Development at the University of Michigan, Lehigh Valley Hospital, and the Dalian Road Development.

RAFAEL VINOLY

USA

Born in Uruguay in 1944. At the age of 20, had already become a founding partner in one of the largest architectural firms in Latin America. Relocated to the U.S. in 1978, and served as guest lecturer at the Harvard University Graduate School of Design. Settled in New York in 1979 and established own firm there in 1983. After opening a second office in London, the firm now employs over 170 people.

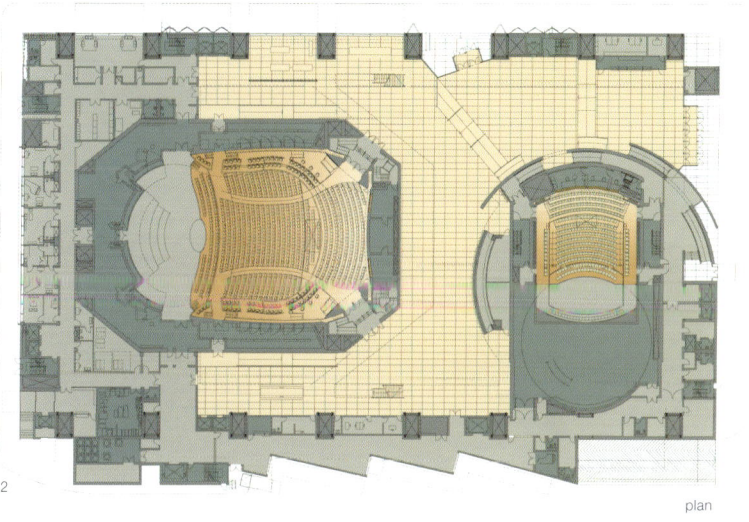

1, 2, 3 Kimmel Center for the Performing Arts   2001 / Philadelphia, Pennsylvania
photo: ©Roman Vinoly

RAFAEL VINOLY

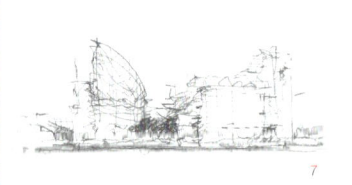

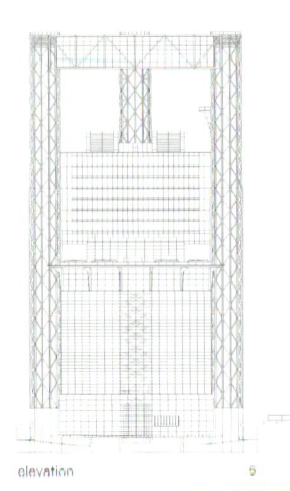

4, 5   Samsung Jong-ro Tower   1999 / Seoul
      photo: ©Kim Jung Oh

6, 7   Tokyo International Forum   1996 / Tokyo

8   Lehman College Physical Education Facility
    1994 / Bronx, New York
    photo: ©Peter Margonelli

9, 10   Princeton University Stadium
      1998 / Princeton, New Jersey
      photo: ©Michael Moran

11   Boston Convention & Exhibition Center
     2004 / Boston, Massachusetts

12, 13   David L. Lawrence Convention Center   2003 / Pittsburgh, Pennsylvania
         photo: ©Roman Vinoly

14   Jazz at Lincoln Center   2004 / New York
         photo: ©Brad Feinknopf

15   Penn State University, School of Information Sciences & Technology
         2003 / University Park, Pennsylvania
         photo: ©Joseph David

16   University of Chicago, Graduate School of Business   2004 / Chicago, Illinois
         photo: ©Brad Feinknopf

17   Carl Icahn Lab of the Lewis - Sigler Institute for Integrative Genomics at Princeton University
         2003 / Princeton, New Jersey
         photo: ©Synectics

18   Nasher Museum of Art, Duke University
         2004 / Durham, North Carolina
         photo: ©Brad Feinknopf

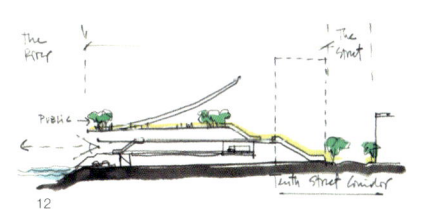

295

Rafael Vinoly

19 Residential Building at Casares & Gelly   2002 / Buenos Aires, Argentina
20 Bard College, Center for Science & Computation / Annandale-on-Hudson, New York
21 Leicester Theater and Performing Art Center / Leicester City, UK
22 Tampa Museum of Art / Competition

19

20

21

22

Rafael Vinoly is one of the most celebrated architects of the era. Although completely unknown in Japan at the time, he managed to win the Tokyo International Forum competition, the first International Union of Architects-approved project in Japan. And not only did the finished building, a huge structure, become one of Vinoly's representative designs, it drew many to his rich body of work.
Born in Uruguay in 1944, by the time Vinoly was 20, he had already become a founding partner in one of the largest architectural firms in Latin America, Estudio de Arquitectura. While working at the company's headquarters in Argentina, he decided, at the age of 34, to relocate to New York. After serving as a guest lecturer for a brief period at the Harvard University Graduate School of Design, he settled in New York in 1979, and established his own firm there in 1983.
In addition to the Tokyo International Forum, I have had the opportunity to visit Vinoly's Kimmel Center for the Performing Arts, David L. Lawrence Convention Center, Lehman College Physical Education Facility, Princeton University Stadium, and the Lewis-Sigler Institute for Integrative Genomics at Princeton University. All of these buildings are large-scale works and all of them feature a unique form and structure.
Judging from what I have seen, the charm of Vinoly's architecture lies in his dynamic structures. With a length of 208 meters and a huge roof topping the 57.5-meter building, the Tokyo International Forum is a particularly impressive example. The breathtaking roof, supported by a series of ship-bottom-shaped, cast-iron ribs, is part of a tremendous structural system bolstered by two huge spindles with a maximum diameter of 4.5 meters.
The Kimmel Center, located in Philadelphia, also boasts an absolutely stunning structural system. The large space within the gigantic, glass barrel vault that covers the site, which occupies one entire block, is created by a cornice-shaped Vierendeel truss. Within it are two concert halls in separate buildings. The urban environment has been taken inside the transparent vaulted building to create a "city within the architecture."
The Lawrence Convention Center in Pittsburgh is equipped with a suspension-bridge-type roof that was inspired by the city's many bridges. The roof element, with a long streaming appearance similar to a bolt of cloth, gives the riverside landmark its unique appearance.

23 Edificio Acqua / Punta del Este, Uruguay
24 UCLA, Nanosystems Institute / Los Angeles
25 Beijing National Swimming Center / Competition
26 Visual & Performing Arts Library in Brooklyn / Competition
27 Zuidoost - Kavel 17 Office Tower / Amsterdam
28 World Trade Center / Competition

photos : Courtesy of the Architect except ©Synectics

The Samsung Jong-ro Tower in Seoul is another awe-inspiring building. Three cylinders equipped with cross braces elevate an "urban canopy" high in the air. This high-tech machine, standing at an urban intersection, has a tremendous visual impact and symbolizes the technological innovations made in the electronic industry by the Samsung Corporation.

As with each of these buildings, Vinoly's works are notable for the original structural form he evolves for each project. In addition, just from looking at a photograph, it is easy to detect a unique form and structure in buildings such as the Boston Convention and Exhibition Center, Nasher Museum of Art at Duke University, Fortabat Collection, Van Andel Institute, John Edward Porter National Neurosciences Research Center, Princeton University Stadium, and the Lewis-Sigler Institute.

Vinoly often makes a good showing in large-scale competitions, but what sort of design methodology does he use? He is fond of saying, "Architectural projects are realized as a result of numerous restrictions. These constraints and obstructions, which are perhaps the very subject of the design, are the root of creativity." Over the last more than 20 years, Vinoly's firm has developed a methodology that supersedes the restrictions of a project. A good design is achieved through the systematic development and evaluation of a variety of proposals which emphasize a host of different aspects in the project.

In fact, for a single project, Vinoly's firm studies anywhere from three to twelve design proposals. A three-dimensional model is created for each design, which is then evaluated in terms of a number of parameters such as functionality, operation, construction cost, urban importance, and public compatibility.

In April 1990, I interviewed Vinoly for a magazine after he had won the Tokyo Forum competition. He said that as an architect he had felt a strong attraction to that large space. But as the resulting work proves, Vinoly's forte is bringing out the allure of a large space with a unique structure. Even more attractive to an anonymous journalist like me, however, was Rafael Vinoly himself, who I found to be a likable person who was unfailingly cordial and always offered friendly, humorous responses.

West 8

The Netherlands

Landscape architecture group based in Rotterdam and comprised of architects, urban planners, and designers. Adriaan Geuze, the principal of West 8, was born in Dordrecht, the Netherlands in 1960. Completed a postgraduate degree at the Agricultural University of Wageningen in 1987, and established West 8 the same year. Edits the architecture magazine _Archis_, and served as landscape supervisor for Schiphol Airport. Teaches at Delft University of Technology and Harvard University.

1 Interpolis Garden 1998 / Tilburg, The Netherlands
   photo: ©Synectics
2 One North Park 2006 / Singapore
3 Jubilee Garden / London

300

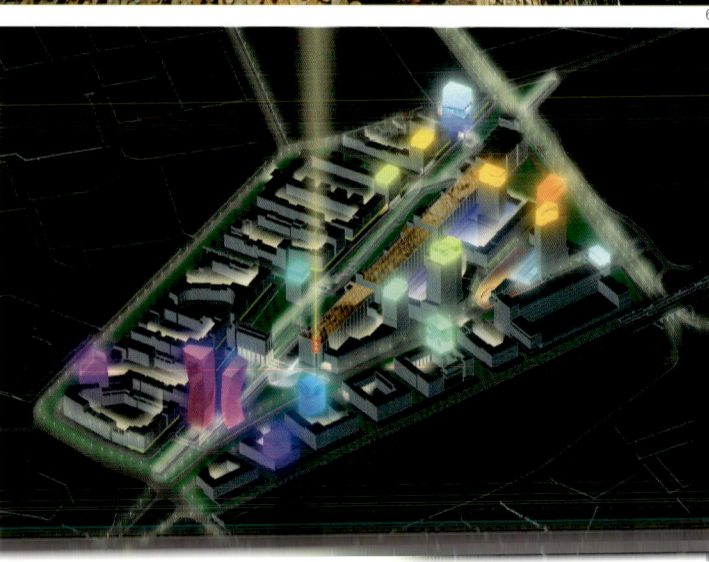

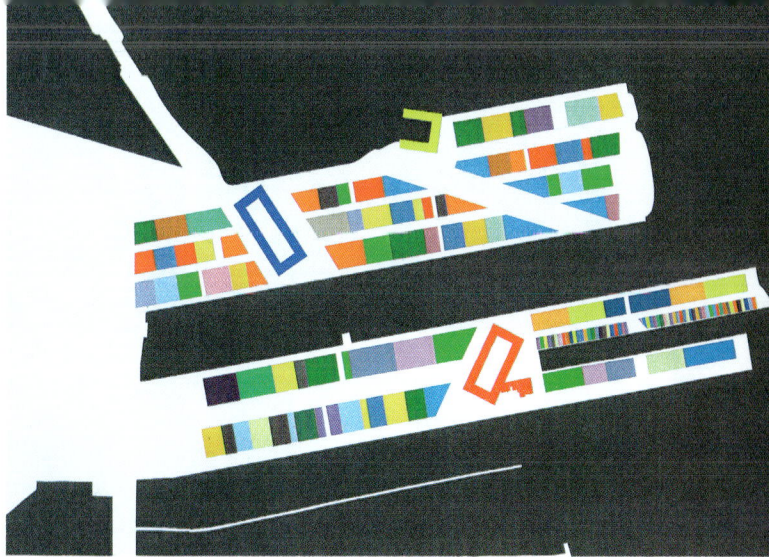

4, 5   Borneo Sporenburg   1997 / Amsterdam
       photo: © Jeroen Musch
   6   Sund Garden   2001 / Malmo, Sweden
   7   Park Strijp / Eindhoven, The Netherlands
   8   Lensvelt Garden   1999 / Breda, The Netherlands
   9   Courtyard Garden at Utrecht University Library   2005 / Utrecht, The Netherlands
  10   Chiswick Park   2000 / London
  11   Manzanares Linear Park / Madrid
  12   Swiss National EXPO'02   2002 / Yverdon-les-Bains, Switzerland

13 Tokyo Canal Project / Tokyo   design: West 8 + tele-design
   CG: ©Hajime Ishikawa with Kashmir 3D
14 Luxury Village   2000 / Moscow
15 City Theater Plaza   1996 / Rotterdam
   photo: ©Jeroen Musch
16, 17 Ypenburg de Singels   2002 / Ypenburg, The Netherlands

18 High Botanic Bridge
19 Porta Nuova / Milan
20 Kanaaleiland   2002 / Bruges, Belgium
   photo: ©Jeroen Musch

photos : Courtesy of the Architect except ©Synectics and ©Hajime Ishikawa with Kashmir 3D

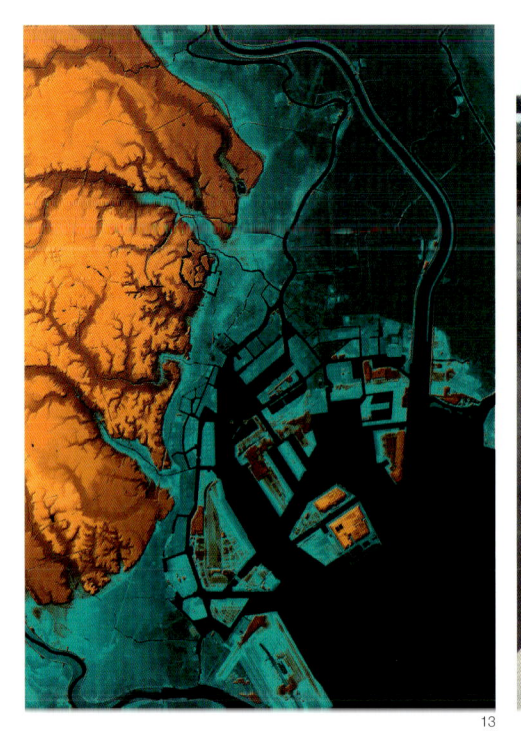

13

14

15

16   elevation

17

18

The Eastern Docklands Redevelopment Project was intended as the finale to an urban development plan that the city of Amsterdam had begun in the 1980s. In addition to the city's fundamental objective to increase residential housing, the project, which included the islands of KNSM, Java, and Borneo/Sporenburg, proposed that a large number of young architects be recruited and that they be given the opportunity to design many things.
Adriaan Geuze, the principal of West 8, was given the important role of designing the master plan for Borneo Sporenburg. Faced with the challenge of making a low-rise, high-density housing block of 100 three-level units in a one-hectare area, Geuze arrived at a solution that afforded people the maximum amount of privacy by placing a courtyard in the center of each unit. It was around this time that the name West 8 first started to become known.
Established in 1987, West 8 is not simply a landscape design firm. Comprised of a multi-disciplinary staff of architects, urban planners, designers, and landscape architects, West 8 is engaged in design and development related to every aspect of the city, including contemporary culture, urban identity, architecture, and public space.
The firm responds to an urban context with a consistently hybrid and multi-disciplinary approach. Out of this earnest, optimistic response comes solutions that would normally never be imaginable. The Borneo/Sporenburg masterplan called for the creation of spaces that respected private and personal identity within the large urban-scale of the docklands. This adept approach made it possible for both the large and the small scale to coexist.
West 8 is considered to be one of the top urban design firms in Europe. But the best indicator of its capability is the work the firm has done with prominent architects, including Enric Miralles, Richard Rogers, Steven Holl, Dominique Perrault, Norman Foster, Rem Koolhaas, Herzog and de Meuron, UN Studio, and Massimiliano Fuksas.
The work that made the greatest impact on me personally was the Interpolis Garden in the Dutch city of Tilburg. The appearance of the randomly shaped, large slate panels overlapping like fish scales is truly impressive. Unlike typical gardens with plants and trees, West 8's designs are often quite dry.
This approach has parallels with the work of noted landscape architects such as Lawrence

19

20

Halprin, Peter Walker, and Martha Schwartz. But West 8's approach is much more avant-garde. Take, for example, City Theater Plaza, located in the center of Rotterdam. Only an amateur would think that because the site is right downtown, an abundance of greenery would create an oasis where residents could relax. West 8, on the other hand, opted for no greenery at all; instead, the firm went the urban route, covering the entire square with boards and placing a parking area underground. The most surprising touch, however, was several tall, moveable lighting units, which West 8 installed on top of the plaza.

To West 8, in order to give an urban development a unique identity, it is necessary to adopt a drastic and easy-to-understand concept. This is not achieved with ready-made objects, but through the passage of time and an accumulation of richness and beauty. To accomplish this, West 8 continually refers to the context, history, landscape, and ecosystem in the local area, while also making use of market criteria and political realities. With this approach, the design itself is never such an important element.

Instead, the surveys, development parameters, and sociopolitical methods enrich the design, and guarantee quality on many levels. This generates a strong identity and fosters a mindset that will secure commercial investment. West 8 believes that urban design is a contribution to our cultural heritage.

Among the firm's representative works are many and various masterpieces, including Sund Garden in Sweden, Chiswick Park in England, and the Swiss National Expo '02 in Switzerland. Along with the three designs mentioned above, other Dutch works include Lensvelt Garden, Park Strijp, and the Courtyard Garden in the Utrecht University Library.

In recent years, West 8 has engaged in many foreign projects. Those already completed include Kanaaleiland in Belgium, Luxury Village in Moscow, and One-North Park in Singapore, and those currently underway include Jubilee Gardens in London, and Manzanares Linear Park in Madrid. In Japan too, several years ago, West 8 collaborated with Tele-design on the Tokyo Canal Project.

Tod Williams Billie Tsien

USA

Tod Williams was born in Detroit in 1943. Graduated from Princeton University in 1965, and completed a postgraduate degree in Fine Arts at the same university in 1967. Currently serves on the advisory board of the Architecture School at Princeton University. Billie Tsien was born in Ithaca, New York in 1949. Graduated from the Fine Arts Department at Yale University in 1971. Currently, the two serve as advisors to the Architectural League of New York, the Public Art Fund, American Academy in Rome, and the Lower Manhattan Development Corporation.

1   American Folk Art Museum   2001 / New York
    photo: ©Michael Moran
2,3 Mattin Center at Johns Hopkins University   2001 / Baltimore, Maryland
    photo: ©Michael Moran

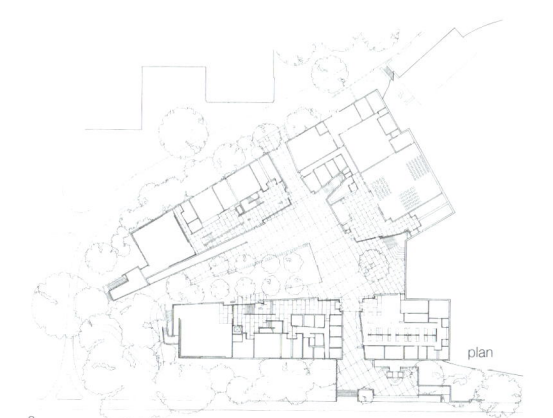

plan

3

4 Neurosciences Institute   1996 / La Jolla, California
   photo: ©Synectics
5 The New College at the University of Virginia   1992 / Charlottesville, Virginia
6 Phoenix Art Museum & Little Theater   1996 / Phoenix, Arizona
   photo: ©Synectics
7 Feinberg Hall at Prinston University   1986 / Princeton, New Jersey

8 BEA Associates Citicorp Office   1979 / New York
9 The Downtown Branch of the Whitney Museum   1988 / New York
   photo: ©Michael Moran
10 Cranbrook Natatorium   1999 / Bloomsfield Hills, Michigan
   photo: ©Michael Moran

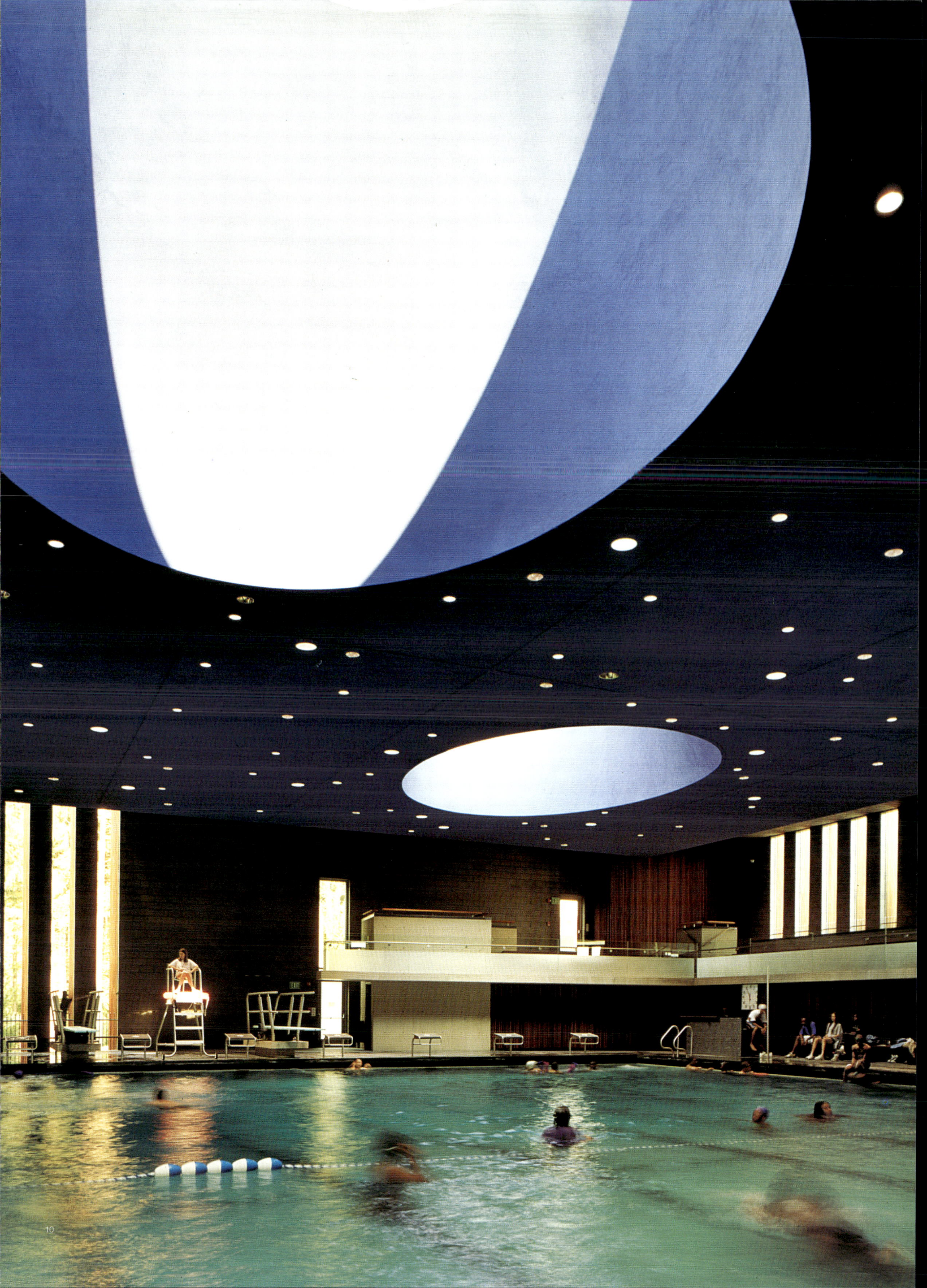

Tod Williams Billie Tsien

11 House on Long Island 1998 / Long Island, New York
   photo: ©Michael Moran
12 House on Shelter Island 2003 / Shelter Island, New York
   photo: ©Michael Moran
13 Asia Society Hong Kong Center / Hong Kong
14 The Quandt Rosenblat Loft 1991 / New York
15 Spiegel House Indoor Pool 1988 / Long Island, New York
16 Architecture Tomorrow 1989-1991 / Whitney Museum, New York, etc.
17 New York City House 1996 / New York
18 The Amphitheater in Guadalajara / Guadalajara, Mexico

To the immediate left of the main entrance to New York's Museum of Modern Art (MoMA) stands the American Folk Art Museum. With a facade that consists primarily of a metallic material, the building creates a fantastic first impression. Since the building was completed in 2001, its design, by Tod Williams Billie Tsien, has been hailed not only in the American architecture world, but in architecture magazines around the world. Compared to MoMA, the twelve-meter frontage of the building is small, but the sculpted exterior is more eye-catching than the flat facade of MoMA. The form is an abstraction of the "hand," the tool which creates folk art, and is covered with panels of tomabsil (a form of whitish bronze) used for propellors and gun barrels.

Even more popular than the building's facade is its elaborate interior. The key to the Williams-and-Tsien style is the selection of a material which is suitable to the quality of the space, and the technique used to distribute the material within it. Williams explains, "The special characteristic of our architecture lies not in the act of looking at a building, but rather in experiencing it. Therefore, the choice of materials and details as well as the construction method and the use of the building become extremely important."

In the same way, the office wing, laboratory, and auditorium at the Neurosciences Institute in La Jolla are fitted with a variety of marvelous materials and arranged in an organic way around a courtyard. As the lot is sloped, the approach leads to the upper section of the laboratory, and by looking over the unique frosted-glass balustrade, one is able to take in all of the building's features including the courtyard – an exquisite touch.

The auditorium, open to the neighboring residential area for concerts, is a particularly gorgeous place with Canadian redwood running through the interior, and an abundance of Texas limestone and Italian marble used in the walls and floors.

Born just outside of Detroit, Williams studied at Princeton and Cambridge before returning to Princeton for a graduate degree, but even as a child he dreamed of becoming an architect. Higher education merely served to finalize his goal. Tsien, meanwhile, is from New York. Initially, Tsien specialized in graphic design and though she liked painting and art, she had no interest or knowledge of architecture. But on a friend's recommendation, she entered the School of Architecture at UCLA and eventually

19 The World Upside Down 1991 / Amsterdam
20, 21 Reva and David Logan Center for Creative and Performing Arts /
Chicago, Illinois
22 Skirkanich Hall at the University of Pennsylvania
2006 / Pennsylvania, Philadelphia
photo: ©Michael Moran

photos : Courtesy of the Architect except ©Synectics

came to embrace the field.
After graduation, Williams worked at Richard Meier's firm, where after six years he became an associate. In 1973, he set out on his own, and in 1986, established his own firm with Tsien. He has taught at Cooper Union, Columbia University, Harvard University and the Southern California Institute of Architecture (SCI-Arc).
Besides UCLA, Tsien also studied at Brown and Yale University, making both of the architects part of the educationally elite. In addition, Tsien has taught at the University of Texas, SCI-Arc, and Harvard Graduate School of Design. Between the two of them, they have worked at every distinguished architecture school in the U.S.
The Neurosciences Institute, however, brought them almost immediate fame. Previous to that, they had designed small-scale works such as the BEA Associates Citicorp Office, Feinberg Hall at Princeton University, the Downtown Branch of the Whitney Museum, the Spiegel House Indoor Pool, and the Quandt Rosenblat Loft. Then in 1992, Williams and Tsien completed the New College at the University of Virginia, followed by the La Jolla work in 1996. After that, the firm really began to take off.
Having gained a certain amount of status in the American architecture world, the architects showed rapid growth with their designs for the Phoenix Art Museum and Little Theater, Cranbrook Natatorium, the Mattin Center at Johns Hopkins University, and the Folk Art Museum. Next, they embarked on their first foreign projects, the Asia Society Hong Kong Center, and the Amphitheater in Guadalajara.
"Architecture is an act of profound optimism. At its base lies the belief that more than anything else, architecture makes it possible to create places on Earth which add a sense of elegance to our lives. We begin our designs not with a concept, but with fragments of thoughts that have been fostered by the actual building." Sincerity is obviously a strength for this duo of architects.

Peter Zumthor

SWITZERLAND

Born in Basel, Switzerland in 1943. Trained as a cabinetmaker under his father in 1958. Studied at the Kunstgewerbeschule Basel in 1963, and at the Pratt Institute in New York in 1966. Worked at the Department for the Preservation of Monuments in Graubünden, Switzerland in 1968. Established his own practice in Haldenstein, Graubünden in 1979. Became visiting professor at the Technische Universität in Munich in 1989. Named special member of the Berlin Academy of Arts in 1994, and worked as visiting professor at the Harvard Graduate School of Design in 1999.

1, 2, 3, 4 Thermal Vals 1996 / Graubunden, Switzerland
photo: ©Synectics

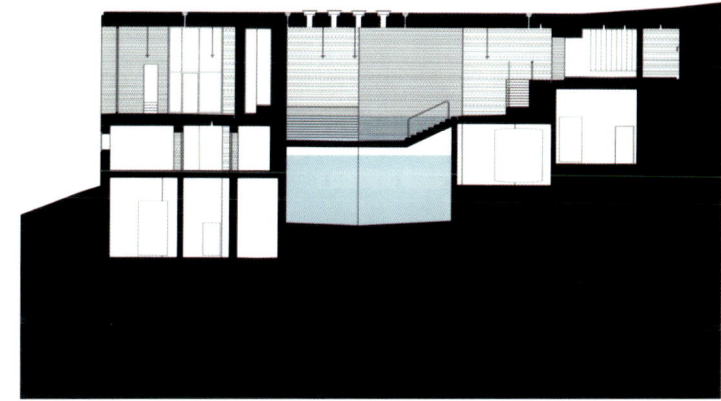

section

311

PETER ZUMTHOR

5, 6, 7   Art Museum Bregenz   1997 / Vorarlberg, Austria
photo: ©Synectics

8   Atelier Zumthor   1986 / Graubunden, Switzerland
photo: ©Synectics

9   Hannover Expo 2000 Switzerland Pavilion   2000 / Hannover, Germany
photo: ©Synectics

10   Connecting Corridor at Art Museum Chur   1990 / Chur, Switzerland
photo: ©Synectics

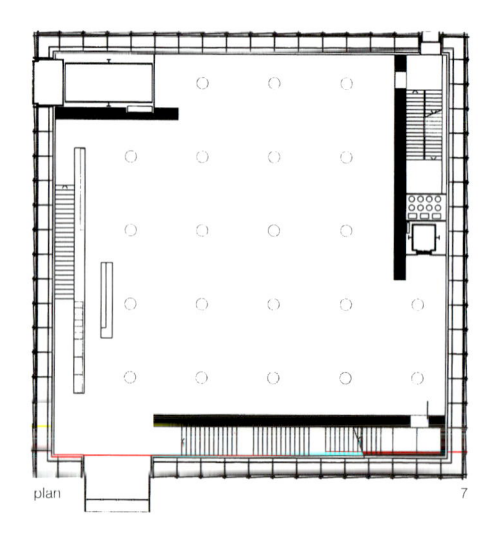

11, 12 Shelters for the Roman Archaeological Site 1986 / Graubunden, Switzerland photo: ©Synectics	15 Renovation of Tower House 1970 / Graubunden, Switzerland photo: ©Hiroshi Kai
13 Elementary School Churwalden 1983 / Graubunden, Switzerland photo: ©Hiroshi Kai	16 Renovation of Casa Communala 1970 / Graubunden, Switzerland photo: ©Hiroshi Kai
14 Renovation of Cafe du Mont 1970 / Graubunden, Switzerland photo: ©Hiroshi Kai	17, 18 Residential Home for the Elderly in Masans 1993 / Graubunden, Switzerland photo: ©Synectics

19, 20, 21 Saint Benedict Chapel   1989 / Graubunden, Switzerland
photo: ©Synectics

19

20

21 plan

Deep in the mountains of eastern Switzerland lies the small village of Vals, where hot springs have been bubbling up for over 100 years. After a hotel was built, and visitors came to test the waters, the town really came into its own. But what has made it even more famous is a bathing facility called Thermal Vals that was designed by Peter Zumthor.
In the singular Swiss landscape, which unfolds against a backdrop of precipitous mountain peaks, Thermal Vals stands submerged on the lot's western slope. The mountain greenery slants downward to become one with the roof of the building. The interior and exterior walls of the structure, about half of which is underground, are made of thinly sliced layers of gneiss from the Vals area. The visibly dense, slate-blue texture is enough to send a shiver through any architect. Only Zumthor could create such a charming appearance simply through his handling of a material. I also understand the attraction of the building, having visited and stayed in the hotel three times and savored the architecture, springs, bar, Zumthor's room, and the landscape. According to Zumthor's wife, who serves as the director of the facility, "In terms of healing power, three days here is equal to three weeks at an Italian resort." My personal feeling, though, is that nothing can compare with the cool, silent inner and outer walls, and the magnificent sight of the remaining patches of snow framed by the terrace.
Peter Zumthor was trained as a furniture craftsman by his father, a professional artisan. After attending art school in Basel, Zumthor graduated from New York's Pratt Institute with a degree in architecture. Needless to say, this explains why Zumthor has such a wealth of knowledge about materials and such a subtle sense of expression. The products of these special talents are Thermal Vals and his next masterwork, Saint Benedict Chapel.
The small church, a wooden structure with a leaf-like planar form, is surrounded by a shingle-thatch exterior wall. Zumthor has been quoted as saying, "By receiving the site of the building, the material becomes a poetic existence." The color of the simple, shingle wall has changed by being exposed to the elements, giving it an appearance that is suited to a rustic, rural chapel. Both the hotel and the chapel are fine examples of Zumthor's poetic way with stone and wood – natural materials which he is especially adept at using –, but for his next important work, the Art Museum Bregenz, the architect proved that he was just as skillful at dealing with artificial materials such as glass and concrete.

22 Topography of Terror
23 Rath House 1983 / Graubunden, Switzerland
    photo: ©Ludwig Abache
24 Gugalun House 1994 / Graubunden, Switzerland
    photo: ©Henry Pierre Schultz
25 Spittelhof Housing 1996 / Basel, Switzerland
    photo: ©Noriko Sato

22 site planning 23

24 25

At the Art Museum Bregenz, located in Austria alongside Lake Bodensee, there is a semi-skeletal exterior wall, which is surrounded by many frosted glass units of the same size. At nightfall, the structure becomes a light box that glows like a firefly. The double skin, with a clear-glass interior wall and a frosted glass interior, has a sustainable design in which fresh air is allowed to flow between the two glass sections.
At the top of each of the building's four floors is a "light room," an artful device which allows natural light from outside to fall across the exhibition rooms through the glass floor (the ceiling of the room below). Structurally independent, the three thick, reinforced concrete bearing walls which stand inside the building support the floor slab on each level in a composition that resembles Mies van der Rohe's Barcelona Pavilion.

In addition to these three, there are many fine Zumthor works, including some early ones, throughout the canton of Grabunden, where the architect also has Atelier Zumthor. In Chur, the capital of the canton, is the Shelter for the Roman Archaeological Site, which formed the basis for Zumthor's masterful handling of wood in the Swiss Pavilion at the Hannover Expo 2000. The work, which uses slender pieces of wood as horizontal members, can be viewed in contrast to the vertical members used in the connecting corridor at Art Museum Chur. Zumthor's Residential Home for the Elderly, which makes use of tufa stone, larch wood and concrete, is located in Masans. The lavish stone and warm wooden design has apparently proved very popular with the people there. Further south of Chur in the mountainous Lumnezia area, one finds numerous early works by Zumthor, created when he was first getting his start as an architect.
Works such as the 1970 Casa Communala, Cafe du Mont, and Chisti Tower House are all renovations of traditional vernacular architecture. Zumthor's craftsmanship is defined by a respect for traditional details and original furnishings, while adding new design elements to arrive at a unified whole. The elementary school Zumthor built on a slope in Churwalden is also filled with his philosophy of engaging in conversation with a place.
In recent years, Zumthor has been engaged in the Kolumba Diocesan Museum (Germany), and Hotel Tschlin and the Private Chapel for a Farmhouse (both in Switzerland). As these works move forward, more hallmarks of Zumor's artisanal expertise, filled with a sense of tranquility, will begin to appear.

315

Works Index

IN ALPHABETICAL ORDER OF COUNTRIES / CITIES.
*Not existed now.

Argentina

Torre Bank Boston   2000 / Buenos Aires   *Cesar Pelli*   **pp.194-16**

Residential Building at Casares & Gelly   2002 / Buenos Aires   *Rafael Vinoly*   **pp.296-19**

Renovation for Corrientes Street   2006 / Buenos Aires   *Miguel Angel Roca*   **pp.212-16**

Spain Plaza   1969 / Cordoba   *Miguel Angel Roca*   **pp.213-17**

Santo Domingo Housing Complex   1975 / Cordoba   *Miguel Angel Roca*   **pp.208-1,2**

Paseo De Las Artes Cultural Center   1979 / Cordoba   *Miguel Angel Roca*   **pp.212-12**

Italia Plaza   1980 / Cordoba   *Miguel Angel Roca*   **pp.212-13**

Plaza de Armas   1981 / Cordoba   *Miguel Angel Roca*   **pp.209-3**

Cordoba Office Center   1993 / Cordoba   *Miguel Angel Roca*   **pp.212-10**

Claustrorum at the National University of Cordoba
1998 / Cordoba   *Miguel Angel Roca*   **pp.212-14**

CPC Route 20   1999 / Cordoba   *Miguel Angel Roca*   **pp.209-5**

CPC Monsenor Pablo Cabrera   1999 / Cordoba   *Miguel Angel Roca*   **pp.213-18**

School of Arts at the National University of Cordoba
2001 / Cordoba   *Miguel Angel Roca*   **pp.209-6**

Faculty of Law at the National University of Cordoba
2001 / Cordoba   *Miguel Angel Roca*   **pp.210-9**

Post-graduate School of Economics at the National University of Cordoba
2001 / Cordoba   *Miguel Angel Roca*   **pp.212-11**

House at Calamuchita   2004 / Cordoba   *Miguel Angel Roca*   **pp.212-15**

Underground Passage between Two Museums in Cordoba
2006 / Cordoba   *Miguel Angel Roca*   **pp.213-19**

Austria

House W   1974 / Graz   *Szyszkowitz-Kowalski*   **pp.265-9**

Kastner+Ohler Department Store Extension   1994 / Graz   *Szyszkowitz-Kowalski*   **pp.265-7**

House K   1996 / Graz   *Szyszkowitz-Kowalski*   **pp.267-21**

Schiessstatte Housing Estate   1999 / Graz   *Szyszkowitz-Kowalski*   **pp.265-11, 12**

Institute for Biochemistry and Biotechnology, Technical University of Graz
2000 / Graz   *Szyszkowitz-Kowalski*   **pp.262-1**

Center of Studies, Technical University of Graz
2000 / Graz   *Szyszkowitz-Kowalski*   **pp.266-15**

Kastner+Ohler Underground Parking   2003 / Graz   *Szyszkowitz-Kowalski*   **pp.265-13**

The Headquarters of the Steiermarkische Sparkasse Bank
2006 / Graz   *Szyszkowitz-Kowalski*   **pp.267-22**

Catholic Parish Center Graz-Ragnitz
1987 / Graz-Ragnitz   *Szyszkowitz-Kowalski*   **pp.264-5,6**

St. Ulrich Cultural Center   2000 / Greith   *Szyszkowitz-Kowalski*   **pp.265-10**

Innsbruck Town Hall   2002 / Innsbruck   *Dominique Perrault*   **pp.199-9**

Electrical Substation   2002 / Innsbruck   *UN Studio*   **pp.276-7**

Karikatur Museum   2001 / Krems   *Gustav Peichl*   **pp.186-4**

EVN Forum   1993 / Maria Enzersdolf   *Gustav Peichl*   **pp.186-8**

Europark   1997 / Salzburg   *Massimiliano Fuksas*   **pp.54-15**

ORF Station in St. Polten   1994 / St. Polten   *Gustav Peichl*   **pp.186-7**

Exhibition Hall and Museum in St. Polten   2002 / St. Polten   *Hans Hollein*   **pp.97-13**

Retti Candle Shop   1965 / Vienna   *Hans Hollein*   **pp.94-1**

Schullin Jeweller I   1974 / Vienna   *Hans Hollein*   **pp.97-14**

Haas Haus   1990 / Vienna   *Hans Hollein*   **pp.95-4**

Rehearsal Stage of the Burgtheater   1993 / Vienna   *Gustav Peichl*   **pp.189-21**

Alte Donau Tower   1998 / Vienna   *Gustav Peichl*   **pp.188-13**

Public School in Donau City   1999 / Vienna   *Hans Hollein*   **pp.99-22**

Millennium Tower   1999 / Vienna   *Gustav Peichl*   **pp.185-3**

Erzherzog Karl Stadt Apartment   1999 / Vienna   *Gustav Peichl*   **pp.189-20**

Generali / Media-Tower   2001 / Vienna   *Hans Hollein*   **pp.97-15**

Vienna Twin Towers   2001 / Vienna   *Massimiliano Fuksas*   **pp.56-21**

Messe Wien   2003 / Vienna   *Gustav Peichl*   **pp.186-6**

Albertina Museum   2004 / Vienna   *Hans Hollein*   **pp.97-17**

Saturn Tower   2004 / Vienna   *Hans Hollein*   **pp.99-23**

Toscanahof   2004 / Vienna   *Gustav Peichl*   **pp.189-18,19**

Art Museum Bregenz   1997 / Vorarlberg   *Peter Zumthor*   **pp.312-5,6,7**

Belgium

Kanaaleiland   2002 / Bruges   *WEST 8*   **pp.303-20**

European Union Headquarters   1998 / Brussels   *Helmut Jahn*   **pp.105-22**

Bolivia

La Florida Park   1990 / La Paz, Bolivia   *Miguel Angel Roca*   **pp.210-7,8**

Uruguay Central District Council   1991 / La Paz, Bolivia   *Miguel Angel Roca*   **pp.209-4**

Canada

St. Mary's Roman Catholic Church   1968 / Alberta   *Douglas Cardinal*   **pp.40-1**

Fairview Elementary School   1975 / Alberta   *Douglas Cardinal*   **pp.45-22**

St. Albert Place   1976 / Alberta   *Douglas Cardinal*   **pp.41-3**

Grande Prairie Regional College   1976 / Alberta   *Douglas Cardinal*   **pp.41-4,5**

Alberta Government Services Building   1976 / Alberta   *Douglas Cardinal*   **pp.45-24**

Cardinal Studio & Residence   1982 / Alberta   *Douglas Cardinal*   **pp.43-10,11,12**

Edonton Space Sciences Center   1983 / Alberta   *Douglas Cardinal*   **pp.41-6,7**

Neeganin Round House & Park   2000 / Manitoba   *Douglas Cardinal*   **pp.45-19**

Grand Traverse Band of Ottawa & Chippewa Indian Civic Center
2001 / Michigan *Douglas Cardinal* pp.41-8

York Regional Headquarters 1992 / New Market *Douglas Cardinal* pp.45-17

Center for Cellular and Biomolecular Research University of Toronto
2005 / Ontario *Gunther Behnisch(B,B&P)* pp.30-5

Iskotew Healing Lodge 2002 / Ottawa *Douglas Cardinal* pp.45-18

Canadian Museum of Civilization 1989 / Quebec *Douglas Cardinal* pp.42-9

First Nations University of Canada 2003 / Saskatchewan *Douglas Cardinal* pp.45-23

Ontario College of Art & Design 2004 / Toronto *William Alsop* pp.12-6

China
Hong Kong Stadium 1983 / Hong Kong *HOK* pp.93-21

Emporio Armani 2003 / Hong Kong *Massimiliano Fuksas* pp.55-20

International Finace Center 2004 / Hong Kong *Cesar Pelli* pp.190-1,2

Jin Mao Tower 1999 / Shanghai *SOM* pp.253-5,6

Shanghai International Expo Center 2001 / Shanghai *Helmut Jahn* pp.104-10

Plaza 66 2002 / Shanghai *KPF* pp.126-3

Fangyuan Mansion 2001 / Shenyang *C.Y.Lee* pp.132-6

Cuba
Villa Armenteros 1950 / Havana *Ricardo Porro* pp.204-4

School of Plastic Arts 1964 / Havana *Ricardo Porro* pp.202,203-1,2,3

School of Modern Dance 1964 / Havana *Ricardo Porro* pp.204-7,8,9

Czech
Kafka Memorial 1966 / Praha *Future Systems* pp.59-5

Denmark
Aarhus Museum of Modern Art(ARoS)
2004 / Aarhus *Schmidt Hammer Lassen* pp.232-5,6

The Danish Royal Library
1999 / Copenhagen *Schmidt Hammer Lassen* pp.234,235-9,10

Nykredit New Headquarters
2001 / Copenhagen *Schmidt Hammer Lassen* pp.236-14

Frosilos Housing 2005 / Copenhagen *MVRDV* pp.165-19

European Film College 1993 / Ebeltoft *Heikkinen-Komonen* pp.72-4

The Frigate Jylland 2005 / Ebeltoft *Schmidt Hammer Lassen* pp.237-18

Sparekassen Ostjylland 2005 / Hammel *Schmidt Hammer Lassen* pp.237-17

Testrup Folk High School 1999 / Marslet *Schmidt Hammer Lassen* pp.237-15

Culture Island in Middelfart 2005 / Middelfart *Schmidt Hammer Lassen* pp.237-16

Egypt
Alexandria Library 2002 / Alexandria *Snohetta* pp.239-2,3

Finland
McDonald's Finnish Headquarters 1997 / Helsinki *Heikkinen-Komonen* pp.75-11

Vuotalo Cultural Center 2000 / Helsinki *Heikkinen-Komonen* pp.73-5

Lume Mediacenter 2000 / Helsinki *eikkinen-Komonen* pp.73-6

Stakes and Senate Properties Office Building
2002 / Helsinki *Heikkinen-Komonen* pp.75-12

Juminkeko Center of Carelian Culture 1999 / Kuhmo *Heikkinen-Komonen* pp.75-10

Emergency Services College Phase IV 1998 / Kuopio *Heikkinen-Komonen* pp.75-13,14

Lappeenranta University of Technology, Phase VII
2004 / Lappeenranta *Heikkinen-Komonen* pp.74-9

Rovaniemi Airport Terminal 1992 / Rovaniemi *Heikkinen-Komonen* pp.71-2

House Kosketus 2000 / Tuusula *Heikkinen-Komonen* pp.75-15

Heureka, Finnish Science Center 1988 / Vantaa *Heikkinen-Komonen* pp.70-1

France
Michel Serres Science Center in Agen 1998 / Agen *Frederic Borel* pp.38,39-14,15,16

Agen Institute for local Development 2002 / Agen *Frederic Borel* pp.34-1,2

VULCANIA 2002 / Auvergne *Hans Hollein* pp.96-11,12

Vassiviere Art Center 1991 / Bess et Saint Anastasise *Aldo Rossi* pp.219-22

Theater & Concert Hall in Blois 1991 / Blois *Frederic Borel* pp.35-4

The Maison des Arts at Michel de Montaigne University
1995 / Bordeaux *Massimiliano Fuksas* pp.54-14

Villa One 1995 / Britanny *Dominique Perrault* pp.200-15

Tax Center at Brive 1999 / Brive *Frederic Borel* pp.37-13

Axe Majeur 1980 / Cergy-Pontoise *Dani Karavan* pp.108-5

Students Dwellings in Cergy Pontoise 1994 / Cergy Pontoise *Ricardo Porro* pp.207-19

College de Cergy-le-Haut 1997 / Cergy-le-Haut *Ricardo Porro* pp.205-10

Dreux Theater 1994 / Dreux *Frederic Borel* pp.35-3

Homage to the Prisoners of the Camp Gurs 1994 / Gurs *Dani Karavan* pp.110-17

SAGEP 1993 / Ivry-sur-Seine *Dominique Perrault* pp.200-17

Dwellings in La Courneuve 1995 / La Courneuve *Ricardo Porro* pp.206-13,14

Aplix Factory 1999 / Le Cellier-sur-Loire *Dominique Perrault* pp.199-8

Maison Folie 2003 / Lille *NOX* pp.174,175-9,10,11

The Faculty of Law and Economics at the University of Limoges
1996 / Limoges *Massimiliano Fuksas* pp.54-13

Venissieux Central Mediatheque 2001 / Lyon *Dominique Perrault* pp.199-7

Hotel du Department des Bouches du Rhone 1994 / Marseilles *William Alsop* pp.12-7

Institute for Neurobiologie in Marseilles   2003 / Marseilles   *Snohetta*   **pp.240-6**

College Fabien   1993 / Montreuil   *Ricardo Porro*   **pp.206-15**

Espace de l'Art Concret   2003 / Mouans-Sartoux   *Gigon/Guyer*   **pp.69-23**

Ricola-Europe SA, Production and Storage Building
1993 / Mulhouse-Brunstatt   *Herzog & de Meuron*   **pp.85-14**

Entrance to the Cave Painting Museum   1993 / Niaux   *Massimiliano Fuksas*   **pp.54-11**

ESIEE   1987 / Paris   *Dominique Perrault*   **pp.198-6**

Housing on Ramponeau Street   1989 / Paris   *Frederic Borel*   **pp.39-17**

Housing on Belleville Street   1989 / Paris   *Frederic Borel*   **pp.39-19**

Hotel Industriel Berlier   1990 / Paris   *Dominique Perrault*   **pp.200-16**

Barracs of the Republican Security Force in Velizy   1991 / Paris   *Ricardo Porro*   **pp.206-16**

Wohnanlage La Villette   1991 / Paris   *Aldo Rossi*   **pp.219-27**

Canal+Headquarters   1992 / Paris   *Richard Meier*   **pp.151-10**

Housing on Oberkampf Street   1993 / Paris   *Frederic Borel*   **pp.37-9,10**

Sports Complex+Parking   1993 / Paris   *Massimiliano Fuksas*   **pp.54-10**

French National Library   1995 / Paris   *Dominique Perrault*   **pp.198-4**

Square of Tolerance-Homage to Yitzhak Rabin   1996 / Paris   *Dani Karavan*   **pp.110-15**

Housing on Pelleport Street   1998 / Paris   *Frederic Borel*   **pp.36-7,8**

School on Moskowa Street   2000 / Paris   *Frederic Borel*   **pp.39-20**

Social Housing Units on Switzerland Street   2000 / Paris   *Herzog & de Meuron*   **pp.84-7**

Nursery School on Recollects Street   2002 / Paris   *Frederic Borel*   **pp.35-5**

Police Headquarter in Plaisir   2006 / Plaisir   *Ricardo Porro*   **pp.207-17**

Reze Cultural Center & Mediatheque   1991 / Reze   *Massimiliano Fuksas*   **pp.54-8**

Restaurant & Hotel, Technical High School in Rouen
2004 / Rouen   *Ricardo Porro*   **pp.207-20**

College Elsa Triolet   1990 / Saint Denis   *Ricardo Porro*   **pp.206-19**

Saint-Exupery College   1993 / Seine-Saint-Denis   *Massimiliano Fuksas*   **pp.54-12**

30 Residential Dwellings in Stains   1991 / Stains   *Ricardo Porro*   **pp.205-11**

Toulouse Provincial Capitol Building   1999 / Toulouse   *VSBA*   **pp.291-24**

Germany

Burda Collection Museum   2004 / Baden-Baden   *Richard Meier*   **pp.151-13**

House H   1993 / Bad Mergentheim   *Szyszkowitz-Kowalski*   **pp.263-2,3**

Berlin Cleansing Department   1978 / Berlin   *Josef Paul Kleihues*   **pp.122-13,14**

IBA Housing at Wilhelmstrasse   1984 / Berlin   *Aldo Rossi*   **pp.219-23**

Phosphate Elimination Plant, Berlin-Tegel   1985 / Berlin   *Gustav Peichl*   **pp.186-9**

Hospital Berlin-Neukolln   1986 / Berlin   *Josef Paul Kleihues*   **pp.122-15**

IBA Housing at Thomas Dehler Strasse   1986 / Berlin   *Aldo Rossi*   **pp.219-24**

Kant Triangle   1994 / Berlin   *Josef Paul Kleihues*   **pp.120-6,7**

Museum of Contemporary Art, Berlin   1996 / Berlin   *Josef Paul Kleihues*   **pp.118-1,2**

Triangle   1996 / Berlin   *Josef Paul Kleihues*   **pp.118-3**

Olympic Velodrome and Swimming Pool   1997 / Berlin   *Dominique Perrault*   **pp.198-3**

Photonikzentrum   1998 / Berlin   *Sauerbruch Hutton*   **pp.226-4**

KITA-Kindergarden   1999 / Berlin   *Gustav Peichl*   **pp.186-5**

GSW Headquarters   1999 / Berlin   *Sauerbruch Hutton*   **pp.227-5,6**

Zumzobel Staff   1999 / Berlin   *Sauerbruch Hutton*   **pp.229-11**

The Royal Norwegian Embassy in Berlin   1999 / Berlin   *Snohetta*   **pp.241-10,11**

IBA Housing at Schutzenstrasse   1999 / Berlin   *Aldo Rossi*   **pp.219-26**

Sony Center   2000 / Berlin   *Helmut Jahn*   **pp.101-2,3**

Neues Kranzler Eck   2000 / Berlin   *Helmut Jahn*   **pp.105-18**

The British Council in Germany   2000 / Berlin   *Sauerbruch Hutton*   **pp.229-13**

Sony Center   2000 / Berlin   *Helmut Jahn*   **pp.101-2,3**

Austrian Embassy in Berlin   2001 / Berlin   *Hans Hollein*   **pp.97-16**

Federal Ministry of Labour and Social Affairs
2001 / Berlin   *Josef Paul Kleihues*   **pp.122-16,17**

Grundgesetz 49   2002 / Berlin   *Dani Karavan*   **pp.108-7**

Berlin Fire & Police Station for the Government District
2004 / Berlin   *Sauerbruch Hutton*   **pp.230-14,15**

Academy of Fine Arts Berlin   2005 / Berlin   *Gunther Behnisch(B&P)*   **pp.31-12**

Hotel Maritim   2005 / Berlin   *Josef Paul Kleihues(Jan Kleihues)*   **pp.123-19**

Hotel Concorde   2005 / Berlin   *Josef Paul Kleihues(Jan Kleihues)*   **pp.123-21**

Museum of Fantasy   2001 / Bernried   *Gunther Behnisch(B,B&P)*   **pp.32-19**

Pharmacological Research Laboratories in Biberach
2002 / Biberach   *Sauerbruch Hutton*   **pp.229-12**

Plenary Complex of the German Bundestag
1992 / Bonn   *Gunther Behnisch(B&P)*   **pp.30-4**

German Art and Exhibition Hall   1992 / Bonn   *Gustav Peichl*   **pp.184-1**

Post Tower   2003 / Bonn   *Helmut Jahn*   **pp.103-6,7**

Kaufhof Galerria   2001 / Chemnitz   *Helmut Jahn*   **pp.105-20**

Ma'alot   1986 / Cologne   *Dani Karavan*   **pp.108-6**

Cologne/Bonn Airport   2000 / Cologne   *Helmut Jahn*   **pp.104-15**

Cologne Media Park Office Complex   2004 / Cologne   *Herman Hertzberger*   **pp.78,79-9,10**

Federal Agency for the Environment   2005 / Dessau   *Sauerbruch Hutton*   **pp.228,229-7,8**

High-Bay Warehouse for Sedus   2003 / Dogern   *Sauerbruch Hutton*   **pp.231-18**

St. Benno Gymnasium   1996 / Dresden   *Gunther Behnisch(B,B&P)*   **pp.31-10**

Max Planck Institute of Molecular Cell Biology and Genetics
2001 / Dresden   *Heikkinen-Komonen*   **pp.75-16**

Mildred Scheel Haus   2002 / Dresden   *Gunther Behnisch(B&P)*   **pp.31-18**

Dialogue   1989 / Duisburg   *Dani Karavan*   pp.110-18

Garden of Memories   1999 / Duisburg   *Dani Karavan*   pp.110-16

Colorium   2002 / Dusseldorf   *William Alsop*   pp.14-13

Library of the Eberswalde Technical School
1999 / Eberswalde   *Herzog & de Meuron*   pp.87-18

Frankfurt Museum for Applied Arts   1985 / Frankfurt   *Richard Meier*   pp.151-9

Museum of Pre- and Early History   1986 / Frankfurt   *Josef Paul Kleihues*   pp.119-4,5

German Postal Museum   1990 / Frankfurt   *Gunther Behnisch(B&P)*   pp.31-14

Museum of Modern Art in Frankfurt   1991 / Frankfurt   *Hans Hollein*   pp.95-5

Messeturm   1991 / Frankfurt   *Helmut Jahn*   pp.105-17

DG Bank Headquarters   1993 / Frankfurt   *KPF*   pp.127-9

Geschwister Scholl Schule   1994 / Frankfurt   *Gunther Behnisch(B&P)*   pp.31-11

Mimaamakim   1997 / Gelsenkirchen   *Dani Karavan*   pp.111-20

IBA Emscher Park Housing Estate   1997 / Gelsenkirchen   *Szyszkowitz-Kowalski*   pp.263-4

Erotic Arts Museum   1997 / Hamburg   *William Alsop*   pp.14-14

Hamburg Music School   2000 / Hamburg   *Enric Miralles Benedetta Tagliabue*   pp.156-7

Alsterfleet Office Building   2002 / Hamburg   *Massimiliano Fuksas*   pp.54-16

Hanse-Forum Offices   2002 / Hamburg   *Massimiliano Fuksas*   pp.55-19

*Hannover Expo 2000 Dutch Pavilion   2000 / Hannover   *MVRDV*   pp.162-6,7

*Hannover Expo 2000 Switzerland Pavilion   2000 / Hannover   *Peter Zumthor*   pp.312-9

North German State Clearing Bank   2002 / Hannover   *Gunther Behnisch(B,B&P)*   pp.29-2,3

Hennigsdorf Town Hall   2003 / Hennigsdorf   *Sauerbruch Hutton*   pp.228-10

Kornwestheim City Gallery   1989 / Kornwestheim   *Josef Paul Kleihues*   pp.121-9

Bayer AG Konzernzentrale   2001 / Leverkusen   *Helmut Jahn*   pp.104-12

LVA State Institute Agency   1997 / Lubeck   *Gunther Behnisch(B,B&P)*   pp.30-7,8

Experimental Factory in Magdeburg   2001 / Magdeburg   *Sauerbruch Hutton*   pp.228-9

Abteiberg Museum   1982 / Monchengladbach   *Hans Hollein*   pp.94-3

Olympic Park in Munich   1972 / Munich   *Gunther Behnisch(B&P)*   pp.32-20

Goetz Gallery   1992 / Munich   *Herzog & de Meuron*   pp.85-13

Kempinski Hotel   1994 / Munich   *Helmut Jahn*   pp.104-14

Munich Airport Center   1999 / Munich   *Helmut Jahn*   pp.104-11

Neues Haus   2001 / Munich   *Gustav Peichl*   pp.189-17

Highlight Munich Business Towers   2003 / Munich   *Helmut Jahn*   pp.105-16

Arianz Arena   2005 / Munich   *Herzog & de Meuron*   pp.84-5

Way of Human Rights   1993 / Nuremberg   *Dani Karavan*   pp.111-21

Air Control Tower Nuremberg Airport
1998 / Nuremberg   *Gunther Behnisch(B&P)*   pp.31-9

Office and Health Center by the City Park
2006 / Nuremberg   *Szyszkowitz-Kowalski*   pp.266-18,19,20

Kalkriese Archaeological Museum and Park
2002 / Osnabruck   *Gigon/Guyer*   pp.66,67-10

Health and Spa Facilities Bad Elster   1999 / Saxony   *Gunther Behnisch(B&P)*   pp.31-13

Hysolar Institute Building   1987 / Stuttgart   *Gunther Behnisch(B&P)*   pp.32-21

Feuerbach Station   1991 / Stuttgart   *Gunther Behnisch(B&P)*   pp.33-25

Reconstruction of the Bayerishe Vereinsbank
1996 / Stuttgart   *Gunther Behnisch(B,B&P)*   pp.33-24

State Clearing Bank   1997 / Stuttgart   *Gunther Behnisch(B,B&P)*   pp.28-1

Mercedes-Benz Museum   2006 / Stuttgart   *UN Studio*   pp.275-5,6

Ulm Exhibition and Assembly Hall   1993 / Ulm   *Richard Meier*   pp.149-3

Aktion Poliphile   1992 / Wiesbaden   *Studio Granda*   pp.260-14,15

Greenland
Culture Center   1997 / Nukk   *Schmidt Hammer Larsen*   pp.234-7,8

Guinea
School for Chicken Farmers   1999 / Kindia   *Heikkinen-Komonen*   pp.73-7,8

Villa Eila   1995 / Mali   *Heikkinen-Komonen*   pp.71-3

Hungary
Baks Village Community Center   1988 / Baks   *Imre Makovecz*   pp.140-11

Farkasret Funeral Chapel   1977 / Budapest   *Imre Makoveczpp*   pp.139-10

ING Bank and NN Hungary Offices   1994 / Budapest   *Erick van Egeraat*   pp.284-15,16

ING Head Office   2004 / Budapest   *Erick van Egeraat*   pp.280,281-1

Deak Palace Renovation   2004 / Budapest   *Erick van Egeraat*   pp.285-22

Dobogoko Ski Lodge   1979 / Dobogoko   *Imre Makovecz*   pp.141-16

Eger Swimming Pool   2000 / Eger   *Imre Makovecz*   pp.138-8

Mako Theater   1998 / Mako   *Imre Makovecz*   pp.136,137-4

Paks Roman Catholic Church   1991 / Paks   *Imre Makovecz*   pp.138-5,6,7

Large Auditorium at Peter Pazmany Catholic University
2001 / Piliscsaba   *Imre Makovecz*   pp.138-9

Sarospatak Cultural Center   1983 / Sarospatak   *Imre Makovecz*   pp.136-1

Siofok Lutheran Church   1990 / Siofok   *Imre Makovecz*   pp.141-15

Szazhalombatta Roman Catholic Church
1996 / Szazhalombatta   *Imre Makovecz*   pp.141-18

Szigetvar Cultural Center   1988 / Szigetvar   *Imre Makovecz*   pp.141-12,13

Tokaj Meeting Pavilion   1979 / Tokaj   *Imre Makovecz*   pp.141-17

Mogyoro-hegy Restaurant   1979 / Visegrad   *Imre Makovecz*   pp.141-14

Visegrad Forest Educational Center   1987 / Visegrad   *Imre Makovecz*   pp.136-2,3

Iceland

Skrudas Residence   2004 / Gardabaer   *Studio Granda*   pp.261-23

Bifrost Business School Extension, Cafe and Quadrangle
2002 / Nordurdalur   *Studio Granda*   pp.261-19

Student Accommodation & Research Wing at Bifrost Business School
2005 / Nordurdalur   *Studio Granda*   pp.261-20

Reykjavik City Hall   1992 / Reykjavik   *Studio Granda*   pp.256,257-1

Hofdabakka Highway Interchange   1995 / Reykjavik   *Studio Granda*   pp.259-10

Kringlumyra Footbridge   1995 / Reykjavik   *Studio Granda*   pp.259-11

Supreme Court of Iceland   1996 / Reykjavik   *Studio Granda*   pp.258,259-6,7,8

Skeidarvogs Highway Interchange   1999 / Reykjavik, Iceland   *Studio Granda*   pp.260-18

Reykjavik Art Museum   2000 / Reykjavik   *Studio Granda*   pp.257-4,5

Skefjar Office   2003 / Reykjavik   *Studio Granda*   pp.261-22

Valhalla Summer Residence   2003 / Reykjavik   *Studio Granda*   pp.261-24

Kringlan Shopping Mall Car Park   2004 / Reykjavik   *Studio Granda*   pp.260-13

Stekkjarbakki Highway Interchange   2004 / Reykjavik   *Studio Granda*   pp.260-16

Laugalaekjarskoli Secondary School Extension
2004 / Reykjavik   *Studio Granda*   pp.261-21

Hrolfsskalavor Residence   2006 / Reykjavik   *Studio Granda*   pp.257-2

Three Footbridges over Hringbraut & Njardagata
2006 / Reykjavik   *Studio Granda*   pp.260-17

Iran

Museum of Glass and Ceramics   1978 / Tehran   *Hans Hollein*   pp.95-8

Ireland

Blackwood Golf Club   1994 / Co.Down, Nothern   *O'Donnell+Tuomey*   pp.178,179-1,2

Howth House   2003 / Co.Dublin   *O'Donnell+Tuomey*   pp.183-23

Cherry Orchard Primary School   2006 / Co.Dublin   *O'Donnell+Tuomey*   pp.183-15

Letterfrack Furniture College   2001 / Co.Galway   *O'Donnell+Tuomey*   pp.181-11

Galbally Social Housing   2002 / Co.Limerick   *O'Donnell+Tuomey*   pp.183-16

Hudson House   1998 / Co.Meath   *O'Donnell+Tuomey*   pp.181-9

Crawford Municipal Art Gallery   2000 / Cork   *Erick van Egeraat*   pp.282-6

Lewis Glucksman Gallery   2004 / Cork   *O'Donnell+Tuomey*   pp.182-12

Irish Film Center   1992 / Dublin   *O'Donnell+Tuomey*   pp.180,181-3,4,5

Irish Pavilion   1992 / Dublin   *O'Donnell+Tuomey*   pp.181-10

Photography Gallery   1996 / Dublin   *O'Donnell+Tuomey*   pp.181-6,7

National Photography Archive   1996 / Dublin   *O'Donnell+Tuomey*   pp.181-7,8

Ranelagh Multi Denominational School   1998 / Dublin   *O'Donnell+Tuomey*   pp.182-13,14

Center for Research into Infectious Diseases at University College Dublin
2003 / Dublin   *O'Donnell+Tuomey*   pp.183-24

Israel

Negev Monument   1968 / Beersheva   *Dani Karavan*   pp.107-3

Peres Peace Center   2007 / Jaffa   *Massimiliano Fuksas*   pp.57-30

Way of Peace   1996 / Nitzana   *Dani Karavan*   pp.111-19

Kikar Levana   1988 / Tel Aviv   *Dani Karavan*   pp.106-1

Italy

Anagni Sports Center   1985 / Anagni   *Massimiliano Fuksas*   pp.53-6

Renovation & Extension of the School in Broni   1970 / Broni   *Aldo Rossi*   pp.215-2

Cassino Town Hall   1990 / Cassino   *Massimiliano Fuksas*   pp.54-7

Civita Castellana Cemetery   1992 / Civita Castellana   *Massimiliano Fuksas*   pp.54-9

Two Enviroments for Peace   1978 / Florence   *Dani Karavan*   pp.110-13

Carlo Felice Theater   1990 / Genova   *Aldo Rossi*   pp.216-7

Gallaratese Housing   1970 / Milan   *Aldo Rossi*   pp.218-20

MOdAM   1985 / Milan   *Mecanoo*   pp.147-21

Sandro Pertini Monument   1988 / Milan   *Aldo Rossi*   pp.219-25

Milan Trade Fair   2005 / Milan   *Massimiliano Fuksas*   pp.56-22,23

San Cataldo Cemetery   1984 / Modena   *Aldo Rossi*   pp.215-5

Paliano Gymnasium   1985 / Paliano   *Massimiliano Fuksas*   pp.53-4

Tower Shopping Center   1985 / Parma   *Aldo Rossi*   pp.217-8

Fontivegge Directional & Commercial Center   1988 / Perugia   *Aldo Rossi*   pp.219-28

Jubilee Church   2003 / Roma   *Richard Meier*   pp.150-4

Sassocorvaro Sports Hall   1973 / Sassocorvaro   *Massimiliano Fuksas*   pp.53-3

Tarquinia Nursery School   1982 / Tarquinia   *Massimiliano Fuksas*   pp.53-5

Casa Aurora   1987 / Turin   *Aldo Rossi*   pp.217-9,10

Fagano Olona School   1972 / Varese   *Aldo Rossi*   pp.215-3

Jerusalem, City of Peace   1976 / Venice   *Dani Karavan*   pp.107-4

*Teatro del Mondo   1980 / Venice   *Aldo Rossi*   pp.216-6

*Dutch Pavilion at the 8th Venice Architecture Biennale
2002 / Venice   *Herman Hertzberger*   pp.81-20

Nardini Research & Multimedia Center
2004 / Viconza   *Massimiliano Fuksas*   pp.55-17,18

Solimene Ceramics Factory   1953 / Vietri sul Mare   *Paolo Soleri*   pp.246-5

Japan

Hotel il Palazzo   1989 / Fukuoka   *Aldo Rossi*   pp.215-4

Seahawk Hotel & Resort   1995 / Fukuoka   *Cesar Pelli*   pp.192-3

Mojiko Hotel   1998 / Fukuoka   *Aldo Rossi*   pp.217-13,14

Kyushu University New Campus Masterplan   2005 / Fukuoka   *Cesar Pelli*   pp.194-18

Bereshit   2000 / Kagoshima   *Dani Karavan*   **pp.108-8**

Warehouse C   1999 / Nagasaki   *Roto Architects*   **pp.222-5**

Matsudai Cultural Village Museum   2003 / Niigata   *MVRDV*   **pp.165-21**

Butterfly Pavilion   2006 / Niigata   *Dominique Perrault*   **pp.200-19**

Nakanoshima Mitsui Building   2002 / Osaka   *Cesar Pelli*   **pp.192-7**

National Museum of Art   2004 / Osaka   *Cesar Pelli*   **pp.192-8**

Way of the Hidden Garden   1999 / Sapporo   *Dani Karavan*   **pp.109-10,11**

Ambiente Showroom   1991 / Tokyo   *Aldo Rossi*   **pp.217-11**

Asaba Design Office   1991 / Tokyo   *Aldo Rossi*   **pp.217-12**

NTT Shinjuku Headquarters Building   1995 / Tokyo   *Cesar Pelli*   **pp.192-4**

Tokyo International Forum   1996 / Tokyo   *Rafael Vinoly*   **pp.294-6,7**

Comme des Garcons Tokyo   1998 / Tokyo   *Future Systems*   **pp.60-11**

Atago Green Hills   2001 / Tokyo   *Cesar Pelli*   **pp.192-6**

PRADA Tokyo   2003 / Tokyo   *Herzog & de Meuron*   **pp.84-4**

Roppongi Hills   2003 / Tokyo   *KPF*   **pp.127-5**

Merrill Lynch Japan Headquarters   2004 / Tokyo   *KPF*   **pp.127-6**

Passenger Terminal 2, Tokyo International Airport(Haneda)
2004 / Tokyo   *Cesar Pelli*   **pp.194-17**

Kurayoshi Park Square   2001 / Tottori   *Cesar Pelli*   **pp.192-5**

Takaoka Station Pavilion   1993 / Toyama   *Enric Miralles Benedetta Tagliabue*   **pp.155-4**

Unazuki Meditation Pavilion
1993 / Toyama   *Enric Miralles Benedetta Tagliabue*   **pp.156-11**

YKK Dormitory & Guesthouse   1998 / Toyama   *Herman Hertzberger*   **pp.81-22**

Korea
Cheongyang Catholic Church   1999 / Chungcheongnam-do   *Kim Young-Sub*   **pp.114-7**

Yongmoon Youth Retreat Camp 1996 / Gyeonggi-do   *Kim Young-Sub*   **pp.117-21**

Resurrection Catholic Church   1997 / Gyeonggi-do   *Kim Young-Sub*   **pp.112,113-1,2**

Myunghweewon Rehabilitation Center for the Handicapped
1997 / Gyeonggi-do   *Kim Young-Sub*   **pp.116-10**

Korea Life Insurance, Suji Training Center & Master Plan
1998 / Gyeonggi-do   *Kim Young-Sub*   **pp.117-18**

Balan Catholic Church   1999 / Gyeonggi-do   *Kim Young-Sub*   **pp.113-4**

Chungang Catholic Church   2000 / Gyeonggi-do   *Kim Young-Sub*   **pp.113-3**

Joong-Ang Catholic Church   2003 / Gyeonggi-do   *Kim Young-Sub*   **pp.114-5**

Nanam Publishing House   2003 / Gyeonggi-do   *Kim Young-Sub*   **pp.117-17**

Kookmin Books   2004 / Gyeonggi-do   *Kim Young-Sub*   **pp.117-16**

Chodang Catholic Church   1999 / Kangneung City   *Kim Young-Sub*   **pp.114-6**

J-Residence   1992 / Pusan   *Kim Young-Sub*   **pp.117-15**

Dong-il Women Laborer's Welfare Center and Nursery
1996 / Pusan   *Kim Young-Sub*   **pp.116-9**

Way of Light   1988 / Soeul   *Dani Karavan*   **pp.110-14**

Catholic University Library and Lecture Hall   1995 / Seoul   *Kim Young-Sub*   **pp.116-11**

Restaurant Bamboo House   1995 / Seoul   *Kim Young-Sub*   **pp.116-8**

House for Kim Young-Sub   1997 / Seoul   *Kim Young-Sub*   **pp.117-12,13**

Ikchunggak & Crystal House   1997 / Seoul   *Kim Young-Sub*   **pp.117-14**

Rodin Museum   1998 / Seoul   *KPF*   **pp.127-4**

Samsung Jong-ro Tower   1999 / Seoul   *Rafael Vinoly*   **pp.294-4,5**

Galleria Hall West   2004 / Seoul   *UN Studio*   **pp.277-19**

Liechtenstein
Office & Art Center   1975   *Ricardo Porro*   **pp.204-6**

Sculpture of Mouths   *Ricardo Porro*   **pp.204-5**

Centrum Bank in Vaduz   2003 / Vaduz   *Hans Hollein*   **pp.95-9,10**

Malaysia
Petronas Towers   1997 / Kuala Lumpur   *Cesar Pelli*   **pp.193-10,11**

Malta
Hal-Farrug Church   2005 / Hal-Farrug   *Richard England*   **pp.48-8,9**

St. Joseph Church   1974 / Manikata   *Richard England*   **pp.51-19,20**

Ir-Razzett ta-Sandrina   1993 / Mgarr   *Richard England*   **pp.48-6**

University of Malta Extension   1997 / Msida   *Richard England*   **pp.51-21**

Church of St. Francis of Assisi   2000 / Qawra   *Richard England*   **pp.50-15**

Millennium Chapel   2000 / Paceville   *Richard England*   **pp.50-17**

St. Andrew Chapel   1989 / Pembroke   *Richard England*   **pp.51-18**

A Garden for Myriam   1982 / St. Julians   *Richard England*   **pp.50-14**

LOVE Sculpture   2003 / St. Julians   *Richard England*   **pp.47-5**

Dar il-Hanin Samaritan   1996 / Santa Venera   *Richard England*   **pp.48-7**

Private Villa   1996 / Siggiewi   *Richard England*   **pp.51-23**

White Shadows Sculpture   2002 / Sliema   *Richard England*   **pp.46-2**

Central Bank of Malta   1993 / Valletta   *Richard England*   **pp.47-4**

St. James Cavalier   2000 / Valletta   *Richard England*   **pp.46-3**

Filfla Chapel   2006 / Wied iz-Zurrieq Cliffs   *Richard England*   **pp.49-10,11,12,13**

Mexico

HOUSE LE   1995 / Colonia Condesa   *TEN Arquitectos*   pp.273-17

Televisa Mixed Use Building   1995 / Colonia Doctores   *TEN Arquitectos*   pp.268-2

Educare Sports Facilities   2001 / Jalisco   *TEN Arquitectos*   pp.269-5,6

Moda in Casa   1993 / Mexico City   *TEN Arquitectos*   pp.271-11

HOUSE RR   1997 / Mexico City   *TEN Arquitectos*   pp.273-16

Hotel Habita   2000 / Mexico City   *TEN Arquitectos*   pp.268-1

Espana Park Residential Building   2001 / Mexico City   *TEN Arquitectos*   pp.271-13

HOUSE C   2004 / Mexico City   *TEN Arquitectos*   pp.273-19

Paolo Soleri Theater   1966 / Santa Fe, New Mexico   *Paolo Soleri*   pp.246-6

National School of Theater   1994 / Tlalpan   *TEN Arquitectos*   pp.268-3

Norway

Arnes Street Rehabilitation   2001 / Arnes   *Snohetta*   pp.242-12

Hamar Town Hall   2001 / Hamar   *Snohetta*   pp.240-5

Karmoy Fishing Museum   1998 / Karmoy   *Snohetta*   pp.241-8

Lillehammer Olympic Art Museum   1993 / Lillehammer   *Snohetta*   pp.241-9

Sonja Henie Plaza   1989 / Oslo   *Snohetta*   pp.242-13

Toyen Culture Park   1994 / Oslo   *Snohetta*   pp.242-15

Bjornson's Garden   1996 / Oslo   *Snohetta*   pp.242-16

Olafia Urban Plaza   1998 / Oslo   *Snohetta*   pp.241-7

Artesia   2002 / Oslo   *Snohetta*   pp.243-19

Morild Lighting Design   2002 / Skien   *Snohetta*   pp.243-20

Peru

Interbank Headquarters   2001 / Lima   *Hans Hollein*   pp.95-7

Poland

Royal Netherlands Embassy in Poland   2004 / Warsaw   *Erick van Egeraat*   pp.282-7

Russia

Luxury Village   2006 / Moscow   *WEST 8*   pp.302-14

Saudi Arabia

Jeddah Airport   1982 / Jeddah   *SOM*   pp.255-14

King Khalid International Airport   1983 / Riyadh   *HOK*   pp.91-11

King Saud University   1984 / Riyadh   *HOK*   pp.91-12

Scotland

New Scottish Parliament 2004 / Edinburgh
Enric Miralles Benedetta Tagliabue   pp.154,155-1,2,3

Singapore

One North Park   2006 / Singapore   *WEST 8*   pp.299-2

Slovenia

Lendva Theater   1991 / Lendva   *Imre Makovecz*   pp.141-21

Spain

National Center for Rhythmic Gymnastics
1993 / Alicante   *Enric Miralles Benedetta Tagliabue*   pp.159-18

Olympic Archery Pavilions
1991 / Barcelona   *Enric Miralles Benedetta Tagliabue*   pp.157-15

Igualada Cemetery   1995 / Barcelona   *Enric Miralles Benedetta Tagliabue*   pp.157-14

Barcelona Museum of Contemporary Art   1995 / Barcelona   *Richard Meier*   pp.151-8

Diagonal Mar Park   2002 / Barcelona   *Enric Miralles Benedetta Tagliabue*   pp.156-8,9,10

Barcelona Forum   2004 / Barcelona   *Herzog & de Meuron*   pp.87-21,22

Gas Natural New Headquarters
2005 / Barcelona   *Enric Miralles Benedetta Tagliabue*   pp.159-20

Rehabilitation of Santa Caterina Market
2005 / Barcelona   *Enric Miralles Benedetta Tagliabue*   pp.158,159-16,17

Banco Santandal   1993 / Madrid   *Hans Hollein*   pp.95-6

Endesa Headquarters   2003 / Madrid   *KPF*   pp.129-21

Mirador   2004 / Madrid   *MVRDV*   pp.164-15

Passages-Homage to Walter Benjamin   1994 / Port Bou   *Dani Karavan*   pp.109-12

Vigo University Campus   1999 / Vigo   *Enric Miralles Benedetta Tagliabue*   pp.157-12,13

Sweden

Halmstad Library   2006 / Halmstad   *Schmidt Hammer Lassen*   pp.234-12

Sund Garden   2001 / Malmo   *WEST 8*   pp.300-6

Switzerland

Liner Museum   1998 / Appenzell   *Gigon/Guyer*   pp.85-4,5

Apartment Building along a Party Wall   1988 / Basel   *Herzog & de Meuron*   pp.84-8

Schutzenmatt Housing   1993 / Basel   *Herzog & de Meuron*   pp.84-9

Pfaffenholz Sports Center   1994 / Basel   *Herzog & de Meuron*   pp.84-11

Signal Box   1995 / Basel   *Herzog & de Meuron*   pp.84-10

Railway Engine Depot, Auf dem Wolf   1995 / Basel   *Herzog & de Meuron*   pp.87-25

Spittelhof Housing   1996 / Basel   *Peter Zumthor*   pp.315-25

Office and Retail Building   1998 / Basel   *Richard Meier*   **pp.152-21**

St. Jakob Park Stadium   2002 / Basel   *Herzog & de Meuron*   **pp.87-20**

Shaulager Museum   2003 / Basel   *Herzog & de Meuron*   **pp.87-19**

Connecting Corridor at Art Museum Chur   1990 / Chur   *Peter Zumthor*   **pp.312-10**

Kirchner Museum   1992 / Davos   *Gigon/Guyer*   **pp.64,65-1,2**

Davos Sports Center   1996 / Davos   *Gigon/Guyer*   **pp.68-11**

Davos Workshop Building   1999 / Davos   *Gigon/Guyer*   **pp.68-14**

Restaurant Vinikus Expansion   1992 / Davos   *Gigon/Guyer*   **pp.68-15**

Renovation of Cafe du Mont   1970 / Graubunden   *Peter Zumthor*   **pp.313-14**

Renovation of Tower House   1970 / Graubunden   *Peter Zumthor*   **pp.313-15**

Renovation of Casa Communala   1970 / Graubunden   *Peter Zumthor*   **pp.313-16**

Elementary School Churwalden   1983 / Graubunden   *Peter Zumthor*   **pp.313-13**

Rath House   1983 / Graubunden   *Peter Zumthor*   **pp.315-23**

Atelier Zumthor   1986 / Graubunden   *Peter Zumthor*   **pp.312-8**

Shelters for the Roman Archaeological Site
1986 / Graubunden   *Peter Zumthor*   **pp.313-11,12**

Saint Benedict Chapel   1989 / Graubunden   *Peter Zumthor*   **pp.314-19,20,21**

Residential Home for the Elderly in Masans
1993 / Graubunden   *Peter Zumthor*   **pp.313-17,18**

Gugalun House   1994 / Graubunden   *Peter Zumthor*   **pp.315-24**

Thermal Vals   1996 / Graubunden   *Peter Zumthor*   **pp.310-1,2,3,4**

Historical Villa in Kastanienbaum, Remodelling and Extension
2004 / Kastanienbaum   *Gigon/Guyer*   **pp.69-20**

Broelberg Residential Complex I   1996 / Kilchberg   *Gigon/Guyer*   **pp.66-7**

Residential Complex Broelberg II   2001 / Kilchcerg   *Gigon/Guyer*   **pp.69-18**

Ricola Storage Building   1987 / Laufen   *Herzog & de Meuron*   **pp.87-23**

Ricola Marketing Building   1998 / Laufen   *Herzog & de Meuron*   **pp.87-24**

Rigihof Restaurant Pavilion, Museum of Transportation Lucerne
2000 / Luzern   *Gigon/Guyer*   **pp.69-21**

Renovation and Extension of the Appisberg Complex
2002 / Mannedorf   *Gigon/Guyer*   **pp.68-16**

E,D,E,N, Pavilion   1987 / Rheinfelden   *Herzog & de Meuron*   **pp.84-6**

Kunst-Depot Galerie Henze & Ketterer, Wichtrach
2004 / Wichtrach   *Gigon/Guyer*   **pp.69-19**

Winterthur Museum   1995 / Winterthur   *Gigon/Guyer*   **pp.65-3**

Oskar Reinhart Collection Museum Renovation   1998 / Winterthur   *Gigon/Guyer*   **pp.66-6**

*Swiss National EXPO'02   2002 / Yverdon-les-Bains   *WEST 8*   **pp.301-12**

Single-Family House   1994 / Zurich   *Gigon/Guyer*   **pp.66-8**

Place for the Communication Center of Credit Suisse
1995 / Zurich   *Dani Karavan*   **pp.109-9**

Switching Station   1999 / Zurich   *Gigon/Guyer*   **pp.66-9**

Three Apartment Buildings Susenbergstrasse   2000 / Zurich   *Gigon/Guyer*   **pp.69-17**

Auditorium, University of Zurich   2002 / Zurich   *Gigon/Guyer*   **pp.69-22**

Taiwan

Grand 50 Tower   1992 / Koahsing   *C.Y.Lee*   **pp.132-4**

Tuntex Tower   1998 / Koahsing   *C.Y.Lee*   **pp.133-7**

Chungtai Zen Temple   1998 / Puli   *C.Y.Lee*   **pp.133-8**

Ta-An Public Housing   1987 / Taipei   *C.Y.Lee*   **pp.134-12**

Tung Wang Palace Housing   1987 / Taipei   *C.Y.Lee*   **pp.135-15**

Hung Kuo Office Headquarters   1989 / Taipei   *C.Y.Lee*   **pp.135-18**

Marine Prospect Garden Housing   1994 / Taipei   *C.Y.Lee*   **pp.135-16,17**

Taipei 101   2004 / Taipei   *C.Y.Lee*   **pp.130-1,2,3**

Thailand

Suvarnabhumi International Airport Passenger Terminal Complex
2006 / Bangkok   *Helmut Jahn*   **pp.102,103-4,5**

The Netherlands

Residential Buildings Growing Houses   2002 / Almere   *Herman Hertzberger*   **pp.79-11**

Office 'La Defense'   2004 / Almere   *UN Studio*   **pp.277-17,18**

Urban Entertainment Center Almere   2005 / Almere   *William Alsop*   **pp.12-8**

Alphen aan den Rijn City Hall   2002 / Alphen aan den Rijn   *Erick van Egeraat*   **pp.202-6**

Canadaplein Cultural Center   2000 / Alkmaar   *Mecanoo*   **pp.147-15**

Karbouw Office   1992 / Amersfoort   *UN Studio*   **pp.274-1**

REMU Electricity Substation   1993 / Amersfoort   *UN Studio*   **pp.276-15**

Students' House in Amsterdam   1966 / Amsterdam   *Herman Hertzberger*   **pp.80-16**

Apollo Schools   1983 / Amsterdam   *Herman Hertzberger*   **pp.80-18**

KNSM Tower   1996 / Amsterdam   *Wiel Arets*   **pp.26-16,17**

100 WoZoCo   1997 / Amsterdam   *MVRDV*   **pp.161-3,4**

Piet Hein Tunnel   1997 / Amsterdam   *UN Studio*   **pp.274-3**

Borneo Sporenburg   1997 / Amsterdam   *WEST 8*   **pp.300,301-4,5**

IJ-Tower   1998 / Amsterdam   *Neutelings Riedijk*   **pp.169-9**

Borneo Sporenburg Houses   1999-2000 / Amsterdam   *MVRDV*   **pp.164-16**

Montessori College Oost   2000 / Amsterdam   *Herman Hertzberger*   **pp.77-7**

Borneo Sporenburg Housing Complex
2000 / Amsterdam   *Enric Miralles Benedetta Tagliabue*   **pp.159-19**

Silodam   2002 / Amsterdam   *MVRDV*   **pp.164-13**

"De Eilanden" Montessori Primary School
2002 / Amsterdam   *Herman Hertzberger*   **pp.79-14,15**

Luxury Housing Mauritskade   2002 / Amsterdam   *Erick van Egeraat*   **pp.282-8**

Living Tomorrow   2003 / Amsterdam   *UN Studio*   **pp.276-13**

World Trade Center Extension   2004 / Amsterdam   *KPF*   **pp.129-17**

Waternet Head Office   2005 / Amsterdam   *Herman Hertzberger*   **pp.76-1**

Centraal Beheer   1972 / Apeldoorn   *Herman Hertzberger*   **pp.76-2**

Orpheus Theatre and Conference Center Renovation and Extension
2004 / Apeldoorn, The Netherlands   *Herman Hertzberger*   **pp.79-12**

CODA   2004 / Apeldoorn   *Herman Hertzberger*   **pp.79-13**

National Heritage Museum   2000 / Arnhem   *Mecanoo*   **pp.145-9,10**

Park and Rijn Towers   2005 / Arnhem   *UN Studio*   **pp.279-26**

Extension to Vanderveen Department Store
1997 / Assen   *Herman Hertzberger*   **pp.81-21**

Water-House Torenvalkpad   1998 / Assen   *Herman Hertzberger*   **pp.81-24**

Police Station in Boxtel   1997 / Boxtel   *Wiel Arets*   **pp.24-9,10**

Library Breda and Center for Art & Music
1993 / Breda   The Netherlands   *Herman Hertzberger*   **pp.81-27**

Chasse Theater   1995 / Breda   *Herman Hertzberger*   **pp.77-5,6**

Lensvelt Office & Factory Building   1999 / Breda   *Wiel Arets*   **pp.24-12**

Breda Fire Station   1999 / Breda   *Neutelings Riedijk*   **pp.170-12,13**

Lensvelt Garden   1999 / Breda   *WEST 8*   **pp.300-8**

Popstage Mezz   2002 / Breda   *Erick van Egeraat*   **pp.285-19,20**

Library for the Delft University of Technology   1998 / Delft   *Mecanoo*   **pp.144-7**

D-Tower   2003 / Doetinchem   *NOX*   **pp.172-2,3**

Veenman Printers Building   1997 / Ede   *Neutelings Riedijk*   **pp.170-14**

Euroborg Stadium   2006 / Groningen   *Wiel Arets*   **pp.27-20**

Roads and Waterworks Support Center   1998 / Harlingen   *Neutelings Riedijk*   **pp.168-7**

Moebius House   1998 / Het Gooi   *UN Studio*   **pp.274-2**

AZL Pension Fund Headuquarters   1995 / Heerlen   *Wiel Arets*   **pp.22-4**

Renovation for Glass Palace 'Schunck'   2003 / Heerlen   *Wiel Arets*   **pp.27-21**

Villa VPRO   1997 / Hilversum   *MVRDV*   **pp.161-2**

Lakeside Housing 'The Sphinxes'   2003 / Huizen   *Neutelings Riedijk*   **pp.166,167-1**

Townhall and Theater Ijsselstein   2000 / Ijsselstein   *UN Studio*   **pp.276-10**

Maastricht Academy of Arts and Architecture   1993 / Maastricht   *Wiel Arets*   **pp.23-5**

Herdenkingsplein Housing   1994 / Maastricht   *Mecanoo*   **pp.142-3**

Bonnefanten Museum   1994 / Maastricht   *Aldo Rossi*   **pp.214,215-1**

Ceramic Office Building   1995 / Maastricht   *Wiel Arets*   **pp.22-3**

Maastricht Fire Station   1996 / Maastricht   *Neutelings Riedijk*   **pp.168-6**

Office Building 'il Fiore'   2002 / Maastricht   *Herman Hertzberger*   **pp.77-8**

Stylesuite D&G fashion Store, Maastricht   2005 / Maastricht   *Wiel Arets*   **pp.27-24**

Courtyard Watersnihof(H) and Zwanenhof(C) for Residential Building
2004 / Middelburg   *Herman Hertzberger*   **pp.81-25**

★Dutch H$_2$O EXPO   1997 / Neeltje Jans   *NOX*   **pp.172,173-1**

Blow Out   1997 / Neeltje Jans   *NOX*   **pp.175-13**

Het Valkhof Museum   1999 / Nijmegen   *UN Studio*   **pp.276-11**

Philips Business Innovation Center   2006 / Nijmegen   *Mecanoo*   **pp.146-13,14**

Kruisplein Housing   1985 / Rotterdam   *Mecanoo*   **pp.142-1**

Rotterdam Street Residential Buildings
1996 / Rotterdam   *Herman Hertzberger*   **pp.81-26**

Erasmus Bridge   1996 / Rotterdam   *UN Studio*   **pp.276-8**

Natural History Museum Rotterdam   1996 / Rotterdam   *Erick van Egeraat*   **pp.283-12**

City Theater Plaza   1996 / Rotterdam   *WEST 8*   **pp.302,303-15**

V2-mediaLab   1998 / Rotterdam   *NOX*   **pp.172-4**

Nieuw Terbregge   2000 / Rotterdam   *Mecanoo*   **pp.147-19**

Inholland University   2000 / Rotterdam   *Erick van Egeraat*   **pp.282-4**

Zalmhaven Apartments Towers   2001 / Rotterdam   *Wiel Arets*   **pp.26-18**

St. Laurence Cemetery Chapel   2001 / Rotterdam   *Mecanoo*   **pp.144-8**

Mullerpier Apartment Block 3   2003 / Rotterdam   *Neutelings Riedijk*   **pp.169-10**

Digital Port Rotterdam   2004 / Rotterdam   *Mecanoo*   **pp.147-18**

Montevideo   2005 / Rotterdam   *Mecanoo*   **pp.147-17**

Shipping & Transport College   2005 / Rotterdam   *Neutelings Riedijk*   **pp.169-8**

Mullerpier Apartment Block 7   2006 / Rotterdam   *Neutelings Riedijk*   **pp.169-11**

Son-O-House   2003 / Son en Breugel   *NOX*   **pp.173-6**

Ministry of Social Welfare and Employment
1990 / The Hague   *Herman Hertzberger*   **pp.80-19**

Benelux Merkenburo   1993 / The Hague   *Herman Hertzberger*   **pp.77-4**

The Hague City Hall and Central Library   1995 / The Hague   *Richard Meier*   **pp.151-12**

Officers Hotel De Citadel   2004 / The Hague   *Mecanoo*   **pp.147-22**

Tilburg Row House   1996 / Tilburg   *Neutelings Riedijk*   **pp.171-18**

Interpolis Garden   1998 / Tilburg   *WEST 8*   **pp.298,299-1**

Markant Theater   1996 / Uden   *Herman Hertzberger*   **pp.77-3**

Verdenburg Music Center   1978 / Utrecht   *Herman Hertzberger*   **pp.80-17**

Faculty of Management and Economics at Utrecht University
1995 / Utrecht   *Mecanoo*   **pp.147-16**

Utrecht University Minnaert Building   1997 / Utrecht   *Neutelings Riedijk*   **pp.168-4,5**

School for Fashion and Graphic Industry Utrecht
1997 / Utrecht   *Erick van Egeraat*   **pp.285-21**

Utrecht City Hall   1999 / Utrecht   *Enric Miralles Benedetta Tagliabue*   **pp.156-5,6**

NMR Facility   2000 / Utrecht   *UN Studio*   **pp.276-14**

Prince Claus Bridge   2003 / Utrecht   *UN Studio*   **pp.276-9**

Utrecht University Library   2004 / Utrecht   *Wiel Arets*   **pp.25-14,15**

Courtyard Garden at Utrecht University Library   2005 / Utrecht   *WEST 8*   **pp.300-9**

Sportcampus Leidsche Rijn   2006 / Utrecht   *Wiel Arets*   **pp.27-23**

Police Station in Vaals   1995 / Vaals   *Wiel Arets*   **pp.22-1,2**

Institute for Forestry and Nature Research
1998 / Wageningen   *Gunther Behnisch(B,B&P)*   **pp.30-6**

Hedge House Gallery   1995 / Wijlre   *Wiel Arets*   **pp.27-22**

Hageneiland Housing   2001 / Ypenburg   *MVRDV*   **pp.164-14**

Ypenburg de Singels   2002 / Ypenburg   *WEST 8*   **pp.302-16,17**

Hotel Castell   2004 / Zuoz   *UN Studio*   **pp.279-27**

U.K.

Selfridges Birmingham   2003 / Birmingham   *Future Systems*   **pp.61-2,3**

Cardiff Bay Visitor's Center   1990 / Cardiff   *William Alsop*   **pp.11-5**

L House   1991 / London   *Sauerbruch Hutton*   **pp.226-3**

National Gallery Sainsbury Wing   1991 / London   *VSBA*   **pp.287-3,4**

Broadgate Development   1992 / London   *SOM*   **pp.255-19**

Hauer King House   1994 / London   *Future Systems*   **pp.62-20**

H House   1995 / London   *Sauerbruch Hutton*   **pp.226-2**

Floating Bridge   1996 / London   *Future Systems*   **pp.62-19**

North Greenwich Underground Station, Jubilee Line
1999 / London   *William Alsop*   **pp.15-21**

NatWest Media Center   1999 / London   *Future Systems*   **pp.59-4**

Marni   1999 / London   *Future Systems*   **pp.60-8**

N House   1999 / London   *Sauerbruch Hutton*   **pp.226-1**

Peckham Library   2000 / London   *William Alsop*   **pp.10,11-1,2**

Tate Gallery of Modern Art   2000 / London   *Herzog & de Meuron*   **pp.87-17**

Chiswick Park   2000 / London   *WEST 8*   **pp.301-10**

Victoria House Office Redevelopment   2003 / London   *William Alsop*   **pp.14-15**

Heron Quays DLR Station   2003 / London   *William Alsop*   **pp.14-18**

King's Library at the British Museum   2003 / London   *HOK*   **pp.93-22**

Goldsmiths College   2005 / London   *William Alsop*   **pp.13-9,10**

Turner Center   2005 / Margate   *Snohetta*   **pp.242-14**

Fawood Children's Center   2005 / North London   *William Alsop*   **pp.13-11,12**

House in Wales   1996 / Wales   *Future Systems*   **pp.60-7**

U.S.A.

Dome House   1949 / Cave Creek, Arizona   *Paolo Soleri*   **pp.246-4**

Arcosanti   1970 / Cordes Junction, Arizona   *Paolo Soleri*   **pp.244, 245-1,2,3**

Pumpkin Apse & Barrel Vault (Cosanti)
1971 / Cordes Junction, Arizona   *Paolo Soleri*   **pp.247-11**

Phoenix Art Museum & Little Theater
1996 / Phoenix, Arizona   *Tod Williams Billie Tsien*   **pp.306-6**

Phoenix Municipal Courthouse   1999 / Phoenix, Arizona   *HOK*   **pp.91-9**

Sandra Day O'Connor United States Courthouse
2000 / Phoenix, Arizona   *Richard Meier*   **pp.152-22**

Ceramics Studio (Cosanti)   1958 / Pradaise Valley, Arizona   *Paolo Soleri*   **pp.247-12,13**

Interior Design for Arizona University Cancer Center Chapel
1986 / Tucson, Arizona   *Paolo Soleri*   **pp.247-9**

Gagosian Gallery   1995 / Beverly Hills, California   *Richard Meier*   **pp.152-20**

Museum of Television & Radio   1996 / Beverly Hills, California   *Richard Meier*   **pp.152-14**

ABC Building   2000 / Burbank, California   *Aldo Rossi*   **pp.218-19**

Miracle Manor Retreat   1998 / Desert Hot Springs, California   *Roto Architects*   **pp.224-16**

San Diego Museum of Contemporary Art La Jolla Wing
1996 / La Jolla, California   *VSBA*   **pp.290-16**

Neurosciences Institute   1996 / La Jolla, California   *Tod Williams Billie Tsien*   **pp.306-4**

La Jolla Playhouse at UCSD   2005 / La Jolla, California   *Roto Architects*   **pp.224-14,15**

Pacific Design Center   1975 / Los Angeles, California   *Cesar Pelli*   **pp.194-12,13**

Restaurant Nicola   1993 / Los Angeles, California   *Roto Architects*   **pp.222-6**

The Getty Center   1997 / Los Angeles, California   *Richard Meier*   **pp.151-11**

Carlson Reges House   1998 / Los Angeles, California   *Roto Architects*   **pp.222-7**

UCLA Gonda Neuroscience and Genetics Research Center
1998 / Los Angels, California   *VSBA*   **pp.289-14**

Dominus Winery   1997 / Napa Valley, California   *Herzog & de Meuron*   **pp.85-15**

George R Moscone Convention Center   1981 / San Francisco, California   *HOK*   **pp.89-2,3**

San Francisco International Airport   2001 / San Francisco, California   *SOM*   **pp.255-25**

de Young Museum
2005 / San Francisco, California   *Herzog & de Meuron*   **pp.82,83-1,2,3**

Dorland Mountain Arts Colony
1994 / Temecula, California   *Roto Architects*   **pp.223-11,12**

US Air Force Academy Chapel   1963 / Colorado Spring, Colorado   *SOM*   **pp.254-9,10**

Packard Hall at Colorado College   2005 / Colorado Spring, Colorado   *ARO*   **pp.21-15**

Colorado House   1999 / Telluride, Colorado   *ARO*   **pp.16,17-1**

Greenwich Academy Upper School   2002 / Greenwich, Connecticut   *SOM*   **pp.255-16**

Hartford Seminary   1981 / Hartford, Connecticut   *Richard Meier*   **pp.152-16**

Beinecke Rare Book & Manuscript Library
1963 / New Heaven, Connecticut   *SOM*   **pp.254-11**

Dixwell Fire Station   1974 / New Heaven, Connecticut   *VSBA*   **pp.290-20**

The Anlyan Center Medical for Research and Education at Yale University
2003 / New Haven, Connecticut   VSBA   pp.291-21

Celebration Building   1995 / Orlando, Florida   Aldo Rossi   pp.217-15,16

High Museum of Art   1983 / Atlanta, Georgia   Richard Meier   pp.148,149-1,2

Georgia Archives Building   2004 / Morrow, Georgia   HOK   pp.93-19

Avante Center at William R.Harper College   2004 / Palatine, Georgia   HOK   pp.93-20

First Hawaiian Center   1996 / Honolulu   KPF   pp.129-19

John Hancock Center   1970 / Chicago, Illinois   SOM   pp.252-4

Sears Tower   1974 / Chicago, Illinois   SOM   pp.252-3

James R.Thompson Center   1985 / Chicago, Illinois   Helmut Jahn   pp.104-9

900 N Michigan   1989 / Chicago, Illinois   KPF   pp.129-22

333 Wacker Drive   1993 / Chicago, Illinois   KPF   pp.128-12

Museum of Contemporary Art, Chicago
1996 / Chicago, Illinois   Josef Paul Kleihues   pp.121-10

IIT Student Housing   2003 / Chicago, Illinois   Helmut Jahn   pp.100,101-1

O'hare International Airport United Airlines Terminal 1 Renovation
2004 / Chicago, Illinois   Helmut Jahn   pp.104-8

University of Chicago, Graduate School of Business
2004 / Chicago, Illinois   Rafael Vinoly   pp.295-16

Athenium   1979 / New Harmony, Indiana   Richard Meier   pp.151-7

The Biomedical & Biological Sciences Research Building at the University of Kentucky
2005 / Lexington, Kentucky   VSBA   pp.286,287-1

Mattin Center at Johns Hopkins University
2001 / Baltimore, Maryland   Tod Williams Billie Tsien   pp.304,305-2,3

Boston Convention & Exhibition Center
2004 / Boston, Massachusetts   Rafael Vinoly   pp.294-11

Genzyme Center
2004 / Cambridge, Massachusetts   Gunther Behnisch(B,B&P)   pp.33-22,23

Martha's Vineyard House   2005 / Martha's Vineyard, Massachusetts   ARO   pp.17-2

Palmer Drive Development at the University of Michigan
2005 / Ann Arbor, Michigan   VSBA   pp.291-22

Cranbrook Natatorium
1999 / Bloomsfield Hills, Michigan   Tod Williams Billie Tsien   pp.307-10

Wells Fargo Center   1989 / Minneapolis, Minnesota   Cesar Pelli   pp.195-27

Aronoff Center for the Arts   1995 / Minneapolis, Minnesota   Cesar Pelli   pp.194-15

Expansion of the Walker Art Center
2005 / Minneapolis, Minnesota   Herzog & de Meuron   pp.85-12

Minneapolis Central Library   2006 / Minneapolis, Minnesota   Cesar Pelli   pp.195-25

The Conference Center of the Church of Jesus Christ of Latter-Day Saints
1993 / Independence, Missouri   HOK   pp.90-6,7

Priory Chapel   1962 / St. Louis, Missouri   HOK   pp.88,89-1

The Rehabilitation of St.Louis Union Station   1985 / St. Louis, Missouri   HOK   pp.92-16

Boeing Leadership Center   1999 / St. Louis, Missouri   HOK   pp.91-10

St.Louis International Airport East Terminal   1999 / St. Louis, Missouri   HOK   pp.92-15

New Jersey House   1996 / Barnersville, New Jersey   Roto Architects   pp.222-8,9

Gordon Wu Hall, Princeton University   1983 / Princeton, New Jersey   VSBA   pp.288-7,8

Lewis Thomas Laboratory, Princeton University
1983 / Princeton, New Jersey   VSBA   pp.288-9

Feinberg Hall at Prinston University
1986 / Princeton, New Jersey   Tod Williams Billie Tsien   pp.306-7

Fisher and Bendheim Hall, Princeton University
1989 / Princeton, New Jersey   VSBA   pp.288-10

Princeton University Stadium   1998 / Princeton, New Jersey   Rafael Vinoly   pp.294-9,10

Princeton Parking Garage   2000 / Princeton, New Jersey   TEN Arquitectos   pp.271-12

Frist Campus Center, Princeton University
2000 / Princeton, New Jersey   VSBA   pp.289-11

Carl Icahn Lab of the Lewis - Sigler Institute for Integrative Genomics at Princeton University
2003 / Princeton, New Jersey   Rafael Vinoly   pp.295-17

IBM Corporate Headquarters   1997 / Armonk, New York   KPF   pp.127-10,11

Lehman College Physical Education Facility
1994 / Bronx, New York   Rafael Vinoly   pp.294-8

Spiegel House Indoor Pool
1988 / Long Island, New York   Tod Williams Billie Tsien   pp.308-15

House on Long Island
1998 / Long Island, New York   Tod Williams Billie Tsien   pp.308-11

Lever House   1952 / New York   SOM   pp.254-13

Chase Manhattan Bank Tower & Plaza   1960 / New York   SOM   pp.255-20

Former Pepsi Cola Building   1960 / New York   SOM   pp.255-24

Marin Midland Bank   1967 / New York   SOM   pp.255-21

Richard L.Feigen Gallery   1969 / New York   Hans Hollein   pp.94-2

BEA Associates Citicorp Office   1979 / New York   Tod Williams Billie Tsien   pp.306-8

MoMA Tower   1984 / New York   Cesar Pelli   pp.194-19

Park Avenue Tower   1987 / New York   Helmut Jahn   pp.105-19

World Financial Center   1987 / New York   Cesar Pelli   pp.192-9

The Downtown Branch of the Whitney Museum
1988 / New York   Tod Williams Billie Tsien   pp.306-9

Worldwide Plaza   1989 / New York   SOM   pp.255-22

Carnegie Hall Tower   1990 / New York   Cesar Pelli   pp.194-23

The Quandt Rosenblat Loft   1991 / New York   Tod Williams Billie Tsien   pp.308-14

Art et Industrie Gallery and Sculpture Garden   1995 / New York   ARO   pp.20-12

54 Thompson Street Lobby   1996 / New York   ARO   pp.19-11

Flatiron Loft   1996 / New York   ARO   pp.21-18

New York City House   1996 / New York   Tod Williams Billie Tsien   pp.309-17

Comme des Garcons New York   1998 / New York   Future Systems   pp.60-9

US Armed Forces Recruiting Station   1999 / New York   ARO   pp.18-3,4,5

Capital Z Office   1999 / New York   ARO   pp.19-8

SoHo Loft   1999 / New York   *ARO*   **pp.19-10**

Qiora Store and Spa   2000 / New York   *ARO*   **pp.18-6,7**

PRADA NY Epicenter   2001 / New York   *ARO*   **pp.19-9**

Scholastic Building   2001 / New York   *Aldo Rossi*   **pp.218-17,18**

American Folk Art Museum   2001 / New York   *Tod Williams Billie Tsien*   **pp.304-1**

Baruch College New Academic Complex   2002 / New York   *KPF*   **pp.129-15**

173/ 176 Perry Street Condominium Towers
2002 / New York   *Richard Meier*   **pp.152-18 Two left wings**

Restaurant 66   2003 / New York   *Richard Meier*   **pp.152-19**

Time Warner Center   2003 / New York   *SOM*   **pp.255-23**

Skyscraper Museum   2004 / New York   *SOM*   **pp.255-17**

Jazz at Lincoln Center   2004 / New York   *Rafael Vinoly*   **pp.295-14**

165 Charles Street Apartments   2005 / New York   *Richard Meier*   **pp.152-18 Right wing**

House on Shelter Island
2003 / Shelter Island, New York   *Tod Williams Billie Tsien*   **pp.308-12**

Nasher Museum of Art, Duke University
2004 / Durham, North Carolina   *Rafael Vinoly*   **pp.295-18**

EPA Campus   2001 / Reseach Triangle Park, North Carolina   *HOK*   **pp.89-5**

Allen Memorial Art Museum   1976 / Oberlin, Ohio   *VSBA*   **pp.290-15**

Procter & Gamble World Headquarters   1985 / Cincinnati, Ohio   *KPF*   **pp.129-20**

Crile Clinic Building   1984 / Cleveland, Ohio   *Cesar Pelli*   **pp.195-26**

Lerner Research Institute   1999 / Cleveland, Ohio   *Cesar Pelli*   **pp.194-22**

Owens Corning World Headquarters   1996 / Toledo, Ohio   *Cesar Pelli*   **pp.195-24**

Lehigh Valley Hospital   2005 / Bethlehem, Pennsylvania   *VSBA*   **pp.291-23**

Vanna Venturi House   1964 / Chestnut Hill, Pennsylvania   *VSBA*   **pp.288-5**

Pocono Pine House   1989 / Mount Pocono, Pennsylvania   *Aldo Rossi*   **pp.218-21**

Guild House   1966 / Philadelphia, Pennsylvania   *VSBA*   **pp.288-6**

Franklin Court   1976 / Philadelphia, Pennsylvania   *VSBA*   **pp.290-18**

Institute for Scientific Information Corporate Headquarters
1979 / Philadelphia, Pennsylvania   *VSBA*   **pp.290-17**

One Liberty Place   1987 / Philadelphia, Pennsylvania   *Helmut Jahn*   **pp.105-21**

Clinical Research Building, Pennsylvania University
1991 / Philadelphia, Pennsylvania   *VSBA*   **pp.289-12**

Parelman Quadrangle, Pennsylvania University
2000 / Philadelphia, Pennsylvania   *VSBA*   **pp.289-13**

Kimmel Center for the Performing Arts
2001 / Philadelphia, Pennsylvania   *Rafael Vinoly*   **pp.292,293-1,2,3**

Philadelphia International Airport   2003 / Philadelphia, Pennsylvania   *KPF*   **pp.129-14**

Cira Center   2005 / Philadelphia, Pennsylvania   *Cesar Pelli*   **pp.194-14**

Skirkanich Hall at the University of Pennsylvania
2006 / Philadelphia, Pennsylvania   *Tod Williams Billie Tsien*   **pp.309-22**

One Oxford Center   1983 / Pittsburgh, Pennsylvania   *HOK*   **pp.93-18**

David L. Lawrence Convention Center
2003 / Pittsburgh, Pennsylvania   *Rafael Vinoly*   **pp.295-12,13**

Penn State University, School of Information Sciences & Technology
2003 / University Park, Pennsylvania   *Rafael Vinoly*   **pp.295-15**

Sinte Gleska University   1999 / Antelope, South Dakota   *Roto Architects*   **pp.222-10**

Dallas Galleria   1983 / Dallas, Texas   *HOK*   **pp.90-8**

Rachofsky Art Museum   1996 / Dallas, Texas   *Richard Meier*   **pp.151-6**

Rice University Herring Hall   1984 / Houston, Texas   *Cesar Pelli*   **pp.194-20**

Architecture and Art Building at Prairie View A&M University
2005 / Prairie View, Texas   *Roto Architects*   **pp.220,221-1,2**

National Air & Space Museum, Steven F.Udvar Hazy Center
2003 / Chantilly, Virginia   *HOK*   **pp.93-23**

The New College at the University of Virginia
1999 / Charlottesville, Virginia   *Tod Williams Billie Tsien*   **pp.306-5**

Gannett /USA Today Headquarters   2001 / Mclean, Virginia   *KPF*   **pp.127-7,8**

Seattle Art Museum   1991 / Seattle, Washington   *VSBA*   **pp.287-2**

UW Physics and Astronomy Wings   1994 / Seattle, Washington   *Cesar Pelli*   **pp.194-21**

Hirshhorn Museum & Sculpture Garden   1974 / Washington D.C.   *SOM*   **pp.254-12**

National Air & Space Museum   1976 / Washington D.C.   *HOK*   **pp.89-4**

Washington Mall   1976 / Washington D.C.   *SOM*   **pp.255-15**

Freedom Plaza   1980 / Washington D.C.   *VSBA*   **pp.290-19**

The World Bank Headquarters   1996 / Washington D.C.   *KPF*   **pp.129-23**

National Museum of American Indian
2004 / Washington D.C.   *Douglas Cardinal*   **pp.44-13**

WORLD ARCHITECTS 51
CONCEPTS & WORKS

Date of Publication: The 1st Printing September 20, 2007

Author & Editor: Masayuki Fuchigami

English Translation: Christopher Stephens

Book Design: Hideyuki Fukuda, Issei Ando | Studio Fuku-De

Editorial Collaboration: Maiko Fuchigami, Hikari Koguchi | Synectics Inc.

Publisher: Keiko Kubota

Publishing House: ADP Company (Art Design Publishing Co.)
　　　4-38-17-1003, Takadanobaba, Shinjuku-ku, Tokyo, 169-0075 Japan
　　　Tel: 81-3-5332-2099   Fax: 81-3-5332-6940
　　　http://www.ad-publish.com

Printing & Binding: Everbest Printing Co., Ltd.

©Masayuki Fuchigami 2007
©ADP Company 2007

Distributed by:

Azur Corporation (Worldwide except Japan and China)
5F Aikusu Building, 1-44-8, Jimbo-cho, Kanda, Chiyoda-ku, Tokyo
101-0051 Japan
Tel: 81-3-3292-7601   Fax: 81-3-3292-7602
E-mail:azur@galaxy.ocn.ne.jp
http://www.azurbook.co.jp

Beijing Designer Books Co., Ltd. (China)
Building No.2, Daesheng Office Building, No.3, Babukou, Gulouxi Road,
Xicheng District, Beijing, P.R. China
Tel:
+86-10-6406-7653 (Beijing)　　　+86-22-2341-1250 (Tianjin)
+86-21-5596-7639 (Shanghai)　　+86-571-8884-8576 (Hangzhou)
+86-25-5807-5096 (Nanjing)　　　+86-20-8756-5010 (Guangzhou)
+86-755-8825-0425 (Shenzhen)　 +86-27-5920-8457 (Wuhan)
+86-28-8660-1680 (Chengdu)
Fax: +86-10-6406-0931
E-mail:info@designerbooks.net
www.designerbooks.net

Printed in China
ISBN978-4-903348-07-0 C0052

All right reserved. No part of this book can be reproduced in any form without permission in writing from the ADP Company.